D1745063

Virtue Ethics and Sociology

Also by Kieran Flanagan

*   SOCIOLOGY AND LITURGY: Re-presentations of the Holy
*   THE ENCHANTMENT OF SOCIOLOGY: A Study of Theology and Culture
*   POSTMODERNITY, SOCIOLOGY AND RELIGION (*co-editor with Peter C. Jupp*)

Also by Peter C. Jupp

*   CONTEMPORARY ISSUES IN THE SOCIOLOGY OF DEATH, DYING AND DISPOSAL (*co-editor with Glennys Howarth*)
*   THE CHANGING FACE OF DEATH (*co-editor with Glennys Howarth*)
    INTERPRETING DEATH (*co-editor with Tony Rogers*)
    DEATH IN ENGLAND: An Illustrated History (*co-editor with Clare Gittings*)
*   POSTMODERNITY, SOCIOLOGY AND RELIGION (*co-editor with Kieran Flanagan*)

*   *From the same publishers*

Virtue Ethics and Sociology

Issues of Modernity and Religion

Edited by

Kieran Flanagan
Reader in Sociology
University of Bristol

and

Peter C. Jupp
United Reformed Church Minister
and Visiting Fellow
Department of Sociology
University of Bristol

palgrave

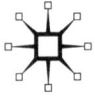

First published 2001 by
PALGRAVE
Houndmills, Basingstoke, Hampshire RG21 6XS and
175 Fifth Avenue, New York, N. Y. 10010
Companies and representatives throughout the world

PALGRAVE is the new global academic imprint of
St. Martin's Press LLC Scholarly and Reference Division and
Palgrave Publishers Ltd (formerly Macmillan Press Ltd).

ISBN 0–333–75010–1

This book is printed on paper suitable for recycling and
made from fully managed and sustained forest sources.

A catalogue record for this book is available
from the British Library.

Library of Congress Cataloging-in-Publication Data
Virtue ethics and sociology : issues of modernity and religion / edited by
Kieran Flanagan and Peter C. Jupp.
       p. cm.
Includes bibliographical references and index.
ISBN 0–333–75010–1
1. Virtue—Congresses. 2. Ethics—Congresses. 3. Religion and
sociology—Congresses. 4. Postmodernism—Congresses. I. Flanagan,
Kieran, 1944– II. Jupp, Peter C.
BJ1531 .V58 2000
306.6'915—dc21

                                                   00–042075

10   9   8   7   6   5   4   3   2   1
10 09 08 07 06 05 04 03 02 01

Printed and bound in Great Britain by
Antony Rowe Ltd, Chippenham, Wiltshire

Contents

Acknowledgements

Virtue Ethics and Sociology emerged from a conference on Religion, Modernity and Ethics held between the 2nd and 5th April 1997 at Clifton Hill House, the University of Bristol, which both editors had organised for the British Sociological Association Sociology of Religion Study Group. The resultant book, our second collaboration, is the fourth recent publication to have resulted from an annual conference of the Study Group and we would like to thank the officers and members for their encouragement at every stage.

The book includes a selection of some of the papers first presented at Bristol, all of which have been substantially rewritten for this volume. From over 40 papers presented, selection was unusually difficult. Nevertheless, we hope that we have represented the spirit of what was a very lively and large conference. Every collection depends on its contributors; we would like to thank our team most warmly for their patient and positive responses to editorial revisions and for dealing so expeditiously and good-humouredly with queries, re-drafts and disk requests.

At the University of Bristol, we would like to thank Elaine Escott and the Computer Centre for help with matching disks to programmes. Kieran Flanagan would especially like to thank his colleague Dr Rohit Barot, who displayed an awesome range of the agenda of virtue ethics, in practice, by assisting with advice, soothing computer panics, and supplying general encouragement. Dr Watts Miller and Theo Nichols, now Distinguished Research Professor, at the Cardiff University, School of Social Sciences, both listened sagely to accounts of the production pains and helped to keep things in perspective. Clifton Cathedral, St Joseph's, Cotham, and Corby United Reformed Church supplied the editors with the (very) necessary spiritual support. The 'real ale' at the Hare on the Hill provided Kieran Flanagan with a more secular form of alleviation whilst The Reform Club, the University of Bristol Senior Common Room and Brown's of Bristol furnished both editors with stimulating culinary contexts for progress meetings. Richard Greatrex, of the SPCK bookshop in Park Street, Bristol lent further encouragement with memories of the last book launch and the one offered for this.

We are both very grateful to Ms Karen Brazier, our editor at Macmillan, for her vigorous support for the venture. Again, we would like to thank warmly our copy-editor, Keith Povey, for his diligence and help with the manuscript. This second editorial venture involved much chasing around with faxes and telephones, but was a highly enjoyable exercise that

x   *Acknowledgements*

necessitated its own display of the virtues of prudence, fortitude, wisdom but above all hope for the success of this collection.

All Souls Day, November 1999   KIERAN FLANAGAN
                                                              PETER C. JUPP

Notes on the Contributors

Margaret Archer is a Professor of Sociology at the University of Warwick. Her previous ten books include *Social Origins of Educational Systems* (1979). Her forthcoming book, *Human Being*, completes a trilogy which started with *Culture and Agency* (1988) and *Realist Social Theory: The Morphogentic Approach* (1995). She was President of the International Sociological Association from 1986 to 1990, chair of its publications committee and a former editor of *Current Sociology*. Currently, she is a counsellor of the newly founded Pontifical Academy of Social Sciences, and is in charge of its publications. In 1997, she became a founding trustee of the Centre for Critical Realism.

Rohit Barot is a Lecturer in Sociology at the University of Bristol. He has conducted fieldwork among Indians in Bristol and Gujarati Hindus in London. He has edited *Religion and Ethnicity: Minorities and Social Change in the Metropolis* (1993), *Racism Problematic: Contemporary Sociological Debates on Race and Ethnicity* (1996) and, with Harriet Bradley and Steve Fenton, *Ethnicity, Gender and Social Change* (1999). He is a member of the Centre for the Study of Ethnicity and Citizenship at the University of Bristol.

Sylvia Collins is a Lecturer in Sociology at Kingston University and has recently completed her Ph.D. at the University of Surrey on young people's religious faith in late modernity.

Pink Dandelion is Associate Director of the Centre for Quaker Studies, at the University of Sunderland; is Honorary Lecturer in the Department of Theology at the University of Birmingham; and is a Tutor in postgraduate Quaker Studies, Woodbrooke College, Birmingham. He is editor of *Quaker Studies* and Convenor of the Quaker Studies Research Association. He has written extensively on the relationship between sociology and Quakerism. His major work is *A Sociological Analysis of the Theology of Quakers: The Silent Revolution* (1996).

Christie Davies is a Professor of Sociology at the University of Reading. His main research interests are in the sociology of morality and the sociology of humour. His publications include *Wrongful Imprisonment* (with Ruth Brandon, 1973), *Permissive Britain* (1975), *Censorship and Obscenity* (with Rajeev Dhavan, 1978), *Ethnic Humour Around the World: A Comparative Analysis* (1990) and *Jokes and Their Relation to Society* (1998). His forthcoming book is *The Mirth of Nations*. He has published a wide number of essays on the sociology of morality and religion.

Kieran Flanagan is a Reader in Sociology at the University of Bristol. His publications include *Sociology and Liturgy: Re-presentations of the Holy* (1991) and *The Enchantment of Sociology: a Study of Theology and Culture* (1996). With Peter C. Jupp he has edited *Postmodernity, Sociology and Religion* (1996). Between 1997 and 2000, he was Chair of the British Sociological Association Sociology of Religion Study Group. Currently he is working on two books: *Seen and Unseen: Tales of Sociology in Theology* and *Virtue Ethics and Vocation: A Sociology of Edification*.

Paul Heelas is a Professor in Religion and Modernity at Lancaster University. He has written extensively on spirituality in the contemporary West. His most recent work is *The New Age Movement. The Celebration of the Self and the Sacralization of Modernity* (1996). He is co-editor (with Scott Lash and Paul Morris) of *Detraditionalization. Critical Reflections on Authority and Identity* (1996). His latest edited work is *Religion, Modernity and Postmodernity* (1998). With Linda Woodhead, his forthcoming book is *Religion in Modern Times*.

David Herbert is a Staff Tutor in Arts, with reference to Religious Studies at the Open University. His main research interest is in the relationships between religion, ethics and modernity, with substantive reference to Islam and multiculturalism in Western Europe. He is also concerned with Christianity, democratisation and human rights in Central and Eastern Europe. He has published essays on these topics in *Studies in Christian Ethics, Islam and Christian–Muslim Relations* and *Modern Believing*. His forthcoming book is *Religion and Civil Society: Multiculturalism, Democracy and Ethics in the New Europe*.

Peter C. Jupp is a Visiting Fellow in the Department of Sociology, University of Bristol. A United Reformed Minister, he is currently minister of Peterborough Westgate Church. He was Director of the National Funerals College, 1992–97. With Kieran Flanagan he has edited *Postmodernity, Sociology and Religion* (1996). He has also edited, with Glennys Howarth, *Contemporary Issues in the Sociology of Death, Dying and Disposal* (1996) and *The Changing Face of Death* (1997) and (together with David Field) the journal *Mortality* (1996–). With Tony Rogers, he edited *Interpreting Death* (1997) and with Clare Gittings, *Death in England: an Illustrated History* (1999).

Jessica Lindohf is a postgraduate student at the Centre for the Study of Theology, Literature and the Arts at the University of Glasgow. Her doctoral thesis is entitled 'A Rebirth of Images', apocalyptic images in film.

Peter McMylor is a Lecturer in Sociology at the University of Manchester. His major book is *Alasdair MacIntyre: Critic of Modernity* (1994) and he has edited, with Peter Halfpenny, *Positivism and its Critics* (1994). His research interests include the connections between historical change and social and ethical thought and the relationship between economic sociology and moral discourse. Currently, he is writing a book with Huw Beynon on the social transformation of British society and is completing a research project on the nature and role of family enterprises in contemporary Russia.

Mark Neal is a Lecturer in Organisation Studies at the University of Aston. His latest book is *The Culture Factor: Cross-National Management and the Foreign Venture* (1998). He has also written (with Christie Davies) *The Corporation Under Siege: The Devices used by Activists and Regulators in the Non-Risk Society* (1998). He has written widely on sociological topics with strong ethical dimensions, including failures of communication between national groups within a multinational firm, gambling, and the pharmaceutical industry.

Keith Tester is a Professor of Social Theory at the University of Portsmouth. He has published widely in the sociology of culture and the sociology of morality. His publications include *Civil Society* (1992), *The Life and Times of Post-Modernity* (1993), *The Inhuman Condition* (1995) and *Moral Culture* (1997). His recent work has focused on the relationship between classical sociology and theological debates, an interest which he is pursuing in forthcoming publications.

W. Watts Miller is a Senior Lecturer in Sociology at the University of Bristol. He is editor of *Durkheimian Studies*. His major book is *Durkheim, Morals and Modernity* (1996). He has edited a critical edition of Durkheim's Latin thesis (1997) and is co-editor of *Durkheim's Elementary Forms of Religious Life* (1998). He is especially concerned with Durkheimian ideas on morality, religion and the sacred. His current project explores the fate of hope in modern secularism.

Introduction

Kieran Flanagan

Life is full of surprises – some being more instructive than others. Somewhere in the West of England, an academic, embroiled in co-editing a worthy volume of essays, decided to buy a large television for rare evening viewing with the added comforts of small (and occasional) whiskies. A local department store, offering £50 with each new credit card, seemed the place to go. The academic, however, was greatly surprised to find his application rejected, despite being debt free. After a Kafkaesque investigation, it transpired that failure to have a continual period on the electoral role formed the statistical basis for the 'cut-off' on the application, determined, as the leaflet unctuously stated, 'by extensive analysis of our experience with previous applications'. In terms of the virtues of stewardship, thrift, discipline, and trust, the character of the sociologist was judged uncreditworthy by statistical fiat and software manipulation.

Leaving aside the narrow purpose of evaluating credit risk, and whether character was being slighted, the exercise is instructive in showing that when it comes to practicalities of money, necessary judgements in a culture of commodification *are* made around elements that pertain to virtue, the traits and dispositions that bear on intrinsic properties of goodness. The issue of trust emerges also in areas of delicacy, where intimacy and sexuality converge, a point which Giddens has pursued in an effort to find a 'pure relationship' of equality without domination and obligation, one fit for life in late modernity. Trust relates to notions of personal integrity, accountability and authority. It deals with what *can* be taken for granted in social relationships, and so for Giddens, 'trust entails the trustworthiness of the other – according "credit" that does not require continual auditing, but which can be made open to inspection periodically if necessary'.[1] This issue of trust occurs in the everyday social experiments of life in late modernity where sexuality has a profound importance. Life is made up of experiencing sexual diversity in apprenticeships of consent. Thus, 'loss of virginity' for a boy is a gain, an inevitable talisman for the future.[2] There is, however, one limit to this libertine notion of diversity: sexual inactivity. Those who preserve their

1

virginity are deemed unreflexive, the implication being that reflexivity, self-awareness, demands they lose that incredible virtue – rapidly. There is no grammar of virtuous self-denial in Giddens' world of intimacy. His is a world of a sexually empowered self desperately seeking 'pure relationships' of mutual convenience and consent. The only sin in this world of intimacy is dominance and the only vice the denial of mutual pleasure. It is a world bereft of character. There is no virtue of disinterested love in these intimate relationships. Discipline is a matter of sexual taste not a property of virtue. This sociological world is one where no tests are made on character, no virtue is forged in adversity, and no moral demand is presented that goes against the inclinations of pleasure that govern its basis. It is a stagnant world of the morally dead for whom virtue is the spectacle of other worlds, ones sociology no longer visits. If sociology has a value in regard to virtue, it is to emancipate the virtuous from their entrapments. Restraint is repression, and governance of the senses is a denial of the promise of a commodified culture, one where any bodily sensibility is to be satisfied – at a price.

Frankly, virtue is not a term to be found in the index of an introductory textbook of sociology. It is not a term of sociological currency. Virtue smacks of something antique, something precious and precarious, artificial and Victorian, perhaps. It is a term of disablement rather than enablement. It belongs to Aristotle and Aquinas, to philosophy and theology, but certainly not to sociology. It is a term of entrapment of women, something attached to attributes of femininity, which feminism has long demolished. Its images are negative. There is something self-satisfied, and falsely superior about the virtuous, which science, psycho-analysis and cynicism have worked dedicatedly to undermine. Whatever the good faith supposedly attached to it, virtue comes wrapped in bad faith. This reflects a maxim of la Rochefoucauld: 'virtue would not go far without vanity to bear it company'.[3] The striving for virtue is riddled with imperfections, doubts and misrepresentations. It is not a matter of sociological value.

The rise of virtue ethics within philosophy, with its stress on community and character, marks a shift of profound importance whose significance sociology has, as yet, failed to scrutinise. This collection is an effort, perhaps the first, to reverse this neglect. It does so in a way that links the issue of virtue to modernity and to religion. Little recent philosophical or sociological attention has been given to the connection between virtue and religion. A single exception is the essay on 'Religion, Virtue and Ethical Culture' by Cottingham. His concerns are with rooting the issue of virtue less in religion than within civic culture, where exemplars are to be cultivated in some communal form.[4] In seeking to connect virtue back to culture, of necessity the issues raised move back to sociology itself. This collection represents its initial response. It is a beginning rather than a completion of an argument about virtue, which promises much in philosophy, but even more in sociology.

Virtue belongs to lost worlds of religiosity, civilisation, refinement and to cultural notions of the value of superiority. In a culture of postmodernity, the judgements of moral distinctions upon which virtue was based have long foundered. Satire made the virtuous the first easy victims of the culture wars. Anyhow, virtue generates a suspicion of deep political incorrectness, for its presumptuous escape from what might be termed vice. Indeed, virtue might symbolise everything life and sexual politics are dedicated to overthrow. It is about discipline and about the denial of appetites and inclinations. As a term, virtue has some profoundly unprogressive attachments and overtones. Virtue is now the vice of the unemancipated. Rather than liberation, the notion of virtue suggests entrapment. It betokens properties laden with hypocrisy and artificiality, traits which reason prescribes as non-rational, emotional, and ripe for enlightened liberation. In short, virtue carries something creepy and artificial compared to the gay abandon which vice invokes. Thus, virtue seems to stand against all current 'isms'. If it operates in its traditional affiliations, it is in the realm of private ambition. Cultural arrogance is the charge laid against the unreticent about the display of their virtues in public. These are not propitious times for the virtuous. In these cultural times, when 'good news' sells little on television or in the newspapers, few want to hear the tales of the virtuous. It is 'bad news' that makes the media flap in delight. Now, if all this is true, why should sociology want to say anything about virtue?

It is a term riddled with opacity, occupying many intellectual territories, from the sacred to the civil. The diversity of settings, meanings and uses begs questions as to who owns the term, its definition and use. Even though few use the term 'virtue', other terms such as heroism, compassion, fortitude and generosity still form part of the image and ambition of culture. In a more democratised form, dignity and worth mark the significance of valued moral traits, the duty and expectation of what is enjoined in the human condition. The marginalisation of the issue of virtue is not to denote that values and moral traits have also been discarded. With cultural wars and identity politics, they might well sail under different ideological colours. But whatever the flag of convenience virtues sail under, there is still the problem of recognition, an issue Herbert has explored in the context of multi-faith and multi-culturalism in three European societies (Chapter 3 of the present volume). Lurking all the time in the issue of virtue is the question of character and trust. It is these concerns that straddle virtue ethics and sociology. Even though virtue has been secularised and has been diffusely relocated, the traits of virtue, of character and goodness still lie around as ambitions in any culture. Indeed, the demand for moral inspection has never been greater, for it is distrust not trust that forms the domain ethical concerns which have emerged from postmodernity. This culture of suspicion seems to suggest that no virtue is possible, nor is any form of moral connection, for all is deemed to be in fracture and transience.

Individualism has accentuated the degree to which the actor is now subject to surveillance and scrutiny. In the rootless, transient world of globalisation there is a greater need to check persons, their moral character and the degree to which they might bear a delegated trust. All manner of technologies are available for checking and minimising risks of misrepresentation. Dating and personnel recruitment agencies endeavour to minimise the risk of certifying fraudulent characters. The costs of failure to do so can be enormous. Thus, a dating agency will fear being sued for inadvertently placing a serial rapist on its books and an employee dedicated to fraud can run up billions on future stocks, if trust has not been adequately certified. The concerns of life politics have increased not decreased the degree to which character is regulated, and one does not require reference to Foucault to observe this point.

Recourse to legislation to govern what is civil in attitude and disposition, to minimise what destabilises the dignity of the marginal, shows endless growth. The governance of character and its social realisation is increasingly a legal matter, enshrined in a bill of rights that enforces a public morality whilst at the same time marking out many of its facets as matters of purely private concern. It is not that the regulation of morality has gone in a post-Christian society. It is now enforced with even greater vigour as part of the inversions realised by a cultural revolution in areas of identity, recognition and entitlement. Legal redress is part of the agenda of lifestyle politics and it is used with force against the untenable judgements of the virtuous, particularly in areas of sexuality and gender. It is not the religious who can claim for 'hurt feelings'; in present civil society they are not deemed to have any, at least in England, that can be given legal recognition and redress. Rights of character are protected in many aspects of public space and failure to know of these 'correct attitudes' can be costly. The dismantling of concern with virtue has been replaced by intensive social engineering to secure and to regulate prescribed attitudes in the work-place and elsewhere. In this prescriptive regime, private attitudes and their public disclosure have become intermingled in a confusing and often duplicitous way.

Despite the machinery of law and technology to check on character and trust, there is a sense of moral drift and unsettlement. There is a feeling that what cultural wars sought to secure as a moral agenda, in areas of identity, sexuality, gender, has not come to pass. Even politicians scent that moral matters have come unstuck. Thus, Blair, at the Labour Party Conference in September 1999, spoke much of a moral crisis in British society. Rights and responsibilities form part of Blair's 'Third Way', as it seeks to impose obligation and commitment on the recalcitrant. People want something better. Crime rates, drug addiction, under-age sex, all form part of a mood of gloom. If sociology is called to articulate public worries and anxieties, then articulating this sense of moral unsettlement is an inescapable part of this duty. But what is it to say? It cannot really say that such speech about morality is foreign to its calling. The deepest traditions of sociology suggest otherwise. Testing the moral temperature, and finding it freezing over under the inexorable growth of modernity, was always the reluctant duty of the fathers of sociology. The loss of a civic morality haunted Durkheim; the relentless growth of calculation and the melting of enchantment vexed Weber; and in the case of Simmel, he uncovered an unresolvable problem of the de-spiritualisation of culture where the god of money was the idol that mattered, that worked a mysterious magic of indispensability from which there was no escape.

In some Islamic societies ministries of virtue operate. Matters have not reached this stage in English society. Virtue is not a term of public reference; there is no moral ecology that seeks to preserve the notion; and there is, as yet, no political argot that would dress the term, and spin it to electoral advantage. One reason for the masked basis of the notion of virtue is that the very moral indifference that has engendered a crisis precludes the term being presented as an antidote, a difference of moral ambition that would matter. It is not that traits of morality that overlap with those of virtue are present or not; it is that they are not given an identifiable focus, a mobilising property that would harness the best that can be retrieved from the present moral drift. Indeed, there is a sense of public unease, that those traits, dispositions and properties of the good, so necessary to preserve the fabric of society, are becoming unstitched and that there is no agreed pattern available to knit them back together again.

This sense of moral unravelment has of late become acute. It could be due to the onset of the millennium, or the decline of religion, or the growth of multi-channel television, or the internet, but for whatever reason, there are unsettlements abroad, distinctive to the age and affecting particularly the younger generation. They seem the unsung casualties of the cultural wars over sexual identity and morals, having high illegitimacy rates, drug taking and, amongst males especially, frighteningly high suicide rates. It is scarcely surprising that in these times of anxiety and uncertainty the fastest growing group amongst students at British Universities is the Christian Union.

Oddly the issue of character and attribute in the 1970s and 1980s did emerge in the gender wars over the supposedly desirable and undesirable moral traits of men and women. Female virtues of compassion, friendship and tenderness were set against more crude male values of violence, insensitivity and the selfishness of the predatory. In the cultural wars, the male sank into a crisis of self-confidence that has only recently become apparent. These efforts, however, to mark difference have sunk into the moral indifference which postmodernity has come to signify. Openness, denial of the right to exclude, to discriminate and to differentiate, rest on a canon of non-judgementalism. In this mechanism of political correctness, the facades of culture have been rearranged and lives go on below the surface in some sort of moral paralysis, where public rhetoric hides an anarchy of private moral states, whose central rule is not to be caught. This anarchy reflects wider fracture and fragmentation. Postmodernity has come to signify life in this perilous, fragmented situation. As obligations and communal commitments have slackened, the social bond, the sense of mutuality which society ought to ordain, but which it cannot enforce, has also been weakened. It is therefore scarcely surprising that the issue of postmodernity should lead into a question of ethics.[5]

A life of waiting, escaping, journeying but never arriving, marks the actor of postmodernity, less living as a tourist in perpetual disconnection than as a prisoner of forces he cannot assimilate, harmonise or transcend. All this returns to a familiar tale, that of Simmel, of the disjunction between forms and content, now exasperated in a state of paralysis in postmodernity, one where the actor is fated to passive marginality, seeking to connect but doomed to disconnection. Seeking to believe without the prospect of belonging marks life in postmodernity.

If there is a mode of resistance to this fate which postmodernity ordains, it comes from religion, particularly in forms of religious fundamentalism. It thrives in an oppositional manner, marking boundaries, imposing obligations and propagating aspirations of virtue in some form of unexpected counter-culture. It presents tunes that make their harmonies regardless of the dissonance blaring out from those who control the mass media. Postmodernity might be about life stuck in endless preludes, where fugues are fated to be discordant, but in such musical games theology tends to play the trump card: God. In all these discontents, these cultural discords and fractures, there lurk wantings to find the Other, to seek roots of obligation and sites for commitments. To redeem the emptiness is to flesh out an identity; and that pursuit is to ask for some form of trustful identification, something secure, something authentic, and something of character. It is against this background that one can discern the way in which modernity, religion and virtue ethics have become partly interlinked. Change and decay have moved them to the fore.

The issues raised in virtue ethics belong to philosophy; they offset the narrowness of an ethics based on Kantian assumptions of reason and consequence; the spirit of calculation of utilitarianism; and the calibration of judgement to outcome, that speak of process, but of no moral substance and of no character or trait of goodness or evil. Kant did write on virtue, but the form it takes in virtue ethics is different. In reaction to the supposed narrowness of ethics and its apparent disconnection from the world as lived, the rise of virtue ethics, with its stress on character traits, on community and formation, and on moral excellence, might have uses in ameliorating the distance of philosophy from the world, but that is not the sociologist's weak flank. Whatever else his weakness, the sociologist lives in the world, and reflexivity enjoins that he speaks from it, to articulate its worries. At present there is a glimmer of an argument that these relate to a sense of moral weaknesses, a loss of virtue. Knowing and uninhibited curiosity carry a price of engulfment and a moral irresponsibility of fatigued capitulation to the chaos of moral choices. A sense of that price can emerge in the randomness of public events, which unexpectedly attract a nation's unwilling attention.

An example of this arose in late August 1999, over a fourteen-year-old boy, who had made a twelve-year-old girl pregnant. This case caused the British prime minister to speak of a moral crisis in the nation. Craftily, the boy denied responsibility for his actions and instead blamed his courses on sex education for corrupting him into thinking of practising sexual permutations which he never realised existed. Instruction had become a form of enticement. The instrument for instilling responsible sexual activity seemingly had confused knowledge, the expansion of possibility, with the failure to implant a wisdom to use it. This boy exemplifies a dilemma of contemporary British life. He raises an awkward question. Who is responsible for moral activities and their immoral effects when traditional cautions about the Tree of Knowledge have lost their plausibility? Increasingly, everybody seems a victim and few wish to exercise moral responsibility. It is scarcely surprising that many feel that a post-Christian society has not managed to deliver the moral goods to either civil or political satisfaction. In these times, indeed, there is a curious ambiguity about morality. At one level, morality matters, and at another it does not.

There is a sneaking suspicion that morality does matter, but at the same time, those who claim to cultivate it are treated with deep suspicion for fostering untenable aspirations. Lurking behind this public mood of affirmation and disaffirmation is the hope that those who conspicuously cleave to an exemplary morality, a life of virtue, will fall from it themselves. It is a hopeless and untenable condition unfit for a cynical age. Yet, the issue of virtue exposes the hypocrisies of postmodernity. It bestows on virtue properties of demarcation which it affects to deny in all other realms of culture. Postmodernity claims to signify the overturning of boundaries, the collapse of belief about belief, and the necessity of coping with nihilism and agnosticism in some noble moral manner of accommodation. Like Simmel's notion of money, the power of postmodernity lies in its colourlessness, its disinterested presentation of what is fated as the human condition. Yet, this disinterest masks a definite assertion, an act of faith, that sites of edification, sites of hope and virtue *are* outside boundaries of conventions in culture which postmodernity arbitrarily draws. The claim that nothing escapes contextualisation or relativism can be turned against postmodernity itself. It masks its own pieties about its articles of faith. Where did these arbitrary exclusions of virtue come from and upon what context-free basis does postmodernity proceed with its own brand of faith in nihilism? Postmodernity fiddles with Pascal's coin, but keeps dropping it lest it be spun. Postmodernity permits all games be played, but not this one of Pascal. If played the wager might lead the self to escape from itself into something better: a life of virtue that leads into the realm of the spiritual.

It is not surprising that the self is in crisis and identity is in chaos. There is nothing to identify with other than the fate of falling, like everybody else. Nothing withstands against this tide of affairs. The issue of identity is *the* business of postmodernity. It has not absolved the need to find an Other to trust, a character with whom to settle in an identification that fulfils. Surely, this is the deeper ambition of life politics? The self has to seek beyond itself, otherwise it risks entrapment, a denial of the means of actualisation in the escape that matters, the giving to others. If the self does not reach beyond itself, it risks going unrecognised and so unloved that it cannot but wither on the vine of culture. Strangely, far from absolving sociology of moral responsibilities, the marriage of reflexivity and postmodernity marks the advent of a greater need to exercise an ethical choice, one where the antino-mies of virtue and vice might loom out of the mist. What modernity lost, postmodernity seems to have regained. This reflects a point that concerned Bauman, that 'morality is the *drama of choice*, the social practice of ethical legislation did everything possible to limit, best of all to *eliminate altogether,* that choice'.[6] Later in the same essay Bauman concludes that 'there is little hope that the plight of the moral self will ever be cured of its intrinsic ambi-valence. Reason and logic offer a cure which is ineffective if harmless, and poisonous if effective'.[7] Anyhow, even if sociology seeks to make no judge-ment in these areas, society demands that it does, and some events impose on the discipline an inescapable duty to arbitrate and to make moral judge-ments. In the face of the gifts of modernity, sociology cannot confine itself to praise of the social surfaces of life and society. Behind the face are pitfalls, deceits and evils, and sociology is enjoined, theoretically, methodologically and morally, to read deeper.

Bauman has shown, to devastating effect in the case of the Holocaust, that sociology cannot just settle for a disinterested, objective account of its social organisation. It might have had routine patterns, but a neutral description of their functions would mock sociology's humanitarian claims. It would be offensively insufficient to treat the events of the Holocaust as a technical matter of disposal which might excite sociological interest in the bureau-cracy of the operation. This bureaucracy was geared to the ordering of mass death. To ignore these ends of the operation would be breathtaking. Some-how, the sociologist has to ask more. What was hidden in what was so routinised and ordinary? How did it come about that a civilisation, endowed with capacities for technical excellence, was uniquely turned to such pro-foundly uncivilised effect: the capacity to industrialise murder?[8] Unfortunately, for some, the only label appropriate to describe these disinterested fruits of modernity, its capacity to calculate without reference to moral ends, comes from the discipline it strove to assassinate: theology. The term it would employ to clarify this state of affairs, albeit one Bauman would resist, is evil.

Whilst Bauman's re-casting of postmodernity into ethical considerations has wide but, as yet, unconfronted sociological implications, MacIntyre, who placed virtue ethics back on the agenda of philosophy,[9] has largely been ignored within sociology, as McMylor and Tester indicate in this collection (Chapters 1 and 2). MacIntyre and Bauman work from different directions, not only theologically but also in their relation to sociology. Bauman proceeds from the limits of sociology to confront the issues of ethics that distinctively emerge from the condition of postmodernity whose significance he has greatly clarified. Sociology is the site of modernity and postmodernity is its maturation. Thus, sociology is implicated in Bauman's account of ethics and postmodernity. On the other hand, MacIntyre, who starts from sociology, turns against it in a devastating critique of its place in the loss of virtue as an ingredient of modernity. In this reading, Goffman and Weber are the scapegoats of his ire. They fashioned a characterless entity of an actor in sociology incapable of distinguishing between the manipulative and the non-manipulative. This actor is removed from the disinterest which the exercise of virtue requires, and sociology legitimises the blindness to distinctions which characterises the present state of moral vacuity. To rehabilitate what sociology cannot grasp, McIntyre returns to the question of virtue in Aristotle and Aquinas. Aware or unaware of postmodernity, MacIntyre blithely seeks the return of a community with its tales and traditions of virtue, its stories of the heroic and of what is worthy of emulation. Not for MacIntyre the fracture of narrative, rather he invokes a theology to rehearse the story. Sociology cannot ignore the issues raised by virtue ethics, not least in the way Weber is placed in the centre of concerns about the moral distortions he laid on sociology, an inheritance which has some dubious overtones. The issue of Weber places virtue ethics in the heart of sociological deliberations. Sociology is placed in the dock and found wanting in virtue. For many, Weber would plead otherwise.

Both MacIntyre and Bauman find uncommon dangers in Weber's account of bureaucratic authority. Despite their differences, both are concerned with the preservation of moral openings in the setting of modernity. Bauman is additionally concerned about its maturation into postmodernity. Each finds a price in the issue of assent to the authority which modernity and the Enlightenment pose. For MacIntyre, it is the telling of tales of character that offers hope of openings. For Bauman, redemption lies in ambiguity. It undermines a totalising belief that risks tyrannising, whether of the Enlightenment or in the revolt it generates, of fundamentalism. It keeps the necessity of choice open. For both, Weber is the villain of the piece. For Bauman, the 'unanticipated consequences' of Weber's approach to bureaucratic rationality, that so exemplified modernity, laid the seeds for what was to come with the Holocaust. Bureaucracy's genius was to re-deploy moral norms in a rationalised manner that gave them an added plausibility. Thus, Bauman records that '*bureaucracy's double feat is the moralization of technology, coupled with the denial of the moral significance of non-technical issues'.*[10] Morality lies in the performance and efficient execution of tasks and not in the moral ends these obtain. Weber was concerned with the unanticipated consequences of reason in modernity, and Bauman asks whether he might even have dimly seen what was to come.[11] In some way modernity, in the shape of a civilisation based on reason, had a particular facilitating and legitimising function in relation to the Holocaust. If this is so, then sociology is in some way morally implicated, for not having a notion of evil (which Bauman would discount). If evil is accepted as a necessary metaphor for the Holocaust, then unless sociology is doomed to a lopsided moral existence, the opposite, good, is a trait that also requires due consideration, and if this so, then the issues raised by virtue ethics creep on to the sociological field.

For MacIntyre, Weber's notion of bureaucratic authority is an emotivist one, where the distinctions between manipulative and non-manipulative social relations are obliterated. It is what is represented in character that is but a mask that disturbs MacIntyre.[12] What is central to MacIntyre is that character provides a moral legitimation of existence. This is a point of convergence between virtue ethics and sociology.

It might seem that the criticisms of Bauman and MacIntyre place Weber totally outside the issue of virtue and, in so doing, also manage to remove its study from sociological scrutiny. Apart from supplying a critical appraisal of his work, McMylor (Chapter 1) indicates why MacIntyre's work has received little sociological notice. It easy to regard his work as a seeking of virtue in terms of a nostalgia and therefore beyond the sociological pale. McMylor criticises such misunderstandings in MacIntyre's account of virtue and goes on to stress the continuity between traditional societies and modernity, whose distinctive traits are then picked out for scrutiny in his writings. He also suggests that although MacIntyre shares with Bauman a distrust of a positivist social science and the structures it produces, the former is more optimistic and radical in his approach than the latter whose analysis is so much darker. For MacMylor, MacIntyre is part of a wider movement to rehabilitate issues of virtue in the conditions of modernity and its maturation into postmodernity.

In chapter 2, Tester turns the tables against MacIntyre to offer a spirited defence of Weber and to defend him against charges of colluding with what he despised – emotivism. Tester's concern is to rehabilitate the ethical duty of establishing moral choice, a position exemplified in Weber's famous lecture, 'Science as Vocation'. The value of Tester's argument is to reveal an unexpected compatibility between Weber and MacIntyre. The ultimate end is an accountability to a 'true self' and here Tester finds a dubious legacy in Weber for any sociology of virtue. It relates to his understanding that science and religion cannot be reconciled. Tester concludes by wondering about the value of a sociology that is so partial and incomplete. Tester also notes the way the theological baggage surrounding Levinas (who is of crucial importance in Bauman's later work) has not been picked up in sociology. It would seem that in dealing with virtue, sociology has to face some hidden theologies. Three other points support the view that the issue of virtue was of deeper significance in Weber than many might think.

First, virtue ethics is at the centre of concern of *The Protestant Ethic and the Spirit of Capitalism*, the classical work of sociology. It examines the elective affinity between virtue, in terms of stewardship and discipline, and the resolution of salvation anxiety. This affinity takes a form where self-accountability has to be resolved in this world. The effect of this calling, that is implicated in the cultivation of virtue, has profound economic and cultural consequences. The mode of argument sets down an exemplary form for later sociology. It establishes that the routinisation and rationalisation of virtues do have uncommon sociological consequences which deserve scrutiny. Secondly, in the area of bureaucracy, Weber was careful to take into account the social factors and effects of recruitment. This could be the weak flank of bureaucracy, for despite its claims to a disinterested pursuit of reason in administration, it had a profound interest in securing conditions of trust in its recruits, that they could be relied upon to share and to implement its values of rational calculation that formed its basis as *the* superior instrument of rule. Examinations were moral and rational instruments of selection. Not only did they certify knowledge, they also certified character in terms of application, diligence and the virtues that came from knowledge, of judgement and respect for the text, the written document. Thirdly, Weber was deeply concerned with the issue of duty, a point which Tester pursues in his chapter. That seeking of an inner calling, and the demand to act on it, both form a crucial strand of Weber's writings. It bestows on the sociologist the duty to reflect on his own ethic and to follow it in a calling, a vocation, that involves in its own way the seeking of virtue, the exercise of character in the use of the sociological gaze.

Bureaucracy is not always subtractive of virtue; in some cases it can facilitate and enhance its basis, a point illustrated in the area of blood donation. It is bureaucracy that facilitates the democratisation of the virtue of blood donation, a form of altruism of the highest order. It is bureaucracy that defends the space for such virtue to thrive, which a free market, based on payment for donation, destroys.[13] In all this, bureaucracy is an instrument and in that regard Weber was correct. But because it is just an instrument, it imposes an increased moral duty on those who use it, to be sensitive to the implications of the legitimacy it commands.

Weber is not the only major sociologist whose interests lie within or adjacent to virtue. It was a major concern for others. Watts Miller has provided an imaginative account of how Durkheim, in the pursuit of a religion of humanity, seemed to exemplify the agenda of virtue ethics in his concern with character, motivation and will.[14]

The legitimacy of the issue of virtue for sociology, whatever the partiality of definitions used, derives less from readings, however plausible, of Weber and Durkheim (and, indeed, Simmel) but from movements regarding the self and its seeking of a holism, one that would reconcile a sense of division between body and soul. This concern points to the rehabilitation of an Aristotelian form of virtue in contemporary life. The seeking of harmony and happiness lies in this pursuit of holism, a value whose use is to be found in New Age religions, medicine, sport and diet, to name a few areas. This seeking seems to reflect a point of Aristotle that 'it is virtuous activities that determine our happiness'.[15] The rise of the sociology of the body, where it is treated as a cultural object, a symbolic resource, involves a property of introspection, scrutiny and stewardship,[16] and although the term 'virtue' seldom arises as an explicit term of reference, issues of health and wellbeing take sociology near its consideration. In all this lies a question of value, one which Davies and Neal (Chapter 4) consider in relation to the issues of risk and moral worth surrounding the person in statistical, potential or full particular forms. Using a variety of settings, from war and executions to the status of the unborn, they also pose some awkward questions about the ethics of risk in relation to pharmaceutical regulation. In all this, what they term statistical persons lose out in relation to a concentration of moral concern on particular persons. The necessity of some sort of judgement and reconciliation of these contradictions governs their chapter which is really concerned with the issue of visibility and recognition of moral worth. In this regard some are more equal than others in relation to the virtue of fortitude and how much sympathy, dignity and virtuous regard they can mobilise. A value of their contribution is the way they show how these contradictions have evolved from the nineteenth century. As applied to the body, technology has brought forward some uncomfortable questions about virtue, its masking and its recognition.

The custody of the body is seen as the root of the means of resolving the identity the self wishes to occupy. Diet, keeping fit, plastic surgery, and efforts to beautify and to maximise appearance all represent efforts of stewardship, opportunities to enhance well-being. Lurking in this issue is the question of the character which the body embodies most notably on the face. Technology can permit the detachment of the face from character and thus from moral scrutiny, and because appearance is so feigned, distrust increases. One wants to attach virtue back to the face through moral endeavour not plastic surgery.

Scrutiny of the body draws attention to its frailty, that, no matter how well the prospect is disguised in worldly pleasures, it is doomed to wither and to die. The traffic of analysis of the body and sexuality seems cast in a one-way direction towards unfettered use unimpeded by discipline, a term that has fallen into disrepute since the writings of Freud and Foucault. Barot, in Chapter 8, supplies a useful antidote to these Western assumptions in his account of celibacy and the Hindu tradition, where renunciation is linked to an awesome regulation of sexual drives.

Barot's essay has a number of unusual features. In linking celibacy to culture, Barot shows the way themes of MacIntyre emerge also in Indian society and religion. Heroism, narratives and a sense of tradition are embodied in the virtues of celibacy and renunciation in ways long lost in the West. Renunciation of sexual activity is deemed an exemplary act of heroism in the Hindu tradition, the realisation of a virtue of great value, for the powers and status it confers, whereas in the West such activities might be deemed lunatic and a denial of everything that sexual politics seeks to overcome. The value of Barot's essay lies in illustrating what has been lost in the endless cult of self-actualisation without inhibitions in the West. The pursuit of bodily pleasure has become a tyranny, one regulated and controlled in a climate of commodity fetishism, in which the body and the self are objects of engulfing dalliances with their own imprisonment. Barot's essay also supplies a useful antidote to the notion that interest in and defence of celibacy is peculiar to Catholicism.

The issue of virtue surrounding the body takes on an even more definite turn in the case of *the* fact of life: death. The final arrangements of disposal embody virtues of mourning, of grief and of how the living may confront life in the absence of the departed. Even in death, la Rochefoucauld finds a mixed motive in the virtues of memoralisation, as one of his maxims notes: 'funereal pomp has more to do with the vanity of the living than the honouring of the dead'.[17] The varying qualities of appreciation and recognition of the person, living and dead, are explored in Davies and Neal (Chapter 4), but Jupp (Chapter 13) examines these in a distinctly religious context, one affected by forces of commodification and secularisation. In marrying changes in memorialisation and forms of disposal, such as cremation, Jupp illustrates the way the Church has lost control of burial rites, an area of supposed indispensability, given that the fate of the departed into the next life is traditionally involved. The commodification of funerals marks a displacement of the power to provide ritual regulation of the virtue of mourning from the clergy to the funeral director and other interested parties and from the values of religious tradition to those of modernity. The issue of the after-life is rearranged and buried with the advent of the do-it-yourself funeral which the burial trade proffers to all without judgement and where the only virtue required is cash in hand.

Paul wrote that 'fruit of the Spirit is love, joy, peace, long-suffering, gentleness, goodness, faith'. He goes on to add that 'if we live in the Spirit, let us also walk in the Spirit' (Gal.5:22 and 25). To these virtues might be added faith, hope and charity and, of course, the cardinal virtues of fortitude, temperance, justice and prudence. It is not wilful to list these virtues in a Christian context, for within virtue ethics and its emergence is a definite streak of Catholicism that is difficult to ignore. The revolt against the

Enlightenment notion of ethics, as being solely imbued with and governed by the spirit of reason, proceeds from Elizabeth Anscombe's famous essay in 1958.[18] Anscombe and MacIntyre are both Catholics, as is Charles Taylor whose work relates to many facets of debate on virtue ethics. Stress on disposition and character, on community, on agency and accountability, on being part of one body, on being morally responsible for one's choices, and on the need to cultivate disposition towards being good, reflect traits common to virtue ethics but ones that are also distinctively of the essence of Christianity. Theology supplies the template for virtue ethics but it also marks a division in the terms of reference within which it operates. Thus, within virtue ethics are issues of choice between revelation and reason; dependence and independence; grace and autonomy; and divinity cast in humanity or adrift as in the manner of Nietzsche.

Nobody would wish to argue that instances of heroism, compassion and the exercise of virtues of bravery and fortitude do not exist outside religion. They emerge in mass accidents and in the unsung activities of those living lives of quiet desperation, caring for the weak. These instances, however, are often exceptional and unrecognised, and their intermittent publicity should not disguise the wider crises of virtue in society, aspects of which have been mentioned earlier. It is the absence of a focused, dedicated interest in the topics associated with virtue that demands sociological attention.

Proverbs 2:1–9 is the first reading at mass for the feast of St Benedict (11 July). The reading enjoins seeking a path of virtue and wisdom to realise happiness. Such an injunction seems proper to theology but alien to sociology, yet in Weber, Durkheim and Simmel, duty, heroism and religiosity bear cultivation. They are ultimate values worthy of rehabilitation. Emancipation and enlightenment, the gifts of modernity, have become soured in postmodernity where the self is trapped, yet seeks escape but on what path? As Tester (Chapter 2) so well indicates, sociology cannot show the way to virtue, save the duty to seek it. It can, however, show how the path to virtue can become overgrown. Pruning of the social is sociology's gift to the ambition to cultivate the virtues. These form the ambitions of civic culture, education and identity politics, for health and well being are also fundamental to the moral commonwealth. The vitality of virtue bears on the soul of culture, which Simmel placed at the heart of the sociological enterprise. If virtues require witness, cultivation, and certification, if they require manifestation in the social, in arrangements that effect their recognition, in institutions, rituals and exemplary communities, then sociology cannot but have a part. Enduring questions of fulfilment and happiness bear on the nurture of virtues. Their roots are frail on a field of culture geared more to up-rooting than rooting. In seeking something deeper, the virtues point to traits of character that ameliorate the vacuity of character of ordained by postmodernity.

The issues that virtue ethics raise for sociology are indeed complex. No single collection, let alone this first sociological response to its existence, can cover all the ground of analysis which virtue ethics generates. A diversity of positions is represented in the collection. Four strands can be found in the collection that are of significance.

The first strand briefly relates to the types of virtues selected. Hope (Watts Miller), celibacy (Barot), mourning (Jupp), fortitude (Davies and Neal, and Archer), justice (Herbert), are the more explicit virtues pursued in the collection. Clearly, other virtues could have been selected for treatment. Virtues in terms of duty, struggle and fidelity are implicit in the other essays in the collection.

The second strand relates to issues of recognition and misrecognition in relation to virtue. Virtue points to a scarce resource of esteem and legitimacy. Far from being unproblematic, as it might seem, virtue is riddled with problems of contestability and claims about the entitlement to be recognised as virtuous. If virtue is about honour, then the question of status it generates can be highly problematic. This becomes especially so when it is valued and appears to be rare. In such cases, the politics of recognition emerge, not only over the issue of who is virtuous, but also in the duty and right to be considered so. This arises in the regulation of behaviour and the appearance of virtue, such as the veiling of women in Islamic societies that utilise legal forms of enforcement through ministries of virtue and public morality. The politicisation of virtue emerges around the question of abortion, where questions of shame and blame arise. Opponents of abortion claim to be protecting the sanctity of life, whilst their opponents deny them such monopolistic entitlements. Such debates are hotly contested in the USA, but far less so in the UK, where abortion has been removed from the political agenda of the three main parties in Parliament. Questions of recognition of virtue emerge in the chapters of Davies and Neal (Chapter 4) and Herbert (Chapter 3). These essays are about the issues of entitlement and the inconsistencies and inequalities that emerge over the recognition of virtue.

These issues of recognition and misrecognition are set in an interpretative context in Flanagan's essay (Chapter 6). He is concerned with the burdens of interpretation, the inconsistencies that emerge around the antinomies of vice and virtue which bedazzle sociology. The incapacity to discern stems from the decadence that emerged with the rise of modernity. As a discipline, sociology tends to despise virtue, in so far as it recognises it, and adores vice in so far as it misrecognises it. Flanagan argues that the slackening of the antinomy between both leads to a moral indifference that undermines agency, accountability and the quest to realise something better in character. Virtue requires struggle to construct, hence its heroic dimension.

In Archer's paper on St Teresa (Chapter 7), the issue of securing virtue is less about representation than misrepresentation. Saints might seem to be cast in plaster as statues for the simple and the superstitious to adore. Archer's account of St Teresa demolishes this form of sentimentality to present the individual and communal struggles that surround her pursuit of heroic virtue, the definitional property of a saint. Recognition of properties of saintliness do not just happen – there are processes of discernment which make their own rules and these have sociological *and* theological bases of scrutiny. Archer displays a range of contradictions and challenges to sociology, not least to Durkheim and Weber, in her effort to defend a theology against what the light of the Enlightenment strove to extinguish. Like Flanagan, she is unapologetic in her Catholic theology and in making sociology subservient to its tenets.

The question of recognition permits Herbert (Chapter 3) to give an unusual variation on MacIntyre's account of virtue by setting it in the issue of multicultural rights of representation, where religion is aligned to politics to seek a place in civil, secular society. Treating Islam in the context of three European societies allows him to draw comparisons with differing forms of assimilation realised in the context of ethnicity and immigration. The value of his essay lies in the way he links the question of virtue, and MacIntyre's reading of it, to issues of the politics of recognition. This locates the question of virtue in a wider framework of ethnicity, religion and culture. It illustrates the potential the question of virtue offers to the critical interests of sociology.

The third strand of the collection points to a division between the contributors about the place of virtue within or outside religion. Secularisation forms a backdrop to this strand. Some virtues are mere forms of civility, such as gentleness and fortitude (such as coping with illness). They can be related to a religious dimension but do not seem to require its exercise. Nor can it be said that heroism is a distinctly Christian virtue. Thus, it is be argued that the issue of virtue can well stand outside religion in its organised form. As definitions of virtue are hazardous and complex, so too are those surrounding religion within the collection. Some positions are well within the contours of traditional religions, in its widest terms, though affiliations to these vary. Thus, Quakerism, Hinduism, Catholicism, New Age religions, and Nonconformist/Anglican positions are treated as explicit reference points (Dandelion, Chapter 10; Barot, Chapter 8; Archer, Chapter 7; Flanagan, Chapter 6; Heelas, Chapter 9; and Jupp, Chapter 13). The issue of Islam is also treated by Herbert (Chapter 3), but less in terms of its theology and more as an issue of religion and ethnicity.

In their assessments of virtue, Barot, Flanagan, Archer and Jupp speak with sympathy from within explicitly Hindu and Christian positions. In the case of Archer and Flanagan, the theological dimensions of virtue and the ambiguities its generates are played back against sociology to mark its limits of analysis. This weakness increases the dependence of sociology on theology. In the remainder of the collection, the response to religion is more complex. In the case of Davies and Neal, and Herbert, the issue of religion is treated less in terms of belief than in terms of the ethics of the person or the ethnic group. This is also the case with Tester and McMylor, whose perspectives might lead further in a religious direction, but this is neither avowed nor pursued.

There is, however, a remarkable contrast in approaches to virtue and ethics within the papers of Watts Miller (Chapter 12), Heelas (Chapter 9) and Collins (Chapter 5). Their approach to religion is decidedly from within a sociological frame of expectations. For Collins, there is a concern to relate invisible religion to the views on virtue of the young people in her sample. This shows a faith that lies within the immanent rather than the transcendent, one that is personalised, individualised and unencumbered by institutional affiliation or commitment. This sets the site for moral decision-making even amongst the committed Christians in her study. In their views on a range of moral issues that relate to virtue, authority was problematic, and in some ways the focus of theology in relation to religious decision-making seems to have become detached, at least in a transcendent and ecclesial form. Her approach provides an interesting contrast with the perspectives of Watts Miller and Heelas who are dealing with religion as detached from a theology.

In Watts Miller's terms, this relates to the site of secularity within which the issue of hope is to be considered. In an effort to seek a commonwealth, Watts Miller follows the issue of hope around Durkheim and Guyau, but also makes genuflections to Marcel and Moltmann. This admits a theological flank to what might seem a purely sociological effort to characterise the issue of hope. Watts Miller uses the notion of hope against hope to preserve an opening, a necessity of struggle, but one that places him, however unwillingly, at the intersections between religion and theology. Religion in some form has its uses in relation to virtue. The issue is: in which form and embodying what belief?

In dealing with issues of cultural extremities, Heelas places faith for their containment in Durkheim's ethic of humanity and its sacralisation in the context of New Age religions. There is an original cast to Heelas' essay which confronts a charge against New Age religions that they seldom consider issues of ethics. Like Watts Miller, Heelas is working within the umbrella of Durkheim's cult of man, whose virtues of heroism denote a vision for sociology. They also offer the prospects of ethics in this context, effecting an amelioration of the extremities of culture. Comparing the two essays, Heelas might seem to be boarding a solution, Durkheim, which Watts Miller is leaving behind. The link between hope and utopia underlines the way both are looking to a future. This forms a distinct concern of several contributors to the collection.

The fourth strand of the collection relates to issues of the link between virtue and the question of secularisation of theology. Whilst Watts Miller accepts the site of secularity as a necessity from which to start the treatment of hope, rather more pessimistic conclusions about the significance of secularisation emerge in the essays of Jupp (Chapter 13), Dandelion (Chapter 10) and Lindohf (Chapter 11). These essays operate in terms of Isambert's notion of internal secularisation. This refers to a reading of the world from within religion, where belief is reorganised so that what is distinctively religious is reordered and rendered problematic. It suggests that secularisation is self-inflicted, the result of the effort of the churches, since the 1960s, to rationalise their relationship to the world.[19] Again this invokes Weber, but in ways that worry about the displacement of the management of virtue, of mourning, of witness and fear of the Last Things, from a traditional theological frame of accountability to one that purely reflects worldly values that seem inadequate. In these three essays, there is a regret at the loss of connection between what is purely religious, what could and should be proclaimed and the needs and fears of the world. These papers are about what is beyond life, the accountability of time to the Second Coming in the case of Dandelion and his treatment of the Quakers; the distinctively theological notion of the apocalypse, ironically discarded by theology only to become a defining image in significant aspects of popular culture in Lindohf's paper; and the commodification of death, where the fate of the dead becomes a matter of earthly proprieties rather than heavenly judgements in Jupp's essay.

Dandelion and Lindohf might seem to be occupying very separate worlds, of Quakerism and contemporary popular culture, yet they both show a concern with the emasculation of theology, where belonging becomes detached from belief in the case of the Quakers, and a failure of theological nerve that enabled a discarded notion of the apocalypse to be reappropriated as a mobilising image in films that made a mark on popular culture. It sacralised that which theology had secularised and had marked as incredible. Where these two papers differ is in their approach to the issue of the structure of ecclesial culture. For Lindhof, this is a mechanism that caused theology to lose contact with the people, whereas for Dandelion its absence left Quakerism naked to the forces of secularity and modernity. His paper provides a fascinating link between time and accountability of witness, one whose evolution points to shifts in approaches to virtue, those peculiar to Quakerism. His metaphor of the alarm clock is tellingly persuasive.

Lindohf's paper provides a detailed account of the way in which the rhetoric and images of apocalypse have been re-cast in films about futures that are profoundly bleak, where social bonds and civilisations have collapsed and where ethics and virtue have to be reinvented. These images of desolation, anarchy and wasteland invoke notions of a First and Second Coming that supplies an interesting contrast to the way they emerge in Dandelion's account of the Quakers. Utopias and issues of hope lie also in these territories. The films Lindohf examines satisfy the needs of large audiences which the Churches seem unable to meet. It is through popular culture that theological images are emerging in ways that reflect fears of a new generation well detached from theological obligations and affiliations, but also their comforts.

There is a property of regret, almost disappointment, in the accounts of Dandelion and Lindhof, over the disintegration of the sites of theological witness, whether of the Quakers, or of Christian theologies in general. In the effort to connect, there has been a fatal disconnection between the liberalisation of theology and worldly expectations. As Jupp, echoing Berger, suggests, Protestantism in the context of modernity has become its own gravedigger, a point which each of these papers in dealing with virtue (faith, fortitude and heroism in relation to time) seems to affirm. Modern churches seem to have had a failure of nerve in dealing with matters that are distinctively their province, their realm of responsibility over mediation and interpretation of matters over which one would presume they had monopolies. Time, hope, death and final judgement are areas where the churches ought to be strong, yet in a culture of postmodernity they are found to be weak. These issues relate to the need to forge character and spiritual ambition, the ground of virtue. In so discarding the centrality of these issues, modernising churches seeking to connect to the common good and planting faith in the city seem to have lost the plot of the question that matters: how to get to heaven. This reflects a common theme of sociologists, of being disappointed in the theologies they scrutinise which endemically seem to misread the needs of the world.

Each paper in the collection displays a command of its appropriate literature, and presents its account in ways that connect to the immediate. There is a property in each paper of coming off the ground in its deliberations that lends a certain vibrancy to the collection as a whole. The contributors are trying to connect to the world as they see and feel it, through the instruments of sociology. None of the contributors would wish what they wrote to be conceived as the last word on the subject. In each, there is a property of wrestling with questions that do not admit of easy resolution in pursuing the link between virtue ethics, religion and modernity. Speaking on behalf of all the contributors, we seem to be stumbling towards the beginning of a set of new questions, all too old for having been forgotten, but all too necessary in our present circumstances. The words, the concepts, the analyses are all needed to keep the wheels of thought rotating as they plough up new fields and, as the furrows are made, sociology has to find its own account of virtue to read the patterns if a fall into the ditch is to be precluded.

Notes and references

1   Anthony Giddens, *The Transformation of Intimacy. Sexuality, Love & Eroticism in Modern Societies* (Cambridge: Polity, 1992), p. 191.
2   Ibid., p. 51.
3   François la Rochefoucauld, *Maxims*, trans. Leonard Tancock (Harmondsworth: Penguin, 1959), no. 200, p. 62.
4   John Cottingham, 'Religion, Virtue and Ethical Culture', *Philosophy*, vol. 69, 1994, pp. 163–80.

5   Zygmunt Bauman, *Postmodern Ethics* (Oxford: Blackwell, 1993).
6   Zygmunt Bauman, 'What Prospects of Morality in Times of Uncertainty', *Theory, Culture & Society*, vol. 15, no. 1, February 1998, p. 13. Italics are his emphasis.
7   Ibid., p. 22.
8   Zygmunt Bauman, *Modernity and the Holocaust* (Cambridge: Polity, 1991).
9   Alasdair MacIntyre, *After Virtue*, second edition (London: Duckworth, 1985). For one of the few sociological appraisals of MacIntyre, see Peter McMylor, *Alasdair MacIntyre. Critic of Modernity* (London: Routledge, 1994).
10   Bauman, *Modernity and the Holocaust*, p. 160.
11   Ibid., pp. 9–11.
12   MacIntyre, *After Virtue*, pp. 23–9.
13   See Richard M. Titmuss, *The Gift Relationship. From Human Blood to Social Policy* (London: George Allen & Unwin, 1970).
14   W. Watts Miller, *Durkheim, Morals and Modernity* (London: UCL, 1996), pp. 10–11. Watts Miller's re-reading of Durkheim needs to be placed alongside a crucial re-casting of Weber's writings by Hennis. He also gives a crucial place to virtue ethics (not his term) in the moral ambitions of Weber's view of sociology. His re-interpretation of Weber stresses his concerns with qualities (virtues) and the fate of these in the context of their routinisation in the inner and outer worlds of the actor, such as the Calvinist. The hazardous task of reconciling these worlds in the fated circumstances of modernity lent a moral purpose to Weber's approach to the actor, whose personality and character were compromised by an irresistible growth of calculation and consequent disenchantment. See Wilhelm Hennis, *Max Weber. Essays in Reconstruction*, trans. Keith Tribe (London: Allen & Unwin, 1988). For an illuminating review essay that suggests a need to re-read Weber in the light of the growth of virtue ethics, see Brad Lowell Stone, 'The Newest Weber', *Sociological Forum*, vol. 5, no. 4, 1990, pp. 669–676.
15   Aristotle, *The Ethics of Aristotle*, trans. J. A. K. Thomson (Harmondsworth: Penguin, 1976), p. 83.
16   Mike Featherstone, Mike Hepworth and Bryan S. Turner, *The Body. Social Process and Cultural Theory* (London: Sage, 1991).
17   La Rochefoucauld, *Maxims*, no. 612, p. 121.
18   G.E.M. Anscombe, 'Modern Moral Philosophy', in Roger Crisp and Michael Slote (eds), *Virtue Ethics* (Oxford: Oxford University Press, 1997), pp. 26–44. For an excellent collection of essays, see Daniel Statman (ed.), *Virtue Ethics. A Critical Reader* (Edinburgh: Edinburgh University Press, 1997), especially the introduction, pp. 1–41. See also: Gregory Trianosky, 'What is Virtue Ethics All About?', *American Philosophical Quarterly*, vol. 27, no. 4, October 1990, pp. 335–44; William C. Spohn, 'The Return of Virtue Ethics', *Theological Studies*, vol. 53, 1992, pp. 60–75; and Gregory E. Pence, 'Recent Work on Virtues', *American Philosophical Quarterly*, vol. 21, no. 4, October 1984, pp. 281–97.
19   François-André Isambert, 'La sécularisation interne du christianisme', *Revue Français de Sociologie*, vol. 17, no. 4, 1976, pp. 573–89.

1

Classical Thinking for a Postmodern World: Alasdair MacIntyre and the Moral Critique of the Present

Peter McMylor

Any assessment of the likely impact of virtue ethics on sociology must take into account the writings of Alasdair MacIntyre. Sociology, however, has paid little attention to these for reasons that will be explored in this chapter. To draw out the distinctive nature of his contribution, comparison will be made with another writer, Zygmunt Bauman, whose influence in sociology in relation to ethics and postmodernity has been profound. It will suggest that Bauman's positive vision for a contemporary ethics reflects an inadequate, romantic response, all too congenial to the modernity it criticises and this is despite his powerful sociological insights into our social and moral order. This becomes especially clear when comparison is made between his insights and the subversive, yet classically based, virtue ethics that MacIntyre proposes.

MacIntyre is a highly unusual figure in the Anglo-American world, being an Aristotelian Thomist and a convert to Catholicism. As a philosopher of morality, he has made significant interventions in political, social and religious thought. Originally from Glasgow, he was educated at Queen Mary College, London and the University of Manchester. Although MacIntyre is principally a philosopher, he held a chair in sociology at Essex before moving to the USA in 1970, where he has occupied a number of prestigious chairs in philosophy. His key work is *After Virtue*.[1] In a complex historical account of the transformation of moral concepts, he sets out in this study the most cogent version of his view that the moral basis of liberal society has hopelessly fragmented. It is not, he suggests, that we are confused over particular moral questions, although we often are, but rather that we have lost the basis for understanding what a coherent moral argument is.

This is because our moral vocabulary has lost the institutional framework (especially in the form of educational institutions) which contained shared and inherited forms of inquiry and understanding, which in turn provided it with meaning and persuasiveness. But with a moral vocabulary torn from its original context, we are left only with fragments of a once meaningful moral scheme. Nevertheless, these fragments are still used as reference points, so that people continue to act as if there remained an overarching moral framework within which to relate to one another. In practice, MacIntyre suggests, we have a tendency to appeal to the parts of moral discourse that suit us. In this situation moral debate and argumentation take an emotivist form in which persuasion is pursued by non-rational means, and will quickly lead to a culture of manipulation and sophistry.

After Virtue should be of particular interest to sociologists because of its accounts of the debates in moral philosophy. As in all MacIntyre's previous work, these are very carefully situated within their social and historical context. For MacIntyre, there is a need to overcome the asocial and ahistorical blindness of a lot of analytical moral philosophy. Because he sees in sociology much of the self-understanding of modernity, the discipline is part diagnosis and part symptom, of the moral disorder of the modern culture. In seeking to understand MacIntyre, we must always recall that in producing *After Virtue*, he was not simply providing an account of moral philosophy with some social context, despite the book's subtitle as 'a study in moral theory'. Rather he had set out to write two books, one on the fate of morality in the modern world and another on the philosophy of social science. In the process he discovered that the arguments of one book required also the arguments of the other. Thus, he indicates that 'a moral philosophy . . . characteristically presupposes a sociology' and some mode of socially instantiating moral concepts is required.[2] So a successful sociology may well have something to teach us about the nature of that place or period's moral philosophy.

Principal amongst the sociologists that MacIntyre has learnt from in understanding modernity is Max Weber. In Weber's sociology of organisation and bureaucracy, MacIntyre sees, within its conceptual distinction between facts and values, the social embodiment of an emotivist moral philosophy. In bureaucratic organisations, managers are engaged in a competitive struggle for limited resources to put at the service of predetermined ends. About the ends no reasons can be given in the practice of managing. He notes thus, 'Weber's thought embodies just those dichotomies which emotivism embodies and obliterates just those distinctions to which emotivism has been blind. Questions of ends are questions of values, and on values reason is silent.'[3] Managerialism is mainly concerned to operate at the level of technique in clear mean/ends schemas in which substantive matters are pushed to the margin.

There can be no denying that MacIntyre's thought has had a considerable impact in pioneering the examination of the issues raised by the question of virtue. For example, in a recent volume devoted to the study of virtue, MacIntyre receives more references than any other living scholar.[4] Despite his significance in this area, it remains true that within much mainstream sociology his work has been largely ignored, at least in comparison with the continental grand theorists such as Foucault, Habermas and Bourdieu. Some sociologists have expressed interest in MacIntyre's work. For instance, in assessing *After Virtue*, Lukes suggested that MacIntyre 'offered a compelling account of the fragmented moral world of modernity, riven by unsettlable moral conflicts, speaking an impoverished moral vocabulary'.[5] This salutary comment was quite rapidly followed by incomprehension as to the direction and utility of what he terms the work of 'MacIntyre the moral philosopher', with his emphasis on tradition-bound communities, pursuing the virtue-based aspiration towards the common good. A liberal like Lukes felt 'left out in the cold'.[6]

In certain respects, the reasons why MacIntyre has not been taken up by contemporary sociology are not to difficult to see. An obvious reason is that classical thought and philosophy are very far from the conventional reference points of social science. There are, however, more explicit reasons given for rejecting MacIntyre's work and these relate to what Gouldner long ago called the 'domain assumptions' of sociology, ones that affect the analyses we produce but which we are always in danger of ignoring.[7] In examining some of the motives for rejecting MacIntyre, a light is cast on the dominant liberal assumptions of much of our contemporary sociology.

Alongside the sympathetic bafflement of Lukes, probably the most common reaction in print from sociologists has been to respond to MacIntyre's work via outright rejection, seeing it as no more than an exercise in nostalgia for a lost age – thankfully lost. Perhaps its most extreme expression is to be found in Robertson's essay entitled, in direct opposition to MacIntyre, 'After Nostalgia', in which 'the classical ideal' is seen to haunt social theory from its origins, with MacIntyre and his 'Grecophilia' but the latest example of a tradition of backward-looking organicist thought.[8]

In essence much of the criticism of MacIntyre comes from those with the strongest attachment to liberalism. This should not, of course, surprise us for he is one of the strongest contemporary critics of liberalism. It will be argued that the liberalism evinced in these criticisms will always find itself more comfortable with the kinds of ethics for which Bauman argues. As will be explained below, the very absolutist purity of Bauman's conception of ethics pushes morality once again into the deepest recesses of individual conscience, and stretches, almost to breaking point, the connections between the 'facts' of everyday social practice and the 'values' of an ethical judgement made purely for the sake of the *other*. Such a morality is likely to shine as a distant and fine ideal, but far above the irredeemably fallen world of everyday practice.

MacIntyre as pre-modern or postmodern? Nostalgia as a concept

The charge of nostalgia has regularly been brought against MacIntyre in relation to his earlier and, perhaps, more fundamentally sociological work,

Secularisation and Moral Change[9] – a work that Tester is probably right in seeing as a good introduction to MacIntyre's work, from the perspective of the sociologist.[10] Criticisms of MacIntyre reflect a perplexity that have categorised him as 'against modernity and its "moral philosopher" Nietzsche, and for nostalgia'.[11] For some critics, such as Poole, this latter property was particularly damaging. Thus he noted that 'what is valuable in MacIntyre has to be rescued from the nostalgia which pervades his work'. He went on to add that, despite its many virtues, 'MacIntyre's project of recovery collapses into antiquarianism and eccentricity. Like all nostalgia it provides a way of accommodating to the world, not a reason for changing it.'[12]

In essence these types of claim involve the view that MacIntyre is operating with a simple *Gemeinschaft* and *Gesellschaft* distinction between pre-capitalist and capitalist societies, the former possessing an organic unity which the latter rapidly loses. In reality MacIntyre was always aware of the dangers of too easy a contrast between these social worlds. In *Secularisation and Moral Change*, he qualifies the point himself when he states, 'the homogeneity of pre-industrial life is, of course, easily exaggerated, but the sharpness of the transition from the values of pre-industrial society to the values of life in the Industrial Revolution can scarcely be exaggerated'.[13]

The whole issue of the contrast between traditional and modern societies is dealt with in a more sophisticated and nuanced way in *After Virtue*. Here MacIntyre is quite explicit about the difficulty of using contrasts between past and present that rely on the older sociological models of organic unity versus differentiation. He notes that there are many myths surrounding our understanding of the medieval world, of which, 'none is more misleading than that which portrays a unified and monolithic Christian culture and this not just because the medieval achievement was also Jewish and Islamic. Medieval culture, in so far as it was a unity at all, was a fragile and complex balance of a variety of disparate and conflicting elements.'[14] Thus he suggests that to understand the role of the virtues in both theory and practice we need to recognise the variety of potentially conflicting strands within the medieval world, all of which are capable of imposing different strains on the whole edifice.

MacIntyre's entire argument in this work is based on an analysis of the role of the virtues in a whole range of pre-modern societies: Homeric Greece, classical Greece, the so-called heroic societies of northern Europe and the medieval world. Crucially, not only are some of these societies descended from one another but the values they inherit from diverse sources are frequently in considerable conflict with one another. The statement of Stauth and Turner that 'medieval Europe was not made up of a set of coherent nation-states each with its own unified morality and religion. Rather we have to imagine medieval civilisation as a collection of oases surrounded by a waste land of pre-literate, pre-Christian and oppositional cultural movements'[15] is, while probably rather overdrawn, by no means incompatible with MacIntyre's picture of these societies. Indeed it could be argued that MacIntyre's sense of the conflicts and contradictions of medieval societies is sharper than this rather crude sociologising of a division between upper-class (or town-based) Christian culture, and rural paganism, for he suggests that the paganism of the heroic societies survived and continued to inform the practices of the upper classes of medieval Europe and that, in some respects, the Church had to come to terms with this.

Thus MacIntyre's argument is fundamentally misconstrued if it is assumed to rely upon a seamless organic moral unity lodged in the past. What is really at stake in his argument is an attempt to delineate what is distinctive about modernity itself. MacIntyre is not claiming that past societies were not full of conflicting views that could not or would not be reconciled with one another, such as Jewish and Christian communities in medieval Europe. He claims, rather, that these views were embodied in communities, perhaps competing ones, that within themselves shared a common conception of what the pursuit of the good life was, or what had been inherited from the past, from other conceptions of the pursuit of the good life that were in contradiction with their then contemporary conceptions, such as the Pagan warrior values of heroic society with the Christianity of the early Middle Ages. What all these forms had in common was an ability to link the individual, via a socially defined role, with the pursuit of human goods, and so MacIntyre asserts:

> in much of the ancient and the medieval worlds, as in many other premodern societies, the individual is identified and constituted in and through certain of his or her roles, those roles which bind the individual to the communities in and through which alone specifically human goods are to be attained; I confront the world as a member of this household, this clan, this tribe, this city, this nation, this kingdom. There is no 'I' apart from these.[16]

The contrast with the situation in modernity is very stark. Here the modern social world, as partly constituted by the liberal state, is an arena in which the individual pursues his or her own private good. This is not to be understood as suggesting that the importance of the social role in modern societies has been diminished, but rather that the concept of the social role has been redefined in such a way as to sharply demarcate the societies of liberal modernity off from virtually all others. I say 'virtually', because it is possible for those anxious about the question of origin to find intimations of this modern conception in the work of some the philosophers of classical Greece, as Nietzsche was to find in the Sophists. MacIntyre also looks to contemporary sociology to find clues to this redefinition of social role, for he sees in the sociology of Erving Goffman an account of what he termed a 'spectral self' flitting from role to role, but in a sense standing out against each one and finding 'freedom' in an indifference to and an awareness of the ultimate contingency of each of them.[17] For MacIntyre, this is the central point at issue which consists of the generalising and operationalising of this distinctive re-definition of the role of the social actor as 'the individual' who

> in modern society is the name of a status and a role. 'The individual' is the name of a piece of social fabrication, of a social role created in the sixteenth and seventeenth centuries in order to abstract human beings from certain aspects of their beliefs and circumstances. So it is not human individuals as such, bearing with them the complexities of belief and circumstance, including their allegiance to some theory of the good and their membership of social groups espousing such a theory, who are the agents who appear in modern practical reasoning. It is the individuals *qua* individuals of whom I am speaking, individuals viewed by themselves and by others as inhabiting the role of 'the individual'.[18]

Enough has been said to show that MacIntyre's relationship to the classical dichotomies of sociology is, to say the least, complex and considerably more so than conventional sociological responses to his work might indicate. What is really at stake in his writings is the issue of comparative analysis, although not in the form we normally associate with such exercises in historical sociology. What is unusual about MacIntyre is his use of moral culture as a means of understanding of the past and other societies. Thus, concentrating on the rhetoric of nostalgia as a means of criticising MacIntyre's strategy towards understanding the significance of virtue ethics is not helpful. The concept of nostalgia is too all-encompassing and is in danger of locking us in to the present and into very particular views of the future in a quite uncritical manner. The late American historian and social critic Chrisopher Lasch argued that nostalgia is an ideological by-product of the much more prominent ideology of progress, one which prevents us from making intelligent use of the past. In relation to the politicising of the idea of nostalgia, he notes that 'in societies that clung to the dogma of progress, no other term was more effective in deflating ideological opponents'. He sees, as MacIntyre does, that, 'nostalgic representations of the past evoke a time irretrievably lost and for that reason timeless and unchanging'. Lasch goes on to argue that there is a key distinction to be made between nostalgia and memory. Nostalgia freezes a past out of a time that is gone forever and in the end, reluctantly, reconciles us to an apparently inescapable present. On the other hand, memory operates rather in the way the concept of tradition does for MacIntyre. It 'sees', as Lasch observes 'past, present and future as continuous. It is less concerned with loss than our continuing indebtedness to a past, the formative influence of which lives on in our pattern of speech, our gestures, our standards of honour, our expectations . . . our basic disposition toward the world.'[19]

But perhaps Lasch's contribution in relation to MacIntyre's work lies in his linking these points about the nature of nostalgia to important criticisms of the determinism inherent within much of modernist sociological discourse. He calls for the outright rejection of modernisation theory and discourse, pointing to the work of Charles Sabel and Jonathan Zeitlin to argue against any notion of the inevitable triumph of large-scale production in the nineteenth and twentieth centuries and the general 'necessitarian habit of thought' that views modernity as a kind of package deal to be accepted or rejected as a whole.[20] The central point at issue is the baleful influence of all varieties of technological determinism in relation to our capacity to make moral judgements about the nature of our future lives. Taylor also commented on these negative features: 'I believe these strong theories of fatality are abstract and wrong. Our degrees of freedom are not zero. There is a point of deliberating about our ends, and whether instrumental reason ought to have a lesser role in our lives than it does.'[21]

The key idea to be taken from all this in regard to MacIntyre's work is that simple-minded periodisation that rules out of court a complex re-articulation of ancient and traditional, moral, philosophical and religious discourses in relation to our present condition is mistaken. So what then is the relationship between MacIntyre's thought and our late-modern or postmodern world?

Practices, tradition and the elusive universal

Perhaps the principal lesson that Milbank has taught us is the dependence of social theory on prior conditions of theological and philosophical formation.[22] It is clear that MacIntyre wants first and foremost to say to sociologists that they are, or should be, part of a socially embodied tradition of rational inquiry with deep and complex roots in different traditions. From this, it follows that there is no way of conducting rational inquiry from a standpoint independent of the particularities of a tradition. MacIntyre represents and recommends for philosophers, and then also for sociologists, the standpoint of Thomist-Aristotelianism with the allied concepts of the virtues and the notion of a practice informed by an adequate concept of narrative tradition. The virtues are settled dispositions, acquired by practice, which enable us to behave in ways that allow us to flourish, whilst engaged in human activities, which are themselves vehicles for pursuing the good life. A practice then is defined by MacIntyre as a

> coherent and complex form of socially established co-operative human activity, through which goods internal to the form of activity are realised in the course of trying to achieve those standards of excellence which are appropriate to, and partially definitive of, that form of activity, with the result that human powers to achieve excellence, and human conceptions of ends and goods involved, are systematically extended.[23]

Now it is clear from MacIntyre's account of the concept of a practice, that although such a conception is perhaps marginal to our political and social life today, it is at least recognisable in such activities as playing a game, writing serious poetry, or engaging in an academic subject. It is also clear that it is not only in modern society but also in ancient and medieval ones that practices may be complex and highly diverse in character. What crucially flows from this understanding of the centrality of practices as arenas for the enactment and development of the virtues is a commitment to the ineliminable narrative unity of a human life and it is this that separates it from postmodern critiques of the inadequacies of modernity. This life contains criteria of intelligibility and accountability which it possesses in part because it is also embedded within wider social narratives which we understand as histories. This is another way of saying that a human life is also the bearer and explorer of a tradition of understanding even if, at present, it is an inchoate one.

There is no doubt that there are parallels with postmodernism in terms of the overall frame of MacIntyre's critique of and rejection of the Enlightenment project and that this has allowed some postmodernists to deploy his work for their own purposes.[24] MacIntyre's understanding of the limitations of the Enlightenment attempt to reconstruct moral thought and, following from this, the flawed attempts to construct a positivistic and predictive social science,[25] do have clear parallels with the critical account of these processes to be found in some of Bauman's works.[26] Both see the rise of the conventional social sciences as part of a modernist project which, at best, has had ambivalent results and, at worst, has led to forms of bureaucratic domination that have effaced and marginalised ethical understandings. These processes created the space for the organisational and moral indifference that allowed the Gulag and the Holocaust to occur.

Where MacIntyre and Bauman do differ, however, is over the question as to whether it is still possible to find sources of authority in our lives, especially over the issue of the self as tradition bearing. MacIntyre is committed to a view that we can distinguish between genuine and sham authority in the tutoring of human nature, via the virtues, in the pursuance of particular practices informed by a particular tradition. MacIntyre would see in Bauman's comment, on trusting 'the wise (the code name of the mighty) to do good autonomously',[27] a dangerous slippage to indiscriminate reductionism and perspectivism. Nor would MacIntyre accept the sense of almost existential pathos that suffuses much of Bauman's writing on morality. In this respect MacIntyre takes a different view as to social reality. He refuses to treat modernist conceptions of self and society as exhaustive of human reality, or to accept that even within modernity we are without resources to understand and to act differently. For Bauman, postmodern ethics are a piecemeal response to the obliterating power of modernity in its attempts to create the ideal and the perfect. Postmodernity is '*modernity without illusions*.[28] It turns back to the most simple of human relations, 'I' and the 'Other'. The classical sources of a premodern tradition are not seen as available by Bauman. His remains a sociological account of morality which is both bewitched and horrified by modernity, but in the end his is an internal critique that seeks to temper what is seen as our present horizon.

MacIntyre is more radical in his doubts about modernity's self-image and its reflection in social science. He seeks to escape (as indeed does Bauman in his own way) what Bauman understands so well as the complicity of modernist and liberal sociology when it replicates the achievements of legislating power in positivist social science. For MacIntyre, the achievements of positivist social science and its complicity with bureaucratic and market power are largely illusory, albeit with real effects in the world. The manager and the therapist are necessary dramatic roles within modernity but their cultural and intellectual underpinning are seen as hollow.[29] He would argue that the narrative quality of a human life and the continuing reality of premodern cultural and intellectual traditions means that we are not without resources to challenge our world.

For Bauman the situation is much darker. Past traditions are not available to him to deploy as they are for MacIntyre. Modernity is both registered and constituted by the modernist social scientific conception of structure and so for Bauman 'this precarious regularity has been an achievement and the decisive defining feature of social organization'. Structure, as a technical concept and a lived reality,

> consists in subjecting the conduct of all units to either instrumental or procedural criteria of evaluation. More importantly still, it consists in delegalizing all other criteria, and first and foremost such standards as may render behaviour of units resilient to uniforming pressures and thus autonomous.

Bauman suggests the moral capacity is central amongst the standards marked for suppression, for he points out that, 'the autonomy of moral behaviour is final and irreducible: it escapes all codification, as it does not serve any purpose outside itself'.[30] The importance of morality, for Bauman, consists in its capacity to allow human beings to leap out of the constraints of modern structure and hence its centrality in the postmodern critique of modernity.

In essence Bauman's postmodern understanding of ethics represents the kind of radicalising of Kant that Rosen sees as so characteristic of all postmodern thought.[31] As Bauman puts it in relation to his chosen moral philosopher of the period, 'Levinas draws a most radical conclusion from Kant's solution to the mysteries of "moral law inside me", but only such radicalism may give justice to Kant . . . the concern for the Other *for the Other's sake*'. The attitude to the Other, before the commencement of any relationship, is vital for Bauman, indeed it is the crux of the matter. Morality is an encounter with the Other in ways that form an unequal relationship, an undemanding reciprocation, and an indifference to gain. It is these 'unbalanced' elements that 'make the encounter a moral event'.[32] Further still, in a statement of apparently asocial moral purity, Bauman states 'moral phenomena are inherently "non-rational". Since they are moral only if they precede the consideration of purpose and the calculation of gains and losses, they do not fit the "means–end" scheme.'[33] This property of absence of calculation in morality provides a remarkable contrast with the notion of 'pure relationships' in Giddens's approach to intimacy. His is a proximity without morality.

The realm of real human activities can never be genuinely moral on this view. MacIntyre's virtue ethics and the practices which are so necessary for their realisation must involve some aspects of instrumental reason for, it cannot be emphasised too strongly, these were not invented by modernity but are a part of all societies. For the Aristotelian, modernity merely generalised instrumental reason excessively throughout human society. This would seem to indicate that Tester is surely right to identify Bauman with a commitment to culture as opposed to civilisation. This distinction was first developed by German Romanticism in its search for a purified subjectivity in contrast to abstract and mechanical civilisation.[34] Such a critical turn has therefore been with modernity since its inception. The moral purity of the individual act in relation to the Other is potent and moving, even inspiring, but it has been successful marginalised by purposive rationality for at least two centuries. It is difficult not to feel the justice of the remark by that old Aristotelian, Karl Marx, that 'the bourgeois viewpoint has never advanced beyond the antithesis between itself and the romantic viewpoint, and the latter will accompany it as its legitimate antithesis up to its blessed end'.[35] The postmodern position, at least in this form, represents a clear example of what Rose, borrowing from Hegel, has called that of 'the beautiful soul', an inner purity or pietism that 'separates itself from history, taking the separated "same" of interiority beyond freedom, to a love dirempted from the state which leaves the field of Mars to the love-in-barbarism it abhors'.[36] Later, she argues that 'Bauman's defence of personal "morality" can only claim an existential sacrality; for he distrusts the risk of sociological authorship: that while no knowledge or politics may be generally available or correspond to its insights, sociological reconstruction is still staked on comprehension and on practice.'[37]

It would be difficult to imagine a conception of ethics more distant than the Bauman/Levinas one from MacIntyre's Aristotelian conception of the virtues. MacIntyre from his earliest writings through to *After Virtue* and beyond, has set himself the task of criticising and exposing the limitations of just this kind of position. As early as 1958, he was pointing out the limitations of the revived liberalism so popular with disillusioned post-Stalinist, ex-Communist Party intellectuals. In reaction to the limitations of a

Marxism that swallowed moral judgements into an all-forgiving productivist notion of historical progress – crimes against individuals being apparently forgivable in terms of the supposed happiness of future generations – many were tempted by a liberalism that asserted the centrality of independent and individual moral judgements. As MacIntyre stated, again in 1958,

> it is the essence of the liberal tradition that morality is taken as autonomous ... it is the doctrine that moral principles can have no non-moral basis. Our judgments on specific moral issues may be supported by the invocation of more general principles. But in the end our most general and ultimate principles, because they are that in terms of which all else is justified stand beyond rational justification. In particular, they cannot be justified by any appeal to facts, historical or otherwise.[38]

Both the classical conception of the virtues, and the practices they inhabit, seek always to make practical judgements about the relationship between means and ends and hence to be completely at home in the world, even if that world is not in reality quite as modernity itself construes it. This is why MacIntyre is concerned to stress the difference between his Aristotelian critique of the Enlightenment and what he terms 'the Romantic rejection of the Enlightenment'.[39] MacIntyre shares with liberals a fear that romanticism will glorify emotion and individual preference, untutored by Aristotelian reasons and the virtues. An asocial purity of motive in moral judgement that precedes context can make no sense to Aristotelians, for the development of the virtues is in their own interests as well as those of the wider community.

For the Aristotelian, the resources of practical rationality and their application in the shared life of virtue, are to be sustained and developed in areas of life and in institutions that must be insulated from the modernity of Weberian formal rationality, e.g. in charities, voluntary organisations, churches, monasteries, and even in universities. Their importance lies, in the first instance, in what they are for themselves, that is attempts to realise their purposes via the practice of the virtues, but, also, because they provide a ground upon which a critique of modernity could emerge. It is surely from here, in institutions and practices that have an adequate conceptual and moral grasp of their social form and purpose, that MacIntyre hopes his new St Benedict will arise.

Aristotelian virtue ethics should not be seen as the distant endeavour recently resuscitated by MacIntyre from long-dead sources. It is rather a live tradition which has had many distinguished exponents in the twentieth century, such as Jacques Maritain, Peter Geach and, in certain respects, Martha Nussbaum. But this is not something that has been very widely noticed even within the discipline of philosophy let alone that of the social sciences. Perhaps the greatest contribution that MacIntyre has made is the manner in which his considerable intellectual authority has been able to bring disparate bodies of work into relation with one another, in a way that has commanded attention. By deploying historical and sociological materials to reveal how moral categories have been shaped and influenced by context, he made for a contextually richer moral philosophy, though, by using the concepts of classical and medieval thought, he raises a questionmark over the post-Cartesian provincialism of modern social science. If postmodern thought has cast doubt on the sovereignty of modern reason then it may be that the time has come for social theorists to investigate the classical and medieval sources of reason to examine afresh what was accepted and rejected with the birth of modernity.

Notes and references

1   Alasdair MacIntyre, *After Virtue* (London: Duckworth, 1981).
2   Ibid., p. 22.
3   Ibid., pp. 24–5.
4   Indeed MacIntyre exceeds all other authorities save Aristotle. See John W. Chapman and William A. Galston, *Virtue*, NOMOS, XXXIV (New York: New York University Press, 1992).
5   Steven Lukes, 'Alasdair MacIntyre: The Sociologist versus the Philosopher', in Steven Lukes, *Moral Conflicts and Politics* (Oxford: Clarendon Press, 1991), p. 253.
6   Ibid., p. 256.
7   Alvin Gouldner, *The Coming Crisis of Western Sociology* (London: Heinemann, 1970), pp. 31–60.
8   Roland Robertson, 'After Nostalgia? Willful Nostalgia and the Phases of Globalisation', in Bryan Turner (ed.), *Theories of Modernity and Postmodernity* (London: Sage, 1990), p. 50. See also discussions on MacIntyre in: 'Against Nostalgia: Talcott Parsons and a Sociology for the Modern World', in Robert J. Holton and Bryan Turner, *Talcott Parsons on Economy and Society* (London: Routledge, 1986), pp. 204–34.; Bryan Turner, 'A Note on Nostalgia', *Theory, Culture and Society*, vol. 4, no. 1, 1987, pp. 147–56.; George Stauth and Bryan Turner, *Nietzsche's Dance: Resentment, Reciprocity and Resistance in Social Life* (Oxford: Blackwell, 1988); and Ross Poole, *Morality as Modernity* (London: Routledge, 1991). Amongst those who see MacIntyre as on the wrong track, we must include the late Gillian Rose. She would never be so crude as to charge him with nostalgia. In the end, she sees Weber and Nietzsche as essential for the renewal of modernity and clearly disagrees with MacIntyre on this. See especially her book *Mourning Becomes the Law*, especially for the criticism of the latter. Her own attitudes to theology were complex and her reception into Christianity generated much controversy. For an appraisal of her work, and also excerpts from her final notebooks, see the special issue of *Women: A Cultural Review*, vol. 9, no. 4, Spring 1998, pp. 6–18.
9   Alasdair MacIntyre, *Secularisation and Moral Change* (Oxford: Oxford University Press, 1967).
10   Keith Tester, *Civil Society* (London: Routledge, 1992), p. 169.
11   Holton and Turner, 'Against Nostalgia', p. 215.
12   Poole, *Morality as Modernity*, p. 150.
13   MacIntyre, *Secularisation and Moral Change*, pp. 12–13.

14 MacIntyre, *After Virtue*, p. 155.
15 Stauth and Turner, *Nietzsche's Dance*, p. 47.
16 MacIntyre, *After Virtue*, pp. 160–1.
17 Ibid., p. 31.
18 Alasdair MacIntyre, 'Practical Rationalities as Forms of Social Structure', *Irish Philosophical Journal*, vol. 4, 1987, p. 13.
19 Christopher Lasch, *The True and Only Heaven: Progress and its Critics* (New York: Norton, 1991), p. 83.
20 Ibid., p. 155.
21 Charles Taylor, *The Ethics of Authenticity* (Cambridge, Mass.: Harvard University Press, 1991), p. 8.
22 John Milbank, *Theology and Social Theory: Beyond Secular Reason* (Oxford: Blackwell, 1990).
23 MacIntyre, *After Virtue*, p. 175.
24 John Gray, *Enlightenment's Wake: Politics and Culture at the Close of the Modern Age* (London: Routledge, 1995).
25 Peter McMylor, *Alasdair MacIntyre. Critic of Modernity* (London: Routledge, 1994).
26 See especially Zygmunt Bauman's works: *Legislators and Interpreters* (Cambridge: Polity Press, 1987); *Postmodern Ethics* (Oxford: Blackwell, 1993); and *Life in Fragments: Essays in Postmodern Morality* (Oxford: Blackwell, 1995).
27 Bauman, *Postmodern Ethics*, p. 30.
28 Ibid., p. 32. Italics are his emphasis.
29 MacIntyre, *After Virtue*, second edition, 1985, pp. 30–1.
30 Zygmunt Bauman, 'The Social Manipulation of Morality: Moralizing Actors, Adiaphorizing Action', *Theory, Culture and Society*, vol. 8, no.1, 1991, p. 143.
31 Stanley Rosen presents a devastating attack on postmodernism, which he reveals to have deep continuities with modernism, which in turn reflects a radicalisation of Kant's philosophy. See his book, *Hermeneutics as Politics* (Oxford: Oxford University Press, 1987), pp. 19–50. In this book, Rosen argues that 'Kant's actual first principle, spontaneity conceived as freedom, legitimates Nietzsche's first principle of health understood as creativity. In the case of Nietzsche, each person who exemplifies the philosophy of perspectivism asserts his uniqueness in the very act of becoming Nietzsche's disciple. In the case of Kant, my "calling" to respect myself or legislate for myself turns out to be the expression of my respect for Kant, and for his right to legislate or enforce by the will of his interpretation of human nature my "right" to self-legislation' (p. 35). In this sense, Bauman's acceptance of the triumph of modernity, even within his postmodern critique and its consequent limitation on the moral resources he can deploy, becomes more explicable. This is because the underlying premises of modernity are being ironically tweaked and played within postmodernity in ways that do not seriously put them in question.
32 Bauman, *Postmodern Ethics*, pp. 48–9.
33 Ibid., p. 11.
34 Keith Tester, *Moral Culture* (London: Sage, 1997), note, pp. 143–5.
35 From *The Grundrisse*, cited in Raymond Williams, *Politics and Letters* (London: New Left Books, 1979), p. 116.
36 Gillian Rose, *The Broken Middle: Out of Our Ancient Society* (Oxford: Blackwell, 1992), p. 257.
37 Ibid., p. 296. Like MacIntyre, Rose refuses the postmodern identification of reason with modernity. See, especially, her book, *Judaism and Modernity: Philosophical*

Essays (Oxford: Blackwell, 1993). For MacIntyre's understanding of reason and rationality, see *Whose Justice? Which Rationality?* (London: Duckworth, 1988).

38   Alasdair MacIntyre, 'Notes from the Moral Wilderness', *New Reasoner*, no. 7, Winter 1958–59, pp. 91–2.

39   Alasdair MacIntyre, 'A Partial Response to My Critics', in John Horton and Susan Mendus (eds), *After MacIntyre* (Cambridge: Polity, 1994), p. 303.

2
Disenchantment and Virtue: An Essay on Max Weber

Keith Tester

Despite the pretensions of many of its practitioners, sociology is often a remarkably parochial affair. The discipline tends to be very inward-looking and texts which should warrant and reward sustained attention are frequently ignored because they are not presumed to 'fit' preconceived agendas. Until recently, such has been the sociological fate of virtually the entire corpus of Alasdair MacIntyre's work.[1] This neglect does not do any credit to the discipline of sociology, since MacIntyre's moral philosophy is one which is indebted to explicitly sociological themes and concerns. It contains and proposes 'a depth-historical sociology of culture' and many of MacIntyre's claims about the prospects for virtue and ethics in the contemporary present serve to 'inform moral discourse with a fitting sociological perspective'.[2] MacIntyre is a moral philosopher whom sociologists should be able to find rather congenial, or at least worthy of some sustained interest.

The likelihood that the sociological neglect of MacIntyre owes a lot to disciplinary parochialism should not be underestimated. In this regard perhaps MacIntyre is not ignored so much as simply not known. Levine, however, points towards a more substantial reason for the absence of an encounter with MacIntyre from much of the resurgent debate within sociology about morality and ethics, when he says that in *After Virtue*, at least, MacIntyre offers a 'misleading representation of modern sociology'.[3] Nowhere is that representation more misleading than in its account of the themes and concerns of Max Weber. The fundamental problem is that MacIntyre approaches Weber without paying adequate attention to the full implications of his famous distinction between statements of facts and statements of values.[4] MacIntyre's reading of Weber seems to be bedevilled by the problem that he reads Weber's statements about the 'is' as if they were barely disguised statements of the 'ought'. In other words, MacIntyre reads Weber as an advocate and he misses the richness and complexity of Weber's unflinching (and, as this essay will show, deeply principled) value neutrality.[5]

For MacIntyre, Weber is one of the leading advocates for the contemporary condition of emotivism in which all statements of morality are in fact little more than statements of preference. MacIntyre evidently takes Weber to be such an advocate because he refuses to pass judgement; later in this chapter it will be shown *why* Weber refuses to judge. For MacIntyre, the rise of emotivism is also about the decline of virtue. Yet MacIntyre is simply wrong with his reading of Weber; Weber is no more an advocate of emotivism than MacIntyre is himself. The inaccuracy has been emphasised by Levine who says, baldly, that MacIntyre 'lacks the patience to grasp the complexities of Weber's argument and thus...simplifies Weber's views to the point of distortion'.[6] Perhaps this is the reason why MacIntyre fails to see that in many ways Weber actually anticipates and supports much of the case that he wishes to develop and present. It is actually reasonable to suggest that Weber and MacIntyre are closer to one another than they are distant. What they similarly provide is a compelling and profound analysis of the state of contemporary moral discourse and, by extension, moral practice. Weber and MacIntyre share a concern to highlight the parlous state of morality in the contemporary present and they both try to work towards resolutions of the situations and issues that they identify. However, their respective attitudes towards the problem of the contemporary present could not be more different. MacIntyre tries to stand against the tide of the present and he advocates a return to traditional modes of thought. Weber, by contrast, would have probably labelled MacIntyre's turn (perhaps ungenerously) as a kind of failure of nerve. For Weber, it is incumbent upon the analyst to confront the contemporary present on its own terms. As he stated, 'it is weakness not to be able to countenance the stern seriousness of our fateful times'.[7]

Undoubtedly the contrast between Weber and MacIntyre – the one refusing to reject the present, the other restating the validity of traditional modes of thought – has much to do with their different theological attitudes. It became very clear in the books that immediately followed *After Virtue* that MacIntyre's position contains a considerable measure of Catholic thematisation[8] whilst, notwithstanding his own personal attitude towards religion, Weber's work contains deeply Protestant intimations. The relationship between Weber's thought and German Liberal Protestantism should not be terribly surprising to anyone who has read Marianne Weber's biography of her husband. That book makes it clear that Weber's intellectual development was very much within a Protestant milieu; in terms of pietism through his mother and in terms of theology through regular and close contacts with books such as Strauss's *Life of Jesus*, the essays of William Ellery Channing and through personal encounters and discussions with the likes of Ernst Troeltsch.[9] Yet the relationship between Weber's thought and Protestantism is something that sociologists appear to be very reticent to discuss. Once again the possibility of disciplinary parochialism seems to emerge, this time perhaps because any suggestion that Weber's work might owe debts to theology would shatter the confident secularism of the discipline of sociology.[10]

It is the intention of this chapter to take seriously MacIntyre's account of the collapse of moral discourse and practice into emotivism, but also to try to go some way towards rescuing Weber from MacIntyre's misrepresentation. As such, in the background of this paper is a presumption that the story that MacIntyre tells in *After Virtue* is broadly valid. In particular, it is possible to contend that Weber was struggling to deal with the problem of the failure of the Kantian project of justifying morality without, however, giving up on Kant.[11] In the foreground is an attempt to outline Weber's importance for any sociology of virtue in the contemporary present. It is my claim that the key to unlocking Weber is provided by Robert Musil who, in his massive novel *The Man Without Qualities*, wrote a chapter entitled 'Ideals and morality are the best means of filling the big hole that one calls the soul'.[12]

My discussion of Weber will concentrate on his lecture 'Science as a Vocation'.[13] The lecture is one of Weber's most important and yet difficult legacies to sociology. It is a text that seems to justify a number of readings on account of the tension that runs through it between, on the one hand, Weber's despair in the face of the contemporary present and, on the other hand, his uncompromising commitment to the belief that every individual subject can will to develop and possess a 'true self' which, in the name of the dignity of human reason, needs to be emancipated from the traps of falsity.[14] Karl Jaspers said of Weber: 'what provided his scientific activity with its axis was that *man* was at the center of his preoccupations, not man as an empty abstraction, but man as a concrete reality in historically changing society'.[15] This is precisely the context in which Weber becomes relevant for any sociological consideration of the issue of virtue.

The essay has two substantive parts. Firstly, I will rehearse Weber's arguments about the relationship between science and the present. For Weber, science is identified with disenchantment and this is a process embedded in the emancipation of human reason in the world. But disenchantment has also produced a malaise of meaninglessness. Secondly, the Protestantism of Weber will be recalled in a discussion of his strategy of turning towards the individual in an attempt to overcome the contemporary condition of incommensurability. With that turn to the individual, Weber does not, as MacIntyre might have it, gesture towards emotivism, rather he moves towards the thesis that the dignity of the individual is realised in duty towards the ideal of reason. Weber's problem is one of the subjective meaningfulness of a world that is meaningless. The virtue of the vocation of science is his proposed resolution of this dichotomy.

The philosopher and the present

Weber's ideal of science is only fully intelligible in terms of Plato's image of the first philosopher. Weber's benchmark is Plato's story about the person who escapes from his fetters in the cave and who, instead of seeing only the shadows on the wall, sees the sun. This first philosopher takes upon himself the duty of leading into the light and away from the shadows those who remain chained in the cave: 'he is the philosopher; the sun, however, is the true science, which alone seizes not upon illusions and shadows but upon the true being'.[16] Plato's philosopher is mocked and ridiculed by those who remain inside the cave and yet his vocation of telling of the truth is accomplished to the extent that he is able to persuade them either to cast off their chains and join him in looking at the sun or, if they are afraid of freedom, to stop believing in the reality of the shadows and believe instead in the truth that he has discovered. Yet Plato only provides 'a wonderful image'. What Weber tries to do in 'Science as a Vocation' is to analyse the current historical situation of this philosopher. As such he talks about the external conditions of science in the universities and he compares the American and the German circumstances. But he also implies that whereas the philosopher of Plato attends to the universal, the scientist in the contemporary present is fated to attend only to the particular: 'not only externally, but inwardly, matters stand at a point where the individual can acquire the sure consciousness of achieving something truly perfect in the field of science only in case he is a strict specialist'.[17]

The philosopher has been historically transformed into the scientific specialist and science has risen to a position of pre-eminence thanks to what Weber calls the 'process of disenchantment, which has continued to exist in Occidental culture for millennia'. He identifies disenchantment with the intellectualisation of the world. Now, an overly straightforward reading of Weber's account of disenchantment would lead to the suggestion that it means that the world has ceased to be explained in terms of resorts to the mysterious or the supernatural. Yet Weber makes it clear that this is not what he means at all. Disenchantment does not refer to something that *has happened*, rather it refers to a *possibility* of intellectualisation: 'it means the knowledge or belief that if one but wished one *could* learn . . . [knowledge of the conditions under which one lives] at any time'. Weber goes on to suggest 'hence it means that principally there are no mysterious incalculable forces that come into play, but rather that one can, in principle, master all things by calculation'.[18] When he identifies disenchantment as a process that *can happen and is happening* rather than as an event that has happened,[19] Weber is creating a space in which the dignity of the philosopher-cum-specialised-scientist can be promoted. The dignity consists in duty towards the process of disenchantment that stands over and above any given individual, which makes the work of that individual of nothing more than utterly temporary relevance[20] and which yet means the dominance of reason and the emancipation of humanity into freedom and out of what Weber, following Plato, identifies as the shadows of superstition and imprisonment.

The problem that confronts Weber is, however, that the universalist promises and pretensions of disenchantment seem to be remarkably incompatible with the contemporary situation. He uncovers what amounts to a crisis in the legitimacy of science and, therefore, a crisis in the legitimacy of the vocation of the philosopher. Instead of the movement of humanity into a subjectively meaningful milieu of disenchanted reason, Weber can see only a world that is characterised by conflict and confusion. Weber seems to see this situation as a product of the tendency of science to destroy the validity of previously taken for granted – and subjectively meaningful – forms of conduct and disposition without, however, offering anything definite in their stead. Here the last few pages of Weber's study of the Protestant Ethic are in the background once again. Weber shows that the virtue of the secularised calling is not universal and not at all necessary. He shows that it is historically contingent and, therefore, he identifies its disposition towards hard work and the accumulation of wealth as a trap that imprisons humanity as a moral aspiration and individuals as concrete beings. But what does Weber offer in the place of this conflict and confusion? It might be said, nothing beyond romantic conventions.[21] The fundamental difficulty that Weber comes to realise by the time of 'Science as a Vocation' is that the science towards which he is ethically and subjectively committed does not provide any meaning beyond itself. Science, in fact, promotes meaninglessness.

Weber explores the relationship between science and meaninglessness by looking towards Tolstoy.[22] 'Science as a Vocation' contains two direct references to Tolstoy. The first deals with the problem of the implications of disenchantment for the subjective meaningfulness of death. Weber tacitly supports Tolstoy's argument that 'for civilized man death has no meaning'. According to Tolstoy, death has come to be deprived of any subjective meaningfulness because life itself has been placed into an infinite progress that goes beyond the individual, continuing after her or his own decease. For Tolstoy, this means that, 'there is always a further step ahead of one who stands in the march of progress'. What any individual can know or achieve is fated to become redundant, 'and what he seizes is always something provisional and not definitive, and therefore death for him is a meaningless occurrence. And because death is meaningless, civilized life as such is meaningless.'[23] This theme was obviously on Weber's mind when he said that, 'in science, each of us knows that what he has accomplished will be antiquated in ten, twenty, fifty years. That is the fate to which science is subjected; it is the very *meaning* of scientific work.'[24] Clearly, then, as soon as the social and cultural milieu is seen as historical and, moreover, as soon as that historical dimension is linked to a process, the individual human subject is deprived of any semblance of dignity or, for that matter, any necessary meaning. All that remains is a hole where the soul used to be. Whatever the individual subject might or might not achieve and accomplish is of no great consequence since the world will go on after her or his death, burying her or his memorials under more recent monuments. There is no subjectively meaningful salvation because there is no subjectively meaningful damnation; nothing can carry that depth of meaning and significance all the time that there is a presumption of 'infinite progress'.[25]

Weber's second reference to Tolstoy cuts further to the heart of the matter of the problem of meaningfulness in the contemporary present. He quotes Tolstoy's dictum that 'science is meaningless because it gives no answer to...the only question important for us: "what shall we do and how shall we live?"' Science cannot answer the 'only question important for us' because it is incapable of talking about values. By extension therefore, science is incapable of justifying any judgements and it cannot be the basis of any identifications of the virtuous or the vicious. Science has no provenance over those domains and, to the extent that science is dominant in the contemporary present, nor can the present justify any judgements. As Weber explains, science is concerned with the logical understanding and interpretation of that which exists. Science is practised in terms of the presupposition that such intellectualisation is worthwhile, but that presupposition is itself beyond justification: 'for this presupposition cannot be proved by scientific means. It can only be *interpreted* with reference to its ultimate meaning, which we must reject or accept according to our ultimate position towards life.'[26] As an example of this argument Weber mentions the case of medicine. He says that medicine is practised in terms of the presupposition that life is always worth living and that the medical specialist has a consequent duty to save life, and yet, '*whether* life is worthwhile living and when – this question is not asked by medicine'.[27] Equally, Weber pointed out that disciplines such as aesthetics or the social and cultural sciences interpret certain artefacts, texts or practices but whether they are actually worthwhile (whether they 'ought' to be) is impossible to say from within those fields. The 'ought' is a province that is beyond the competence of science and, therefore, so is judgement. The possibility of value as a universal criterion of judgement necessarily collapses into statements of personal preference.

To this extent, Weber reveals the relationship between disenchantment and what MacIntyre subsequently labelled emotivism. Indeed, Weber seems to imply that statements of preference are all that can possibly remain in the wake of the crisis of legitimacy that disenchantment involves and attenuates. Yet Weber does not at all approve of this situation. In fact he repudiates it. This is very clear in his disparaging comments about German youth who have, he believes, responded to the meaninglessness of science with a flight towards sensation. What Weber calls 'youth' appears to represent the undignified other within the text of 'Science as a Vocation'. This is what Weber is struggling against. According to Weber, the Platonic identification of science with reason and freedom is seen as quite incredible by 'youth'.

He understands youth to believe that, 'the intellectual constructions of science constitute an unreal realm of artificial abstractions, which with their bony hands seek to grasp the blood-and-the-sap of true life without ever catching up with us'. Weber seems to be bewildered by the view of 'youth' that, 'here in life, in what for Plato was the play of shadows on the walls of the cave, genuine reality is pulsating'.[28]

Weber thinks that 'youth' confronts the crisis of the legitimacy of science at its sharpest and that they turn away from it and towards that which seems to remain sure beyond any rational justification; the irrational. In so doing they prove that they are possessed of that weakness which is the inability to confront these times. As Weber saw the matter: 'they crave... experience as such. The only thing that is strange is the method that is now followed: the spheres of the irrational, the only spheres that intellectualism has not yet touched, are now raised into consciousness and put under its lens.' He warned that 'this method of emancipation from intellectualism may well bring about the very opposite of what those who take to it conceive as its goal'.[29] Moreover, the abyss of meaninglessness that disenchantment opens up is believed by Weber to lead 'youth' to search for a leader in whom they can, presumably, invest a supreme meaning and overcome the problem of their own freedom (through a kind of return to the cave). Weber rejected this irrationalism because it is incompatible with his fundamental commitment to principles of reason and human emancipation.

There is running through the text of 'Science as a Vocation' a commitment to the freedom of the individual human subject. This means that it is wrong for the scientist to pretend to be a leader because such a claim infringes the reason and the freedom of others, and because anyone who does so pretend is nothing more than a fraud, for Weber argues that 'in the field of science... the man who makes himself the impresario of the subject to which he should be devoted, and steps upon the stage and seeks to legitimate himself through "experience"... is no "personality"'. Rather, such playing for effect 'is a crowd phenomenon, and it always makes a petty impression and debases the one who is thus concerned'.[30] The irrational – whether it takes the form of sensation, the search for a leader, easy mysticism or crowd-pleasing – is seen by Weber to be at once a defining trait of the moral discourse and practice of the contemporary present but also the most powerful condemnation of it.

With his diagnosis of the state of moral discourse in the contemporary present, Weber anticipates MacIntyre's account of incommensurability. Weber would agree with MacIntyre's thesis that, in the present, there prevails a multiplicity of different, various and competing ethical systems each of which possesses its own criteria of the excellent and the good. And he would also agree with MacIntyre's contention that it is impossible to appeal to any existent universal standards in order to judge between these different positions.[31] As Weber said: '"scientific" pleading is meaningless in principle because the various value spheres of the world stand in irreconcilable conflict with each other'.[32] There is no court of appeal. Weber articulated this in an example that was especially pertinent given the time of his lecture, 1918, and after four years of competing claims about who held the moral high ground in Europe: 'I do not know how one might wish to decide "scientifically" the value of French and German culture; for here...different gods struggle with one another, now and for all times to come.'[33] Yet Weber glimpsed the possibility that worrisome attempts might well come to be made to try and resolve the struggle of the different gods, through a flight to the irrational (which in Weber's terms demeans the dignity of humanity) or through the more elemental exercise of force.

The recovery of science

It is worth pausing and pulling the threads of the preceding discussion together. It is also worth thinking back to Musil's sentence about ideals and morality being the way of filling the hole of the soul (when I use the word 'soul' I want to refer to the possibility of subjective meaningfulness that is apprehended as pertaining beyond contingent time and place and, therefore, as transcendent). Now, Weber's account of disenchantment and his emphasis upon the inability of science to answer the important question does suggest the decline of the universal credibility of any conception of the subjective meaningfulness of the social and historical world. The soul is subjected to a double dissolution at least. First, it is dissolved through the rise to dominance of a narrative of progress; the possibility of the soul of any given individual is subsumed within a broader process that goes on without stopping for any subjective reason. Transcendence does not at all reside in subjectivity, in excellence or in a commitment to some next world; instead it resides in this world itself. Transcendence becomes immanent. Secondly, the soul is dissolved into irrationalism. The meaninglessness of science leads to a turn towards this-worldly properties and qualities of being as the source of all legitimacy and validation. The subjectively meaningful transcendent therefore collapses (or at least becomes inconsequential) and leaves only incommensurability. As Weber said: 'so long as life remains immanent and is interpreted in its own terms, it knows only an unceasing struggle of...gods with one another'.[34]

It might be said that Weber offers a sociology of the demise of the soul in the contemporary present and, therefore, of the rise of an emptiness within the individual. But, in Musil's phrase, Weber consequently shows how ideals and morality can fill the hole that remains. For Weber then the problem is one of how to recover reason, the freedom of humanity, and the possibility of subjective meaningfulness, whilst also accepting the fate of these times of disenchantment and meaninglessness. This is why 'Science as a Vocation' is a text that offers a critique of moral discourse and practice in the contemporary present alongside an emphasis on the demands which are made upon the individual by the calling of science.

Weber has to identify subjective meaningfulness as the only possible resolution of the crisis of legitimacy that is implied by disenchantment. He cannot turn to traditional modes of thought or practice and, indeed, Weber's whole sociology contains within it a tendency to deny the time-immemorial. In Weber's own terms this would be one reflection of his refusal to turn away from the challenges of the contemporary present. But it can be suggested that this refusal to entertain the traditional is at least partly due to the Liberal Protestant strain that can be detected in his thought. For example, like Troeltsch, Weber saw Christianity as one religion amongst many. The difference is, of course, that whereas Liberal Protestantism sees Christianity as the highest *existent* form of religion within this plurality, Weber could not turn to any judge or arbiter between the competing positions and therefore all he could do was register incommensurability. More generally, Weber's own debts to Kant[35] meant that he shared the concern to establish humanity over and above nature, in a form possessed with the dignity of reason and freedom.

It is at least partially this context that explains why, when Weber sought to fill in the hole where the soul used to be, he had to turn to the individual. Tradition offers no solution because it is contrary to the spirit of the present. Habit offers no solution because, as the analysis of the Protestant Ethic had demonstrated, it is a false and particular entrapment of the freedom of humanity (it is, in other words, a kind of superstition). Equally, the example of 'youth' offers no solution because in their struggle to elevate their own truth and freedom they are, in effect, achieving precisely the opposite for 'today, youth proclaims ... redemption from the intellectualism of science in order to return to one's own nature and therewith to nature in general'.[36] But for Weber, humanity cannot return to nature because that is contrary to reason and the freedom of humanity.

The individual becomes the only place to which one can turn. And, whereas Protestantism involves an emphasis upon the individual believer, justified by faith, so Weber's 'Science as a Vocation' contains a very secular emphasis upon the individual scientist, justified by his or her quest and struggle with and for disenchantment. Implicit in Weber's thesis is a belief that it is only in a self-willed (and therefore subjectively meaningful) disposition towards the excellence which science demands that the individual can be free of the various demands of desire, self-interest and popular esteem. Moreover, it is only in this way that scientists can distinguish themselves from 'youth' and offer it an example of what can be done. Here, then, there is something approaching a subjectivisation of the Kantian equation of Enlightenment with maturity.[37] Or, as Weber put it, scientists must be aged – not young and youthful – if they are to confront the devil in the contemporary present. Thus, he writes, 'this does not mean age in the sense of the birth certificate. It means that if one wishes to settle with this devil, one must not take flight before him . . . First of all, one has to see the devil's ways to the end in order to realize his power and his limitations.'[38]

In order to provide a legitimate context for that turn to the mature individual who can see the devil of the present and all its works, Weber has to redefine the meaning of science. Weber has to establish science on a ground that is primarily ethical rather than dogmatic. As such it is no surprise to find passages in 'Science as a Vocation' where science is identified as a subjectively meaningful existential situation rather than simply as a series of rational procedures and methods. This enables Weber to stress what he calls the 'inward calling' of science. Thus, he warns, 'whoever lacks the capacity to put on blinders, so to speak, and to come up to the idea that the fate of his soul depends upon whether or not he makes the correct conjecture at this passage of this manuscript may as well stay away from science'. The person who cannot achieve that overwhelming sense of subjective meaningfulness found on a page, 'will never have what one may call the "personal experience" of science. Without this strange intoxication, ridiculed by every outsider; without this passion . . . you have *no* calling for science and you should do something else.' Weber concluded: 'for nothing is worthy of man as man unless he can pursue it with passionate devotion.'[39] But it must be noted that this is not a passion that leads the individual into a kind of megalomania. It is a passion that involves a wager on subjectivity and, in that wager, the possibility of meaningfulness is put at the mercy of the enthusiasm that might – or presumably might not – be inspired by a manuscript or a conjecture. For Weber then, nothing is 'worthy of man as man' unless it forces him to engage in subjectively meaningful practices that no outsider can ever understand, that the crowd-pleasing 'impresarios' would mock and which yet enable that individual to stand aboard the train of the contemporary present and, thus, passionately devote himself to the mission of disenchantment, reason and human emancipation. Weber says that, 'an inner devotion to the task, and that alone, should lift the scientist to the height and dignity of the subject he pretends to serve'.[40] Once again the message is clear. In so far as science is a motor of the processes that are defining of the contemporary present, then science, even in the face of meaninglessness and incommensurability, requires a certain virtue: the virtue of the duty to reason and to human freedom.

The acceptance, embrace and the performance of that duty means that the scientist becomes a beacon of disenchantment rather than simply an agent of it. In this way, Weber stresses the aims of science as a virtue. First, it 'contributes to the technology of controlling life by calculating external objects as well as man's activities'. Again, there is an implicit attack on any kind of emotivism in this passage; Weber is advocating control and calculation not preference and popular influence. Secondly, science provides 'methods of thinking, the tools and the training for thought'. Here, then, the scientist does not give in to impulses or taste; for Weber what makes us truly human is reason, is thought; and thought has to be trained. It is a hard achievement, not something that is given. Thirdly, and it would appear for Weber most importantly, science involves clarity.[41] Clarity means the knowledge that when one has taken a practical stand and when one value has been given pre-eminence over all others, the individual has to determine to serve that particular end in the full recognition of the fact that, 'figuratively speaking, you serve this god and you offend the other god when you decide to adhere to this position. And if you remain faithful to yourself, you will necessarily come to certain final conclusions that subjectively make sense.'[42]

As such the meaninglessness and incommensurability that dominate moral discourse and practice in the contemporary present can be overcome by the individual who wills to serve one 'god' at the expense of all others and who then subordinates all of his or her other impulses or desires to that end. But, at this point, Weber takes the goal of science beyond the individual and he reconnects the scientist in the contemporary present both to his or her contemporaries and to the Platonic archetype. Thus, he asserts: 'if we are competent in our pursuit . . . we can force the individual, or at least we can help him, to give himself an *account of the ultimate meaning of his own conduct*. This appears to me as not so trifling a thing to do, even for one's own personal life.'[43] For Weber, intellectual integrity means the clarification of the ultimate standpoint that one has chosen for oneself and through which one makes the present subjectively meaningful and gives oneself to the performance of duty to the god of reason and human emancipation. In all of that resides virtue, despite and because of the conflicts and confusions of the contemporary present.

Conclusion

In his essay on Robert Musil, Berger makes the point that, for the Austrian novelist, if 'a "true" self was possible, it would not be a given, a *datum*, but rather something to be attained, achieved as the result of an enormously difficult effort'.[44] This is precisely the conclusion that Weber had already anticipated. For Weber, the 'true' self is the product of a difficult struggle to overcome through an enhanced clarity and knowledge (and enhanced reason) the emptiness, contingency and incommensurability that is the almost necessarily dominant defining trait of the contemporary present. Weber points to the demise and confusion of judgement and moral practice in the contemporary present and yet he manages to recover the possibility of virtue. However there is a strange paradox about this Weberian recuperation of virtue. The 'true self' of the virtuous scientist ends up remarkably like the first philosopher of Plato. Perhaps, then, 'Science as a Vocation' is not quite as able to stare the present resolutely in the face as Weber would like to believe.

Or, put differently, Weber leaves the question in abeyance: is virtue possible in the context of the conditions and circumstances of our disenchantment?[45]

But about one thing Weber is very sure indeed. Without the virtue that is associated with the vocation of science, sociology is trivialised. This is, perhaps, the point at which Weber's account becomes subjectively meaningful for him. One of Weber's recurrent concerns was to try to clarify his own 'ultimate standpoint'.[46] 'Science as a Vocation' could not have been delivered by a man who was able to rest easily with himself. Weber is attempting to justify himself to himself. And in that attempt he discovers the virtue of virtue. It fills the hole where, in different historical circumstances, he might have been able to find his soul. As such, Weber might not know if virtue is possible, but he is sure that it is necessary. It might be said that in this way Weber offers a Kierkegaardian solution to a problem he has with Kant.[47] He knows that the Kantian problematic towards which he is dedicated is unsustainable. Weber cannot provide any rational or sociological justification for his own ultimate standpoint.

The point is that Weber does not at all doubt the Kantian thesis that the dignity of humanity is to be found in freedom and in the struggle for emancipation from the pressures and demands of the external and the contingent (that is to say, Weber accepts Kant's project of autonomy and the critique of heteronomy).[48] Yet Weber's sociological project reveals the improbability of any such emancipation. Weber's sociology undermines what MacIntyre calls Kant's 'two deceptively simple theses': 'if the rules of morality are rational, they must be the same for all rational beings ... and if the rules of morality are binding on all rational beings, then the contingent ability of such beings to carry them out must be unimportant – what is important is their will to carry them out'.[49] However, the analysis of the Protestant Ethic and, indeed, the knowledge of the process of disenchantment, shows the variability of the rules of morality. For Weber it follows that either morality or humanity is not rational. Consequently, it also becomes sociologically inappropriate to contend that the rules of morality are universally binding. The only option that is left for Weber, if he is to be able to cling on to his Kantian commitment to human freedom, is a personalisation of the will to carry out the demands of morality. This is Weber's Kierkegaardian moment: 'the act of choice had to be called in to do the work that reason could not do'.[50] But it is absolutely wrong to contend that Weber thereby falls into the trap of emotivism. He does not. Rather, for Weber, this act of choice represents the only possibility that remains for the individual who would will to do his or her duty to the demands of human freedom and thereby attain a 'true self'. This is not a choice that the individual *prefers* to carry out. Weber identifies it instead as one that the individual is *obliged* to carry out, regardless of personal inclinations.

Weber's legacy to any sociology of virtue is at once profound and yet highly problematic. He provides a most demanding and compelling insight into what it might mean to be a sociologist who makes a wager on the self as opposed to simply playing to the crowd.[51] Yet his concern with the project of the attainment of a 'true self' means that the more sociological horizon of the relationship of that self to others is somewhat lost to sight. To this extent, the sociology which goes one step further to reject the Kantian problematic offers a counterpoint to Weber. In particular the sociology which orients itself around the postmodern has tended to emphasise the fact that relationships between self and others are of absolutely central moral and ethical significance. The point has been emphasised by Zygmunt Bauman. For Bauman postmodernity offers the hesitant possibility that individuals might be able to practice a kind of moral subjectivity in the world which embraces the infinite pre-social demand of a responsibility to care for the Other. Levinas, not Kant, thus becomes the philosophical inspiration for the sociological project.[52] But the turn to Levinas has unfortunate implications for sociology. First, the importation of any imagination of a pre-social ethics into sociology leads to the development of a too straightforward Manichaeism in which the social, cultural and historical becomes little more than a distortion of the pre-social truth.[53] Secondly, if the responsibility to care for the other is pre-social then it is not liable to any kind of narration since that narration will necessarily stand as nothing other than an illicit socialisation of that which is not social. Thirdly, it is noticeable that the sociology which turns to Levinas tends to read him in a very particular way. Levinas is taken to be the philosopher of an ethical demand which individuals feel and act upon independently of any weight of tradition. Hence the distinct possibility that any turn to Levinas ultimately and inevitably leads to theology is ignored.[54] Sociology and religion are kept apart.

The separation is due to the very basis of sociology itself. The lesson of Weber is that sociology and religion cannot be reconciled. The former is a knowledge and a discipline of disenchantment and therefore it generates only ethical meaninglessness. The latter is a knowledge and a discipline of meaningfulness which, from a sociological point of view, cannot be justified. But perhaps sociology cannot be justified either. That is what Weber's 'Science as a Vocation' reveals despite itself.

Notes and references

1 Exceptions to this general rule are: Robert T. Hall, 'Communitarian Ethics and the Sociology of Morals: Alasdair MacIntyre and Emile Durkheim', *Sociological Focus*, vol. 24, 1991, pp. 93–105; Peter McMylor, *Alasdair MacIntyre* (London: Routledge, 1994); and Paul du Gay, 'Alasdair MacIntyre and the Christian Genealogy of Management of Critique', *Cultural Values*, vol. 2, no. 4, 1998, pp. 421–44.

2 Donald N. Levine, 'Sociology after MacIntyre', *American Journal of Sociology*, vol. 89, no. 3, 1983, p. 700.

3   Ibid., p. 700. See also Alasdair MacIntyre, *After Virtue. A Study in Moral Theory*, 2nd edition (London: Duckworth, 1985).
4   Max Weber, *The Methodology of the Social Sciences*, trans. and ed. Edward A. Shils and Henry A. Finch (New York: The Free Press, 1949).
5   Indeed, MacIntyre is rather dismissive of attempts to draw fact-value distinctions. See his *After Virtue*, pp. 56–8. I have explored MacIntyre's reading of Weber in 'Weber's Alleged Emotivism', *The British Journal of Sociology*, vol. 50, no. 4, December 1999, pp. 563–73.
6   Levine, 'Sociology after MacIntyre', p. 170.
7   Max Weber, *From Max Weber. Essays in Sociology*, trans. and ed. Hans H. Gerth and C. Wright Mills (London: Routledge & Kegan Paul, 1948), p. 149.
8   See Alasdair MacIntyre, *Whose Justice? Which Rationality?* (London: Duckworth, 1988), and *Three Rival Versions of Moral Enquiry* (London: Duckworth, 1990).
9   Marianne Weber, *Max Weber: A Biography*, trans. Harry Zohn (New York: John Wiley, 1975).
10 On the secularism of sociology, see John Milbank, *Theology and Social Theory. Beyond Secular Reason* (Oxford: Blackwell, 1990).
11 MacIntyre, *After Virtue*, pp. 43–7.
12 Robert Musil, *The Man Without Qualities*, vol. 1, trans. Eithne Wilkins and Ernst Kaiser (London: Martin Secker & Warburg, 1954), chapter 46, 'Ideals and morality are the best means of filling the big hole that one calls the soul', pp. 218–20. For a useful appraisal of Musil, see Peter L. Berger, *A Far Glory. The Quest for Faith in an Age of Credulity* (New York: Doubleday, 1992), for an essay entitled 'Excursus: Robert Musil and the Salvage of the Self', pp. 105–22. My claim that Musil offers a key to unlocking Weber is due to my reading of this essay by Berger.
13 Weber, *From Max Weber*, pp. 129–56.
14 To this extent, 'Science as a Vocation' has close moral affinities with the theme of entrapment (or, in more Kantian terms, heteronomy) which runs through the last couple of pages of Weber's study of the Protestant Ethic. See Max Weber, *The Protestant Ethic and the Spirit of Capitalism*, trans. Talcott Parsons (London: George Allen & Unwin, 1930).
15 Karl Jaspers, *Leonardo, Descartes, Max Weber. Three Essays*, trans. Ralph Mannheim (London: Routledge & Kegan Paul, 1965), p. 230.
16 Weber, *From Max Weber*, p. 140.
17 Ibid., p. 134.
18 Ibid., p. 139.
19 Here there are traces of Kant's dictum that this is not an enlightened age, but that it is an age of Enlightenment. See Immanuel Kant, *Political Writings*, second edition, ed. Hans Reiss (Cambridge: Cambridge University Press, 1991), p. 58.
20 Weber, *From Max Weber*, p. 138.
21 Weber, *The Protestant Ethic*.
22 Weber once planned to write a book about Tolstoy. See Marianne Weber, *Max Weber*, p. 466.
23 Max Weber, *From Max Weber*, p. 140.
24 Ibid., p. 138.
25 This is a theme that is explored to considerable effect by another author Weber greatly admired, Dostoevsky. See Fyodor Dostoevsky, *Notes from the Underground*, trans. Mirra Ginsburg (New York: Bantam, 1974).
26 Weber, *From Max Weber*, p. 143. Emphasis added.

27 Ibid., p. 144. Emphasis added.
28 Ibid., p. 141.
29 Ibid., p. 143.
30 Ibid., p. 137. This sentence seems to imply a Kierkegaardian strain in Weber's thought. See Soren Kierkegaard, 'The Present Age', in Robert Bretall (ed.), *A Kierkegaard Anthology*, trans. Alexander Dru (Princeton: Princeton University Press, 1946), pp. 258–69.
31 For a useful summary of his position, see Alasdair MacIntyre, *How to Seem Virtuous Without Actually Being So* (Lancaster: Centre for the Study of Cultural Values, 1991).
32 Weber, *From Max Weber*, p. 147.
33 Ibid., p. 148.
34 Ibid., p. 152.
35 I have gestured towards Weber's debts to Kant throughout this essay. The debts are well revealed in Milbank, *Theology and Social Theory*. See also Immanuel Kant, *Critique of Practical Reason*, trans. Thomas Kingsmill Abbott (London: Longmans, 1909).
36 Weber, *From Max Weber*, p. 142.
37 Kant, *Political Writings*, p. 54.
38 Weber, *From Max Weber*, p. 152.
39 Ibid., p. 135.
40 Ibid., p. 137.
41 These three aspects of science are discussed in Weber. See *From Max Weber*, pp. 150–1.
42 Ibid., p. 151.
43 Ibid., p. 152. Original emphasis.
44 Berger, *A Far Glory*, p. 113.
45 Other sociologists have sought to recover to clarify precisely this question of the relationship between sociology and virtue. See, for example, Kieran Flanagan, *The Enchantment of Sociology. A Study of Theology and Culture* (Basingstoke: Macmillan, 1996).
46 See Edward Bryan Portis, *Max Weber and Political Commitment. Science, Politics and Personality* (Philadelphia: Temple University Press, 1986).
47 This way of making the point was intended deliberately to recall Alasdair MacIntyre, *After Virtue*, p. 41.
48 See Immanuel Kant, *Groundwork of the Metaphysics of Morals* ed. Mary Gregor (Cambridge: Cambridge University Press, 1998).
49 MacIntyre, *After Virtue*, pp. 43–4.
50 Ibid., p. 47.
51 The phrase 'wager of the self' is derived from Kieran Flanagan's essay, 'Postmodernity and Culture: Sociological Wagers of the Self in Theology', in Kieran Flanagan and Peter C. Jupp (eds), *Postmodernity, Sociology and Religion* (Basingstoke: Macmillan, 1996), pp. 152–73. It might be said that in Weber's work there is a theological wager on the self in sociology, but a wager that Weber – as a sociologist – was fated always to lose.
52 Bauman has used Levinas in a number of texts, but perhaps the more important are: *Modernity and the Holocaust* (Cambridge: Polity, 1989); *Modernity and Ambivalence* (Cambridge: Polity, 1991); and *Postmodern Ethics* (Cambridge: Polity, 1993). The turn to Levinas is also well represented in Barry Smart, *Facing Modernity: Ambivalence, Reflexivity and Morality* (London: Sage, 1999). These concluding

comments refer to points I make at greater length in chapter 4 of my book, *Moral Culture* (London: Sage, 1997), pp. 113–45. The difficulty is that the turn to Levinas tends to fall into the trap of emotivism because it leads to a somewhat voluntaristic (and therefore preferential) account of the basis of the ethical demand. These comments can also be read as a critique of some of the claims about ethics made in my earlier book, *The Life and Times of Post-Modernity* (London: Routledge, 1993).

53   This point has been made to good effect in Ross Abbinnett, 'Postmodernity and the Ethics of Care: Situating Bauman's Social Theory', *Cultural Values*, vol. 2, no. 1, 1998, pp. 87–116. See also his book, *Truth and Social Science. From Hegel to Deconstruction* (London: Sage, 1998).

54   For example, I can think of no text in the now widespread sociological literature on Levinas which contains any movement towards Simone Weil's ideas of patience and of waiting.

3
Virtue Ethics, Justice and Religion in Multicultural Societies

David Herbert

This chapter assesses the contributions of Alasdair MacIntyre to understandings of virtue ethics in the context of issues of public policy, particularly those arising from the presence of religious minorities in multicultural democratic societies. Is collective representation as a religious group an appropriate form of public recognition for these groups and, if so, in what ways and in what contexts? It will be answered with special reference to Muslims in Britain, France and the Netherlands.

Collective representation can take place at a number of levels, from local authority groups, such as the Standing Council on Religious Education[1] in Britain to migrant consultative groups in the Netherlands through to national government bodies. It raises questions about politics and constitutional affairs, such as the issue of multi-faith representation in a revised Upper House for the United Kingdom. Such representation forms part of a wider pattern of recognition – of which public funding for religiously-based schools, the distribution of welfare resources and the collection of national and local statistics are examples. This recognition can be seen as an acknowledgement by society that Muslim groups have a place, and that their religious and cultural identity needs to be secured. Beyond its symbolic significance, representation can also ensure that Muslim interests are taken into account in public decision-making processes. A sense of exclusion from these may exacerbate a sense of deprivation which Muslim groups feel they suffer.[2] For Muslims, demands for public recognition arise in response to a sense of exclusion from the public sphere, that is from those forums for debate and expression of interest separate from the state, but through which public policy is influenced and partly shaped.[3]

As a result of this perception of exclusion, various demands for public recognition, including more definite forms of collective representation, have been made by Muslims in Western Europe since the 1980s. These demands stemmed from particular public controversies about their cultural and religious rights, and the issues of tolerance and recognition they generated. Thus, in France there was the issue of the *foulard* ('headscarf') where

Muslim rights to proclaim a religious identity clashed with the prevailing civil regulations, which precluded such forms of representation in the classroom. This generated much controversy about the status of Islam in France and its rights of cultural and religious recognition. Failure to grasp Islamic sensibilities arose in England over the offence generated by Rushdie's *The Satanic Verses* controversy which again suggested that their collective representations were not being adequately recognised. This failure to understand also lay behind the unsympathetic response to their claims for separate schools, rights granted to other religious groups, but which Muslims had been denied up to recently.

In this setting, 'recognition' is a complex term: it means both that one's views and feelings have not been properly understood, and that the place of understanding has been usurped by prejudice. This often becomes manifest as a rejection of one's views and of oneself as trivial, irrational, or barbarous. Taylor has traced the history of this sense of recognition[4] and established a debate on its contemporary significance.[5] He discerns a counter-Enlightenment tradition which runs from Rousseau through Romanticism, Hegel and Herder to nineteenth-century nationalism and which insists on the importance of the recognition of distinctive collective identities for the well-being of individuals and societies. This contrasts to the emphasis in the Enlightenment and its stress on the importance of the universal and abstract individual. The need for recognition of one's identity is not unique to modernity, yet it has created conditions – in particular, unprecedented global interaction – in which recognition can become problematic.

Applying this analysis to contemporary identity politics, Taylor describes the importance of recognition in the following terms:

> our identity is partly shaped by recognition or its absence, often by the *mis*recognition of others, and so a person or group of people can suffer real damage, real distortion, if the people or society around them mirror back to them a confining or demeaning or contemptible picture of themselves.[6]

On this basis, one can see how Muslims might suffer as a result of neglect or distortion of their collective identity, and also how one might proceed to justify the institutionalisation of recognition. Yet such demands for recognition are strongly contested. In particular, it may be argued that recognition of religious groups will give undue power to their leaders, who, in turn, may not represent the view of their supposed Muslim constituencies, especially women and the religiously unorthodox.

This chapter examines the demands for collective representation by Muslims in Britain, France and the Netherlands. Each has different forms of recognition, which are closely related to state policies on the integration of ethnic minority groups, and also to historic patterns of religion–state relations.

In spite of this diversity, there emerges a common pattern of demand for collective recognition on a religious basis by Muslims, which contrasts with resistance to such recognition by the largely post-Christian majority. This provides the context for our discussion of ethical theories and their interaction with social critiques. It leads to a question of how can any set of institutional arrangements meet the apparently conflicting demands here presented?

Taylor's political theory provides a useful starting point for answering this question. His writing on identity politics can link Muslim demands for recognition to a tradition in modern political theory and practice. Virtue ethics can build on this connection, for, in contrast to rival traditions of ethics, it emphasises formation of character rather than the abstraction of principles (deontology) or the calculation of consequences (consequentialism). This emphasis focuses attention on the differential development of individuals, and hence the social conditions under which this takes place, in contrast to the tendency to abstract individualism in alternative approaches. It gives virtue ethics an affinity with those, including Muslims, who seek recognition for the role of family, community, religion and other social institutions in the development and sustenance of character, and hence in the moral life of society.

Collective representation: support and opposition

We now turn to consider evidence both for the demand for collective representation by Muslims, and the opposition to this idea. A different form of evidence will be drawn from each country. In France we consider survey-style interviews undertaken between 1988 and 1989 by Leveau.[7] Although a decade old, this study has the advantage of being undertaken before the *foulard* (headscarf) affair, the 'Islam of France' debate, the Rushdie affair and the Gulf war which so polarised public opinion,[8] and hence arguably may be taken as more indicative of underlying attitudes than subsequent surveys. Here, in the context of a strong laicist tradition and individualist concept of citizenship, Leveau found that 'Muslims in France are starting to ask for a political modification on a community basis'.[9]

For the majority of Muslims, such a modification was seen as a route to integration within French society, rather than a form of looking back to links with their countries of origin. Thus 72 per cent, more among the young than old, of those interviewed wished that Muslims in France could have their own representatives. Additionally, 60 per cent were in favour of choosing such representatives democratically from amongst Muslims living in France. Only 13 per cent wanted them to be appointed from the country of origin. By contrast, 82 per cent of non-Muslims felt that the Muslim religion ought to be kept a private matter, while 52 per cent agreed with the proposition that 'the more one is integrated in French society the less one remains a Muslim', with only 30 per cent being against this proposition.

Our Dutch evidence comes from a study of the representation of Muslim groups on local authorities. Feirabend and Rath considered the city of Rotterdam, where the local council reluctantly entered into critical dialogue with Islamic associations on the grounds of a perceived need for 'co-operation with the groupings that are nearest to migrants' hearts. For Turks and Moroccans these are clearly the mosque.'[10]

In 1983, representatives of Islamic associations were invited to join the Working Party on the Self-Organisation of Migrants, a move which led to the public subsidisation of Islamic groups and, in 1988, the eventual formation of an umbrella body of Islamic associations. This contributes to the overall forum for migrants and is consulted by civil servants and local authorities over issues such as religious education, mosques and general migrant matters. This representation was not achieved without overcoming opposition, both from mainstream (left-wing and liberal) political parties and from secular migrant organisations. In another city, Utrecht, such opposition had proved sufficient to prevent the formation of an equivalent representative body. This opposition needs to be understood against the historic background of the relation between religion and politics in the Netherlands. Although there is a constitutional separation of church and state, there is also an historic mode of integrating religious groupings, Catholic and Protestant, into society. This has been accomplished through the promotion of separate institutions along religious lines. This process is effected through the policy of 'pillarisation'. Since the 1960s, this system has partly broken down. Yet, it still persists in various forms, including the constitutional right to the public funding of religious schools.

It is against this background that the opposition of local politicians to the political representation of Muslim groups needs to be understood. This opposition is illustrated in two sets of comments. The first comes from a Christian Democrat councillor in Utrecht. He stated:

I am also a member of a church community, that community also has a minister. But what I mean is I will not address myself to him if I have a housing problem. Then I go to the housing department, I do not go to my minister. That is the way things were in the past, I mean those days are gone.[11]

The second comment comes from a liberal party (D'66) councillor, also from Utrecht, who noted that

the laws of the Morocco-men are interwoven with their religion, well that is a problem. I do believe it has to be clear to everyone how Dutch society functions. We keep church and state separated, and I consider that an acquired right which should not be changed. And that has to be made very clear towards mosque organisations. Once that is clear, well, I think we can live together very well.[12]

These statements suggest a scepticism towards the democratic credibility of Muslims in the Netherlands, and perhaps also towards the compatibility of Islam with democracy.

Our British evidence comes from Muslim self-organisations. A variety of initiatives from Muslim groups indicate a demand for collective representation along religious lines. These reflect a diversity of actions, from the Muslim Institute initiatives, the Muslim Manifesto and Muslim Parliament, to the campaigning work of the UK Action Group on Islamic Affairs. The last is an umbrella body representing a range of Muslim organisations, which presented a publication entitled *Need for Reform* to the Home Secretary in 1993 at the time of the review of the 1975 Race Relations Act.[13] This marshalled a range of sources arguing for the recognition of Muslims as a distinct religious and cultural group requiring recognition in various areas of British law. These efforts to realise recognition have generated a certain amount of opposition. Thus the Runnymede Trust's report on the place of Muslims in British society concluded that

> the expression of anti-Muslim ideas and sentiments is increasingly respectable. They are a natural, taken-for-granted ingredient of the common sense world of millions of people every day.[14]

In each of these countries, the Muslim desire for collective representation faces public opposition. This is particularly striking given the ethnic diversity of Muslim populations and the very different levels of recognition accorded to them in each case. In the Netherlands, the largest ethnic groupings are Turkish and Moroccan; in France, Algerian, Moroccan and Tunisian; and in Britain, largely South Asian, although there are significant minorities from elsewhere in each case.[15] There is a diversity in the agenda and forms which these quests for recognition take in terms of group religious identity. This can take various forms, including representation on local and national government consultative bodies, public funding for religiously-based schools, the distribution of welfare resources and the collection of national and local statistics. In the Netherlands recognition takes place in all of these cases (though to varying extents according to locality), in Britain in some, and in France in none.[16]

These contrasting patterns of recognition stem from contrasting histories of policy towards religious diversity, and contrasting ways of incorporating immigrant groups. The French laicist tradition, stemming from the Revolution and reinforced by the 1905 decision to ban public funding of religious bodies in most *départements*,[17] effected a ban on the self-organisation of non-national immigrant groups effective from the 1930s to 1981. This contrasts with the Dutch use of collective religious identity as the key to social integration under the policy of pillarisation.[18] Soysal has analysed incorporation patterns of migrants into Western European societies, and concluded that French, Dutch and British systems represent three contrasting types – of statist, corporatist and liberal respectively.[19]

Thus, in spite of the different histories of these societies, the different origins of their Muslim communities, and the different incorporation regimes through which the authorities in each have sought to integrate Muslim immigrants, each country shows evidence of two common conflicting features. First, there is a demand by a significant proportion of the Muslim population for some form of collective recognition in the public domain, be that political, social or cultural. Secondly, there is a resistance on behalf of the majority post-Christian population to such forms of collective recognition. Against this background, we turn to ethical theory to see what light it can shed on resolving the dilemmas of Muslims seeking effective policies for their representation and recognition.

Virtue ethics and social policy: an unlikely combination?

Virtue ethics forms one of three major types of ethical theory. It deserves attention in the analysis of policy because: (i) in contrast to alternatives, it is agent-centred and offers dynamic models of agent–environment interaction, and hence, potentially, offers greater possibility for dialogue with the social sciences; (ii) other approaches have serious shortcomings, especially when used in isolation, and (iii) it may be constructively combined with other approaches to provide a more holistic approach to ethics. As well as outlining three forms of ethical theory, we shall also distinguish between four levels of social critique[20] which can help us to think about different ways in which ethicists might engage with policy issues. This will help to introduce MacIntyre's virtue ethics, which will then be brought into critical dialogue with alternative approaches.

Contemporary ethical theories can be classified in three main types: consequentialist, deontological and virtue ethics. In some ways these approaches are so different that one may question whether they are theories of the same thing at all.[21] This can be seen by contrasting their approaches to questions of justice in policy or in relation to institutional arrangements of a particular society. Characteristically, the consequentialist asks whether the *consequences* of a policy or set of arrangements are just; the deontologist whether the *principles* informing them are just; and the virtue ethicist, whether this is the kind of policy or arrangement which a just *agent* (individual, community or society) would produce. In practice the three approaches may not be mutually exclusive – the difference is rather one of priority.

On the above description, virtue ethics appears agent-centred. In contrast, the other approaches share an abstract individualism which neglects the complex web of life, one where 'principles' and 'consequences' form only a part. Although virtue ethics more readily leads to a consideration of social and cultural processes, this has not developed into consideration of specific policy issues to the extent of exploring and providing alternative approaches. This may be because of its broad approach, but it also arises from its intellectual isolation.[22] There are, however, deeper reasons why both virtue ethicists and deontologists tend to step back from immediate policy issues.

First, there is a scepticism about the consequentialist assumption that it is possible to predict accurately in advance the consequences of actions in complex social settings. Consquentialists share many assumptions with the positivist social scientific methodologies which tend to inform policy studies. An example of this overlap between both is rational choice theory (RCT), which holds that individual agents will behave so as to maximise their own advantage. At first sight, RCT may appear agent-centred, like virtue ethics, in that its self-description proceeds from the supposed action of agents. It is, however, more accurately described as consequentialist, since it proceeds from an *assumption* about the action of agents, rather than making this the subject of *critical investigation*, as in virtue ethics. Thus, its emphasis is on the prediction and measurement of consequences, given certain assumptions about the way people generally behave. This approach has found it difficult to make sense of some kinds of behaviour – including political behaviour.[23] This is because political behaviour seems to be influenced by factors other than those of narrow self-interest, for example those of group solidarity, and what emerges in social processes of negotiation and discussion.

More widely, as Bauman has argued,[24] the Promethean premise of social engineering has been called into question by the failure of socialist projects both east and west of the former Iron Curtain, as well as by postmodern developments within academia which undermine the 'legislative' claims of 'experts'. In this context, the broadening of democratic participation in policy formulation and decision-making represents an increasingly attractive alternative to the technocratic management of market forces.

Secondly, consequentialism lacks substantive moral content. For example, RCT provides no critical judgement on the maximising behaviour of individuals, while utilitarianism, which transfers the assumption of maximising behaviour from the individual to society, can provide no critical interrogation of its maxim 'the greatest happiness of the greatest number'. Rather, such principles have to be imported from elsewhere, usually from deontology. Thus, 'bottom-loaded utilitarianism' imports the concept of rights from deontology to qualify the utilitarian maxim with the statement 'provided certain minimum rights of individuals are protected'. However, the credibility of the deontologists search for incontrovertible principles on which to base ethical life has also seemed increasingly questionable, as the foundations for such an enterprise continue to prove elusive.[25]

Thus, at least negatively, problems with alternative approaches make the relationship between virtue ethics and policy appear worthy of investigation. More positively, virtue ethics would seem to be a promising potential source of the substantive ethical content absent from consequentialism. It would also supply a more dynamic model of the individual in relation to others in the context of developing traditions in contrast with the static subject and elusive foundations of deontological ethics. There may then be a basis for constructive interaction between the approaches.

The different kinds of contribution which ethical theory might make to policy may be illuminated by considering different levels of social critique. Dryzeck distinguishes between four such levels: metatheoretical, which concerns itself with the epistemological assumptions of social analysis; pure, which contrasts a description of actual conditions with an ideal situation; indirect, which reconstructs an actual situation as it would be if an ideal model operated within it, and contrasts this with what actually happens; and constructive, which proposes alternatives to existing arrangements.[26] As we shall see, MacIntyre operates largely at the metatheoretical level, so that a constructive critique of policy issues, such as the collective representation of religious minorities, often has to extrapolated. In this process a sociologically-oriented virtue ethics such as MacIntyre's may be complemented by critiques operating at different levels of analysis, and by drawing on other ethical theories.

MacIntyre: virtue ethics and social criticism

MacIntyre provides an unusual example of a virtue ethicist with sociological competence and therefore might seem to offer a means of searching for links between virtue ethics and the formulation of policy in relation to rights of collective representation and recognition. He would, however, be sceptical of such a linkage of policy and virtue ethics, for he sees the bureaucratic structure of modern states through which such policy would be mediated as inimical to the cultivation of virtue. Thus, in the conclusion to *After Virtue* he writes:

> the tradition of the virtues is at variance with central features of the modern economic order and more especially its individualism, its acquisitiveness and its elevation of the values of the market to a central social place . . . it also involves a rejection of the modern political order.[27]

Indeed, the heart of MacIntyre's dual critique of modern moral philosophies and modern societies is that both have abandoned (in theory and social practice respectively) the teleological account of humanity central to virtue ethics. Ethics needs an account of the moral development of human beings in terms of substantive virtues – not the Kohlberg's cognitively biased[28] nor the ethnocentric version developed from Piaget[29] which underlies Habermas' communicative ethics.[30] Without such an account, moral philosophy is reduced to forms of calculation devoid of substantive values (consequentialism), or an assertion of principles which cannot be justified in relation to an account of human nature or society (deontology). The consequence of the latter, which MacIntyre sees as a key failure of the Enlightenment project, is a belief in the 'irreducible plurality of values' which enters the sociological tradition as 'an insistent and central Weberian theme'.[31] In this context, the government of modern societies becomes a matter of containing plurality behind a mask of 'effective' management and bureaucracy.

Thus, one interpretation of MacIntyre is that he would view the kinds of representation for Muslim groups discussed above as subject to this general critique. It is not that he either supports or opposes such institutions specifically, but rather that the larger structure of state or fabric of society, of which they would form part, stands condemned. Such a total critique can itself be condemned as a refusal to engage with social reality. However, several strands of his work point away from this interpretation. First, he immediately qualifies his negative remarks on modern politics by noting that:

> this does not mean that there are not many tasks only to be performed in and through government which still require performing:... But each particular responsibility has to be evaluated on its own merits.[32]

What, then, are the merits of the case in hand? There is some justice in criticising MacIntyre for failing to elaborate on what his gesture towards 'the construction of local forms of community within which civility and the intellectual and moral life can be sustained through the new dark ages which are already upon us'[33] means in social practice. His contribution remains largely a metacritical one. Nonetheless, there are sufficient hints for extrapolation that help the concerns of this essay. These emerge in two ways. First, he identifies some existing American religious communities as sustaining traditions of virtues, including

> some Catholic Irish, some Orthodox Greeks, and some Jews of an Orthodox persuasion, all of them communities that inherit their moral tradition not only through their religion, but also from the structure of the peasant villages and households which their immediate ancestors inhabited on the margins of modern Europe.[34]

On these grounds, one might also plausibly identify contemporary Muslim communities in Western Europe as sustaining traditions of virtue, since they also inherit their moral traditions, not only from their religions, but from the communities of their ancestors in North Africa and the Indian subcontinent. Thus, on MacIntyre's account, it seems that the distinctive traditions of Muslim communities are something that should be supported. By extension, forms of recognition which enable Muslim communities to sustain their traditions are also good. However, in so far as this may lead to integration into the political mainstream, MacIntyre's account sounds a warning, for the latter has been identified as corrosive of traditions of virtue.

Secondly, in *Whose Justice? Which Rationality?*[35] MacIntyre develops a theory of traditions in interaction which can be used as a framework for analysing the situation of minority religions in majority post-Christian societies. His argument attempts to steer a course between the deontological search for universal principles as a foundation for ethics, or knowledge more generally, and a relativist resignation to the culture-boundedness of all knowledge, moral or otherwise.[36] It is that participants in different traditions, finding themselves in situations where social contexts are partially shared – as immigrants and others frequently find themselves in multicultural democracies – may come to understand one another's traditions in much the same way as they learn to understand one another's languages. Hence, if their own tradition has difficulty formulating a solution to a particular problem:

> when they have understood the beliefs of the alien tradition they may find themselves compelled to recognise that within this tradition it is possible to construct from the concepts and theories peculiar to it what they were unable to provide from within their own conceptual and theoretical resources, a cogent and illuminating explanation – cogent and illuminating, that is, by their own standards – of why their own intellectual tradition was unable to solve its own problems or restore its coherence.[37]

In this way traditions may develop commonalities – shared conceptions, shared practices – at certain points, while remaining quite distinct at others. Thus the model provides a way of thinking how differences between traditions might be resolved while each tradition retains its integrity; indeed, each tradition retains its integrity precisely by drawing on the resources of another.

The model has significant problems which become apparent when one tries to reconstruct social reality in its terms, of which we shall consider just two. First, it becomes difficult to see how the intellectual coherence attributed to traditions matches the reality of either religious or cultural traditions in highly differentiated societies, or even in traditional forms, given the historic diversity of religious traditions. Secondly, it seems to assume a symmetry of power between traditions, whereas relationships between immigrants and host societies are likely to be radically asymmetrical, as the language analogy suggests. However, while traditions may be far more piecemeal than MacIntyre appears to allow, the model enables us to make sense of the holistic aspirations of some religious traditions, and their coherence may be reinterpreted on an individual, psychological level as a narrative framework which helps one to make sense of the world and which is partly shared by others. Furthermore, while power is unequally shared, the model gives us a way of thinking about how immigrant religions and cultures can become sources of resistance to dominant ideologies and values. It also urges the basic beliefs and values of society to enter the public sphere, to justify and renew themselves.

This last point, however, draws attention to MacIntyre's lack of attention to the possible benefits of modern moral and political traditions, in particular those of equality, personal autonomy and participative democracy. In the next section, we shall see how these developments might be brought into dialogue with MacIntyre's work to engage with the question of collective representation for religious minorities.

Alternatives to MacIntyre: political philosophy and cultural diversity

Earlier, we introduced Charles Taylor's formulation of the problem of recognition in modern societies. Taylor sees group recognition and individual autonomy as in permanent tension: increases in one will have costs for the other. Societies must therefore strike a balance, and in his view modern societies are tilted too far in the direction of individual liberty. Thus, in the liberal–communitarian debate in North American political philosophy, he counts as a communitarian. By contrast, Will Kymlicka is a liberal, but one who has devoted much attention to questions of community, culture and multiculturalism, especially in a Canadian context, where he has addressed the rights of indigenous and linguistic minorities.[38] Kymlicka's approach to ethics is an eclectic one from the perspective of our three-fold typology: he is centrally concerned with the formulation of principles to inform practice (deontology), but also with anticipating the consequences of policy (consequentialism), and to an extent with the formation of character (virtue ethics). He has argued that liberalism need not be neglectful of the significance of community for the flourishing of individuals, and thus he provides an interesting alternative perspective to MacIntyre.

Kymlicka views the contemporary wariness of any recognition of collective rights by liberals as a specifically post-war phenomenon, especially as a reaction to Nazi race policies. Perhaps because religious minorities, at least non-Christian or politicised ones, are less prominent in Canada than in Western Europe he has devoted less attention to these than to national and cultural ones. Nonetheless, two aspects of Kymlicka's work are highly relevant to our case. The first concerns special group representation rights in political assemblies, for example in the provision of reserved seats for Maoris in the New Zealand Parliament.[39] He argues that only two criteria should qualify groups for such rights. These are claims to self-government, and systemic disadvantage in the political process. While the first does not apply to Muslims in Western Europe, the second may, especially where their non-national status deprives them of the right to vote in national or local elections.[40] In this instance, his conclusion coincides with that which can be derived from MacIntyre.

A second relevant feature of his work, however, exposes differences between the two approaches. This lies in his discussion of the liberal state's approach to non-liberal minorities' conduct of their own internal affairs. This is relevant to the point of this chapter, as both Dutch and French evidence suggests part of the objection of non-Muslims to the collective representation of Muslims is scepticism about the democratic qualities of Muslim representatives. A key question here is whether recognising the leadership of what is perceived to be an illiberal order colludes in entrenching their illiberal ways, and does so at the cost of oppressing individuals within that community.

Kymlicka pursues this question in relation to Canadian and American legal judgements concerning Amish, Hutterite and Mennonite communities. He argues that liberals should uphold the principle of individual autonomy – understood as the right of the individual to revise his or her fundamental ends, including religion.[41] But he does not believe that upholding the primacy of autonomy necessarily entitles liberals to impose their views on illiberal minorities. Rather, he distinguishes between three kinds of illiberal minorities, and grades the degree of intervention that is justifiable accordingly. These groupings are national minorities, such as Francophones in Quebec; historic minorities such as the Amish in Wisconsin or Hasidic Jews in New York; and recently arrived immigrants, which would include most Muslims in Western Europe. He argues that internal interference should be limited in the first case, cautious in the second, but that for the third

> it is more legitimate to compel respect for liberal principles, ... I do not think it is wrong for liberal states to insist that immigration entails accepting the legitimacy of state enforcement of liberal principles, so long as immigrants know this in advance, and none the less voluntarily choose to come.[42]

Hence Kymlicka's view is directly contrary to the one derived from MacIntyre. How might one choose between them?

For Kymlicka, recognition of Muslim leaders in some state-related consultancy capacity would require some assurance of liberal attitudes and democratic credentials. It is difficult, however, to see how this could be achieved in practice, even if representatives are elected. Instead, it may be better to try to achieve a plurality of representative voices rather than exclude some from the political arena entirely. It is important to make the point that recognition of collective religious identity in a democratic context does not exclude recognition of other forms of identity. For example, the representation of Islamic associations on the advisory boards of Dutch local authorities does not exclude the presence of secular migrant organisations or women's groups, although with finite resources such recognition does mean that other organisations will lose out to some extent. Thus, if different voices within minority communities can be represented, and a system of individual rights is firmly in place, it seems possible to give greater collective recognition to religious groups without compromising the rights of dissenting minorities within those groups.

The final ethicist which we shall consider is Jürgen Habermas. While much of Habermas' work has been at a metatheoretical level, the 'asylum debate' in Germany in 1993 drew him into comment on issues of direct concern to us here. A particular strength of Habermas' work is its abiding concern with participative democracy. So how does he see this best being served in the present case? His answer is through extension of the scope – and more effective actualisation – of individual rights. For example, he writes:

> a correctly understood theory of rights requires a politics of recognition that protects the integrity of the individual in the life contexts in which his or her identity is formed. This does not require an alternative model that would correct the individualistic design of the system of rights through other normative systems. All that is required is the consistent actualisation of the system of rights. There would be little likelihood of this, of course, without social movements and political struggles. We see this in the history of feminism, which has made repeated attempts to realise its legal and political goals in the face of strong resistance.[43]

Several points require exposition here. The historical example underlying Habermas' model is the women's movement over the last hundred years, and one may ask how well this example matches understandings of the aims of recognition for religious minorities. His argument is that the women's movement has effectively campaigned against inequalities on the basis of collective mobilisation, but that their goal has been recognition as equal individuals, not that of collective difference. This is contestable as a reading of the aims of diverse women's movements, but it is even more problematic when applied to religious minorities, where recognition of collective difference on the basis of fundamental equality may be exactly what is sought.

The analogy between women's movements and religious minorities is problematic because where the reconstruction of gender relations necessarily has implications for the whole of society, so that support can potentially be mobilised on a society-wide scale, it is not clear that the problematisation of the terms of equality by religious minorities has the same broad relevance or appeal. Thus, the goals of such a movement may be much more difficult to achieve through the political mainstream.

Exposition of what is meant by 'protect[ing] the integrity of the individual in the life contexts in which his or her identity is formed' is also necessary. For example, such protection does not extend to attempts to guarantee the survival of cultures: for Habermas, such survival should only be through the active choice of those who share a culture. Thus he writes:

> the ecological perspective on species conservation cannot be transferred to cultures. Cultural heritages and the forms of life articulated in them normally reproduce themselves by convincing those whose personality structures they shape, that is, by motivating them to appropriate productively and continue the traditions. The constitutional state can make this hermeneutic achievement of cultural reproduction of life-worlds possible, but cannot guarantee it.[44]

However, as Taylor argues against Kymlicka, it may be precisely this survival down through the generations that minority communities most crucially seek to ensure[45] – not just the conservation of culture for their own generation. This brings us to a crucial difference between MacIntyre and Habermas, in terms of their understanding of tradition. For Habermas, reason is the ultimate arbiter, communicatively constructed but individually exercised, and in a way which is assumed to be able to transcend tradition. The basis of trust in tradition 'was destroyed [by] the gas chambers...mass murder...was even dependent on the normality of highly civilised social intercourse. The monstrous occurred, without interrupting the steady respiration of everyday life.'[46] For MacIntyre, by contrast, it is the idea of reason disembedded from tradition which is most dangerous. The production-line atrocities of the Holocaust are not so much a failure of tradition, as a possibility always inherent in modernity.[47] This is because modernity undermines moral traditions, which alone can establish a binding link between past and future generations, and thus provide a basis for historical conscience.

Perhaps here we are only seeing another variant of the conflict between the Protestant emphasis on conscience and the Catholic emphasis on binding tradition. If so, it would seem to provide confirmation of the Protestant character of modernity and, if MacIntyre is correct in surmising of a necessary link between virtue and tradition, perhaps a further reason for the neglect of virtue ethics in modernity – a neglect which may prove costly.

In this chapter, it has been argued that virtue ethics promises to takes us deeper into the moral sociology of human behaviour than alternative approaches. In terms of the specific question set at the outset, MacIntyre's account of virtue ethics can help do justice to claims for recognition by religious minorities, by exposing the connections between moral community and the formation of character. For the same reasons, it warns against an excessive absorption into the political mainstream. In the context of more detailed analysis of this kind of situation by political theorists, virtue ethics can help provide a more nuanced account of the issues involved, but suffers in its MacIntyrean form from an unbalanced account of the moral-political forms of modernity, and in particular, of autonomy, equality and participative democracy. A consideration of these factors drawing on other ethical approaches suggests that the collective representation of religious minorities needs to be balanced by a plurality of alternative voices within representative forums, in particular of those who have been historically marginalised within religious traditions.

Notes and references

1 These councils were created by the 1988 Education Act. They include representatives of local religious communities to advise the Local Education Authorities on the religious education syllabus used in local state schools.
2 Tariq Modood *et al.*, *Ethnic Minorities in Britain: Diversity and Disadvantage* (London: Policy Studies Institute, 1997).
3 Jürgen Habermas, *The Structural Transformation of the Bourgeois Public Sphere* (Cambridge: Polity, 1989). Habermas describes the modern public sphere, which historically emerged in Europe at the end of the eighteenth century, as 'a forum in which the private people come together to form a public, readied themselves to compel public authority to legitimate itself before public opinion'. See p. 25.
4 Charles Taylor, *Sources of the Self: The Making of Modern Identity* (Cambridge, Mass.: Harvard University Press, 1989).
5 Charles Taylor with Amy Gutmann (ed.), *Multiculturalism: Examining the Politics of Recognition*, expanded edition (Princeton: Princeton University Press, 1994).
6 Ibid., p. 25.
7 Rémy Leveau, 'Islam in France: New Perspectives', in Wasif A. R. Shahid and Sjord van Konigsveld (eds), *The Integration of Islam and Hinduism in Western Europe* (Kampen: Kok Pharos, 1991), p. 123.
8 Catherine Wihtol de Wendel, 'Muslims in France', in Wasif Shahid and Sjord van Konigsveld (eds), *Muslims in the Margin: Political Responses to the Presence of Islam in Western Europe* (Kampen: Kok Pharos, 1996), pp. 52–65.
9 Leveau, 'Islam in France: New Perspectives', p. 122.
10 Jeroen Feirabend and Jan Rath, 'Making a Place for Islam in Politics', in Shahid and van Konigsveld (eds), *Muslims in the Margin*, p. 248.
11 Ibid., p. 254.
12 Ibid., p. 255.
13 United Kingdom Action Committee on Islamic Affairs (UKACIA), *Need for Reform: Muslims and the Law in Multi-Faith Britain* (London: UKACIA, 1993).
14 *British Muslims and Islamophobia* (London: The Runnymede Trust, 1997).
15 Jørgen Nielsen, *Muslims in Western Europe* (Edinburgh: Edinburgh University Press, 1992).

16   It is controversially planned to include questions on ethnicity for the first time in 1999 in the French national census, though only for a 1:50 sample. See Jane Marshall, 'French Row Over Race Poll', *Times Higher Education Supplement*, 27 Nov. 1998, p. 56.

17   Norman Ravitch, *The Catholic Church and the French Nation* (London: Routledge, 1990).

18   Ruben Gowricharn and Bim Mungra, 'The Politics of Integration in the Netherlands', in Shahid and Van Konigsveld (eds), *Muslims in the Margin*, pp. 114–29.

19   Yasmin Soysal, *Post-National Citizenship* (New Haven: Yale University Press, 1994).

20   This scheme follows John Dryzeck, *Discursive Democracy* (Cambridge: Cambridge University Press, 1990) and 'Critical Theory as a Research Programme', in Stephen White (ed.), *The Cambridge Companion to Habermas* (Cambridge: Cambridge University Press, 1995), pp. 97–119.

21   Marcia Baron, Philip Pettit and Michael Slote, *Three Methods of Ethics* (Oxford: Blackwell, 1997).

22   Ibid., p. 175.

23   Dryzeck, *Discursive Democracy*, pp. 111–15.

24   Zygmunt Bauman, *Legislators and Interpreters* (Cambridge: Polity, 1987) and *Intimations of Postmodernity* (London: Routledge, 1993).

25   See Bauman, *Intimations of Postmodernity*.

26   Dryzeck, *Discursive Democracy*, p. 109, and his essay 'Critical Theory as a Research Programme', pp. 30–2.

27   Alasdair MacIntyre, *After Virtue*, second edition (London: Duckworth, 1985), pp. 254–5.

28   Carol Gilligan, *In a Different Voice: Psychological Theory and Women's Development* (Cambridge, Mass.: Harvard University Press, 1982), pp. 18–21 and 25–32.

29   Steve Fuller, *Science* (Buckingham: Open University Press, 1997), p. 122.

30   Stephen White, *The Recent Work of Jürgen Habermas* (Cambridge: Cambridge University Press, 1989), pp. 58–68.

31   MacInytre, *After Virtue*, p. 109.

32   Ibid., p. 255.

33   Ibid., p. 263.

34   Ibid., p. 252.

35   Alasdair MacIntyre, *Whose Justice? Which Rationality?* (London: Duckworth, 1988).

36   For an extended comment on MacIntyre's *Whose Justice? Which Rationality?*, see the essay review by Stephen Turner, 'Whose Tradition About Tradition?', *Theory, Culture and Society*, vol. 7, no. 4, 1990, pp. 175–85.

37   MacIntyre, *Whose Justice? Which Rationality?*, p. 364.

38   Will Kymlicka, *Liberalism, Community and Culture* (Oxford: Oxford University Press, 1989), and his *Multicultural Citizenship* (Oxford: Oxford University Press, 1995).

39   Kymlicka, *Multicultural Citizenship*, pp. 147–9.

40   Yasmin Soysal, *Post-National Citizenship*, p. 128.

41   Kymlicka, *Multicultural Citizenship*, p. 160. Kymlicka rejects Rawls' political liberalism on its distinction between public and private identity, because the illiberal groups, whose participation in democratic politics Rawls is trying to encourage by making this distinction, themselves reject it.

42   Ibid., p. 170.

43 Jürgen Habermas, 'Struggles for Recognition in the Democratic Constitutional State', in Taylor with Gutmann (ed.), *Multiculturalism*, especially p. 113.
44 Ibid., p. 130.
45 Taylor with Gutmann (ed.), *Multiculturalism*, pp. 40–1. His argument refers specifically to demands for cultural survival by Canadian Indians and French Canadians.
46 Jürgen Habermas, in Peter Dews (ed.), *Autonomy and Solidarity: Interviews with Jürgen Habermas*, revised edition (London: Verso, 1992), p. 238.
47 Bauman also argues, for independent reasons, that industrialised genocide is a danger always inherent in modernity. See Zygmunt Bauman, *Modernity and the Holocaust* (Blackwell: Oxford, 1989).

4
Ethics and the Person: Risk, Moral Recognition and Modernity

Christie Davies and Mark Neal

Perhaps the central moral value of modern western democratic industrial societies with a free market capitalist economy is the sanctity of the individual person, the protection of whose life, health and safety is given priority over all other goals. It is no longer the sanctity of life as such that is stressed, for these societies are increasingly permissive with regard to abortion and even euthanasia, but rather the preservation of individuals from harm, pain and suffering. This change has profound implications for the setting in which virtue is tested, recognised and regulated.

The loss of life is simply one of the greatest of these values, for it extinguishes an individual person who has consciousness, plans, expectations, hopes and relationships. The justification of these new preoccupations and priorities is either made in terms of the form of short-term negative utilitarianism known as 'causalism', which sees the goal of society as the minimisation of harm to the aggregate of individuals who make up that society, or it is made in terms of rights – the right of each individual to be protected from certain kinds of harm. Yet, this right is subject to numerous contradictions, in relation both to entitlements and to risk. These contradictions throw light on the issue of virtue in a postmodern society and suggest that uncomfortable inconsistencies are not new, but have become exasperated in a culture where there is no sense of moral limit. They amplify concerns discussed in the earlier chapters but in a definite manner that presents inescapable dilemmas which seem incapable of resolution in the absence of a moral consensus as to the value of life for the statistical as against the particular person. A particular facet of the ethical question of risk is explored in this chapter in relation to the moral quandaries that the issue of the statistical, the particular and the potential person poses.

The central moral concern of the modern democratic capitalist world is the minimisation of the suffering of each person. We are increasingly unwilling to inflict pain on an individual through harsh punishments, such as the deprivation of life, or by trapping an individual in a horrid future through harsh ethical demands and exhortations to fortitude. Today abortion is permissible; shooting army deserters is unthinkable. This marks a massive cultural shift from the situation at the beginning of the twentieth century, and even more so from earlier times when suffering was something to be endured, when savage punishments were routinely inflicted and when inflexible moral rules were upheld regardless of the consequences for particular individuals. The execution or flogging of a woman who killed her illegitimate child soon after birth was once seen as a justified moral act, yet the very knowledge that this occurred is shocking to modern sensibilities. Now we are a softer society, in part because premature death is much less common and we increasingly have the pharmaceutical means to conquer pain. Death is a release from senility and the chronic disabling and demeaning diseases of old age. When it is not a release from suffering, when it is part of suffering, when it means the cutting off of an individual's plans, hopes, expectations and relationships, then it is horrifying and unacceptable. Against this moral shift in sensibilities, abortion and even euthanasia are allowable because they diminish suffering.

In practice, though, all persons are *not* assigned the same degree of consideration when decisions are being made about which lives should be sacrificed, saved or ignored, or to what level of harm or risk a person should be exposed. In modern societies, there are essentially three unequal categories of person to be considered – full particular persons, statistical persons and potential persons.

A full person has a particular identity that is known to others. Here is Bert Smiggs or Mabel Hawkins, people who are distinguishable from all other persons, who have distinct genetic, personal and social characteristics and a unique, coherent self whose existence others can discern, understand, appreciate and respect (even if they dislike that particular individual).

Statistical persons also possess these properties but, since no one knows who they are, their personhood is less visible, vivid and capable of comprehension. If the public is told that one person in every ten thousand will be killed in a traffic accident in a particular conurbation next year, this will not have the same impact as the death in a Mercedes of Diana, People's Princess of Wales.[1] She was a full particular person to those who knew her, even though in many cases that was only through the media. On the other hand, the people within the aggregate traffic data are mere statistical persons, random accidents waiting to happen, anonymous, without characteristics other than their chance of death. Understandably, perhaps, such persons usually count for less in our calculations than full particular persons.

Finally, there are potential persons – foetuses, babies and even very young children, who also count for less in our calculations because they lack self-consciousness, awareness, plans, expectations and rational connectedness. They do not yet possess a recognisable, coherent 'self', which is the defining characteristic of a full particular person; they are mere potential persons who are not considered to be entitled to the same rights or degree of consideration as full particular persons.

Particular persons are prized above statistical persons

As suggested above, statistical persons usually rank lower in our hierarchy of concerns than full particular persons. The British Medical Association summarised this position regarding exposure to risk when it stated that

> everyday experience shows us that as a community we are willing to spend far more on some lives than on others and this has very little to do with how economists might value those lives ... cost–benefit analysis is always liable to moderation on a case by case approach with the importance of the individual generally being believed to be paramount. Unlimited resources might be released to save the life of a miner trapped underground with his plight clearly visible to the nation through the news-hungry media. Yet nearly a miner a week dies in Britain from routine accidents (1980s). Take another rather more complicated example of individual exposure to risk. Imagine that a huge food store required fumigation to prevent the growth of a mould which could result in the death, over the next 20 years of (say) a dozen people. However, the necessary fumigant chemical (for which there was no alternative) was hazardous to the workers to the extent that one or two would be likely to die within this period. It is unlikely that this fumigant would be permitted for use, although there would be a net community gain, because the near certain death of one or two people is regarded generally as a matter of much greater concern than the possible death of more people but among a very large number.[2]

Such a conclusion is far from being universally true; indeed, in a socialist or fascist society it might be regarded as mere bourgeois sentimentality. Nonetheless the BMA's authors have made an accurate point about the particular society in which they live and other societies like it.

Particular persons in wartime

The special sanctity of the full particular person in Western society is even more powerful in times of war when there is large-scale killing and an expectation that military personnel will be willing to risk being killed. One sign of this is the unwillingness of Western politicians and military leaders to order the killing of their enemy counterparts, as can be seen from the recent controversy when British plans to assassinate Hitler were revealed.[3] In terms of cost–benefit analysis it is difficult to see how anyone could have objected to the removal of such a monster: it would have eliminated a highly effective 'charismatic leader' to whom military officers had sworn a personal oath of loyalty and it would also have created a divisive conflict over who should succeed him as Fuehrer. Yet, largely without moral qualms, the British devoted far more effort to destroying German cities and the civilians, women and children who lived there. A hundred thousand people were killed in a fire-storm in Hamburg in a single night, but only Bishop Bell, the Bishop of Chichester, had the courage publicly to say anything strongly critical about this.[4] That Hitler could be held more sacred than the ordinary people of Hamburg is a measure of the force of our greater unwillingness to inflict harm on full particular persons than on mere statistical ones. Likewise, RAF bombers and commandos, landing from the sea, attacked St Nazaire on the Atlantic coast of France and other naval and U-boat bases, but no one entered the nearby German naval headquarters in the chateau of Kernevel on the same coast to assassinate the German admirals.

A further indication of the sanctity of the full particular person in the West is to be found in the horror and incomprehension with which Japanese kamikaze attacks on Allied planes, ships and tanks during the Second World War were regarded. Westerners hold it to be wrong to send a full particular person to absolutely certain death, however desperate the situation, even though they routinely send troops into action where it is known that there will be heavy casualties but not precisely who is going to be killed. It is a distinction that has been well made by the French sociologist Jean Baechler.[5]

The willingness of Japan's Second World War military commanders to sponsor, encourage, permit and in some cases force pilots to crash on the deck of an enemy ship, or naval men to ride a torpedo released from a submarine to instant and certain death, shocked Westerners because, we suggest it ignored and nullified the distinction between full particular persons and statistical persons. Full particular individual persons with known identities were erased with certainty rather than simply being exposed along with a mass of their comrades to a high risk of becoming casualties. Although Japan, even then, was a modern, technically sophisticated industrial society with a well-developed division of labour, the leaders of Imperial Japan and their followers did not give that special priority to the full particular individual person that was then, and remains today, a central moral assumption of Western democratic societies.

What this demonstrates is that the strength of this priority varies from one culture to another. It is not an automatic product of a particular stage in economic development defined in terms of modernity but rather it is an aspect of a particular Western philosophy derived from the Protestant religious tradition and from a liberal democratic ideology. Despite Japan having become an industrial society by the early twentieth century, it had remained a militant society (to use Herbert Spencer's term) in its spirit and outlook, a society governed by the warrior code of *bushido* in which respect for the individual was subordinate to the requirements of a militant hierarchical collectivity.[6]

Ironically, Spencer, the prophet of individualism, had himself advised the Japanese to retain their hierarchical traditions and to use them as a vehicle for creating a modern industrial society in Japan.[7] His Japanese readers and admirers who consulted him may have expected him to argue that individualism and modernity are inextricably linked, but Spencer was sufficiently flexible and sufficiently versed in comparative sociology to be willing to set aside his own ideology and to give what he considered to be objective advice.

At the same time, it should not be supposed that the wartime Japanese leadership was entirely unconcerned with the fate of particular individual persons. When designing human torpedoes the Japanese naval leaders had tried hard to design an escape hatch like an ejector seat that would release those riding the torpedo before it struck its target.[8] Of course, they would probably have been killed by the blast anyway, but for moral reasons the Japanese naval commanders wanted if possible to avoid sending particular known individuals to certain death.[9] Even in the world of the kamikazes there was some respect for the distinction between full particular persons and statistical persons.

The tendency for dilemmas caused by extreme military situations to overwhelm the distinction between full particular persons and statistical persons has not been confined to Japan. On 1st September 1914 during the First World War the British Cabinet minister Charles Hobhouse wrote in his diary:

> we are told to expect Zeppelins over London at any night ... Churchill has sent 100 aeroplanes to Dunkirk to watch for them. In the last resort the officers in charge of aeroplanes will charge the Zeppelins but in view of the certain death have arranged to draw lots for the task.[10]

Clearly, it was not considered acceptable to order particular known individuals to undertake a task involving certain death, nor to call for volunteers. Rather the British pilots had to be converted into statistical persons by reintroducing the element of chance into the situation, using the impersonal anonymous statistical procedure of drawing lots.

Executing particular persons to save the lives of statistical persons

One case where particular known individuals were deprived of their lives with inexorable certainty occurred when the British military authorities during the First World War executed soldiers for military offences, notably desertion. This measure proved to be extremely controversial even during the war itself, and even more so in the 1920s – which led to the death penalty for these offences being abolished by 1930.[11] The controversy continues today, many decades later, with new political demands for the individuals concerned to be granted full pardons.

The British military leadership justified the executions both during the war and in the debates of the 1920s purely in terms of deterrence and denied that any element of retribution was involved.[12] This was actually borne out by the decision at the end of the war not to execute men condemned to death during its last months and awaiting execution at the time of the Armistice.[13] The military leaders defending capital punishment argued that by executing these men they had warded off military collapse at crucial moments, thus saving the lives of a much larger number of unknown statistical persons and perhaps even preventing the defeat and collapse of state and nation. However, the idea that particular individuals could be executed regardless of culpability in order to save the lives of a mass of unknown statistical persons came to be seen as so repugnant after the war that execution for purely military offences such as desertion was abolished. The inviolability of the individual was now so firmly established that it could not be compromised, even to save the lives of numerous other statistical persons.

In Britain, in the earlier part of the twentieth century, the retention of capital punishment for murder was based on ideas of retribution and just desert, which linked each particular murderer to another particular person, the victim of the murder. There was an equivalence between them, a sense that the execution of one particular person wiped out the outrage done to another particular person. Such arguments were prominent in the debates about capital punishment held in the British Parliament in the 1940s.[14] With the decline of a moralism in Britain that bore the idea that the main purpose of the law is to punish the guilty, to protect the innocent and to reward the virtuous, the arguments about capital punishment became causalist (harm minimising) and were concerned mainly with the question of deterrence. In 1957 Parliament passed the Homicide Act which restricted capital punishment to the kinds of murder held to be deterrable, such as murders using a gun or committed in the course of a robbery. Many of the most heinous kinds of murder such as sex murders or poisoning now became non-capital offences punishable only by imprisonment.[15] In this way the link between the fate of the murderer and horror at the fate of the victim, another full particular person, was broken. The argument from deterrence pays no attention to the full particular person who became a victim but concentrates entirely on the statistical persons whose lives will be saved in the future as potential murderers are deterred by the execution of others and the thought that it might happen to them.

At the time this division of murders into deterrable and non-deterrable was thought to be a stable, rational, causalist resolution of the issue, and the then Archbishop of Canterbury (Fisher) thought it a wise, expedient and enduring measure.[16] However, the provisions of the Homicide Act lasted for only eight years, and capital punishment was effectively abolished in Britain in 1965. In retrospect it is easy to see why the 1957 Act proved to be so unworkable that even the once reactionary and traditionalist House of Lords, including the Bishops and the Law Lords, came to prefer the total abolition of the death penalty to the 1957 distinction based on deterrence.[17]

Not only is the unique deterrent quality of capital punishment unproven but, even if it were demonstrated, it is difficult to justify the killing of a full particular person in order to save the lives of mere statistical persons. An argument based on deterrence without any reference to retribution is bound to fail for this reason and in Britain it failed for murder in 1965 just as it had for desertion in 1930. The American econometrician Ehrlich[18] has argued that as many as eight lives are saved for every execution for murder that is carried out. Even if he is right, it is the potent image of the particular person awaiting execution that prevails in the mind of the decision-making elite. This image is perhaps best conveyed by Dostoyevsky who had himself been sentenced to death and reprieved only when he arrived at the place of execution. He remembered that:

> the chief and worst pain is perhaps not inflicted by wounds but by your certain knowledge that in an hour, in ten minutes, in half a minute, now this moment, your soul will fly out of your body, and that you will be a human being no longer and that that's certain – the main thing is that it is certain. . . . Take a soldier and put him in front of a cannon in battle and fire at him and he will still hope, but read the same soldier his death sentence for certain and he will go mad or burst out crying. Who says that human nature is capable of bearing this without madness? Why this cruel, hideous, unnecessary and useless mockery? Possibly there are men who have sentences of death read out to them and have been given time to go through this torture and have then been told, 'you can go now, you've been reprieved'. Such men could perhaps tell us.[19]

By contrast, no such strong image can be summoned up by the exponents of deterrence, for future victims are by definition unknown and their sufferings cannot be given a particular form. It is this, rather than the related Kantian consideration that people should not be used simply as a means, that has made it impossible to restore capital punishment in Britain on the basis of deterrence alone.

Capital punishment has survived in much of the United States because America is a much more religious, moralistic and democratic country, where it is held both that murderers deserve to be executed and that capital punishment is a stronger, more effective deterrent to murder than its alternatives. Yet, Americans are reluctant to execute and only 2 per cent of American murderers get executed. Their risk of execution is very small. The minority, who are executed, are chosen according to structured criteria approved by the US Supreme Court, based not on deterrence but on culpability.[20] Thus, justification is shifted back to the victim, the full particular person who was murdered.

The rise of concern for the particular person

The rise of the special regard afforded to the particular person and the need to protect him or her from suffering is not a new or recent phenomenon or the product of so-called 'late-modernity' or 'post-modernity'. It is part of a long process of change within Western democratic countries stretching back through the nineteenth century and noted with disapproval by the distinguished Italian sociologist, Vilfredo Pareto,[21] who saw it as irrational sentimentality. It is the working out of older ideas of progressive liberal individualism which perceive each person as having at any point in time a special unique self that must be respected.

In the late twentieth century the commitment to and application of this view has intensified in the West with an increased emphasis on individual rights, even in cases where this results in the net infliction of harm on (statistical) people in general and leads to restrictions on the power of the state to use force against individuals, even though the state's bureaucratic powers have immensely increased. It has also led to the near collapse of the total institution, one of whose central tactics was to strip away the personal identity of particular persons by turning them into anonymous numbers. There was no direct economic imperative behind these changes; whilst monasteries and other religious orders, lunatic asylums, mass conscript armies, orphanages, prisons, kibbutzim and boarding schools are economically ineffective, that is not the main reason for their decline.

These changes were rather the product of the marked loss of centrality and importance of the non-economic sacred hierarchies of the Churches and the military which had stood for an alternative tradition to individualism, that of service and sacrifice in the interests of a collectivity and a tradition. Banks have prevailed over the 'musical banks'.[22] This is mainly a question of ideology, as can be seen from the contrast with the socialist former Soviet Union where it was long held acceptable to sacrifice particular persons today – through executions, slave labour, the seizure of the peasants' food, obsessional investment in heavy industry, psychiatric political prisons and brutal military conscription[23] – in order to strengthen a hierarchical collectivity and supposedly to benefit the statistical persons of some utopian future generation. Political elites make these choices according to their ideology.

Potential persons and particular persons: abortion and infanticide

There is a third category of person who is the object of disputes over ethical issues. This is the potential person. The potential person, by reason of immaturity, lacks the moral significance of the full particular person who has had time to develop unique personal characteristics, expectations and relationships. Nonetheless there are circumstances when the potential person can take precedence over mere statistical persons.

The decline of the importance of the sanctity of life, and the rise to supremacy of the right of the full particular person to autonomy and to being shielded from suffering, are shown clearly by the massive liberalisation of the laws relating to abortion throughout the Western world. The permitting of abortion in the West was not an economic measure aimed at population control, maintaining a balanced demographic profile or controlling female participation in the labour force, as it had been in the Soviet Union and Eastern Europe, China and Japan. It was not about statistical persons. Rather, it was about the rights of particular mature persons to self-determination or privacy even if this meant sacrificing the continued existence of potential persons. Potential persons cannot have rights, nor can they suffer; they only feel pain in the sense that a lowly animal does. They lack an ability to reflect upon their situation and their future.

There has thus been a major change from the situation that existed in the recent past. In Britain, under section 58 of the 1861 Offences against the Person Act, it was stated that:

> every woman being with child who, with intent to procure her own miscarriage, shall unlawfully administer to herself any poison or other noxious thing or shall unlawfully use any instrument or other means whatsoever with the like intent . . . shall be guilty of an offence, and being convicted thereof shall be liable . . . to imprisonment for life.[24]

In theory, at least, a very severe penalty could be imposed on the woman herself for seeking to destroy a potential person. No external 'exploiter' needed to be involved, nor was the measure enacted to protect the mother, for at the time there were no laws to stop women who were not pregnant from ruining their health by taking any noxious substance they chose. In any case the imposition of life imprisonment was an odd way to protect someone from the risk of self-harm. Only in the case where the mother's life was at risk was abortion permitted.

There could not be a greater contrast with the (British) Abortion Act of 1967 which permitted abortion on condition that:

> (a) that the continuance of the pregnancy would involve risk to the life of the pregnant woman or of injury to the physical or mental health of the pregnant woman or any existing children of her family greater than if the pregnancy were terminated or, (b) that there is a substantial risk that if the child were born it would suffer from such physical or mental abnormalities as to be seriously handicapped.

In determining whether the continuance of a pregnancy would involve such a risk of injury to health as is mentioned in paragraph (a) of sub-section 1 of this section, account may be taken of the pregnant woman's actual or reasonably foreseeable environment.[25]

Here the emphasis is obviously on the suffering of full particular persons, a suffering that mere potential persons cannot experience.

It is only if they are damaged and survive to be born and to grow up that potential persons can in any real sense suffer; then it is suffering at its worst, for it will be life-long. This accounts for the horror felt at the deforming effects of the teratogen thalidomide which resulted in the biggest ever change in Britain in the level of regulations governing pharmaceutical products, a change enacted in the interest of preventing harm to full particular persons.[26] Whilst abortion has become widespread and accepted, there is now an increased disapproval of the woman who takes drugs, drinks to excess or smokes during pregnancy or who refuses to take tests for genetic abnormality or to seek an abortion if an abnormality is indicated. Already, legal action has been taken against amniocentesis laboratories for failing to spot a serious genetic defect such that a pregnancy resulted in a defective live birth rather than an abortion.[27] In the future such offspring could well (on the basis of their sufferings as full particular persons) sue their mothers for failing to carry out their moral and legal duty to abort them.

The change in attitudes to the relative standing of potential persons and full particular persons in Britain has indeed been massive but is not quite as abrupt as implied above, as may be seen from the history of the law relating to infanticide. The killing of a very young child is generally regarded as a horrid crime but the murder is a crime not so much against the child but against its mother, who suffers the most at the sudden breaking of a very strong emotional tie. The child is hardly aware of its own existence. Indeed that existence overlaps so much with that of the mother that it is not yet really a fully separate person. But how then do we judge the case where a mother kills her own child?

In the past, she would have been sentenced to death for murder, but in the course of the nineteenth century it became difficult to get juries to convict mothers who had killed their own very young children. Even if a sentence of death was imposed, it was never carried out.[28] Among the reasons advanced 'why infanticide should be considered less reprehensible than other killings' was that 'the injury done to the child was less, for it was *incapable of the kind of suffering which might be undergone by the adult victim of a murder*'[29] (italics added).

From 1922, the killing of a newly born child by its mother was treated not as murder but as the lesser crime of infanticide, and in 1938 the time period for the rule reducing murder to infanticide to apply was extended to twelve months. Another reason for this leniency was also advanced, namely that the mother's responsibility was presumed to be reduced by the disturbance to her mind caused by birth or lactation. Yet, as Smith and Hogan noted in their standard text on the criminal law, 'the relationship of incomplete recovery from the effects of childbirth to the child-killing is remote'.[30] It is equally difficult to see why there should be an automatic presumption that the mother's mind is disturbed rather than the defence being expected to produce evidence to this effect in court, as is the case in many American states. In some cases the mind of the killer may be disturbed; in others not. It cannot be presumed. It seems likely that the law was fudged on this point because of sympathy with the suffering of the mother as a full particular person filled with a sense of guilt and horror at her own action and a corresponding legal disregard for the mere potential person who had been killed.

The same point may be made in relation to mothers who kill their older children. Between 1900 and 1949, 45.7 per cent of all death sentences for murder in England and Wales were commuted or respited, but in the case of female murderers the proportion commuted was much higher at 90.8 per cent.[31] In explaining this disparity the Royal Commission on Capital Punishment commented that:

> among the comparatively few murders committed by women the proportion of heinous cases is far smaller than it is among the much larger number of murders committed by men. The great majority of murders committed by women are cases of women killing their children in conditions of misery and stress where a reprieve follows almost as a matter of course. Indeed of the 130 women sentenced to death for murder 102 had killed their child. Two of the 130 were insane and one had her conviction quashed on appeal. In 116 of the remaining 127 cases or 91% the sentence was commuted.[32]

Thus we can see that the bias in public sentiment and in the application of the law in favour of the full particular person (with a life of his or her own to lead and a capacity for suffering derived from an ability to reflect upon and connect past, present and future) relative to the mere potential person is of long standing in Britain. Nonetheless the bias has grown over time, as people have come to be less willing to tolerate suffering and correspondingly to be less concerned with the preservation of life at the margins of human existence.

In the United States, a more religious and a more populist society than Britain, the same changes have taken place but have encountered stronger opposition, leading to a bitter *kulturkampf* over abortion, between moral and cultural factions with strongly opposed ideologies about suffering, that have led them to consider the relative standing and interests of full particular persons and potential persons in quite contrary ways.[33] Potter, noting that the shift to a world that freely permits, and in some circumstances even encourages abortion is part of a more general social and moral change, observed that

> the willingness to accept and transcend allotted afflictions through the power of redemptive suffering has faded in public consciousness to the point that it can seldom induce willing imitation. For many people there is simply no meaning in putting up with an unwanted circumstance when recourse is available (to abortion) without a high probability of temporal retribution.[34]

A similar point has been made by Luker on the basis of her empirical study of abortion activists in the United States. She argues that

> pro-choice people do not see suffering as either ennobling or as spiritual discipline. In fact they see it as stupid, as a waste and as a failure, especially when technology exists to eliminate it . . . given their ability to alter Nature, it is immoral not to do so, especially when those activities will diminish human pain.[35]

The acceleration of the long shift in Western industrial society towards a world in which the full particular person is sacred, and suffering is the ultimate evil, has crushed, or at least very severely threatened, one of the pre-existing core religious traditions of Western society. Christian fortitude is no longer a central virtue. Once again the point is clearly made by Potter. He noted that

> at stake in the abortion debate is not simply the fate of individual women or even the destiny of individual nations and cultures . . . Abortion does not merely contradict specific mores and moral teachings pertaining to sexuality, marriage and procreation or endanger a system of law built upon 'respect for life'. It implies the rejection of a world view which has sustained a way of life, a mode of being in the world, a pattern of response to the human condition. Abortion is a symbolic threat to an entire system of thought and meaning.[36]

Statistical persons do not enjoy the same total moral advantage over potential persons enjoyed by full particular persons (the mother and her existing children). We can see this from the restrictions placed on experiments on human embryos carried out by doctors or scientists, despite the immense indirect benefits these could bring to statistical persons through the increased knowledge that could be brought to bear on the treatment of genetically based diseases, cancer, senility and infertility. In Britain the 1984 Warnock report strongly recommended that no experiments should be allowed on human embryos more than fourteen days old,[37] as if they suddenly became in some sense human at that point. For a report that did not in any way challenge Britain's existing liberal laws on abortion, it was a rather strange conclusion. In the United States, attitudes are even more restrictive, which is why the world's first test-tube baby, Louise Brown, was born in England. British ethical assumptions and perhaps ethics committees were more secular and permissive than those of the more religious, moralistic and populist Americans. In Britain, priority has been given to the needs of particular infertile would-be parents over traditional fears and constraints. However, these individuals seeking medical help are full particular persons. Mere statistical persons still count for much less.

The effect of pharmaceutical regulation on statistical persons: the ethical dilemma of thalidomide

Nowhere has the balancing of the relative moral claims of full particular persons, statistical persons and potential persons been more problematic than in the regulation of the pharmaceutical industry, where there is a difficult trade-off to be made between minimising harm to particular persons and encouraging product innovation which will benefit statistical persons. The industry is also particularly significant because it provides the material underpinning to modern ideas about the progressive conquest of suffering. Painkillers (other than opium and alcohol), tranquillisers, anti-depressants, birth-control pills and safe abortifacients are all relatively recent products of pharmaceutical discovery and innovation. What can be cured need not be endured. Again, fortitude ceases to be a 'natural' virtue and even to be a central one. The minimising of harm, pain and suffering has become a more credible and convincing doctrine even if it is ultimately futile because of our poor and highly imperfect design, our fallen state and the relentless war waged against us by our cruel stepmother, Nature.

The distinction we have drawn between mere potential persons and full particular persons is very clearly illustrated by the thalidomide tragedy of the early 1960s when 4,500 babies were damaged and deformed as a result of their mothers taking thalidomide as a sleeping pill.[38] Tellingly, the sense of moral outrage that followed was not concerned with the harm done to potential persons as embryos, but with the later effects of the tragedy on two classes of full particular people: the children themselves, who would have to grow up and cope with their deformities; and their mothers who had gone through the physical and emotional trauma of giving birth to their damaged children, and now had to cope with the emotional, social and practical difficulties of bringing them up.

If the drug had caused the *death* of the foetuses this would have been damaging for each potential mother, but it is certain that the level of outrage among the public, the media and politicians would have been at a far lower level. A number of factors would have ensured this. First, the potential persons would never have made it to full particular personhood – they would have lived and died invisible, unseen, unheard, without individual characteristics, tastes, visible appearances or goals. Secondly, at the time, miscarriages were common and were understood to be unfortunate but in the end 'normal' developments. For a drug to cause the death and spontaneous abortion of the foetus could thus have been understood within the context of risk of miscarriage, rather than as the killing of a person, albeit only a potential person. Thirdly, whereas the birth of a disabled infant had life-long implications for the mother, the death of a foetus would have been a regrettable but discrete event. It would not have bound the woman to a continuing set of caring and nurturing responsibilities. Furthermore, the memory of the incident could have been set to one side, and would not necessarily have affected the mother's continuing intention and ability to have children.

Because of these considerations, had thalidomide been *more* destructive, had it resulted in the elimination of the foetus, it is likely that the tragedy would have had *less* of an impact. In modern Western cultures most people would prefer the death of a potential person to the infliction of damage on a full particular person.

In the risk-fearing, risk-averse, risk-obsessed world of the end of the millennium it can seem shocking that before the 1960s the British pharmaceutical industry was almost entirely unregulated. In the wake of the thalidomide tragedy, the government's initial reaction was to establish in 1964 the Dunlop Committee on the Safety of Drugs which, by modern standards, was relatively toothless.[39] Its main function was advisory. It did not have the power to force companies to adopt stricter testing regimes.

This reluctance to impose emergency regulations was in line with the willingness to accept everyday risks that characterised British society at the time. Many people had lived through hard times – the slump and poverty of the 1930s, and the hardships and casualties of the two world wars. Although the risks of premature death or serious harm or illness had fallen dramatically since the turn of the century, many had inherited the stoical acceptance of risk of previous generations, a view of life that had been necessary in times when early death, including that of infant and mother, had been common and when death had been fully visible rather than sanitised and segregated by the welfare state, the national health service and the availability of crematoria.

Had the thalidomide tragedy resulted in different, less visible, less lasting, patterns of harm, then the response of establishing a powerless committee might have been enough to calm public fears. Indeed, had thalidomide resulted in the mere death rather than the damage of a large number of foetuses and thus subsequently of full particular persons, then it is likely that there would not have been a surge in public anxiety about future drug development.

Thalidomide, however, produced a continuing, lasting tragedy. People, who had been horrified at the initial news pictures and footage, were again shocked when they encountered a thalidomide-damaged child in their own neighbourhood. The tragedy was thus not a discrete occurrence, nor one that people could get over and forget. It developed and deepened as the children grew to be conscious of their plight, and struggled to come to terms with their circumstances. For this reason, the issue did not disappear. The public, the politicians and the media now demanded tougher and more comprehensive safety legislation. This led to the 1968 Medicines Act, when the government introduced regulations that laid out in fine detail the testing requirements for all new medicines. The Act met with very little effective opposition, for in the wake of the tragedy it was difficult to argue for the pre-existing *laissez faire* system. Time and time again, in the public and political debate, reference was made to the full particular persons who were the victims of the tragedy, and descriptions of their plight were used to strengthen pro-regulation arguments. Because of the continuing and visible nature of the tragedy, the British public demanded and obtained some of the tightest regulations in the world.

Most of the public and some of the politicians who supported the 1968 Medicines Act did so for reasons concerned with ensuring the safety and welfare of the British people. A great deal of the debate and the rhetoric was cast in these terms. Most of these supporters of the new legislation, however, either did not understand, or simply did not care about, the effects of the new regulations on the functioning of the British pharmaceutical industry. The overriding rationale for the new regulations was to ensure the safety and efficacy of new drugs, regardless of the effects these would have on the ability of the industry to provide new life-saving or life-enhancing products.

It is possible to argue that strict regulations actually depress the general welfare of the British people who, as a consequence, have beneficial products denied them and who receive fewer life-saving or life-enhancing products.[40] All regulations carry costs, and those of pharmaceutical regulation are high.[41] In laying down comprehensive safety regulations, the state has forced the industry to commission expensive scientific studies and to comply with new bureaucratic regulations and delays. This has imposed new costs on pharmaceutical companies,[42] a development that is reflected in the vast increase in the costs of producing a new drug,[43] which, in 1992, were around a hundred and fifty million pounds.[44]

The new controls on drug development have not only had an impact upon the costs of producing a new drug, but they have also meant that drug development takes much longer.[45] In 1960, it took only 2 years, on average, to develop a drug from conception to production; now it takes around 12 years. Hartley and Maynard have estimated that increased safety regulation accounts for between 25 and 50 per cent of the additional costs of producing a new drug today compared with the past.[46] Because of the enormous increase in the costs of developing drugs, the number of new drugs coming out on to the market is much lower than it might have been. In 1970, 22 new major pharmaceutical products were introduced on to the market at a cost of £222 million. In 1990, 24 major new products were introduced at a cost of £1,082 million.[47] Thus, there has been an enormous increase in expenditure on development with no significant increase in the number of important new drugs coming on to the market.

The ethical conflicts between a concern for particular persons and the welfare of statistical persons are clear from a perusal of the present regulations and of the effects of these kinds of changes on general welfare. The Medicines Act was a response to the visible tragedy afflicting the 4,500 full particular people who had been severely damaged by thalidomide. The aim of the Act was to ensure that there would never be a recurrence, that we would never again be faced by such a large number of full particular persons being damaged or killed through taking medicines. However, the pursuit of this goal has contributed to escalating costs, lengthening development times ('drug lag') and fewer medicines reaching those who need them. A wish to avoid inflicting harm on full particular persons has thus taken precedence over any concern about the harmful effects the regulations may have had on a far greater number of invisible statistical persons.

The benefits we all have gained from our most widely used painkillers, aspirin and paracetemol, were only possible because these products were developed and marketed *long before* the new tighter regulations came into force. Under the present regulatory regime neither aspirin nor paracetemol would have gained a product licence; aspirin would have been banned because of its effects on the lining of the stomach; paracetemol because of its high toxicity. Under the present regulations, these would have been just two of an unknown number of 'invisible drugs', medicines which are withheld from the public without publicity or comment or any assessment of the harm done to the unknown persons who have been denied them. Harm to particular persons has once again taken precedence over harm to statistical persons and feared risks have taken priority over unknown lost benefits.

A good example of the priority given to protecting full particular persons at the cost of denying benefits to statistical persons can be seen in the controversy over the non-steroidal anti-inflammatory drug (NSAID) benaxoprofen, or 'Opren'. By 1980 Opren had been used successfully to treat a variety of inflammatory disorders and was preferred by patients; they had found it to be safe and effective. Then, on 8 May 1982, a doctor published a report suggesting a link between the drug and five or maybe six deaths from kidney and liver failure.[48] This was followed by a flurry of further fearful reports, and media attention soon led to a full-blown public panic. Concerns about the drug were raised in the House of Commons, and enormous political pressure was brought to bear upon the Committee on the Safety of Medicines. In August 1982 the drug was withdrawn.

Since then it has become clear that the drug was quite safe for people who did not already have renal problems. Indeed, the Drugs Safety Research Unit (DRSU) carried out a research project involving 24,000 patients, in which they investigated 54 cases of liver or kidney failure. In their report, they could find only *one* of these deaths that could be attributable to the drug.[49] As Professor Bill Inman, the head of the DSRU observed:

> I have always held the rather unpopular view that the removal of 'Opren' was inappropriate and robbed some patients of treatment which was sometimes highly effective. All that was necessary was to warn against sun exposure and advise care with the dosage of elderly patients or those with suspect renal function.[50]

We can see how a concern to avoid in the future the kind of harm already done to full particular persons overrides any concern about the invisible benefits withdrawn from statistical persons. In the panic about this drug, the sentimentality about deceased or damaged full particular persons led to widespread public and political pressure for a ban, to ensure that no further full particular persons – no Mr Martyn Donovan, aged 67 of Galway Close, retired builder; no Mrs Kay Gore, aged 72, relict of Nigel Gore – were harmed. The emphasis given to full particular persons resulted in the withdrawal of a beneficial product, meaning that thousands of invisible statistical persons were forced to transfer to other medicines which may have been less effective and less safe.

Anti-risk campaigns and the 'perfect' particular person

In public debate, as we have seen earlier, dead or maimed children can become resources for pushing through or tightening up safety regulations, or for gaining support for anti-risk campaigns. A relatively recent example of the political potency of dead children in campaigns for regulation comes in the form of the Dunblane tragedy in 1996 when sixteen schoolchildren and their teacher were shot dead by a local resident. The popular shock and revulsion at this event were understandable, and the popular press duly responded with sentimentalised characterisations of the victims, referring to them as the 'Dunblane Angels'.

Soon those concerned about the victims began looking for someone or something to blame. The murderer was dead, having killed himself, and anyway, our society has become curiously unwilling to blame particular persons, however wicked their conduct. Instead, blame fell upon 'the system' that had 'allowed' the tragedy to happen. The laws governing gun control enacted by successive Firearms Acts between 1968 and 1994, and the relatively libertarian line taken by The Firearms Consultative Committee (FCC) became the subject of denunciation.

In the public debate that followed, the Dunblane mothers became a power-ful political force, and those people who enjoyed pistol-shooting and tried to defend their pastime could not gain a fair hearing. As with medicines, it proved impossible to retain the previous workable and effective system of controls. Dunblane had been a freak event but it was no longer morally acceptable to use this category to describe a human tragedy of this kind.

The sentimentalisation of the victims reached its highest point a year later when a local Dunblane musician recorded Bob Dylan's song, 'Knockin' On Heaven's Door' with some of the surviving children, and added to it an original verse of his own. It ran:

> Lord these guns have caused too much pain
> This town will never be the same
> So, for the bairns of Dunblane,
> We ask, please, never again.

The song topped the Christmas charts and the proceeds went to the campaigning charities.

Those who sought to defend the right to possess and use handguns in Britain now faced an impossible task, for their opponents used powerful and emotive rhetoric and images involving the prospect of (and everyone's potential 'responsibility for') future child deaths and maternal bereavements. It was impossible to win an argument against the pleas of the full particular persons most closely affected by the tragedy – the Dunblane mothers – and against those who invoked the memory of perfect particular persons – the 'Dunblane Angels' themselves. The defenders of Britain's then existing gun laws which were already more rigorous than in most countries were inevit-ably defeated and the gun control laws were made yet more stringent.

Perfect particular persons and anti-drug campaigning

The premature deaths of youthful and appealingly perfect particular persons loved by their parents make potent media stories, and can become the foci of angry campaigns. A further such case involved Leah Betts, a young woman who died in 1995 as a result of taking an ecstasy tablet (MDMA). Whereas death at this age through infection or accident would have been commonplace in the past, by the 1990s in Britain it was rare and thus shocking. Today, when someone succumbs to risk, a 'cause' of the tragedy has to be identified and remedied almost as a moral act. In the early days of the Leah Betts tragedy, everybody concerned with her death, her parents, their lawyers, and the media, pinned the blame on to the ecstasy tablet she had taken, and thus on the person who had supplied her with the drug. But as now often happens, a second more powerful wave of blame with a much more diffuse target followed. Soon, the blame shifted from the immediate supplier to the inadequate education of young people about drugs. Within a week of her funeral Leah Betts became the spearhead of an anti-drugs campaign which tried to use her premature death to shock those who might be tempted. One particularly tasteless poster campaign used a picture of Leah Betts with the slogan 'Sorted' (drug-culture jargon for having been supplied with drugs for the night).[51] Before her death, Leah Betts was just another (full particular) person, but after she died she was promoted to being a *perfect* particular person. She was everything a young woman should be. A visible perfection was assured by the particular unchanging photograph of her that was always used by the media. The now famous picture did not need commentary, but posed a simple question – why did such a perfect girl die? It was later discovered that Leah Betts had not died from the drug, but from an overdose of water (albeit taken in response to the drug).[52] Furthermore, it was not the first time she had taken ecstasy. She was thus not a perfect person but a more normal and ordinary girl, but her image had served its purpose for the campaigners.

Perfect persons: a special kind of particular person

Perhaps the best way to view perfect persons is as a special kind of particular persons. Just as the particular person is more visible, more real, than the mere statistical persons, so too the perfect person is the most visible, most well-known of particular persons. We live in a paradoxical society in which the relations between individuals become more and more impersonal and a smaller proportion of the people we meet are well known to us than was true in the past. The void is filled by the perfect persons provided by the mass media. Princess Diana is the most striking recent example of this. When she died, she took on untouchable perfect particular status and any sense of proportion in issues related to Diana was lost.[53] Any criticism or disrespect was instantly denounced, with even the Prime Minister (Blair) adding his bit of indignation.[54] The causes she had associated herself with – particularly the banning of landmines – took on an irresistible moral impetus. If an urban neighbour dies in a car crash, it is not usual to go to the funeral, for he or she is almost unknown to us, a particular person sliding into the insignificance of a statistical person. Yet if celebrities such as Diana, or Princess Grace of Monaco, die in the same way, 'a nation mourns' and indeed a television-watching world mourns because celebrities are visible, because the media have revealed to us such intimate details of their lives as to make us think we know them. When they die, media canonisation makes them into perfect persons, young, glamorous people cut off in their prime whose particular qualities are well known and on whom an entire array of virtues has been imposed.

Ethical decisions about capital punishment, abortion or pharmaceuticals are skewed towards giving priority to the visible particular person over the invisible unknown statistical persons. The perfect persons take the argument one stage further for they become the vehicles through which the rules themselves get changed, the vivid single individuals whose fate carries more weight than any number of unknown statistical persons. Their death can sway bureaucracies and determine new regulations.

In conclusion, it is argued that the central moral goal of the institutions that compose modern societies is the minimising of suffering to persons, a goal justified either in 'causalist' utilitarian terms or in terms of an ideology of rights. As we have shown, however, an important distinction is made between categories of persons, such that full particular persons are afforded a greater degree of importance and consideration than mere statistical persons or potential persons. Once this is understood, many of the seemingly paradoxical changes that have occurred in modern societies such as the abolition or restricting of capital punishment, the permitting of abortion and the over-regulation of the pharmaceutical industry can be seen to be part of a consistent pattern. Thus in the case of abortion only a potential person exists, not a full particular person, and that person has no rights and has no mental existence which is the necessary underpinning of human suffering. We still treat murder as a more wicked and severely punishable crime than say torture, maiming or blackmail which involve more direct pain, because murder involves depriving full particular persons of their existence in the prime of life – almost the worst possible infliction of suffering. Yet thalidomide which maimed full particular persons and inflicted suffering on them and on their families created a far greater sense of horror than if it had merely caused the miscarriage of potential persons. The decision by Mrs Sherri Finkbine to seek an abortion after she had taken thalidomide now seems an essentially moral act and indeed it was one of the factors leading to the liberalisation of the abortion laws in the United States.

In such a world the people who often lose out are the statistical persons who are relatively invisible. Particular persons are highly visible. Perfect persons are super-visible and indeed their demise leads to moral or techno-moral panics and gives enormous leverage to those wanting new and sometimes oppressive legislation. Particular persons are the subject of more moral concern than statistical persons because the latter lack a specific identity. The victims of future murderers, whom we choose not to deter with capital punishment (assuming that there is enhanced deterrence), or the patients who die or suffer because the pharmaceutical industry is hindered from developing the new drugs that could save them by a degree of regulation stimulated by the past individual fate of tragic particular persons, are both examples of this neglected and uncared for category. There is thus an inner contradiction within our modern 'caring' morality which claims to minimise harm and yet which sometimes reasonably, sometimes with sentimental fakery,[55] gives the fullest consideration to the protection of visible particular individuals, while neglecting the possibility that this will lead to the greater suffering of mere statistical persons.

Notes and references

1   See Tony Walter (ed.), *The Mourning for Diana* (Oxford: Berg, 1999).
2   British Medical Association, *Living with Risk* (Chichester: John Wiley, 1987), p. 163.
3   See Daniel Johnson, 'Why We Should Have Killed Hitler', *The Times*, 24 July 1998, p. 20, and Bruno Bokun, *Spy in the Vatican, 1941–45* (London: Vita 1973), p. 56.
4   Christie Davies, 'Religion, Politics and the "Permissive" Legislation', in Paul Badham (ed.), *Religion, State and Society in Modern Britain* (Lewiston: Edward Mellen, 1989), pp. 319–40.
5   Jean Baechler, *Suicides* (Oxford: Blackwell 1979), pp. 331–2. See also: Fitzroy Maclean, *Eastern Approaches* (Harmondsworth: Penguin, 1991), p. 193; and Major General Sir Edward Spears, *Assignment to Catastrophe*, vol. II, *The Fall of France, June 1940* (London: Heinemann, 1954), p. 238.
6   Jay Rumney, *Herbert Spencer's Sociology* (New York: Atherton, 1966), pp. 76–8.
7   Herbert Spencer, letter to Kentaro Kaneko, 21 August 1892, in David Duncan, *The Life and Letters of Herbert Spencer* (London: Methuen, 1908), pp. 319–20.
8   Baechler, *Suicides*, p. 409. See also Edwin P. Hoyt, *The Kamikazes* (London: Panther, 1985), p. 137.
9   Baechler, *Suicides*, p. 409, and Hoyt, *The Kamikazes*, p. 35.
10 Edward David (ed.), *Inside Asquith's Cabinet, from the Diaries of Charles Hobhouse* (London: John Murray, 1977), p. 187.
11 Christie Davies, 'The British State and the Power of Life and Death', in Richard Whiting and Simon Green (eds), *The Boundaries of the State in Modern Britain* (Cambridge: Cambridge University Press, 1996), pp. 341–74.
12 *Report of the Interdepartmental Committee on Proposed Disciplinary Amendments of the Army and Air Force Acts*, Cmnd 2376 (London: HMSO, 1925), p. 5, para. 13.
13 Julian Putkowski and Julian Sykes, *Shot at Dawn* (London: Leo Cooper, 1992), p. 263.
14 Christie Davies, *Permissive Britain* (London: Pitman, 1975), and Christie Davies, 'The British State and the Power of Life and Death'.
15 See: Christopher Hollis, *The Homicide Act* (London: Gollancz, 1964), pp. 54–5; Viscount Kilmuir (The Lord Chancellor), *Hansard, House of Lords*, vol. 201, col. 1168–9, 21 February 1957; and Elizabeth Orman Tuttle, *The Crusade Against Capital Punishment in Britain* (London: Stevens, 1961), pp. 157–61.
16 Archbishop of Canterbury (Geoffrey Fisher), *Hansard, House of Lords*, vol. 201, col. 1194, 21 February 1957.
17 By 204 votes to 104. See in particular Lord Morris of Borth-y-Gest, *Hansard, House of Lords*, vol. 268, cols 535–8, 19 July 1965, and Lord Parker of Waddington, *Hansard, House of Lords*, vol. 269, col. 541, 26 October 1965.
18 Isaac Ehrlich, 'The Deterrent Effect of Capital Punishment, A Question of Life and Death', *American Economic Review*, vol. 68, June 1975, pp 397–417.
19 Fyodor Dostoyevsky, *The Idiot*, trans. David Magarshack (Harmondsworth: Penguin, 1955), pp. 47–8. See also pp. 86–8.
20 Christie Davies, 'The British State and the Power of Life and Death', pp. 355–7.
21 Vilfredo Pareto, *Sociological Writings* (London: Pall Mall, 1966), p. 232.

22 'The musical banks' are Samuel Butler's term of satire of the churches. See Samuel Butler, *Erehwon or Over the Range* (London: Jonathan Cape, 1927), pp. 150–64.

23 See: Robert Conquest, *The Great Terror* (Harmondsworth: Penguin, 1974); Rudolf J. Rummel, *Lethal Politics, Soviet Genocide and Mass Murder since 1917* (New Brunswick: Transaction, 1990); and Rudolf J. Rummel, *Death By Government* (New Brunswick, Transaction, 1990).

24 A. C. Smith and Brian Hogan, *Criminal Law*, 4th edition (London: Butterworths, 1978), p. 342.

25 Ibid., p. 345.

26 Ibid., see notes 38, 39, 40.

27 It is suggested that it is seen as worse to suffer the consequences of such a defect than to be aborted.

28 Smith and Hogan, *Criminal Law*, p. 338.

29 Ibid., p. 338.

30 Ibid., p. 228.

31 *Report of the Royal Commission on Capital Punishment 1949–53*, Cmnd 8932 (London: HMSO, 1953), pp. 13, 326.

32 Ibid., p. 326.

33 Christie Davies, 'Moralism, Causalism and Rights: The Contrasting Arguments about Abortion, Capital Punishment and the Law that are Used in Britain and America', in Paul Badham (ed.), *Ethics at the Frontiers of Human Existence* (New York: Paragon) (in press).

34 Ralph B. Potter, Jr., 'The Abortion Debate', in Ralph B. Potter, Jr. (ed.), *The Religious Situation* (Boston: Beacon, 1969), pp. 128–9.

35 Kristin Luker, *Abortion and the Politics of Motherhood* (Berkeley: University of California Press, 1984), p. 189.

36 Potter, 'The Abortion Debate', p. 128.

37 *Report of the Committee of Inquiry into Human Fertilisation and Embryology*, Cmnd 9314 (London: HMSO, 1984). See also A. T. H. Smith, 'Warnock and After: The Legal and Moral Issues Surrounding Embryo Research', in Mark Ocketton (ed.), *Medicine, Ethics and the Law*, ARSP Beiheft 32, 1986, pp. 744–75.

38 See: Michael Burnstall and Bryan Reuben, *Critics of the Pharmaceutical Industry* (London: Remit Consultants, 1990); and Henning Sjostrom and Robert Nilsson, *Thalidomide and the Power of the Drug Companies* (Harmondsworth: Penguin, 1972).

39 Alan Maynard and Keith Hartley, 'The Regulation of the Pharmaceutical Industry', *Symposium on Pharmaceutical Economics* (Berlin: Liber Forlag, 1984), pp. 123–37.

40 Mark Neal, *Keeping Cures from Patients: The Perverse Effects of Pharmaceutical Regulations* (London: SAU, 1995).

41 Ibid., p. 11.

42 Ibid., p. 9. See also ABPI, *ABPI Facts and Figures* (London: Association of the British Pharmaceutical Industry, 1992).

43 Neal, *Keeping Cures from Patients*, p. 11.

44 Ibid., p. 11.

45 Joe di Masi, 'Rising Research and Development Costs for New Drugs in a Cost Containment Environment', *Pharmaco-Economic*, 1 (Supp.), 1992, pp. 13–20.

46 Keith Hartley and Alan Maynard, *The Costs and Benefits of Regulating New Product Development in the UK Pharmaceutical Industry* (London: Office of Health Economics, 1982).

47 *ABPI Facts and Figures*.

48 Bill Inman, '30 Years in Post-Marketing Surveillance: A Personal Perspective by Professor Bill Inman', *PEM News*, no. 8, November 1993, pp. 26–8.
49 Ibid., p. 26.
50 Ibid., p. 28.
51 Nicholas Saunders, *Ecstasy Reconsidered* (Exeter: BPC Wheatons, 1997).
52 Ibid., p. 26.
53 Walter, *The Mourning for Diana*.
54 Later on Tony Blair, whilst undertaking political duties in Saudi Arabia, somehow found time to publicly and unfairly denounce the critics of the mourning for Diana, following the publication of Professor Anthony O'Hear's thoughtful essay, 'Diana, Queen of Hearts, Sentimentality Personified', in Digby Anderson and Peter Mullen (eds), *Faking It. The Sentimentalisation of Modern Society* (London: SAU, 1998), pp. 181–90.
55 Ibid.

5
Faith, Ethics, Young People and Late Modernity

Sylvia Collins

During 1993 the British public heard about the murder of two-year-old James Bulger by two ten-year-old boys. This murder is now one of the most infamous cases of recent years. Naturally, there was a sense of moral outrage at the time that a young child had lost his life in such a tragic way but, equally, there was incredulity that the two murderers were themselves still children.[1] Since then the media have presented numerous reports reflecting a public concern with young people's sense of morality.

One of the responses to this concern has been to highlight the role of the Church and religious education in schools, as providers of young people's moral values. This reflects a belief that, in some way, religion is the basis for moral decision-making.[2] In the case of links with the Church, this connection is less close than might be thought. For instance, the 1981 European Values Survey indicated that only 37 per cent of people thought the Church was giving adequate answers to moral problems and the needs of individuals.[3] Trends in secularisation have been associated with a move away from an absolute morality based on religious values to a more relative, situationally based style which may reflect an uncertain and subjective form of spirituality, or no supernatural belief at all. This chapter explores this change which has profound implications for understanding the link between virtue ethics, religion and modernity. Data from an empirical study of British youth forms the material used for this account.[4] Before discussing the results of this study, what do we know already about young people's faith?

The literature presents a complex picture in terms of secularisation trends across Western Europe.[5] In general, indicators such as those of church membership and attendance have shown a decline in mainstream institutional Christianity,[6] particularly over the last fifty years[7] and especially amongst young people. Data from the European Values Survey shows that weekly church attendance amongst 18–24-year-olds fell from 43 per cent in 1981 to 18 per cent in 1990.[8] More locally, the large-scale survey of 12–16-year-olds in England, by Francis, indicates that few young people think Church is very important (22 per cent), that few of their best friends go to Church

(18 per cent) and that many think church services are boring (50 per cent).[9] Comments from studies which include qualitative data re-enforce these points.[10] There is reason to suppose that this Church decline reflects a generational change rather than simply a stage in the life-cycle.[11]

Despite decreasing levels of institutional religious affiliation, however, Christian belief has not disappeared altogether. Table 5.1, for example, suggests that the majority of respondents in the European Values Survey, including a sizable number of young people, believes in God. The soul (increasingly), heaven and sin also retain a reasonable number of believers, although fewer believe in hell, the devil and reincarnation.[12]

Table 5.1   European religious change 1981–90 based on data from the European Values Survey

Believe in	Total (%)		18–24-year-olds (%)	
	1981	1990	1981	1990
God	73	70	77	67
A soul	58	61	63	65
The devil	25	25	26	23
Sin	57	57	57	51
Heaven	40	41	43	39
Hell	23	23	23	20
Reincarnation	21	21	27	26

Sources: Total %: Davie, 1998, p. 236; 18–24-year-olds: Ashford and Timms, 1992, pp. 126–7.

Francis and Kay, in their study of 13,000 13–15-year-olds in England and Wales, found a high degree of religious uncertainty amongst young people, but still around a third believed in God and other aspects of the supernatural.[13]

Since the late 1960s a small proportion of young people in their late teens and twenties have been attracted to new religious movements that allow unorthodox religious expression.[14] Paradoxically, non-traditional organisations of evangelical Christianity, particularly those associated with the charismatic movement, have a younger age profile than other Churches, and are growing.[15]

The picture of young people's faith presented in the literature is therefore far from straightforward; still less is the effect of faith on morality. The 1981 European Values Survey indicated that young people are less likely than older people to find the Church's moral teaching helpful in their lives.[16] The 1991 Survey shows only 18 per cent of young people believe in absolute good and evil. Francis and Kay found just 19 per cent of 13–15-year-olds agreed with the statement 'I believe God punishes people who do wrong'.[17] Nevertheless, they also found that young people who do believe in God have a clearer idea of right and wrong and are more likely to accept a strict moral code compared with atheists or agnostics. Halman and de Moor, commenting on European and North American data, however, warn against drawing simplistic conclusions. They point out that whilst religiously minded people tend to be less permissive[18] than others there are many factors apart from religion that determine the moral climate of a society.

Given the contested nature of both religiosity and its relationship to morality, the aim of the current study was to explore the faith of young people further and to consider how it relates to their opinion on ethical issues. Since the Church is in decline, the notion of faith was not limited to what is defined in institutional religions. Instead a more functional approach was taken in line with Luckmann's notion of 'invisible religion'[19] and Giddens' analysis of ontological security and the self in late modernity.[20] In this regard, faith refers to the subjective investment of trust in referents (which may or may not be organised into a coherent system) which provides ultimate meaning to young persons' life experiences. It is what informs who they are and gives them hope and purpose for the future by bracketing out the doubts and uncertainty which would otherwise undermine their 'courage to be'.[21]

The study that forms the basis of this chapter involved a structured survey of 1,090 young people, aged between thirteen and sixteen years, drawn from three schools in the South of England, followed by in-depth semi-structured interviews with thirty-six of the respondents from Years Ten and Eleven (fifteen and sixteen-year-olds). The main purpose of the survey was to establish a basic picture of young people's faith referents and moral views which were explored in more depth during the interviews. The survey asked questions relating to traditional Christian beliefs and practices and various forms of 'common' or 'folk' religion (such as belief in horoscopes and luck). Items from the questionnaire were factor-analysed to produce a scale of Christian commitment and interviewees from each school were selected according to their score on the scale. This resulted in three groups: (i) eleven interviewees that had a high degree of commitment to Christian beliefs and practices; (ii) thirteen that had a moderate degree; and (iii) twelve that had little or no Christian commitment.

Analysis of the data indicated two models of faith. Most of the young people – that is those with medium to low levels of Christian commitment – located faith in human relationships. More specifically, faith was structured around an internally referential system of family, close friends and the reflexive self.[22] The majority of the youngsters had developed mutual bonds of trust between themselves, family members and close friends. It was the trust invested in these relationships which gave the young people their meaning, identity, hope and purpose. In their faith structure, they did not show a need for a permanent transcendent referent, such as God or a supernatural power. As such this model of faith can be referred to as 'immanent' since it is located in the concrete relationships of everyday life. This is not to say that these young people had given up notions of transcendence altogether. In line with the studies mentioned above, there was a great deal of uncertainty, but few were prepared to reject transcendent ideas outright. Some read their horoscopes and watched *The X-Files* whilst entertaining the vague possibility that there might be some supernatural truth 'out there'. Many even retained the possibility that the Christian God might exist, although they had little interest in the Church. This 'openness' to a transcendent reality, however, was articulated more in terms of idle curiosity than seekership, and was balanced by a heavy dose of scepticism. The only time transcendent beliefs were likely to be taken seriously was during a personal crisis when the organisation of immanent faith was threatened by a broken relationship through death or circumstance. Even then there was no commitment to the transcendent as such. Transcendent referents were simply utilised on an *ad hoc* basis, 'just in case', but without any sense of conviction. The majority of young people did not completely reject the supernatural outright, nor did they incorporate it into their faith structure in any meaningful way so as to derive their 'courage to be' from it.

The second model of faith was articulated by the few young people who had a high degree of Christian commitment. This model built upon the immanent faith structure and included family, close friends and the reflexive self amongst its referents. In addition, however, transcendent referents were a permanent locus of faith. These young people invested trust in God not in the abstract but in terms of a concrete relationship. God, or Jesus, for these young people was a 'person' to whom they related as they might to a trusted friend or family member.[23] Indeed, God was sometimes described as a 'best friend'.[24] Thus, for the committed Christians, and in contrast to the majority of young people, the transcendent was an integral part of their faith. As such, this model is referred to as 'transcendent faith'. The transcendent, though, was an addition to, not a replacement of, trusted human relationships as a source of meaning, identity, hope and purpose. So how were the young people's ethical choices informed by their faith?

To examine this question, the data were used to consider the young people's notions of good and evil and four areas of moral concern that Giddens identifies as being important in the late modern world: survival and being; transcendence; cooperation; and personhood.[25]

The young people's concepts of 'good' and 'evil' suggested a moral continuum from good to bad with evil being an extreme version of 'bad'. The interviewees' understanding of good and evil was directly related to their faith, reflecting the young people's ultimate concern with trustworthy relationships. Thus good meant 'caring for people', 'helping people', 'being kind and polite' or, rather more vaguely, 'being a nice person'. A secondary understanding of good was linked to the reflexive self and was more to do with personal commendation. For example, good was 'enjoyment', 'something you like' and 'achievement'. Good therefore referred to those actions and values which promoted faith in relation to trusting others and the self. As such, good reinforced ontological security. Only six of the young people, not all of whom were committed Christians, went beyond this immanent understanding of good, to God. Thus, whilst God was regarded as good, good did not necessarily refer to God.

In comparison, evil was that which destroys faith by betraying trust in human relationships. Murder, child abuse, criminal acts and general acts of cruelty and hatred were examples of evil. Only nine of the interviewees linked evil with transcendent themes, and these were taken from the Christian symbolic universe (the devil, hell and sin). There was no secondary, individual understanding of evil. Personal failure through dishonesty or dissatisfaction, for instance, was seen as bad rather than evil.

In terms of moral choices, the young people felt that every person had the capacity for good or evil within them. This meant that everybody had an individual responsibility to choose between acting for good or evil. There was a consensus that 'right' choices were those made in accordance with good. Since good related both to others and the self, there could sometimes be a conflict in deciding what these right choices were. Without any reference to an absolute transcendent moral order, the young people expressed a minimalist criteria – right choices involved 'being nice' or at least 'not harming anyone else'. Another guideline the young people suggested was 'authenticity', that is, adopting a course of action that was true to the self. This points to the importance of autonomy and the reflexive self belonging to the notion of an immanent faith. Indeed, authenticity was important, even in the few cases where there was an absolute authority to refer to, as the following comment from a committed Christian illustrates: 'good is following what's right and what you think is the moral thing to do, and evil's the opposite'.

There was also an awareness amongst the young people that whilst an action based on good was the most desirable course to follow, evil was an inevitable, perhaps even a necessary part of the human condition. This 'fallen humanity' was not seen as being in need of redemption but only required acceptance that 'that is how things are'. Thus, another respondent noted: 'if you're good you're still going to have a bit of evil in you because nobody can be totally good'.

On the whole, therefore, morally good actions were those which respected and strengthened the trust between individuals and towards the self: that is to say, the basic immanent faith structure. Evil actions were interpersonal and attacked the potential for trust in human relationships. That self-harm does not feature as a realm of evil raises an interesting question about the scope of actions an individual allows herself in relation to her own personhood, as against the actions that are acceptable when others are involved. Whilst abuse of others was regarded as morally reprehensible, self-abuse (for example through the consumption of harmful drugs) could be seen as an amoral area. Turning to the different moral spheres Giddens identifies, Table 5.2 provides a summary of the questionnaire results that emerged from the study.

Table 5.2 Summary of the questionnaire results

Moral area	Belief	Overall	Degree of Christian commitment			Cramer's V ($p < 0.05$)*
			High	**Medium**	**Low**	
			(Transcendent faith)	*(Immanent faith)*		
Survival and Being	Protecting the environment and avoiding pollution is *less* urgent than often suggested	9 (1083)	7 (168)	8 (625)	12 (290)	0.06
Transcend-ence	Abortion is wrong except where the life of the mother is at risk	39 (1084)	51 (168)	39 (625)	33 (291)	0.16
Coopera-tion	All war is wrong	59 (1077)	56 (168)	63 (618)	52 (291)	0.08
	Rich nations should have a lower standard of living to help poorer nations become wealthier	42 (1080)	61 (168)	38 (621)	39 (291)	0.16
Personhood	It's wrong to have sexual intercourse outside marriage	12 (1087)	41 (168)	7 (628)	6 (291)	0.32
	Homosexual (gay and lesbian) relationships are wrong	32 (1085)	40 (169)	30 (626)	31 (290)	0.06*
	It's alright to use soft drugs like marijuana (hash or pot)	36 (1086)	19 (168)	33 (626)	55 (292)	0.18

*Correlations marked with an asterisk were *not* significant at the $p < 0.05$ level.

The first moral area, 'survival and being', refers to the decisions which surround the ethical use of natural resources. Over the last two decades there has been an increasing public awareness of the damage caused to the environment and the problems that continue to be brought about through the development and use of technology. When asked directly about their attitude towards pollution in the survey, only 9 per cent of the young people agreed that environmental protection and pollution control was *not* an urgent issue while 77 per cent suggested it was. This accords with figures produced by Francis and Kay[26] and fits with Ester, Halman and Seuren's results from the European Values Survey.[27] In the light of the interviews, however, these figures may be somewhat misleading if taken at face value for, in terms of the young people's lifestyle decisions, the environment held little real significance. Indeed, given the publicity that 'green issues' have had in recent years it was surprising that they did not highlight environmental issues to a greater extent than they did. In fact, environmentalism was hardly mentioned at all and it did not constitute any part of the answers to the question 'what is the most important thing in life?' There was little indication that these young people would accept a lower standard of living to help the environment and there was little association between the environmental attitudes of young people and their faith.

The second moral area, 'transcendence', is concerned with the ethical decisions about life and death, particularly as they relate to reproduction. The process of creating human life has to a large extent been brought under human control, raising moral questions in regard to contraception, abortion, *in vitro* fertilisation, artificial insemination and genetic engineering. This issue is also of importance in the light of Giddens' concern with the growth of 'plastic sexuality' as a characteristic of late modernity.[28]

In terms of their life plans, most of the interviewees mentioned that they expected to have children of their own one day (reflecting the importance of the family to them) but regarded the decision as a matter of personal choice rather than something governed by God. In this respect they suggested individuals have a responsibility to use contraception to limit the risks of unwanted pregnancy. Should an unwanted pregnancy occur, 39 per cent of the young people agreed with the statement 'abortion is wrong except where the life of the mother is at risk'. During the interviews some of the youngsters elaborated on their views of unwanted teenage pregnancies. Few of these interviewees were in favour of unqualified abortion or were completely against it under all circumstances. Most of them regarded the decision as a very personal one which should be made in relation to the individual's circumstances. In other words, there was no moral absolute which could determine the right course of action for all people. However, there were some implicit guidelines for such a decision which had its roots in immanent faith. In instances where it was likely the child would be born into a situation devoid of security and family intimacy, abortion was seen as being more appropriate than in other situations. In other words, the absence of trustworthy relationships would seem to render life not worth living. Similarly, abortion was more acceptable if the pregnancy would have a negative effect on the mother's existing trusted relationships or projects for self-realisation (for example through educational or career attainment). If the pregnancy was the result of rape (itself an act which undermines interpersonal trust) and would be a constant reminder of the uncertainties of life and so a threat to the mother's ontological security, then abortion would again be acceptable to some young people. Under these circumstances abortion was not seen as evil because it was a means of maintaining the mother's faith in herself and others. The other justification for abortion was that if the foetus could not feel anything then termination could not be seen as contravening the minimal moral criterion of avoiding harm to another.

From the above, the main basis for moral decisions in this area is immanent faith. Only one of the interviewees made a direct reference to the transcendent sanctity of life. The survey, as might be expected, did show that the young people with transcendent faith were more likely to object to abortion than the others. However, such an objection was not overwhelming and the correlation between Christian commitment and attitude on this item was weaker than might be expected. For young people with transcendent faith an autonomous reflexive self was also important. Even when these young people saw abortion as morally wrong in relation to an absolute authority, they were reluctant to 'push their faith' on to somebody else. In other words, the 'absolute authority' boiled down to 'absolute' only for the individual. Thus as one respondent noted: 'I don't agree with it [abortion] but I don't think you can really judge people if they do go ahead with one because it's up to the individual really. But I personally would never do that.'

The third moral area, 'cooperation', considers the relationship between the individual and society. Violence and the ethics of wealth distribution fell into this category. In terms of violence, 59 per cent of the youngsters indicated that 'all war is wrong' and there was little difference between them in terms of their Christian commitment. None of the interviewees showed any concern about the possibility of annihilation through nuclear war which Giddens suggests is a late modern source of existential angst. A few made reference to the conflict in the former Yugoslavia, describing it as being a 'stupid' state of affairs, but it was not something that directly affected them or caused them concern. The issues that did worry them were far more local – bullying and racism. Bullying undermines immanent faith since it destroys the individual's reflexive sense of self-worth. Consequently, it was a morally unacceptable form of behaviour for the young people. Some of the interviewees were asked what they would do if they saw somebody being bullied. Their responses again reflected immanent faith in that they were more likely to help a bullied individual if they were a close friend or family member than if they were a stranger.

On the other hand, some of the young people admitted to having been bullies themselves under the force of peer pressure. This again can be understood in terms of immanent faith in that going along with peers can sometimes be a means of securing a trusted friendship within the group. Undermining somebody else's faith outside that group may be preferable to risking one's own faith structure.

When it came to wealth distribution, 42 per cent of the youngsters felt that 'rich nations should have a lower standard of living to help poorer nations become wealthier'. Committed Christians were more likely to agree with this statement than the others. From the interviews and given the importance of consumerism in late modernity, there was a surprising degree of reluctance to admit to the significance of money. The young people said that they valued family and friends above money – several argued along the lines that 'money can't buy you love'. Indeed, in talking about the National Lottery the young people said that they would not like to be '*really* rich' in that they would never be sure that people liked them for 'who they are' rather than for their money. Being accepted for 'who one is' was an important element of immanent faith.

Charitable giving provides an opportunity for the active redistribution of wealth and some of the young people were involved in this way. The young people would only give, however, if their own needs and the needs of family and close friends had been met first. The choice of the charities they supported also tended to reflect immanent faith in that the young people would often support charities which had familial significance. The exception to this was widespread support for things like Comic Relief. These sorts of charitable events are a late modern phenomena and, importantly, make a link between the global and the local. Electronic media bring the charitable cause into the young person's home and offer something like a 'relationship' with the person in need. The emphasis at these events on raising money in an entertaining way with family and friends accords with the importance young people place on relationships and personal happiness as part of the process of self-realisation. In other words, charitable events of this kind can strengthen immanent faith through shared activity and by establishing personal satisfaction through fund-raising achievements. The rapid dissipation of the 'global community' after the event, and the lack of opinion the interviewees had in relation to on-going social problems, testified to the localised nature of a morality based on an immanent faith.

The final moral area of 'personhood' considers the decisions surrounding the achievement of a sense of self. This includes ethical decisions relating to how the young person treats his own body. Two aspects of personhood were considered – the expression of sexuality and the use of drugs. The issue of sexuality is closely related to reflexivity and identity in the context of late modernity.

Generally the youngsters indicated liberal attitudes towards heterosexual intercourse outside marriage. Seventy-two per cent disagreed with the statement 'it's wrong to have sexual intercourse outside marriage' (12 per cent agreed). Their only hesitation as far as moral injunctions on sex was concerned was that the partners should at least like each other, and that they should take appropriate precautions against disease and, as mentioned earlier, unwanted pregnancy. Apart from these provisos, most of the young people thought it was really up to individuals to determine their own behaviour for themselves without outside interference.

The few youngsters who took some exception to this view were those with transcendent faith. For them, sex was regarded as a sacred act, ordained by God for married couples. In this respect they saw sex very much as part of the organisation of faith – under the right circumstances. The intimacy of sexual expression could enhance the trust between partners, but if used indiscriminately, sex was devalued and its capacity to enhance trust was diminished. Some of the interviewees indicated, however, that peer pressure might encourage them to become sexually active. As with bullying, responding to peer pressure can be seen as an attempt to maintain the trust between friends.

The liberal attitudes of the young people in terms of heterosexual expression were not matched by their attitudes towards homosexuality. Overall, a third of the youngsters thought gay relationships were wrong and there was no significant difference between them in terms of Christian commitment. The reason for this was clear: it was, largely, dependent on the structure of immanent faith. To 'come out', or even hint at oneself as being gay, would leave the young person open to bullying and ridicule (especially amongst the boys) and consequently faith would be put under a great deal of pressure.

When it came to the use of soft drugs most of the young people felt the decision should be left to the individual. Abstinence on the part of interviewees was largely pragmatic in that either they were concerned about the harm drugs might cause them, or they had been ineffective or unpleasant when they had tried them. It was only the committed Christians who related abstinence to a transcendent authority as they thought drug-taking was contrary to the will of God.

What can we conclude from this study about the relationship between religion and morality? First of all, moral decision-making does appear to be related to faith, but primarily in an immanent rather than a transcendent form. In accordance with the logic of immanent faith, ethical decisions are seen to be primarily the responsibility of the individual, bearing in mind circumstances and advice from those in the immanent faith structure (family and close friends) and the need to secure an authenticity to the self. External institutional authorities, such as the Church, are not significant. Tolerance of the attitudes and behaviours of others (provided they do not impose on the self, family and friends) is important for maintaining the faith and the ontological security of others and, reciprocally, of oneself. Even for those young people who did have a strong Christian commitment, the transcendent realm (God, the Bible, etc.) was just one aspect of a broader immanent basis for moral decision-making. Hence there was quite a degree of similarity between the committed Christians and the other young people in terms of their moral reasoning and opinions.

Having said that, the second point to note is that a morality based on immanent faith does not necessarily contradict Christian morality. Indeed, its origins are Christian, for the morality of immanent faith is derived from parental religiosity, the sort characterised in Davie's terms as 'believing without belonging',[29] a form of faith that takes Christianity for granted, that renders the Church subjectively redundant, but lays great store on the importance of 'being a good neighbour'.[30] The religious underpinning becomes separated from the moral framework in this context and increasingly so for the second generation. Without repeated and explicit contact with religion in a world largely governed by secular rational utility, it is not surprising that the majority of young people in this study paid little attention to a transcendent authority when making moral decisions. Nevertheless, there remains some fragment of cultural religiosity that implicitly affirms the Ten Commandments[31] and informs notions of good and evil and right and wrong, even if most of the young people in this study did not associate these views with divine injunctions.

Given this situation, religious educators face a difficult task if they are asked to re-establish a model for ethical decision-making that is explicitly based on religious authority, especially since many young people do not accept the authority of the Church and largely see it as being out of touch with the real decisions they face on a daily basis. Indeed, Bruce points out the near impossibility of restoring a shared religious memory once it has been eroded.[32] This might be the crucial question governing the intersection between virtue ethics, modernity and religion, and one which sociology is in a unique position to explore further. From this study it seems that any attempt to re-establish an explicit link between religion and morality again needs to start where young people are – that is, with immanent faith and its logic of morality – and then build upon that to facilitate young people's own authentic exploration of the transcendent realm.

Notes and references

1   Blake Morrison, *As If* (London: Granta, 1997).
2   For an exploration of this theme, see Robin Gill, *Churchgoing and Christian Ethics* (Cambridge: Cambridge University Press, 1999).
3   See Stephen Harding and David Phillips with David Fogarty, *Contrasting Values in Western Europe: Unity, Diversity and Change* (Basingstoke: Macmillan, 1986), p. 44.

4   It is realised that young people do not form a homogenous group and that issues of gender, ethnicity and class will complicate understandings of their responses to problems raised about virtue ethics. Clearly, these variables would need to be expanded in further studies. Likewise, for practical reasons, the institutional religion used is Christianity. See Peter Brierley (ed.), *UK Christian Handbook. Religious Trends 1998/1999* (London: Christian Research, 1997), p. 12.

5   See David Martin, *A General Theory of Secularization* (Oxford: Blackwell, 1978), and Grace Davie, 'God and Caesar: Religion in a Rapidly Changing Europe', in Joe Bailey (ed.), *Social Europe* (London: Longman, 1998), pp. 231–53.

6   For a critique of institutional indicators, see Steve Bruce, *Religion in the Modern World: From Cathedrals to Cults* (Oxford: Oxford University Press, 1996), pp. 25–7.

7   For an overview of these trends, see Wade Clark Roof, Jackson W. Carroll and David A. Roozen, *The Post-War Generation Establishment Religions: Cross-Cultural Perspectives* (Boulder: Westview Press, 1995).

8   Sheena Ashford and Noel Timms, *What Europe Thinks: A Study of Western European Values* (Aldershot: Dartmouth, 1992), p. 124.

9   Leslie Francis, 'Christianity Today: The Teenage Experience', in Jeff Astley and David Day (eds), *The Contours of Christian Education* (Great Wakering: McCrimmons, 1992), p. 352.

10 See, for example: Phillip Richter and Leslie J. Francis, *Gone But Not Forgotten: Church Leaving and Returning* (London: Darton, Longman & Todd, 1998), pp. 124–5; and a much earlier study, Bernice Martin and Ronald Pluck, *Young People's Beliefs* (London: General Synod Board of Education, 1977), pp. 16–17.

11 Grace Davie, 'God and Caeser', p. 239.

12 See, for example, Michael P. Hornsby-Smith, *Roman Catholic Beliefs in England: Customary Catholicism and the Transformation of Religious Authority* (Cambridge: Cambridge University Press, 1991), p. 90.

13 Leslie J. Francis and William K. Kay, *Teenage Religion and Values* (Leominister: Gracewing, 1995), pp. 137, 152.

14 These movements have not made up for the loss from the Churches. Bruce notes that in 'the 1980s alone more than five million people were lost to the mainstream churches but the total membership of new religious movements in Britain was less than five or six thousand'. See his study, *Religion in the Modern World*, p. 188. For membership figures for new religious movements in the UK, see Brierley, *UK Christian Handbook. Religious Trends 1998/99*, pp. 106–108.

15 Peter Brierley, *Christian England: What the English Church Census Reveals* (London: Marc Europe, 1991), p. 99.

16 Harding and Phillips with Fogarty, *Contrasting Values in Western Europe*, p. 44.

17 Francis and Kay, *Teenage Religions and Values*, p. 137.

18 'Permissiveness' in this context refers to a willingness to accept that other people have different standards, rather than a lax morality. See Loek Halman and Ruud de Moor, 'Religion, Churches and Moral Values', in Peter Ester, Loek Halman and Ruud de Moor (eds), *The Individualizing Society: Value Change in Europe and North America* (Tilburg: Tilburg University Press, 1993), pp. 37–66.

19 Thomas Luckmann, *The Invisible Religion* (London: Collier-Macmillan, 1967). See also Sylvia Collins, 'Immanent Faith: Young People in Late Modernity', in Leslie J. Francis (ed.), *Sociology, Theology and the Curriculum* (London: Cassell, 1999), pp. 165–74.

20 Anthony Giddens, *Modernity and Self-Identity: Self and Society in the Late Modern Age* (Cambridge: Polity Press, 1991).

21 Paul Tillich, *The Courage To Be* (London: The Fontana Library, 1962).
22 This accords with some of the themes surrounding Luckmann's notion of 'invisible religion'. This concept has sometimes been criticised for being too broad to be useful. The results of this study, however, go some way towards justifying its use.
23 See also David Day and Phillip May, *Teenage Beliefs* (Oxford: Lion Publishing, 1991).
24 Psychologists might interpret this conceptualisation as a stage of faith to be superseded by a more abstract understanding later on. It is, however, a style of faith that is in tune with wider late modern sociological trends that stress the value of personal relationships and intimate experiences over and above the impersonal bureaucracy of institutional religion.
25 Giddens, *Modernity and Self-Identity*, p. 227.
26 Francis and Kay, *Teenage Religion and Values*, p. 70.
27 Peter Ester, Loek Halman and Brigitte Seuren, 'Environmental Concern and Offering Willingness in Europe and North America', in Ester, Halman and de Moor, *The Individualizing Society*, pp. 163–83.
28 Anthony Giddens, *The Transformation of Intimacy. Sexuality, Love & Eroticism in Modern Societies* (Cambridge: Polity Press, 1993), p. 2.
29 Grace Davie, *Religion in Britain Since 1945: Believing Without Belonging* (Oxford: Blackwell, 1994).
30 See Edward Bailey, 'The Religion of the People', in Tony Moss (ed.), *In Search of Christianity* (London: Firethorn Press, 1986), p. 184.
31 Harding and Phillips with Fogarty, *Contrasting Values in Western Europe*, p. 59. It is noteworthy, from the 1981 European Values Survey, that the majority of people accepted the last seven of the Ten Commandments as applying to themselves. The first three, which are explicitly religious, were not accepted to the same extent.
32 Bruce, *Religion in the Modern World*, pp. 230–4.

6
Vice and Virtue or Vice Versa: A Sociology of Being Good

Kieran Flanagan

The other night, from cares exempt,
I slept – and what d'you think I dreamt?
I dreamt that somehow I had come
To dwell in Topsy-Turveydom! –
Where vice is virtue – virtue, vice:

This poem of W. S. Gilbert might seem to embody all the dreams of post-modernity.[1] Nostalgia, ambiguity and escapism are the marks of this culture of sophisticates which so ably inverts vice and virtue in playful indifference to consequence. Postmodernity exults in the indifference to difference. All moral matters are turned around and around. Virtue is the vice of the dull; and vice is the virtue of the liberated. In these endless inversions and reversions, the fruits of decadence so assiduously planted in modernity have come to a complete but tasteless ripeness. Indeed, so ripe do they seem, that they may be past their 'sell-by date'. They have long lost their original bloom, the colouring that invoked pleasures of temptation. Now there is a nostalgia for times when blasphemy effected a sense of violation. With the indifference to difference, nobody cares much about virtue and vice. As antinomies, they arouse no curiosity, they bear no testing and they certify no character. Somehow this dream invokes rueful reflection on times when distinctions did matter, but now no longer. They are subjects of neither philosophical nor sociological discourse. As Foot observed, 'for many years the subject of the virtues and vices was strangely neglected by moralists working within the school of analytical philosophy'.[2]

There used to be a bravery, a pioneering property to those who manipulated inversions of virtue and vice. Effecting rearrangements that detached morality from appearance in the interests of pleasure was the hallmark of decadence. Inversions realised a peculiarly satisfying sense of transgression. This involved de-sacralising images to feed the satisfactions of an aesthetic but profaning gaze. Unfortunately, the private, almost subterranean exercises of inverting virtue and vice in a confusion of images moved from the salon to the supermarket and the gods of consumption took over from the God of religion. Thus it came to pass that everybody could invert and transgress images of vice and virtue and anything could be exchanged in the marketplace, for that was the miracle of commodification which money consecrated. Further opportunities for detaching appearance from morality, thus blurring distinctions between virtue and vice, came with visual technology – for instance, with digital packages for computer-made icons and images. No social space was required for their construction or consumption, so that if virtue and vice were disassembled, this was a private matter of taste, with no public form of accountability. All, whether sacred or profane, in image and likeness could be fragmented and reassembled.

Postmodernity is the term that denotes this capacity to break asunder what God has joined together: virtue and vice. In all this, virtue and vice are lazily decontextualised and disembedded in a culture of pastiche. The 'real' and the 'virtual' have become interchangeable and no reference is required to the originals. The moral template upon which they were cast as differences has long been broken. What can be rendered counterfeit, what can be detached from its original, now sets the criteria for judging the authenticity of cultural artefacts in use and appreciation. This is a culture that exults in ambiguity and its heroes are the androgynous, those who pass between virtue and vice, but in a purposefully indefinable manner. In all this wonder world of the counterfeit, suspicion is a necessary instrument of survival. Disbelief is the language of belief.

Political correctness scorns those who seek to make demarcations based on notions of vice and virtue. Such boundary-making involves moral judgements and principles of exclusion, offensive to some in a culture where life and sexual politics seek their eradication in the interests of some rainbow-like notion of inclusion. Marking differences between virtue and vice, and sorting entitlements to the attributes both carry whiffs of hypocrisy and moral conceit. They undermine the agenda of life and sexual politics, of affirming the dignity and rights of the individual to pursue *any* identity that harms no one else. All civil rights of identity are to be granted[3] save to those who wish to judge and to exclude. In giving voice to the marginalised, the virtuous are reduced to whispering on the margins, hoping not to be subject to the scorn of the mighty. In all this, matters have been turned about. The vice-ridden occupy the high moral ground of politics and the mass media. The virtuous play little part in the factories of culture where images are cast.

Yet, all this is not as new as it seems. Augustine gazing at the culture of Rome made a declaration that could characterise the present values regarding the status of virtue and vice. He stated that

full publicity is given where shame would be appropriate; close secrecy is imposed where praise would be in order. Decency is veiled from sight;

indecency is exposed to view. Scenes of evil attract packed audiences; good words scarcely find any listeners. It is as if purity should provoke a blush, and corruption give ground for pride. But where else should this happen but in devils' temples, in the resorts of delusion? The object is, by the one device to ensure the capture of the honourable minority, and by the other to prevent the reformation of the corrupt majority.[4]

Planting issues of vice and virtue back on to the field of a culture of post-modernity seems like a dream. It invokes the sort of nostalgia to be condemned in a culture of suspicion. It involves a retreat to a land of purity, heroism and virtue that never existed. This sense of wanting to retreat is well captured in Arnold's poem 'Rugby Chapel'. Musing in the gloom of an Autumn evening, he thought back to his youth, to what gave him strength, when the burden of duty to choose between good and bad was carried with innocent zeal. Recalling those times, he wrote of his dead father's leadership:

> Still, like a trumpet, dost rouse
> Those who with half-open eyes
> Tread the border-land dim
> 'Twixt vice and virtue; reviv'st,
> Succourest![5]

Now there is no border-land, no twilight zone for moral testing, for reason has made all things light and clear. Following on from the maturation of modernity that so enlightens, postmodernity abjures the differences incarnated in these antiquarian distinctions between virtue and vice. These attentions to moral differences invoke worlds well discarded, of good and evil, of duty and judging and of being judged and being excluded. They conjure up virtues so misapplied on Flanders' fields, of fortitude and courage and a misguided heroism which satire has long demolished. These are terms of the dead, whose mute memories are lettered in such rhetoric on the public school chapel wall. They invoke times when religion made all too uncomfortably definite what now seems so comfortably indefinite.

Postmodernity licenses an abdication of the struggle, the unspringing of the tension between vice and virtue (or is it the other way around?). The dream of Gerontius is not fit matter for the sociological imagination. His dreamful flight into theological fancy involved close encounters with angelic and devilish kinds. Listening to the latter's cries, he remarked: 'how sour and how uncouth a dissonance', almost as if speaking prophetically of the culture of postmodernity. It was, however, the impotency of devlish evil that fascinated his soul as he heard them chant 'virtue and vice, a knave's pretence, 'tis all the same'.[6] This is now the canon of postmodernity. Tables are turned and now it is only the knavish and the foolish who mention such distinctions. Nobody would think that the ability to make such distinctions could be a condition of bestowing trust. Few would smile at Johnson's comment: 'if he does really think that there is no distinction between virtue and vice, why Sir, when he leaves our houses let us count our spoons'.[7]

The unwillingness or incapacity to make such distinctions leaves a lot of moral business unfinished. It carries a price which postmodernity signifies, of living on a cultural landscape bereft of moral markings. It is, however, surely an elementary question for sociology to ask on this landscape – what is the character of he who comes? It is the sort of question Simmel would have well understood. It is also the question of the agenda of virtue ethics and its emergence in philosophy.[8] Such a philosophical shift of emphasis in relation to virtue might suggest a friendliness to sociology, for both face a common agenda. Unfortunately, one of the main exponents of virtue ethics, Alasdair MacIntyre, as other contributors have indicated, indicts two of sociology's heroes: Weber and Goffman. They are charged with sustaining and effecting emotivism, that is the obliteration of distinctions between manipulative and non-manipulative social relations.[9] Earlier in the volume Tester has addressed these charges against Weber, although in the case of Goffman they are well proven. It cannot be said that character and virtue are part of Goffman's little world of petty manipulation where the fooled deserve to be misled.

Sociology might accept the agenda of virtue ethics, its concern with character and community, but not the theological and philosophical overtones to which it is attached. Yet, outside the artificial worlds of postmodernity, issues of good and evil and of virtue and vice are present in events that horribly unfold. Wars in Kovoso and massacres in Rwanda reproduced too many horrors on the screen for the sociologist to ignore. There was no playful virtual reality in these events. Sadly, they reflected life in the global village in all its evilness. Whether it is invoked as a metaphor or something more direct, only theology seems able to supply the appropriate language to characterise what so demeans humanity in those events where virtue fled and vice ruled. Sociology would lose all its moral claims if it denied that distinctions were to be made there.

Even in these settings, virtues of bravery, fortitude and charity are to be found, sprung from religion or a common sense of humanity. Rumours of compassion fatigue seem misplaced. Moral frameworks of identification of good still exist and, as Watts Miller has argued in his chapter, there is still a spirit of hope against hope. It is curious that the postmodernity that sought to reduce the actor to a mere spectator on life, the perpetual tourist, seems to have presided over the return of the self, identity and moral quest to the sociological agenda. In these issues so unexpectedly returned, lie questions of choice, the making of identity, the finding of bases of trust, the seeking of communities of affiliation and commitment, but above all the question of character. Identity asks a question the self cannot avoid: 'what am I to be?'.

Such a query brings back the issue of accountability for choice. Dealing with virtue and vice has its uses, for in their inversions lie issues of identity and identification, points of character and its need to struggle. If virtue ethics is to have its sociological uses, it has to be grounded in dilemmas of choices, sites of recognition and misrecognition.

Forming part of a wider project,[10] this chapter explores the way virtue and vice might offer themselves for sociological scrutiny in three forms – as cast asunder, as mutually implicated, and as counterproductively cast even for the good and the holy. These inversions and reversions present pleasing conundra for sociological inspection. They are pleasing because they are unresolvable, and they are significant because they characterise the inescapable divisions of the human condition. These are issues of choice, to be good or evil. Such choice has to be realised on the ground of culture, where sociology squats, and not on the high mountains occupied by Milbank and the acolytes of radical orthodoxy, who read from their texts and see post-structuralist visions in the night with no field in sight.

The purpose of these three readings is to draw out the necessary tensions of the antinomial relationship between virtue and vice. As unresolved ambiguities, vice and virtue entail questions of judgement, of character and of searching for something better. They carry a necessary part of what it is to struggle, to be tested, in short to be human, but with a prejudicial spin, cast into a theology, Catholicism in this case. It is the implicit value judgement of the essay, the agenda of reflexivity it contains.

The sundering of virtue and vice: a sociological inquest

Among his many admonitions of Wormwood, Screwtape was particularly scathing about his underestimation of the significance of gluttony. As he wrote:

> one of the great achievements of the last hundred years has been to deaden the human conscience on that subject so that by now you will hardly find a sermon preached or a conscience troubled about it in the whole length and breadth of Europe.[11]

The sins of the flesh identified as vice have long slipped away as matters of serious moral concern. This passing marks the triumph of secularisation and the liberation it promises. Their vanishing also marks a success in re-labelling, so what was pejorative has become part of a life style, the displacement effecting some unquestioned legitimacy, some entitlement of identity and condition. Indolence has been re-cast as leisure; sloth has become fatigue at the stresses of life; lust has become a necessary right of sexual politics; and greed is but the exercise of consumer choice. Even the lazy 'couch potato', guiltily, uselessly and vacantly staring at the television set, has been re-cast on the moral scale as being visually challenged, hence being shelved from life. Sin has been eclipsed. It is no longer a condition of evil, for the term itself has been demolished. As hell has also been dismantled by fiat, there is no sting in vice. It carries no spiritual tribulations, no burden of guilt and no sense of displacement from the good of society. Vice has been cut into a thousand exemptions, all of which fracture its basis. Conditions of moral turpitude are now states of addiction, all for cure in the medical model. If this exemption does not apply, then vice belongs to entrapment in the social conditions of life. In all this, there is no culpability, no need to confess, and nothing to be guilty about. As sexuality has become a central part of cultural identity, it has become well detached from issues of vice. Prostitutes are sex-industry workers; homosexuality is a lifestyle choice; and anybody can be transgendered into any bodily form, even one unimaginable to the sophisticated anthropologist. Identity has become politicised, and the pursuit of its realisation is a civil right, one to be defended, where dignity, recognition and inclusion are entitlements, with no moral price to be paid. Sexual politics have removed the sting from vice and, indeed, have made sure it is well removed from the public sphere too as a term of any currency. Restraint is a vice of the unliberated. In the burgeoning sociology of sexuality, discipline is a sado-masochistic treat, not an instrument to extinguish vice.

In his excellent study of *The Seven Deadly Sins*, Lyman points to the way the study of evil in sociology has been subsumed under 'the embarrassing, neutered morality of "deviance"'.[12] Unfortunately, the advent of postmodernity has marked the disappearance of deviance as a branch of sociology. Lifestyle politics are about the emancipation of groups from the fringes of society where, formerly, they were treated as deviant. Disbelief in any binding norms has meant abdication of belief in the right to exclude. Terms such as vice and evil stand disconnected from sociology. They represent everything it seeks to overturn: prejudice, superstition and dark religious traditions. They bear a rhetoric of the night incompatible with sociology's status as the discipline of the day. Secularisation has marked the demise of such rhetoric, and lifestyle politics are established to perpetuate its extinction.[13] These traits of vice and evil do not exist, for all is a social construction, a process without moral judgement. Thus, within sociology and anthropology, there is a deep reluctance to treat of events in terms of evil, even in the case of child abuse, where arguments about Satanic aspects emerge.[14] Anyhow, as Luhmann observes, sociology cannot establish moral norms. Sociology is not ethics, and vice versa. With the issue of good and evil floating off, the habitus of original sin has also diminished.[15]

The deconstruction and decay of vice as a social entity is a function of modernity and civilisation, the very entities that facilitated the rise of sociology itself. Unfortunately, these entities do not absolve sociology from some need for judgement and accountability, as Bauman shows well. Thus, in his account of the Holocaust, sociology is placed in the dock as a defendant, but it is also a witness for the prosecution, for no other discipline so understands the makings of modernity from within. Progress requires a judgement and the Holocaust enforces one. Bauman argues that the disguise of the need for choice in a system of convention, cast in the smooth reasons of the values of civilisation and their bureaucratic ordering, can mean that humanity is the main loser, and so he writes:

> evil can do its dirty work, hoping that most people most of the time will refrain from doing rash, reckless things – and resisting evil is rash and reckless. Evil needs neither enthusiastic followers nor an applauding audience – the instinct of self-preservation will do, encouraged by the comforting thought that it is not my turn yet, thank God: by lying low, I can still escape.[16]

It is in the realm of normality and conventionality that evil seems to thrive. Sociology deludes itself if it confines its moral judgements to the surface of life. Possibilities of escaping, failure of commitment and self-centredness, are marked as the symptoms of postmodernity and these have come to be mirrored in the present state of sociology itself. It suffers a paralysis of ethics and imagination. Living by the mirrors of a world of virtual reality means that the ability to decipher has become impossible. There is no tradition, no narrative, no tale to invoke, to see something better. In this paralysis, the burden of disbelief is increasingly hard to bear. In an insightful work, Beaudoin has explored what it is to live outside religion but with a disbelief, a distrust, in the solutions of the 1960s. He sees in the generation of the 1990s a sadness and anger about suffering expressed in psychological and spiritual crises of meaning. Thus:

> clothing styles and music videos suggest feelings of rage, with the videos expressing this in apocalyptic images. Despair is common and occasionally leaps overboard into nihilism.[17]

A generation has been sold out on a capacity to believe. It is trapped in a liberation laid down in another generation, and what previously seemed a release now imprisons, as Etzioni well illustrates in his references to the guidelines laid down at Antioch College to secure 'pure relationships' of intimacy without harassment, and sexuality without unwanted violations. These bureaucratised rules of trust generated ridicule and revolt. As he argues, what was 'originally conceived as sexual liberation, enhanced freedom and growing sexual equality ended up being experienced by many as troubling, uncertainty and confusion'. It exasperated the individualism of moral accountability which the application of reason to rules of intimacy was supposed to regulate. In the privatisation and emptying of trust, seeking communal attachments through a rehabilitation of virtues is now necessary. This marks a return to issues of moral autonomy. Thus, for Etzioni, dialogue, civility, and virtue form his concern with remaking the moral fabric of community.[18]

In the making of trust lies the issue of judgement over vice and virtue, one which Giddens has inverted in his approach to understanding the management of intimacy. Neither vice nor virtue are his terms. In so far as they relate, he would echo the maxim of la Rochefoucauld, that 'we are so biased in our own favour that often what we take for virtues are only vices disguised by self-love'.[19] It is what the self wants that counts for the failure to calibrate differences, if any, between virtue and vice. There are other reasons not to calibrate, which Bauman has pursued. In his writings the need to make judgements is at tension with the risk of being subsumed into affiliation with a totalising belief system, which always betrays, by evolving into totalitarianism. This risk of domination, that justifies a reluctance to commit, emerges also in Giddens. The extension of mutual obligation and expectations of commitment into intimate relationships risks undermining the purity of self-interest that governs his conception of these bonds. For him, the crucial issue of intimacy in late modernity is the democratisation of personal relationships based on negotiation and consent, forms that debar moral judgements. These belong to oppressive pasts and emotional inequalities that 'allocated a central role to male sexuality, linking virtuous women to marriage, separating them from the various categories of fallen women – prostitutes, courtesans and harlots'.[20] Intimacy is defined in terms of equality and this transcends all other considerations. It is about gaining an equality of emotions for both sides of the relationship. In this regard, virtue and vice would denote a capacity to divide and conquer in a manner at odds with these values. Virtue no longer has a claim on the regulation of intimacy. Bizarrely, it introduces an impurity in relationships by inserting expectations of difference and dominance.

For Giddens, sexuality has become 'plastic' or de-traditionalised as the act becomes detached from reproduction. Whereas Catholicism regards this as unnatural and regressive, Giddens treats it as progressive, as a trait of personality that is bound with the self and which can be an instrument inserting an equity in sexual relationships, where the male no longer supplies all the rules of power.[21] Thus, sexuality forms a crucial strand of the project of reflexivity. This entails a self-awareness of the resources, ranging from therapy to self-help manuals, that enable the actor to realise the project of intimacy as a form of 'pure relationships'. These also entail the securing of consent, the ambition to realise co-dependence and the negotiation of means to ameliorate risks of misuse of power and dependence. The actor is accountable for the realisation of this project not in terms of ethics, or virtue, but in utilising information that will best secure mutual satisfactions. Sexuality, not tradition, or romance, or love, much less religion, governs the reflexive project of identity, one characterised by openness, not opacity, disclosure rather than enclosure and a freeing in a mutuality of interest agreed equally by both parties. Traditional notions of virtue and vice are jettisoned in this purity of relationship. Thus Giddens affirms an escape from the imprint of heterosexuality. Emancipation from the 'unnatural', where it was treated as a perversion of the natural, enables Giddens to regard 'gays as pioneers, particularly in the sphere of relationships'.[22] This promotion of homosexuality from a condition of vice, to one exemplifying virtue in the pursuit of 'pure relationships', underlines the inversion of the ordering of these moral attributes. It is a notion that has nevertheless been treated with a certain scepticism.[23]

Few other issues exemplify his inversion of vice and virtue as much as those of shame and addiction. In Catholicism, virtue is about firm attitudes and dispositions that seek a morally good life,[24] whilst vice is linked to domination by disordered passions, and the resulting perversions denote a condition of evil and loss of grace.[25] What might belong to the issue of vice, such as excessive sexual activity, is moved by Giddens into an issue of addiction. This is treated as a negative property, not so much in terms of an intrinsic moral disorder, but as a compulsion that hinders the actualisation of the self. It is an offence not so much against a notion of a Divine law, but of a human one, one that lends an injunction to reflexivity (self-awareness) to seek to alleviate burdens and barriers that hinder self-actualisation. In this setting, shame is related to a lack of self-esteem; it is what limits the individual's ability to approach adults as emotional equals. Thus, for Giddens, shame is what detracts from the reflexive project of the self; it is a failure of duty to seek escape from entrapment in addiction.[26] The shame lies in the effect of the act, not in its objective and intrinsic characteristics. In this notion of shame, there is neither condemnation nor culpability, except that of not seeking its eradication in therapy to alleviate what disables the self and its project of constructing its own narrative. In late modernity, the only tale to tell is of the self. Issues of virtue and vice are not part of this agenda of reflexivity, rather they are impediments to self-actualisation. They are the dead tokens of a tradition of religion which late modernity seals in its grave.

Although Giddens is concerned with exploring conditions of trust in late modernity in the setting of intimacy, the arguments for securing its basis seem unpersuasive. In his idea of 'pure relationships', there are no external communal supports or traditions to invoke. These 'pure relationships' have to be found in a mutuality based on individualism and the moral engagements of the two persons involved in the seeking of intimacy.[27] In their endeavours, there is no quest for community, for nothing social exists outside their seeking of pleasurable pairings founded on notions of equality and consent. It is a life of choice, of pick-and-choose with no obligation to stay if pleasure is not given.

For Giddens, trust is about a 'vesting of confidence in the other and also in the capability of the mutual bond to withstand future traumas'.[28] The agenda of trust is about minimising risk and anxiety amongst strangers seeking intimacy. Yet, as sexuality has become instrumental and available outside marriage without moral censure, mistrust abounds. Revealing a disillusion with the 1990s, Meghan Daum reflected on two decades of permissible sexual pleasure, and concluded that 'we're still told not to trust each other. We've entered a period where mistrust equals responsibility, where fear signifies health.'[29] It is, however, not surprising that the world of 'pure relationships' which Giddens portrays is devoid of character. His world is one of negotiation without ambivalence, without risk of failure, or the need for moral struggle. In the world portrayed by Giddens, of the impersonal couplings of lonely strangers, life is boringly transient. These are worlds of mutual pleasure and when that dissolves, so do the relationships. Although earlier in their text, the Becks have spoken of 'old female virtues' of understanding, tolerance, willingness to compromise, and the courage to start again, no virtue in restraint is admitted in their later account. No vice is recognised, for only the acts of connection to alleviate loneliness matter, and these admit no inhibition in a world of love. This is proclaimed as 'our secular religion' and makes 'its own rules out of sexual desire now unhampered by moral or legal obligations'.[30]

As relationships become purified in calculation, the need to let go in love is undermined. In the world of intimacy of Giddens, 'pure relationships' are founded on minimising the giving of love. Contingency becomes a virtue and in the chaos the dreading overtones of vice vanish. There is no tragedy in these worlds where love is so easily lost and seldom gained. The tensions and drama of mutuality unravel as the agenda of 'pure relationships' gains ascendance. They take the risk and anxiety out of affairs of the heart, by making them unambiguous. What is ambiguous is an impediment to this charter of purity and consent – it licenses something to be held back, to be unclarified. Yet, as Bauman elegantly argues, 'the pathos of love feeds on mystery. But the mystery it feeds on is one it hopes to crack. Curiosity is the hope of knowledge – and when the hope wanes, curiosity gives way to indifference.' Thus, rather against Giddens, Bauman claims 'ambivalence is the daily bread of love. Love needs a duality that stays insurmountable.'[31] Mystery and ambiguity are the centre of moral life for Bauman; they prevent enclosure in a total belief system that can only corrupt. Thus, for him, 'to act morally means to face up to that incurable ambivalence' of indifference, where responsibility dies, and or where it degenerates into coercion.[32]

Living a life of coping with ambivalence legitimises a state of indifference, but it too breeds intolerable limits, of being encased in cynicism and disconnection. What seems to liberate – the eradication of difference – seems to have wrought a state of indifference. Instead of connecting to where life is, the actor has to live where it is denied. Knowing of entrapment is to demand release, and that is found in the re-invention of a concern with difference, of facing ambiguities in terms of forging choice. All this returns to the polarities of good and evil. Evil is permitted as a metaphor, for speech of its existence is denied; it is the difference that is treated with indifference, but good is always sought in its intrinsic worth. It is the property of holism, of the self-made man, the actor of postmodernity, gazing but never realising. Living in life without contrasts, with an antinomy of good and evil ruptured, is his emptiness, his failure of commitment all that surprising? Dead to himself, parading as a sponge soaking up but never absorbing, gazing but never finding, crisis-ridden in identity with no capacity to meaningfully identify, where else has the actor of postmodernity to return, but to the antinomies of virtue and vice? Such retreatism, such nostalgia, breaches the code of disembodiment promulgated in postmodernity. At least, in preaching the acceptance of belonging without believing, of living on moral tick, postmodernity bears a nobility of stoicism, a Neitzsche-like super-human stiffness, unlike the ignoble retreatants, the surpliced sitting in their choirstalls in permanent retreat from moral life. The latter flee life, which the former confronts, but then postmodernity makes its own mythologies, however much it denies the narratives of others.

Virtue and vice as mutually implicated

It is foolish to believe that religion offers a form of escape from the antinomies of vice and virtue. It is in the nature of the human condition to be tempted. In facing the allures of vice, there is the prospect, the hope, of victory gained. The seed-bed of character lies in what emerges from testing, and from this there is no escape. Self-knowledge generates its own moral reflexivity, where choice has to be made in what to struggle over. In this spiritual and moral wrestling the self comes to know what it despises and this forms the platform for seeing something better. Virtue needs vice to know what it wants to reject and vice needs virtue to realise its pleasures. Living with each other has uses for the holy and the unholy. Thus, virtues require their opposite for their manifestation, and it is hard to think how fortitude could emerge, save on the back of the cussed. If the antinomies of vice and virtue are cast asunder, then something of the human condition has been lost. This is the capacity to be subtle, for as des Esseintes noted, artifice is 'the distinctive mark of human genius'.[33]

In the case of the antinomies that vice and virtue represent, artifice lies in the virtuous endeavour to rise above the fleshly imprisonment of human nature. To the sophisticated, these efforts at moral elevation are self-evidently risible, if not inconvenient, for they draw attention to the vacuity of worldly values. They cast back an aura of guilt on to the emancipated. Yet, without the efforts of the virtuous, the vice-ridden find their foci of transgression have melted away. They need the virtuous to violate and to trespass on their aura, for without these activities of the good, the pleasures of vice seem devoid of focus.

The trouble is that vice has become so popular. It is no longer unrespectable. As Skolnick has noted, vice is a subject of endless social transformation, where what is forbidden becomes industrialised, as in the case of gambling and lotteries. Vice presupposes a moral ambivalence for, as he adds, it represents a form of 'conduct that a person may enjoy and deplore at the same time'.[34] In his reading of vice, therefore, pleasure and wickedness combine. With the dismantling of virtue as a moral ambition, one neither deplores nor enjoys activities of vice. It is now a humdrum event devoid of excitement, risk, curiosity and condemnation. This was a point the pioneers of decadence, the parents of modernity, well understood.

Esseintes had a genius for the pursuit of pleasure, that involved the obsessive collection of aesthetic objects, including those proper to religious ceremonies. This caused him to wonder had he committed blasphemy in their profaning accumulation. But then he reflected:

> this idea, that he was possibly living in a state of sin, filled him with a certain pride and satisfaction, not unmixed with delight in these sacrilegious acts.[35]

These recondite forebodings might seem redundant to those, such as Giddens, pioneering 'pure relationships' in late modernity, yet within these inversions of vice and virtue were sown the seeds of modernity. Baudelaire and Huysmans were fascinated with the issue of evil, and what is best forgotten by many, and is unforgivable for some, is that in the end both these exemplary *flâneurs* of modernity strolled back to Catholicism. The return was not surprising. What other retreat was possible?

Modernity was derived from the capacity to transgress and to invert, and evil was its focal point of experimentation. Vice needs virtue if for no other reason than that the pleasures of decadence lie in doing what is forbidden. As la Rochefoucauld observed, 'hypocrisy is a tribute vice pays to virtue'.[36] But with vice discarded and evil unrecognised, all is now emptiness. Modernity has lost its foil of playing vice against virtue, and the upshot is the condition of postmodernity. It involves living on a field of chaff, where nothing roots. The trouble is that secularisation has removed the sting of Divine retribution, or so it thinks, and sexual politics has rendered vice incompatible with the religion of self-actualisation where any activity is to be dignified as a civil right. Unfortunately, the foil of virtue has been subject to boundary removal, and vice finds itself, as the new religion, marked with the indifference which seemed to have sunk its more traditionally cast predecessor, a religion linked to a theology. Modernity kills the things it loves. Thus, vice has become a victim of its success. It is no longer thrilling. A state of boredom and fatigue has now settled. Curiously, vice, uninhibited by the guilty aura virtue casts, gives no pleasure. Postmodernity is the intensification of boredom. It is an irredeemable state of complete moral paralysis, hence the reason Bauman and others start to think of ethics and means of escape. No one is obliged to anyone and the face of the Other has frozen in disbelief. It is now uninteresting to gaze at, for it lacks a character.

Paradoxes are endurable, if some resolution is proffered for the future. But the eternal present of postmodernity offers no such thing. The past is incredible and the future indecipherable, so that one is punished with living in the immediate, where all solace, all originals and nostalgias have vanished. It is not surprising, as Watts Miller writes in this collection, that some form of hope is required to survive life in a secularised morality. Bauman offers no hope. For him, 'the defining feature of the postmodern idea of the good life is the lack of definition of the good life'.[37] This hardly seems good enough. Moral ambitions still abound; issues of character flaws bedevil political careers; and there is always the embarrassing question which the children might pose: *why* be good?

Cynical responses seem inadequate. This perpetuates the moral inactivity that denotes a particular characteristic of postmodernity. Thus Bewes sees cynicism as 'enlightened false consciousness'. This refers to a sensibility formed by a particular discourse, but then estranged from it. It embodies a fatalism, a justification of melancholic retreat. In this regard, Bewes also sees the blasé as a necessary fatigue, a boredom with the world that justifies a defeatist retreat from encounters with its all too meaningless basis. In this sense of weariness, Simmel and Huysmans saw much in common in terms of what was coming, which postmodernity has sealed with a loveless kiss.

A typical character invoked by Bewes is des Esseintes. He is treated as a prototypical consumer of virtual-reality technology, who captures the notion of cynicism which Bewes sees as so central to the character of postmodernity.[38] In the end, all issues return to character and to the interior it occupies, the being in that skin and in that consciousness facing the limits of a self. Working against the background of Blair's vision of socialism, as having 'a moral purpose of life', a belief in society, Bewes argues that

> inner emigration is a viable metaphor for this process of depoliticization, first, because the moral individual derives his or her justification not from action, or the effects of action, but from interior rationalization, from the finely gradated but ultimately indeterminate realm of human motivation.[39]

As the self migrates into inner engagement, it retreats from judgement, accountability and engagement. It moves away from the social sphere in a manner sociology can only deplore. As it travels further within, it collides with a niggle: what does it value? The mundane tires the cynical and nihilism dissolves into nullity. It has no option but to re-invent itself, and when the self shrinks to vanishing point, it hits the walls of the human spirit and uncoils back out again. It demands metaphors that will speak for a sufficiency and these might force a humiliating retreat back to religion, well plundered, dead perhaps, but still viable for theft. Oddly, religion is still the larder of modernity, and as postmodernity runs out of food it slinks back to the cupboard, which – strangely enough – is not bare. Thus, it is not surprising that the issue of the sacred hovers as a metaphor around the tribe, aesthetics and the body.

Renewed interest in Durkheim centres on the way the values of humanity are to be sacralised to provide a sense of worth, somewhat scarce in the culture of postmodernity. The idea of the sacred has come to signify a basis of trust to a society that has lost belief in itself. Although the antinomies of vice and virtue have become unravelled, the need to transgress still persists, even if the targets have vanished. As Jervis has noted, 'the fascination with the body boundaries and transgressions involved in sexuality can be seen, in effect, as a search for transcendence in a secular and materialist age'.[40] The urge to seek returns, but here we face a peculiarity. In embodiment, the self and the body meet in a manner that invites scrutiny. One seeks to inspect to find something of value. In this inspection, there is the risk that reflexivity becomes an intensified form of knowing of emptiness.

Ascetics tame the body for fashionable display as an object of worship. It shines with health and sensuality, but in such display it becomes the victim of the entrapping gaze, fodder for the stalker's stare. Intolerance of such objectifications focuses attention on alternative identities. As unfettered sexuality becomes disenchanting, enchantment lies in chastity and modesty, and the rediscovery of these values can take on the properties of a moral adventure, perhaps all the more unexpected when they emerge from New York brands of feminism.[41]

Clean living without chemical dependencies or sexual imprisonments offers to a new generation a concern with purity and independence which operates as conditions of revolt and resistance against past dalliances with vice. Virtue is the 'new' creation of a new order of youth whose virtuous claims terrify the greying survivors of the 1960s. These might be just fashionable fads of the young. Yet one gets a sense that, for them, de-spiritualisation has gone as far as it can go. Their revolution is to seek to repair the disjunction between virtue and vice and to turn it around, so that the pursuit of the former arises from an escape from the latter.

If sociology marked the cultural turn with deep enthusiasm a decade ago, the spiritual turn is just on the horizon and the search for a rhetoric for its characterisation has only just started. As the turn to the East marked the pioneers of the 1960s, those of the year 2000 look West, to the spiritual traditions where virtue was formed by professionals, the men and women, often young, who left the world to face the self with little communal solace in lives of enthusiastic self-denial. If efforts at rehabilitation of virtue come to be recognised, the writings of these pioneers will come back into fashion. What they will show is that misrecognitions and confusions abound, that choice still has to be made, for even in angelic life on earth, the flesh is weak, especially in seeking virtue. Keeping the virtues heavenside up is no fine art; it requires as much guile as the commission of vice. Accurately deciphering the vice versa of vice and virtue has implications for the after-life, but it also involves an earthly art worthy of sociological attention.

The virtue of vice and the vice of virtue for the saintly

To attribute the properties of virtue to vice, or vice versa, generates obvious objections. Clearly, virtue and vice are discrete in their metaphysical essences and it would go against all the tenets of Christianity to suggest that the latter can dominate the former. They have a proper order in theology. To fall from virtue into vice calls for an effort to redeem the situation. As Aquinas has argued, in the context of penance, 'every special virtue expels the habit of the opposed vice; just as white expels black from the same subject'.[42] So why signify the confusion, having railed against the inversions wrought by postmodernity?

At one level, the mixing is counterproductive, for it could be argued that attributing the properties of one to the other permits hypocrisy to flourish as a beneficiary of this misapplication. Successful efforts at misattribution, as in Goffman's world, suggest that there is no difference between the two, hence justifying indifference to both. If one had to choose, vice is more interesting. It is all about ventures and risks. It is about misadventures, and losses. Virtue is about going nowhere and playing safe in not moving. One hears few tales of adventures in the pursuit of virtue. This would be to miss the point. The seeking of virtue does not absolve the actor from the imperfections of the human condition, rather it forces him to confront them. It does not absolve the actor from the need to test, to purify and to scrutinise to retrieve the virtuous from rocks of vice, even when they appear confused and difficult to separate. Risks of misreading have their purposes. The very confusions of virtue and vice elicit virtues in handling them. One thinks of fortitude and patience, and the denial of despair to find room for hope that from the wresting better will come in character. Virtue is not about a contraction of knowing of the human condition, but more about its expansion.

Knowing of virtue makes the virtuous prone to endemic misunderstandings, scruples, burdens and pains. In seeking virtue, the idea that it is some form of escape is nonsense. It is about confronting the contradictions of the human condition and getting severely mixed up in the process. Virtue might have its own reward, but it does give rise to adventures in seeking it. Those seeking virtue face risks and burdens that make their own demand on character.

The road to virtue is riddled with its own confusions and misattributions, but these are burdens the virtuous are called to bear. Muddles between virtue and vice come at fine and exceptional points of sociological significance. Virtue can mask vice and take on misleading properties. By reading the surface of virtue, one might get confused. Agency permits misattribution, thus the scribes and the Pharisees ' outwardly appear righteous unto men, but within ye are full of hypocrisy and inequity' (Matthew 23: 28). They are the beneficiaries of virtues they do not possess, which underlines the danger of reading their attributes on the surface, and not leaving to God alone the reading of the secrets of the heart. This opens out a sociological interest and dilemma: that the display of virtue is riddled with the potential risk of vice, not merely the vice of hypocrisy, but also of narcissism, vainglory and the cultivation of rewards of esteem and honour in this life rather than in the next. A degree of virtuous dissimulation is required if a character of virtue is to be sustained.[43] Being good is a fraught risky business and misattributions can often occur in its display. The virtuous need to give witness, but in so doing they need to avoid pride in display. As in other instances, there is a thin line between certain virtues and vices. Thus the virtue of prudence can carry a vice of cowardice, the 'real' reason for not acting. Finding a purity of motive in dealing with virtues enjoins a peculiar sociological reflexivity. Anger might seem a vice, but then it can be a virtue, a necessary one, for as John Chrysostom warned, 'he who is not angry when he has cause to be, sins. For unreasonable patience is the hotbed of many vices.'[44] Efforts to realise a life of virtue can attract many unwanted vices.

For instance, some Catholic nuns in their religious habits, those unmodernised prior to Vatican II, felt that a false set of virtues was being displayed. Rather than charity and chastity being displayed, they felt themselves to be the beneficiaries of false claims, of vices of unfair protection and presumption, and a degree of pride in pious display that placed them above humanity and in some unidentified with it. Even more oddly, some nuns felt that this display of virtuous clothing elicited hostile comments from the vice-ridden. In seeking to symbolise the avoidance of vice, they seemed to become an occasion for its arousal in others.[45] No matter what the ambitions the virtuous have, they seldom escape from the issue of vice and its temptation. Indeed, lives of denial generate particular temptations and inclinations, where the flesh feels even more those very deprivations that disturb the virtuous in their endeavours to find a peace of the spirit. There is no escape from the divisions of human nature and its propensity to weakness, as John Donne warned in a sermon at Lincoln's Inn: 'he that retires into a monastery upon pretence of avoiding temptations, and offences in this world, he brings them thither, and he meets them there'.[46]

The pursuit of virtue often involves knowledge of vice. This is to go back to the issue of double knowledge represented in the apple-tree in the Garden of Eden, which signified that only God can transcend both. To recognise the way one flows into the other is to draw attention to the issue of agency and will, but above all the hope of escape from vice into virtue. The issue of misrecognition of vice and virtue relates to their interdependent properties, that one is necessary for the growth of the other and, even if it is easy to confuse both, there is hope of escaping from these dilemmas. Thus, as la Rochefoucauld noted wisely, 'vices have a place in the composition of virtues just as poisons in that of medicines: prudence blends and tempers them, utilising them against the ills of life'.[47] This bears on a point of Donne, in a section of paradoxes and problems at the end of the third elegy on jealousy (ironically written around the theme of the loss of his mistress's chain). Reflecting on how much faith and belief is required to assure that virtues are not counterfeited, he wrote with a certain sociological prescience:

> for it is the same to be and to seem virtuous. Because he that hath no virtue can dissemble none. But he that hath a little may gilt and enamel, yea, and transform much vice into virtue. For allow a man to be discreet and flexible to companies – which are great virtues and gifts of the mind – this discretion will be to him the soul and elixir of all virtue. So that, touched with this, even pride shall be made civil humility, and cowardice, honourable and wise valour.

In conclusion, he adds:

> so that virtue which must be loved for herself, and respects no further end, is indeed nothing; and riches, whose end is the good of the body, cannot be so perfectly good as the end whereto it levels.[48]

Undermining discrete differences between virtue and vice points to a particular form of reflexivity, one not so much a project of self-awareness as of self-knowing. First, the sociological contribution to understanding virtue ethics lies in the social processes of rescue which the agent undertakes to prevent virtue sliding, intentionally or otherwise, into its opposite, a form of vice. Secondly, a theological point is underlined, that the human condition is one of imperfection. Those with spiritual scruples come to know this, for the realisation of virtue is adjacent to the vice of its greatest danger: pride. Thirdly, there is a distinctive property of knowing in relation to virtue and vice that opens out all manner of interesting dilemmas which a culture of postmodernity masks. These relate to a wider but under-explored issue, the sociology of the transmission of virtue. In looking for a phenomenology of virtue and vice, Williams rightly suggests that

> the insights obtained from descriptions of virtues and vices are varied; they include an acquaintance with attitudes associated with virtues;

knowledge of the objects of virtues, of the kinds of situations in which virtues are or are not exemplified, of obstacles to possessing them, and of distinctions between them and near relatives.[49]

In an essay on teaching postgraduates, Dowd sees these students as a form of elect, predestined to shaping analytical insights. This re-conception necessitates some aesthetic of sociology, to add on to its positivist affiliations. What is added on is an interpretative remit which gives sociology new directions 'less to discover social laws and more to discover – and to appreciate – social lives'.[50]

With virtue and vice seemingly cast asunder, the issue of guilt has vanished and with it the prospect of solidarity and resistance, which for Bauman and Tester represents the plimsoll-line of moral integrity. Looking over a world of savagery, Tester comes to the gloomy conclusion that 'if any moral message can be extracted from the present, it is the message that the present seems to make no definite moral sense whatsoever'. Blaséness has become an instrument of self-deception and it might be the task of sociology to indicate how spiritually damaged society is, in its failure to effect a moral solidarity.[51]

Living in postmodernity has only exacerbated this condition of moral blindness, where the instruments of distinction have become glazed over. Postmodernity proffers neither solutions nor redemption and to that degree it does not claim, nor does it realise, an improvement in the moral fabric. It is about a state of predicament of finding choice where there are no rules of arbitration. As Bauman has argued often, 'confronting the choice between good and evil means finding oneself in a situation of ambivalence'.[52] Journeying but never arriving, fixing what is doomed to be unfixed, seeing but not belonging, living as the perpetual tourist, are the dilemmas Bauman uncovers in his approach to postmodernity which takes on an increasing concern with ethics. Unfortunately, in this state everything becomes unstuck. Thus, in his gloomy account of finding an Other to face to find oneself, his alternative solutions are comfortless. Living with death, coping with the fragility of the body, and dealing with conditions of distrust, all suggest a logic to flight to escape from the burden of the social. In this effort to escape, the 'well constructed and durable identity turns from asset into liability. *The hub of postmodern life strategy is not identity building, but the avoidance of being fixed.*'[53] Perhaps the greatest accomplishment of postmodernity is to convey the notion that no deposit is required to escape from the human condition and to live as the perpetual tourist, never having to stick around sufficiently long to make a moral choice. There is no cost to this condition. As Bauman elegantly writes, postmodernity preaches delay on payment. Thus, 'if the savings book was the epitome of modern life, the credit card is the paradigm of the postmodern one'.[54] Yet, everything had a price in modernity and the bills still stand in postmodernity.

However virtue and vice are cast, whether mutually implicated or counterproductively cast in forms of misrecognition that afflict the scrupulous,
the issues of inversion point to endemic problems of agency in securing
choice. Agency, choice, and commitment to endeavour to be good are the
domain items of virtue ethics. Whether realised in independence or dependence, a heroic endeavour is required to realise the agenda of virtue ethics.
Testing of character, discernments, the cultivation of a culture of scrutiny,
not suspicion, are all part of the means of forging the virtuous in their
endeavours to cope with recognitions and misrecognitions. Those who try
to be good lead lives in isolation. In sociology, they have no voice. In the
humility stakes they win hands down, but for them their dreams are of
surmounting difference. They have their own antinomies, as mysterious as
they are 'real' to them, of denial being a form of liberation and discipline
being an opportunity to realise freedom. With their own paradoxes, the
virtuous face down ambivalances that lurk in virtue and vice, and, stretching the spiritual capacities of the self, with grace, they reach to the heavens,
for there the issue of vice versa matters not. They have climbed out of the
human condition and that is the ultimate adventure in dealing with virtue.
There are some young students one meets who are making a lonely, much-
mocked endeavour to construct a life of goodness, to preserve a virginity, to
keep a discipline of virtue and to have a purity of endeavour that is as heroic
as it is unexpected. They have no place in the sociological sun, yet their
constructions and endeavours to do good deserve the deepest admiration
and respect. It is for them that one dreams their voice will be heard: that it is
virtue over vice and not vice versa as the present world would suggest.

Notes and references

1   William Schwenck Gilbert, *The Bab Ballads* (London and New York: George Routledge, 1898), p. 368.
2   Phillipa Foot, *Virtues and Vices, and Other Essays in Moral Philosophy* (Oxford:
Blackwell, 1978), p. 1. For one of the best collections on the topic, see Ellen
Frankel Paul, Fred D. Miller, Jr. and Jeffrey Paul (eds), *Virtue and Vice* (Cambridge:
Cambridge University Press, 1998).
3   For a useful account of the emergence of the politics of identity, see Robert
G. Dunn, *Identity Crises: A Social Critique of Postmodernity* (Minneapolis: University of Minnesota, 1998), pp. 19–30.
4   St Augustine, *City of God*, trans. Henry Bettenson (Harmondsworth: Penguin,
1984), p. 83.
5   C. B. Tinker and H. F. Lowry (eds), *Arnold. Poetical Works* (London: Oxford University Press, 1950), pp. 287–8.
6   John Henry Newman, *The Dream of Gerontius and Other Poems* (London: Oxford
University Press, 1914), pp. 18–21.
7   *The Oxford Dictionary of Quotations*, second edition (London: Oxford University
Press, 1955), no. 10, p. 271.

8 For an excellent overview of the agenda of virtue ethics, see Robert B. Kruschwitz and Robert C. Roberts (eds), *The Virtues. Contemporary Essays on Moral Character* (Belmont, California: Wadsworth, 1987), and Lester H. Hunt, *Character and Culture* (Oxford: Rowman & Littlefield, 1997).

9 Alasdair MacIntyre, *After Virtue*, second edition (London: Duckworth, 1985), pp. 23–9 and 114–17.

10 Kieran Flanagan, *Virtue Ethics and Vocation: A Sociology of Edification* (forthcoming).

11 C. S. Lewis, *The Screwtape Letters*, revised paperback edition (New York: Collier, 1982), p. 76.

12 Stanford M. Lyman, *The Seven Deadly Sins*, revised and expanded edition (New York: General Hall, 1989), p. 3.

13 Lyman sees the Protestant background to Parsonian sociology as marking the secularisation and marginalisation of the notion of sin and judgement. The fault for this lay in sociology itself. See ibid., pp. 277–98.

14 See J. S. La Fontaine, *Speak of the Devil. Tales of Satanic Abuse in Contemporary England* (Cambridge: Cambridge University Press, 1998). For a work that links Satanism, alchemy and children in a study of evil, which caused the author to flee from the study of vice into a pursuit of virtue, see J. K. Huysmans, *La Bas* (Lower Depths) (London: Dedalus, 1986).

15 Niklas Luhmann, 'The Sociology of the Moral and Ethics', *International Sociology*, vol. 11, no. 1, March 1996, p. 32, and footnote 4, p. 36.

16 Zygmunt Bauman, *Modernity and the Holocaust* (Cambridge: Polity Press, 1989), p. 206.

17 Tom Beaudoin, *Virtual Faith. The Irreverent Spiritual Quest of Generation X* (San Franciso: Jossey-Bass Publishers, 1998), p. 97.

18 Amitai Etzioni, *The New Golden Rule. Community and Morality in a Democratic Society* (London: Profile Books, 1997), pp. xiii–xiv.

19 François La Rochefoucauld, *Maxims*, trans. Leonard Tancock (London: Penguin, 1959), no. 607, p. 120.

20 Anthony Giddens and Christopher Pierson, *Conversations with Anthony Giddens. Making Sense of Modernity* (Cambridge: Polity Press, 1998), p. 119.

21 Anthony Giddens, *The Transformation of Intimacy: Sexuality, Love and Eroticism in Modern Societies* (Cambridge: Polity, 1992), p. 2.

22 Giddens and Pierson, *Conversations with Anthony Giddens*, pp. 144–6.

23 Lynn Jamieson, 'Intimacy Transformed? A Critical Look at the "Pure Relationship"', *Sociology*, vol. 33, no. 3, August 1999, p. 487.

24 *Catechism of the Catholic Church* (London: Geoffrey Chapman, 1994), pp. 400–6.

25 Ibid., p. 394 and pp. 411–12.

26 Giddens, *The Transformation of Intimacy*, pp. 70–4 and 175–6.

27 See Zygmunt Bauman, *Life in Fragments. Essays in Postmodern Morality* (Oxford: Blackwell, 1995), chapter 2, 'Forms of Togetherness', pp. 44–71.

28 Giddens, *The Transformation of Intimacy*, pp. 138–9.

29 Meghan Daum, *The New York Times*, 21 January 1996, cited in J. Francis Stafford, 'The Religious Sense', *Communio*, vol. 25, no. 4, Winter 1998, p. 666.

30 Ulrich Beck and Elisabeth Beck-Gernsheim, *The Normal Chaos of Love*, trans. Mark Ritter and Jane Wiebel (Cambridge: Polity Press, 1995), pp. 77 and 194.

31 Zygmunt Bauman, *Postmodern Ethics* (Oxford: Blackwell, 1993), p. 95.

32 Bauman, *Life in Fragments*, p. 66.

33 J. K. Huysmans, *Against Nature*, trans. Robert Baldick (Harmondsworth: Penguin, 1959), p. 36.
34 Jerome H. Skolnick, 'The Social Transformation of Vice', *Law and Contemporary Social Problems*, vol. 51, no. 1, 1988, p. 10.
35 Huysmans, *Against Nature*, p. 91. Des Esseintes felt that as he loved these articles and had not put them to depraved uses, he might not be guilty. On the same page, Huysmans wrote, 'he beguiled himself in this way with prudent, cowardly thoughts, the uncertainty of his soul preventing him from perpetrating overt crimes, robbing him of the necessary courage to commit real sins of real iniquity with real intent'. The trouble with dalliances with vice is that they pose risks of redemption.
36 La Rochefoucauld, *Maxims*, no. 218, p. 65.
37 Bauman, *Life in Fragments*, p. 79.
38 Timothy Bewes, *Cynicism and Postmodernity* (London: Verso, 1997), pp. 30–7. Curiously, Bewes pays little attention to the theological fate of des Esseintes: see Kieran Flanagan, 'J.-K. Huysmans: The First Post-Modernist Saint?', *New Blackfriars*, vol. 71, no. 838, May 1990, pp. 217–29. It is an irony that those who play with deconstruction in postmodernity, which supposedly expels God, seldom realise, as in Pascal's wager, that the coin can spin in a wholly different direction too. See Kieran Flanagan, 'Postmodernity and Culture: Sociological Wagers of the Self in Theology', in Kieran Flanagan and Peter C. Jupp (eds), *Postmodernity, Sociology and Religion* (Basingstoke: Macmillan, 1996), pp. 152–73.
39 Bewes, *Cynicism and Postmodernity*, p. 197.
40 John Jervis, *Exploring the Modern: Patterns of Western Culture and Civilization* (Oxford: Blackwell, 1998), p. 177.
41 Wendy Shault, *A Return to Modesty: Discovering the Lost Virtue* (New York: The Free Press, 1999).
42 Thomas Aquinas, *Summa Theologiae*, trans. Reginald Masterson and T. G. O'Brien (London: Eyre & Spottiswoode, 1965), vol. 60, p. 55. See also Galatians 5: 17.
43 Kieran Flanagan, *Sociology and Liturgy: Re-presentations of the Holy* (Basingstoke: Macmillan, 1991), pp. 122–3.
44 Cited in Peter Kreeft, *Back to Virtue. Traditional Moral Wisdom for Modern Moral Confusion* (San Francisco: Ignatius Press, 1992), p. 134.
45 Kathleen Norris, *The Cloister Walk* (Oxford: Lion, 1999), pp. 329–39.
46 John Carey (ed.), *John Donne* (Oxford: Oxford University Press, 1990), p. 297. In Huysman's semi-autobiographical account of his return to Catholicism, a Trappist monk, speaking of demons and temptation, denied the cloister was a place of peace. Indeed, referring to the devil, he warned that 'no place on earth is more haunted by him than a cell, no one is more harassed than a monk'. See J. K. Huysmans, *En Route*, trans. W. Fleming (London: Daedalus, 1989), p. 250.
47 La Rochefoucauld, *Maxims*, no. 183, p. 60.
48 Carey, *John Donne*, p. 16.
49 Clifford Williams,' Teaching Virtues and Vices', *Philosophy Today*, vol. 33, Fall 1989, p. 198.
50 James J. Dowd, 'Revising the Canon: Graduate Training in the Two Sociologies', *Teaching Sociology*, vol. 19, no. 3, July 1991, p. 321.
51 Keith Tester, *Moral Culture* (London: Sage, 1997), pp. 150–1.
52 Bauman, *Life in Fragments*, p. 2.
53 Ibid., p. 89. (Italics are his emphasis.)
54 Ibid., p. 5.

7
Contemplating Virtue: St Teresa as a Challenge to Social Theory*

Margaret Archer

Both theology and sociology have enormous difficulties in explaining the making of a saint: these are greater when the challenge is a contemplative who seems to have penetrated the sublime. We can see the problem in Bernini's 'Ecstasy of St Teresa' where we realise that the central figures representing Teresa and love were problematic to both the secular and religious powers of her day. The sculpture in Santa Maria della Vittoria is flanked by two opera boxes of *notables* engaged in altercation. It seems from this that explaining Teresa's ecstatic love was no easier to the faithful than to the faithless.

Perhaps, then, it is less surprising that the forms of explanation offered by theology and sociology should parallel one another so closely. These are commonly known as individualist and collectivist explanations: what they have in common is a total failure to accommodate Teresa who is expelled from either version. When theology proffers hagiographic individualism, this quickly becomes the analysis of 'acts' and 'beliefs', as in the canonisation procedure. In this Teresa slips away, again, disaggregated into her beliefs, her doings and her supernatural feats. Yet, of course, she fares no better on hagiographic collectivism where she is merely the earthen vessel of 'amazing grace' and is often painted surrounded by a heavenly host, depicted as the true agents in her story.

Sociological theory offers its own methodological individualism where individuals and their relationships with others are the terminus of explanation thus endorsing an anthropocentricism which can embrace Teresa as a person, providing we expunge the divine. This reduces the sublime simply to 'Teresa's beliefs' – the precise opposite of what she held revelation to be. Alternatively, sociological collectivism makes her of even less interest. As a mere epiphenomenon of her times and circumstances, these shaping forces are more important than the malleable individual who is so shaped.

The difficulties of either the individualist or collective explanations[1] can be illustrated (not allegorised) by telling a story – one whose point demonstrates the deficiencies of both, but whose greater significance lies in pointing beyond this dichotomy to the need for other modes of explaining Teresa herself.

Anthropocentric and socio-centric accounts

The period is 1560–3, the place Avila, and this is the first instalment of the story, which will be told in two parts. The central character in the first part is a professed Carmelite, aged 45, born Teresa Sánchez de Cepeda y Ahumada.[2] She has a supporting cast of a very extended family, a variety of sisters (of both kinds), numerous confessors, sundry nobles, a grand inquisitor and two nuncios. It can be told as 'The Storming of the City' – a sixteenth-century *el alma/el alamo* which begins outside the city walls in the Carmelite Convent of the Incarnation – a place which according to Teresa's autobiography rather resembled a salon.

1. The story begins with a small group of nuns one evening in September 1560, at the Convent of the Incarnation, talking over the origins of the Carmelites (who had no founder – other than the hermits of the Carmel, listening alone like Elijah on Sinai to a small voice after the whirlwind) and of a desire to return to the austerities of the desert fathers – brushed aside by the 1432 Bill of Mitigation, which allowed the previously 'discalced' (religious orders who went barefoot) to put their shoes back on.
2. The vision grew in clarity, of a strict contemplative enclosure, a discalced house for a handful of individually committed religious and lay women. In origin it was *not* born out of discontent, for Teresa wrote in her *Journal* 'I was most happy in the house where I was, for I was very fond of both the house and of my cell, and this held me back'.[3] *Nor* was it envisaged as an evangelistic assault on the city (on society), for it was to be enclosed behind walls and without the city walls.
3. The support which grew depended on personal persuasion, largely by Teresa of her confessors, Francis Borja (Society of Jesus), Pedro de Alcántara (Franciscan) and Pedro Ibañez (Dominican), and often after initial doubts and resistance. Sanctity and stratagem went hand in hand, for the cunningness of serpents equalled the gentleness of these doves. The house was to be purchased by Teresa's sister Juana and brother-in-law Juan de Ovalle, in the names of two lay widows. The plot also contained the wandering made-good brother, Lorenzo, sending in his needed 200 ducats from New World projects for conversion of the property into St Joseph's Convent.
4. The growth of opposition is classic conflict theory in its individualism. Opposition comes from the city where Teresa finds herself discomfited at St Thomas's from the pulpit where the preacher inveighed against 'nuns who left their convents to go and found new orders'. Her sister Juana was refused absolution unless she would give up the idea and she also asked Teresa to do so. She wrote, 'I was now very unpopular throughout my convent

for wanting to found a convent more strictly enclosed. The nuns said that I was insulting them; that there were others who were better than myself, and so I could serve God quite well where I was.'[4] The City Fathers, not wanting another convent, prevailed on the Carmelite Provincial, Angel de Salazar, who opposed the project in view of public hostility.

5. At this point, early in 1562, Teresa was called to a royal house in Toledo to a depressive noblewoman Doña Luisa de la Cerada. She accepted to go as she accepted to return, expecting, reluctantly, as needs required, to become Superior at the Convent of the Incarnation. The project appeared stillborn. Yet it was still gestating, with greater clarity, austerity and uncompromisingness, after Teresa learned that the ancient rule enjoined such poverty as precluded communal possessions – endowments. Henceforth she thought of St Joseph's living on alms *sin renta* in genuine detachment from the world and dependence on God.

6. Much opposition to this new 'extremism' now came from supporters who, she wrote:

> put before me so many contrary arguments that I did not know what to do; for, now that I had learned the nature of the Rule and realized that its way was that of greater perfection, I could not persuade myself to allow the house to have any revenue. True, they sometimes convinced me; but, when I betook myself to prayer again and looked at Christ hanging so poor and naked upon the cross, I felt I could not bear to be rich. So I besought Him with tears to bring it about that I might become as poor as He.[5]

She now had to try to win over her supporters to this more radical vision.

7. Arriving back in Avila, the key players in the narrative were now assembled. Permission was received from Rome authorising the foundation of St Joseph's in the name of two widows (thus outflanking the hostile Carmelite Provincial, Salazar) and placing the convent of St Joseph under the Bishop of Avila, Don Alvaro de Mendoza. The city walls were breached when he was persuaded (very reluctantly) by Teresa to accept a foundation *sin renta* in the knowledge of the public outcry which would ensue at the idea of supporting a new foundation. On August 24th 1562, the first convent of the reformed or discalced Carmelites opened and the first mass was said for its seven sisters.

The story does not end here. So far, it has been told in standard individualist terms – the 'ultimate constituents' have been individuals, the explanatory variables, their dispositions – and the outcome: the result of the conflictual interplay of named 'other people'. In other words, the social context has been presented in reductionist form, a non-reified context describable through the strategy of 'personalisation', involving things like persuasion, information, reluctance and reflection. Yet is this a truly individualist account? For the players have played from roles (monk, Provincial, nuncio, noblewoman, Bishop) and many of the constraints and enablements they wielded rested in the role, not the incumbent; in the institutions, not the individuals; in vested collective interests, not individualistic dispositions; in structured locations of power, not personal powers. Without these social forms the players would not have held the cards they did, nor been able to play in this drama at all.

Let us continue the story, but transform the telling to a collectivist mode. This entails being able to account for the facts of the opposition of the city and why it was intensified. How can we explain it and answer the question Teresa asks in her autobiography 'how everyone thought that twelve women and a prioress (for I must remind those who opposed the plan that there were to be no more) could do such harm to the place when they were living so strictly? If there had been any error in their project it would have concerned themselves alone; harm to the city there could not possibly be, yet our opponents found so much.'[6]

The collectivist would respond, taking up its form of the story.

1. Late-sixteenth-century Spain had a total population of something like less than 8 million. By the end of the century the number of monks alone is estimated at 400,000. Although female religious were less numerous, it was probable that 1 in 12 of the people fell outside the economically active population by reason of vocation; they withdrew family capital in the form of dowries when professed, or required municipal support as members of charitable foundations. The charge on the cities and on society increased with the falling value of money, due to the influx of American gold. This meant the devaluation of their endowments whose inadequacy then threw them back on the city in order to be supplemented by alms or subsidies. And the number of convents continued to grow. At the beginning of the sixteenth century, Avila had four convents; 50 years later there were at least six more and the proposal for Theresa's project. The same battle raged all over Spain as economic decline and the expansion of religious foundations coincided. For example, the same struggle over a new discalced Carmelite House was played out in Madrid several years after Teresa's death (1582). In other words, this is all just part of a pattern produced by the play of socio-economic forces.

2. The Bishop of Avila bowed to the Papal bull which instructed that no authorities, either ecclesiastical or lay, should attempt to hinder the foundation of St Joseph's. Opponents in the Church may have been silenced by the power of Rome, but the city was not – society repudiated the project. Penniless nuns begging beneath city walls, from a surreptitiously planned and then coercively imposed convent, were a slight to the authority of the Corregidor, the *notables*, and the City Fathers. Tradesmen closed their shops to demonstrate and the Inspectorate of Fountains announced that the

convent buildings would interfere with the city's water supply. The City council met in emergency session and some hammered on the doors of St Joseph's, which the nuns then reinforced. The City of Knights pitted itself against the clutch of nuns just outside their city walls.

3. The Bishop sent a representative who read the townsmen the papal bull, insisting on the ecclesiastical and civil authority conferred on him. The militants on the City Council renewed their pressure. Unable to dissolve the convent directly, they referred their case to the Royal Council. Delegates were nominated and funds raised for a protracted lawsuit. Teresa's friends began to pool money (for Teresa had none) and to prepare counter-representations. When the Royal Council official arrived in November to take statements from the contending parties, a compromise was mooted between the City and the foundation. If the Convent was adequately endowed and thus less likely to be a burden on local resources, the City Fathers would tolerate it.

4. Teresa bowed to these powers, accepting that she must yield on the question of endowment. A compromise was worked out for signature, when Teresa suddenly asserted her unwillingness. At prayer she had reflected that once endowed they would be forever constrained to forgo poverty. To silence her opponents, a petition was dispatched to Rome asking specifically for the convent to be allowed to continue *sin renta*. The swift and unusual December papal ruling granted the nuns of St Joseph's the privilege 'to possess no goods, either individually or collectively, but to maintain themselves freely from the alms and charitable assistance which pious Christians may offer and bestow'.

5. The law suit and the Royal Council remained unsettled. Rumblings and menacing continued to drift over the ramparts of the City of Knights. In June 1563, according to records, the case still dragged on. As litigation costs outweighed charitable donations, passions cooled slowly. Avila had finally accepted the small convent.

Why? On this *collectivist* account, because of the two collective entities involved, the Church had overpowered the city and the crown had insufficient interest to act as other than umpire. In this account, we have collective agents alone, whose *positions prises* are determined by their vested interests, and the outcomes of their confrontations are determined by the relative distributions of power and resources. Issues begin when vested interests are invoked and end when continued confrontation literally costs too much. The figure of Teresa is pretextural; the same struggles between city and Church were being played out all over Spain. The reasons for this lay outside Spanish social structure altogether: in the new world's economic devaluation of the old world and in the Eternal City's ecclesiastical hegemony over the cities of western Christendom. In all of these contending social forces, Teresa becomes a tiny spot of local Avilian colour.

Is this social determinist account sufficient? Teresa and the rest of the cast are reduced to *träger*. Are they the marionettes playing out events and never the makers of history, even under times and circumstances not of their choosing? Of the many difficulties of this position, the prime one which this story highlights is the unworkability of the 'passive agent' which collectivism presents. Teresa was not an agent of some reified, homogeneous Church, not a sleeping agent, not an unconsciously prescient pawn of it – she was as much of a nuisance within it as outside it. Her ideas (using Weber's 'switchmen' simile) nudged parts of the Church on to a different line, accentuating the Church's ideal interests over its material ones and actualising the contradiction between Church and city in the country where the possibility of their collaboration has seemed more convincing than anywhere – the country which itself had been welded into a nation state by *los reyes catolicos*.

Yet if we grant that Teresa had some influence on the course of events, through her ideas, then we must take her and them seriously, just as seriously as the time and the circumstances *not* of her choosing. And if we take *both* seriously, then we have to reject reductionism of any kind – of the individualistic version which would make Teresa the mistress of her circumstances, and that of the collectivist version which reduces her to an expression of her times.

If we do take her and her ideas seriously, then we have to ask whether we are dealing only with social reality (in its natural, geographical context). Both forms of reductionism assume we are, for they exclude transcendental reality by always reducing it to social terms, to such things as Teresa's ideas whose referents are properly to transcendence. Thus in individualism, beliefs become merely what believers believe (they are bundled into the individual as personal knowledge). Teresa's claim to have a contemplative relationship with divinity (which is an ontological claim) is *automatically* reduced to 'Teresa's claim'. This is a full-blooded version of the 'epistemic fallacy'[7] which transmutes reality into knowledge. Individualism logically has to commit it, for if the individual is the 'ultimate constituent' of social reality then such reality is necessarily anthropocentric – and obviously excludes the transcendental. Anthropocentricism precludes divine intervention into the human world by theoretical fiat. Without warrant, it dismisses self-subsistent transcendental reality by illicitly making the human individual 'ultimate', and therefore the ultimate source of the beliefs he or she holds.

In parallel, collectivism, which maintains that the ultimate constituents of social life reside in properties of society, has to find society's reasons for the appearance of beliefs like Teresa's. It does so in typical Durkheimian fashion by denying the content and referent of Teresa's beliefs and pointing instead to their social functions. In this case she becomes the mouthpiece of religious institutions. Again this is by theoretical fiat: Durkheim had set out 'to discover the causes leading to the rise of the religious sentiment in humanity' sociologically, thus prejudging the whole issue and prefiguring his own conclusion, namely that if religion 'is at once the symbol of the god and of the society, is that not because the god and the society are only one?'[8] They can of course only be one if the transcendental reality is ruled out of existence and the believers are deemed, by the sociologist, to be mistaken in the true referent of their beliefs.

Hence in *individualism*, listening to Teresa's ideas becomes reduced to 'learning more about Teresa'. In *collectivism*, listening to Teresa's ideas becomes reduced to 'learning more about her society'. What they are ruling out in their anthropocentrism and socio-centrism respectively, is that her ideas *can* be taken seriously.

The light the Enlightenment tried to extinguish

The difficulty with taking Teresa seriously is that this has generally been taken as a matter of taking her *beliefs* seriously, of assessing what evidence is there to support them. But evidential talk is grounded in the explanatory model of modernity's science – a model of matter-in-motion. To Buckley this entailed the disastrous move of substituting impersonal scientific evidence in place of a personal God.[9] Instead of being the result of religious experience, religion became the product of a process of inference, the result of a series of arguments about evidence from the physical world. Trigg has argued that 'the more the material world was seen to operate in its own right, according to its own laws, the easier it was to dispense with God altogether'.[10] To Buckley, what had begun as a search for independent evidence of God became a materialist concentration on the workings of the physical world in their own right. Religion had put itself into the hands of Enlightenment philosophy and then 'philosophy spoke, and its final word was no'.[11]

So let us try a different tack based upon reversing the modernist view of both humanity (like Teresa) and of God. In other words, we *humans* are unlike matter: we have sensibilities which matter does not. Our human *experience* is not that of objects for which external evidence is forthcoming, but turns on the difference that what we do depends on a 'largely inarticulate sense of what is of decisive importance' to us as human beings.[12] Nor is God merely a mover of matter, a physicalist 'first cause' (namely that to which mechanics relegates Him). He is not a depersonalised object but an immanent subject, i.e: His ontological transcendence need not imply absolute unattainable otherness or the indifference of a first cause which had put creation in motion.

The Enlightenment gave a *logocentric* view of human beings. Since truth was defined in terms of formal logical deductions performed on symbolic systems this model was incompatible with explaining morality, which is not fully propositional. Often moral action depends on us having the capacity to have experiences which are not enjoyed by all life forms, let alone machines like digital computers, designed to work inferentially. In the moral domain these are capacities of moral sensibility, for only those with appropriate emotional make-up will understand 'kindness': computers may simulate compassionate behaviour but cannot feel compassion.

Thus the formal model of rationality forces a distinction between *logos* and *pathos*, between our rationality and our sensibility. As the two became pushed apart, it installed the 'head' and 'heart' dualism. On the logocentric model we have emotions and desires: reason acts as the slave of these passions, telling us instrumentally how best to maximise their satisfaction, but is not able to evaluate the ends sought themselves; so there is for us no moral knowledge, no *vertrationalitat*. Therefore we have no moral careers, only emotional responses to aspects of the world: this is Hume's 'emotivism' where morals become a function of taste alone – and *de gustibus non est disputandum*.

So on this model Teresa is just wired up, so that she wants to found a convent because of her religious emotions. All we can do is to look at *how* she went about it, whilst others, differently wired, tried to stop her. This is the *metaphysical* individualism of modernity which lay behind the *methodological* individualistic account given in the first part of this chapter. But we can neither ask nor evaluate *why* she desired it. So the response to Bernini is banal – she is just that way emotionally inclined. Yet, unlike an object, she wants to tell us – she wants to justify herself by giving reasons to her confessors, which is why she wrote her *Life*. On Hume's model it could have gone on a Lutheran's postcard: 'I desired, I could do no other: this was how I worked to achieve my desire.'

The only other explanatory model available was Kant's stern 'Voice of Duty', which is a 'head' versus 'heart' model and depends on 'free will' informing us of our duty which we then must seek to universalise. What this cannot do is explain the will's choice, and why it can move us against our inclinations. But this does not help with Teresa, who is not moved by duty and is in the awkward position of knowing how she thinks she ought to act, but not whether it is her duty to act in this way.[13]

Let us see if we fare any better if we cut through this distinction between reason and the emotions. We will start by accepting that unless we were already cognitive or affective beings, then no amount of knowledge could move us to anything. St Augustine makes this assumption when talking about the incompatibility between apathy and morality: 'if *apetheia* is the name of the state in which the mind cannot be touched by any emotion whatsoever, who would not judge this insensitivity to be the worst of moral defects'.[14] So let us grant that emotions are the basis of our being moved, but now qualify this such that the passions are not blind urges, but involve (*contra* Hume) information and cognition. Now reason has been made implicit in *all* emotions: it has the cognitive task of informing us about how things are in themselves (not how we subjectively take them to be). For example, every-day virtues like 'consideration' or 'generosity' take a lot of cognitive skill (it is not enough for a gift to be the one we would like to receive!).

This means that feelings are not just felt, they relate to the nature of their object, and what makes an emotion appropriate or inappropriate is nothing self-referential but the nature of the emotion's object. Hence the appropriate response to goodness is love, but love of the object itself and not because of its value to us – which makes the moral glory of humanity the fact that we need not be anthropocentric. Love certainly moves one to action and it does so in the sense that the loved object is a moral end in itself. This cuts through the modernist idea that existing beings cannot be moral ends because ends must be abstract entities like propositions, desirable states of affairs, facts or events. It means that the quality in question, here goodness, must inhere in the object, but – and this is the cognitive element – we may of course be wrong.[15] We are fallible and could behave *as if* the object had intrinsic value. This is our problem: many of the faithless would say Teresa was loving and acting as if God existed, that she was wrong and she cannot be proved right by advancing a proof for the existence of God! Are we stuck at this point? The reply is 'No', though it will take two more stages of argument to spell it out.

In concluding with our re-drawn moral agents who are not modernist rational calculators, let us see where this now leaves the reconceptualised Teresa:

1. She is in love.
2. Her emotion is linked to her reason for loving: she loves that most worthy to be loved.
3. She cannot be wrong that the greatest love is due to supreme goodness.
4. When we love we cannot be mistaken about that, though we can love unwisely.
5. She tells us at length about her personal relationship with God, the supreme good.

We will need all of this, but let us work on the last item, her claim for a personal relationship to God.[16] This is the point where we have to take Him out of the grip of the Enlightenment because you cannot love a 'first cause' or relate to a depersonalised causal mechanism. We also have to move beyond natural theology, which again may create a space for the notion of a creator, but it is an empty space containing a being who may be quite indifferent to human beings. If we ask instead how can God bridge the gap between the infinite (His ontological transcendence) and the finite (His creatures), we are dealing anew with a God who acts and can reveal Himself. Ontological transcendence need not imply absolute otherness, since God can actively make Himself known in ways that can be grasped by us. Now if He is granted this power, on the omnipotence argument, then His revelation is a fact about Him and not a feature of our judgement which is a fact about us. This will be granted logically by the faithless who reserve their doubts for His existence in the first place.

The first step of the argument works on the notion of self-revelation through a suggestion of Feuerbach's which he never took seriously since God was, he concluded, an alienated projection of human wants (in yet another anthropocentric theory). The insight is that God is constrained by the nature of his creation because, to Feuerbach, 'in the scheme of his revelation God must have reference not to himself but to man's power of comprehension'.[17] He is constrained if He wishes to communicate Himself because 'my ways are not your ways and my thoughts are not your thoughts'. Now I want to borrow left-handedly from one of our more anthropocentric philosophers, David Wiggins, who regards the idea of non-human persons or communication with them as impossible – here he has in mind Martians and automata, but God fits his category too. We cannot 'make sense of non-human creatures, become attuned to them, or be in a position to treat their feelings as if they were our own'.[18] He goes on to argue that faced with an automaton or Martian we cannot have the expectations which enable us to interpret them, given their inscrutable sources of satisfaction, *unless*, and this is crucial, these creatures were synthesised by carbon-copying the contingencies of our human frame and constitution. That is, we could not understand them and they could not communicate with us, unless by accident or design they conformed to human form and human consciousness.

If we now consider the non-human creature God, desirous of communicating with us, then we come to what I term the *necessity* of the incarnation. Only by 'laying His godhead by' could we understand what divinity was like if it came to us in human form. Because of our human limitations, God's *logos* come to us as *pathos* – in the word made flesh living amongst us. Hence the essential role of Athanasian teaching that Christ was simultaneously fully divine and fully human – the joint conditions of a full revelation of divinity which was fully communicable to humanity. On those conditions Wiggins is right to wonder 'how far the process [of communication] can go'. Teresa is trying to tell her contemporaries, and us, that it is a lot further than has been imagined. Now our faithless modernist will presumably respond that my case and Teresa's is now twice as bad: if they cannot accept a 'first cause' they certainly will not swallow the notion of an incarnate God.

'Anyone who lives in love lives in God' (1 John 4:16)

Here faithless modernists have a moral problem themselves: they will not accept the incarnate Christ, but they cannot deny the historical Jesus.

Indeed people today very readily perform this division when they say 'well, I'm not religious but I do subscribe to His moral code' or 'He was an example of a very good man'. This is household Arianism. Of course such was not Teresa's response: her imitation was of incarnate love. But this is the difficulty for the faithless. She is in love, and they cannot hold her mistaken about her own feelings, but she is in love with the *same person* whose moral qualities they have just deemed worthy of love because of his goodness. They *can* understand her for (a) they understand loving supreme or at least very great goodness and (b) they often themselves love persons they have never met (celebrities), even to the point (c) of fantasising meetings and conversations with them. Teresa is not an enigma to them, but is she simply a fantasist like them? For we admitted that the cognitive basis of our emotions was humanly fallible and therefore corrigible. Here is the big difficulty for the faithful; it seems we have got as far as we can get in gaining assent that she is genuinely in love with a supremely good but dead man, Jesus. We are not going to persuade any of the faithless that she is in loving communication with the Risen Lord, as she asserts.

Yet having conceded this much, how is it then possible to attempt to authenticate her contemplative experiences? What could give authenticity to her claim (a truth claim) that she loves living love, since God is love and she lives close to Him personally? Here the authentication comes from the fundamental notion that 'to live in love is to live in God'. We cannot make anyone assent to her 'living with God' but we can warrant the assertion that someone is living a life of love.

Now the next stage is to build upon the notion of 'loving' itself, by making use of the reconceptualisation of ourselves as creatures of sensibility. We are not logocentric jugglers of symbolic strings, for our moral lives cannot be framed sententially. They are not a matter of pure reason adopting a series of moral propositions – a detachable moral code of 'do's and don't's' which define moral living as *acts* (of commission or omission). Secondly, those sensibilities which give us our orientation to the good are not optional extras because our valuational judgements (the things we care deeply about) are central to *who* we are and to *how* we see our place in the world.[19] Putting the two points together, the moral career which partly defines who we are, yet which cannot be captured sententially, can be termed 'living in love'.

Following on, this can now be linked to the notion of God as immanent in the world in a form which is cognisant of our human limitations. Here it has been argued that the life of Jesus (as way, truth and life) provides the objective conception of what it would be like for our moral judgements to be true, one which is independent of whether we judged matters so or not. The importance of God's *logos* as *pathos* is twofold. On the one hand, when we recommend a life, as it was lived, we accept that the world has not only physical properties but also valuational ones. The life of incarnate love supplied the role-model for 'living in love'. On the other hand, as a moral pattern, the life of the historic Jesus is morally intelligible and often acceptable to the faithless, even though they do not see this as imitating the Son of God. We are not forced to accept one source of morality for the unbeliever and another for the believer, because the two will frequently refer to the same source themselves under different descriptions – but this is the only way in which we can know anything at all.

Finally let us look at this new model of moral being, which has been differentiated from symbolic manipulation, to see how different it is from propositional morality and how it comes with a public standard for authentication. Apparently the majority of Americans believe that the 'golden rule' epitomises Jesus' ethical teaching, namely 'do unto others as you would have them do unto you'. Now this is morally active because it involves seeking the good of others. Nevertheless, it is hardly the highest standard in ethics since (i) our desires themselves may not be morally commendable, (ii) it is quite compatible with self-fulfilment on our own terms, and (iii) it can become merely an ethic of conventional reciprocity designed, like Utilitarianism, to bring about the smooth running of everyday life. It does not call us to any kind of extraordinary goodness. All the same, it is more demanding than the earlier 'silver rule', which can be formulated as 'that which you would not want others to do to you, do not do unto them'. This is more morally passive for it largely places negative constraints on our behaviour, but this very refraining from harming others could be based on purely prudential grounds of self-interest. Although there is no positive admonition to virtue here, the silver standard is still higher than the 'tinsel rule', 'treat others as they deserve', which requires that they have to earn moral treatment, they have to gain respect, and even win their place in the 'kingdom of ends'.

The three rules are a hierarchical structure of increasingly demanding propositions, but simultaneously they disclose the limitations of that which can be expressed sententially. What they miss is the 'platinum standard', the radical demand of one life on others, summed up in Jesus' new commandment to 'love one another as I have loved you'. This is a call beyond convention into supererogation; a call to perfection in a love which includes enemies as well as friends. As such, it is a call to model ourselves on love which cannot be interpreted in terms of mere procedural ethics, as with the other three rules. What has to be emulated is a life in its fullness, and the urge to do so engages all our personal sensibilities in a moral vision of 'discipleship', something defying codification into stateable rules because it has outdistanced banal procedural horizons and has resisted routinisation into the rule-governed.[20]

What does the moral praxis of 'living in love' look like? This notion of 'discipleship' treats moral knowledge as practical wisdom and falls between Ryle's 'knowing now' (as in swimming) and 'knowing that' (which is propositional). 'Living in love' is much more akin to playing music by ear, involving an immersion in the whole musical enterprise, an engagement with its traditions, repertoires and maestros, most of which is not mediated by ratiocination – hence little of which can be distilled into propositions. Indeed, this is where the words run out. All lovers of music, as of wine, communicate at best by metaphors; and talk of 'attacking notes' or of a 'flinty taste' are metaphors which cannot be cashed in.[21] Jesus, the personification of love, spoke in parables, not to clarify but in order to approximate to the articulate. 'Discipleship', then, is in part imitation, in part swimming in the stream of its traditions and exemplars, but it is also developing a reflective self-adjustment, the capacity to make one's own judgements of the appropriateness of actions in new unscripted contexts. This 'living in love' has nothing to do with juggling sentences, but much more to do with acquiring a 'feel' because it is feelings themselves which are moved.[22]

The core skills are nothing mysterious since the historical knowledge on which they are based is found in the canon, whose own constitution Frances Young has interestingly compared with musical composition.[23] Acquiring the basic repertoire entails personal immersion in this thick tradition comprising the core canon and subsequent commentaries which include the lives of proficients themselves. (During Ignatius' recovery, as a young soldier wounded at Pamplona, his moral career might have continued as that of a troubadour if the supply of romances had not run dry. This left him alone with a book of saints which transformed his courtship into discipleship.) The saints are the master musicians in this training and canonisation can be seen as convergent judgements that such lives were indeed conformed to the 'platinum standard'. This living tradition represents the useful element from the collectivist account, for we are indeed inducted into a corpus of knowledge, techniques and practices which are never of our own making since they pre-date us and yet have causal efficacy upon us. No one invents the entire Christian cultural conspectus *de nova*: their Christian lives begin as apprenticeship. (Probably in this delicate task of moral education the reason why some do not develop a moral career is their frail acquaintance with the collective tradition and a lack of contact with sufficient of its living journeymen.)

Simultaneously, the core skills themselves evolve, for there is nothing purely mimetic in discipleship. Proficient lovers increasingly develop their faculty of judgement, including a critical appraisal of their own discipleship, out of which they elaborate novel strategies for living in love in new times and circumstances, where no code of established practice is available. Like musicians with a good 'feel', they improvise creatively on the theme laid down and collaborate together in this evolving improvisation. They acknowledge personal responsibility for creating something novel out of their inheritance in response to new eventualities in the present. They respond to what went before and themselves lay down some of the parameters of what will come next, for tradition itself is elaborative over time.

Thus Teresa produced her *Interior Castle*, St John of the Cross, the works beginning with the *Ascent of Mount Carmel*, as St Ignatius had, slightly earlier, his *Spiritual Exercises*. These innovative texts of discipleship represent the kernel truth of individualism: we are active agents not passive marionettes and the opposition incited from others is correctly seen by individualists as the tension through which tradition evolves. But what is being elaborated are not additions to a sentential code, but new words for describing the essentially wordless practical experience of 'living in love', which represents an educated capacity to improvise on life and not merely to mimic the past.

The 'feel' and the 'ear' involved in this give content to the idea of our immanence in the world, by which the world itself can impose a sense of things to be done or said. It always remains the case that love is known by its fruits and that how to be faithful is a response to the exigencies of the here and now. This forms the ultimate authentication of contemplative experience which is open to inspection by the faithful and the faithless alike, for both can pronounce on the outworkings of 'living in love'. The figures on Bernini's balcony now find Teresa's life intelligible, accessible and even subject to their secular and ecclesiastical evaluations alike. We seem to have come a long way from the beginning.

What the faithless will still deny is her deep adherence to the Master Conductor, to the source of the inner music she hears. Yet secular social theory can live with this and work despite it. Max Weber declared that he was himself 'religiously unmusical', but he did not deny that there was music to be heard, although all he could see were dancers moving to a silent orchestra. He did follow those moving harmoniously through the globe's ballrooms and he had much to say about the pattern of the dance as a way of being in the world. In this he acknowledged the limitations of secular social theory and its inability to grasp or to explain away, but also endorsed its need to incorporate that which social theory could not explain and should not reinterpret in secular terms – the recognition of transcendence on the part of its subjects. From his place in the balcony, did Weber not look on with a certain wistfulness?

Notes and references

* This chapter was produced under the aegis of an ESRC Research fellowship, for which I am most grateful.

1 For the key articles summarising the debate between Methodological Individualists and Collectivists, see John O'Neill (ed.), *Modes of Individualism and Collectivism* (London: Heinemann, 1973). For my own commentary upon this debate, see

Margaret S. Archer, *Realist Social Theory: The Morphogenetic Approach* (Cambridge: Cambridge University Press, 1995), chapter 2, pp. 33–64.

2 Biographies, bibliographical commentaries and historical background on St Teresa include: E. Allison Peers, *Handbook to the Life and Times of St Teresa and St John of the Cross* (London: Sheed & Ward, 1954); Efrén de la Madre de Dios and Otgar Steggink, *Tiempo y vida de Santa Teresa* (Madrid: Biblioteca De Autores Cristianos, La Editorial Catolica, 1968); Alberto Barrientos (ed.), *Introducción a la lectura de Santa Teresa* (Madrid: Editorial de Espiritualidad 1978); Stephen Clissold, *St Teresa of Avila* (London: Sheldon Press, 1979); Noel D. O'Donoghue, *Mystics for our Time* (Edinburgh: T. & T. Clark, 1989); Rowan Williams, *Teresa of Avila* (London: Geoffrey Chapman, 1991).

3 All quotations for St Teresa's *Life* are taken from E. Allison Peers (ed.), *The Complete Works of Saint Teresa of Jesus*, vol. 1 (London: Sheed & Ward, 1982), p. 219.

4 Ibid., p. 224.

5 Ibid., p. 243.

6 Ibid., p. 256.

7 See Roy Bhaskar, *Reclaiming Reality* (London: Verso, 1989).

8 Emile Durkheim, *The Elementary Forms of the Religious Life* (London: George Allen & Unwin, 1964), p. 206.

9 Michael Buckley, *At the Origins of Modern Atheism* (New Haven: Yale University Press, 1987).

10 Roger Trigg, *Rationality and Religion* (Oxford: Blackwell, 1998), p. 179.

11 Buckley, *At the Origins of Modern Atheism*, p. 357.

12 Charles Taylor, *Human Agency and Language, Philosophical Papers 1* (Cambridge: Cambridge University Press, 1985), p. 38.

13 For a summary of the long-running Hume–Kant debate, see Bernard Williams, 'Internal and External Reasons', in his *Moral Luck* (Cambridge University Press, 1981), pp. 101–13, for the neo-Humean position; and Thomas Nagel, *The Possibility of Altruism* (Oxford: Oxford University Press, 1970), on the neo-Kantian side. The debate is economically summarised by Martin Hollis in chapter 6 of *The Cunning of Reason* (Cambridge: Cambridge University Press, 1987), pp. 74–96.

14 St Augustine, *City of God*, trans. Henry Bettenson (Harmondsworth: Penguin, 1972), pp. 564–5.

15 I owe this bold statement of realist ethics to Andrew Collier, *Being and Worth* (London: Routledge, 1999). See especially pp. 52–62.

16 For a consideration of doxastic experiences, see William Alston, *Perceiving God* (Ithaca, New York: Cornell University Press, 1991).

17 Ludwig Feuerbach, *The Essence of Christianity*, trans. George Eliot (Buffalo: Prometheus Books, 1989), p. 207.

18 David Wiggins, 'The Person as Object of Science, as Subject of Experience and as Locus of Value', in Arthur Peacocke and Grant Gillett (eds), *Person and Personality* (Oxford: Blackwell, 1987), p. 71.

19 See Harry G. Frankfurt, *The Importance of What We Care About* (Cambridge: Cambridge University Press, 1988), p. 91. He notes 'especially with respect to those we love and with respect to our ideals, we are liable to be bound by necessities which have less to do with our adherence to the principles of morality than with integrity or consistency of a more personal kind. These necessities constrain us from betraying the things we care about most and with which, accordingly, we are most closely identified. In a sense which a strictly ethical analysis cannot

make clear, what they keep us from violating are not our duties or our obligations but ourselves' (p. 91).

20   The thinking in the last two pages owes much to Douglas V. Porpora, *Landscapes of the Soul* (forthcoming).

21   Janet M. Soskice, *Metaphor and Religious Language* (Oxford: Oxford University Press, 1985); and David Tracey, *The Analogical Imagination: Christian Theology and the Culture of Pluralism* (New York: Crossroad, 1981).

22   Again a debt must be acknowledged, despite our disagreements, to Michael Luntley, *Reason, Truth and Self* (London: Routledge, 1995).

23   Frances Young, *The Art of Performance* (London: Darton, Longman & Todd, 1990).

8
Virtue Ethics and Celibacy:
A Hindu Perspective

Rohit Barot

This chapter focuses on virtue ethics by selecting the Hindu concept of *dharma* and relating it to celibacy as a value that deserves attention. Colonial and post-colonial modernity introduced science and secular thought in India and made an impact on Indian belief systems that began to refashion Indian ideas in a modern context. Indians like Raja Rammohan Roy, Swami Vivekanand and Sri Aurobindo revitalised the tradition of spiritual and philosophical inquiry and, as it were, brought Hindu thinking into a modern framework. The material for this chapter stems from Hindu roots but also the issue of identity and culture when these are planted in alien European surroundings. This relates to a theme which Sarup has explored, of the distinctive problem of securing an identity as a migrant within the culture of confusion embodied in the notion of postmodernity.[1] In this context, it is suggested that Hindu understandings of virtue, celibacy in this case, supply an important, and perhaps neglected, comparative dimension to debate on virtue ethics, which is very much seen as a Christian preserve. The issue of virtue relates to religion, but has some distinctive implications when examined in relation to the Hindu tradition.

In their respective analysis of social life, both Weber[2] and Durkheim[3] examine the part that religion plays in the regulation of human behaviour. Just as Durkheim focuses on religion as a critical factor in the creation of social solidarity and group cohesion, Weber also asserts that 'the most elementary forms of behaviour motivated by religious or magical factors are oriented to *this* world'.[4] It is in reference to this tradition of inquiry into the relationship between religion and society that this chapter examines the concepts of ethics and virtue in contemporary Hindu social life. It concentrates on the basic categories of Hindu life which provide an ethical framework most Hindus are likely to find acceptable. The perspective deployed here focuses on the meaning of their ethical framework without reducing it to any 'objective' basis for social existence. There is a sense in which this framework transcends individuals and groups but here their own subjective understanding is the focus of this inquiry and its explanation.[5] The argument does not assume a Hindu view point as if it was a singularly unilinear influence. In South Asia, traditions have evolved and intertwined over centuries to create various interfaces and fusions of ideas and action. More than 'purity' of a given tradition, the most relevant question for belief is the complexity that underpins various paradigms of order.

First, it is useful to distinguish ethics and virtue and to take ethics as a basis for virtue, as existing in a methodological sense and as persisting as a moral imperative. It is the distinction between the two in the English language that can provide a general guidance to the extent to which similar distinctions can be made in the Hindu context for a comparative perspective on virtue, even if this comparison is limited to differences between linguistic usages. After a brief examination of the distinction between ethics and virtue and what each of these terms mean the chapter can proceed to analyse categories of Hindu thinking which provide the best possible approximation to ideas of ethics and virtue.

When scholars refer to ethics as a category, they may at least refer to two mutually exclusive domains. First of all they may use ethics to highlight the principles of morality to which human beings should comply voluntarily for commonly acceptable standards of behaviour. Such a prescription implies *ipso facto* that humans should refrain on moral grounds from wrongdoing or vice,[6] thus giving us a generally acceptable distinction between virtue and vice. This definition provides a starting point for this chapter. Should ethics refer to a broad moral foundation for social order, then virtue must refer to a whole range of particular moral prescriptions which regulate human behaviour according to both acceptable and unacceptable ethical presuppositions.

Dharma and *adharma* as the basis of Hindu ethical thought

In outlining the significance of *dharma*, this chapter uses the relationship between text and context for two related aims. Some of the Hindu material provides ideas and information grounded in notable texts such as *Vedas*, *Upanishads* and *Bhagavada Gita* – although these are not the only textual sources which inspire virtue and ethics. Hindu religious tradition consists of a plurality of movements which have created a wide range of writing including books of rules[7] which specify acceptable and unacceptable parameters of human behaviour. It may be argued that this plurality of sources touches on some of the underlying ideas and ideals which Hindus believe mark their life. Whatever unity may exist in different movements and organisations, a wide variety of texts and interpretations remains a distinctive feature of Hindu thinking as it has evolved in the modern period. Besides the question of this textual variety, there is the question of the relationship between the values the texts expound and the social implications of these values in everyday life. Everyday living depends on general

and common sense consensual understanding of virtue and ethics in interpersonal encounters.

There is a whole domain of the degree to which these textual bodies
underpin various institutions and resurgences of certain features of Hindu
thinking, for instance, in the recent deployment of ideas about Hinduness
(*hindutva*) in what has come to be known as the politics of Hindu nationalism. This topic falls outside the remit of this chapter. The model of Hindu
virtue and ethics constructed here derives from everyday observation of life
of the Hindus in India and diasporic Indian communities which the author
has studied in various fieldwork contexts.

In responding to Orientalist criticism that Hinduism lacked ethical
content, Sri Aurbindo argued that, if anything, Hindu thought could be
'accused of a tyrannously pervading ethical obsession' as expressed through
the concept of *dharma*.[8] The twin conceptions of *dharma* and its opposite
adharma form the core of Hindu ethical ideas. Therefore it is worth explaining what these distinctions mean and the way in which they underpin the
fabric of Hindu religious ideas and their regulation.

Bearing this complexity in mind, this chapter focuses on the concept of
sanatan dharma translated as universal religion. In his analysis of self-understanding of traditional Hinduism, Halbfass has drawn attention to the fact
that the concept of *dharma* is difficult to define.[9] For other commentators, it
has to be understood as 'a problem rather than a concept, vague, indeterm-
inable, impossible to define without broadening into useless generality or
narrowing it to exclude valid instances'.[10]

Dharma derives from the Sanskrit root *dhr* which means to 'sustain, support and uphold'.[11] As a concept, it encompasses both nature and culture.[12]
It is a conception that refers to the eternal (*sanatan*), a notion of regularity
and harmony that enables Hindus to conceptualise this order as everlasting
sanatan dharma. Gods and goddesses regulate the movement of day and
night and seasons and the entire cosmology including the conduct of
humans. Order and regularity in human affairs generally refer to that which
is customary and as proper, and as Weber had noted in his study of Hinduism, '*Dharma* depends first on sacred tradition', a system of norms developing
over a period of time.[13] Halbfass quotes Gonda's clear formulation on
dharma as follows:

> originally referring to the principle of universal stability, the power
> which sustains, upholds, and maintains the firmly established order, this
> term . . . in general means the lawfulness and regularity, the harmony, the
> fundamental equilibrium, the norm which reigns in the cosmos, nature,
> society and individual existence.[14]

Dharma refers to a notion of duty, responsibility and moral obligation. As
Lipner has noted, 'this is why the word has been variously translated as

"law", "virtue", "merit", "propriety", "morality", "religion", etc.'[15] It signifies what is right, virtuous, meritorious, ethical and socially and culturally
acceptable. Thus, the concept of *sanatan dharma* binds every living creature
to the essence of divinity and offers meaning to an ephemeral human existence bounded by life and death.

Any action that is against *dharma* is *adharma* and is thus inconsistent with
generally acceptable standards of moral norms. The polarity of *dharma* and
adharma[16] is closer in meaning to the distinction between the ethical and
the unethical than between virtue and vice, which has more definite
and specified requirements of prescribed and proscribed behaviour. At first
sight *dharma* may appear to be a dominant functional ideology constructed
to demand compliance and regulation. Far from being a simple set of beliefs
to foster solidarity, narratives on *dharma* demonstrate that it is a *contested*
category. The question of what constitutes true *dharma*, in a particular set of
circumstances, can be a matter of difference of opinion and often a source
of conflict.

The phenomenology of *dharma* relates both to the Hindu aims of life as
well as to lifecycle stages. Besides *dharma*, three aims of Hindu life refer to
artha, wealth creation, *kama*, pleasure, and salvation, which the Hindus
identify by a Sanskrit word *moksha*. It is not uncommon to come across a
hierarchical arrangement of these aims. Which is the most superior aim is
not something that is entirely preordained, as the significance of each aim is
determined according to the socio-cultural context of its definition. The
idea of *varnashram dharma* requires humans to follow the calling of their
social position or *varna*. This concept divides traditional Hindu society into
a fourfold classification of priests, warriors, merchants and workers. There is
an excluded category of untouchables, now identified as Dalits in modern
India. Generally, it is birth which determines who belongs to which *varna*
but the idea of action and merit can also bear on it. Distinction between
birth and action through merit may remain contentious and may not be
fully resolved, as Gandhi's writing on *varna* demonstrates.[17]

Be that as it may, *varna* also related to traditional lifecycle stages according
to which a person passes through four well-known stages (*ashram*): of being
a celibate student, *brahmachari*, a householder, *grahasthi*, and then a forest
dweller, *vanprasthi*, who finally renounces all social ties in order to become a
sanyasin to transcend the material body and death to achieve salvation of
the highest order, *moksha*. *Dharma* and its opposite *adharma* provide a broad
ethical framework for a whole range of virtues of self-control and self-discip-
line which enables each human being to realise his or her potential fully
according to his or her position in the social order. Although it is possible to
argue that *varna* existed as a social system only in ancient India and that the
scheme *varnashram dharma* can no longer be considered relevant to modern
Indian communities, what is remarkable is the continuity of *varna* as an
idea for defining various lifecycle stages. It is not uncommon for Hindus to

refer to stages conceptually and to mark different degrees of engagement and disengagement in their social life.

At this point it is useful to introduce the Hindu concept of *karma*, action. Hindus expect a relationship between *dharma* and *karma*. They believe that in order to avoid action which may fall in the realm of *adharma*, there should be a parity between *dharma* and *karma*, although what forms a proper ethical relationship between *dharma* and *karma* requires a methodical approach that establishes clearly that a particular *karma* is at least broadly consistent with what is right, proper and morally acceptable. Although it is theoretically possible for Hindus to conceive an action that does not have any basis in *dharma*, the concept of *sanatan dharma*, the idea of universal regulation, presupposes a consistent and invariable relationship that must mark both the realm of nature as well as that of culture. Thus, Hindus are most likely to question the idea that the natural and social worlds do not necessarily contain certain fundamental and universal norms which provide order and meaning to human existence.

Having established a broad concept of universality of normative order in *sanatan dharma*, Hindus often proceed to use a set of adjectives to identify particular types of *dharma*. A multiplicity of words may qualify the opposites of *dharma* and *adharma*. In order to signify the fact that *dharma* is something integral to every human being, Hindus deploy the concept of *svadharma*, that is, one's own *dharma* which relates to an individual's own understanding of right and acceptable moral conduct. Distinct from *svadharma* is the conception of *manavdharma* which refers to ethical belief and ideas which should apply to all human beings irrespective of their social status. *Manavdharma*, or the concept that all human beings share ideas of right and proper conduct, provides a basis for order and regularity in a situation where institutional mechanisms to impose order may have broken down. Hindus often present the idea of *manavdharma* to argue that people will behave rightly and properly, even where formal agencies of social sanctions may not exist. Respondents may also use the expressions *sadharandharma* or *samanyadharma* according to which all human beings, irrespective of their social status, should observe standards of moral obligation.

In the context of recent developments of sociological theory, the expression normative order may invoke memories of Parsonian functionalism of the kind in which the concept of normative order emerged as a conservative ideology prescribing cohesion and integration of a social system rather than divisions and conflict which may also characterise a social order. Instead of implying that social orders are always held together by a consensual normative system, the deployment of *dharma* almost invariably points to difficulties inherent in establishing clearly and categorically what it is that constitutes the right *dharma* in a situation which requires a respondent to make a particular choice between different aims. Therefore the relationship between different levels of *dharma* is not necessarily always identical. Moral obligation, which applies at the level of *manavdharma*, may actually conflict with duties which an actor has to perform in particular historical situations. In such circumstances, what constitutes *dharma*-based action is not necessarily self-evident. It is something that has to be established by arguments and counter-arguments before a person can be reasonably certain of his moral obligation.

One of the best examples of the lack of identity between collective and personal levels of moral obligations is provided in a widely accepted Hindu text, *Bhagvada Gita*.[18] Set in a context of conflict between two sides of a patrilineage for the kingdom of Ayodhya, the first chapter of *Bhagavada Gita* focuses on the dilemma that Arjuna faces when he is expected to fight with his own kith and kin for succession and so confronts the 'to be or not to be' situation. This is articulated in his dialogue with his charioteer Krishna. It is one of the best-known examples that demonstrates conflict between Arjuna's *svadharma*, his personal duty which prescribes that it is ethically wrong to kill cousins, and the righteousness of the war for succession to Ayodhya. Irrespective of the question of whether this text refers to any real war or not, it clearly highlights that the question of moral duty can be highly problematic and the outcome of such obligation may be ethically appropriate but not necessarily conducive to integration of the kind envisaged in functionalist social theory. What is ethically acceptable or not may remain highly problematic and may require a methodical analysis before a clear and categorical *dharma* principle can be established for a particular kind of action.

Ethics and virtue in a textual and contextual framework

Using *Bhagavada Gita* as a narrative that primarily concerns itself with the question of what is and what is not right, there is an issue about the texts and the way in which they can influence the normative culture and ideas about right and wrong. In his introduction to *Dialectic in Practical Religion*, Leach raises the question of how classical texts can obscure or even corrupt the idea of religion of everyday life or practical religion. He argues that 'in studies of comparative religion a failure to take into account this distinction between philosophical religion and practical religion has often led to grave misunderstanding'.[19] While anthropologists will regard this distinction as crucial in order to maintain a clear analytical separation between textual and contextual religion, nevertheless it is doubtful if the dichotomy between the two is methodologically useful in instances where text and context stand in close, dynamic and dialectical relationship. In other words, the textual material may mirror the contextual religion and the interplay between the two can form the core of the formation of religious ideas and practices. This relationship does not necessarily contradict Leach's useful distinction, in so far as the text is not reified, as if it was the only source of practical morality.

There is a diverse variety of Hindu textual sources. The tendency to 'semi-tise' a singular source like *Bhagavada Gita* as the only main text of the Hindus is erroneous. Hindus share a whole range of common ideas about the nature of life and death and the meaning of human existence. However, at the same time, different Hindu communities have developed their own particular traditions based on their particular historical experience which is unique to them. It is this uniqueness which combines with commonality and creates both unity in diversity and diversity in unity – a complex pluralism within the tradition that is reflected in textual sources. As for the members of a particular community, whatever rules of conduct may have been approved for them is something which is a part and parcel of their life; the particular constituents of their own *dharma* which cannot be reduced to any mono-lithic model of Hinduism. A further distinction between literary and folk traditions, encompassing the urban–rural divide, points to diversities marked by certain common themes. The distinction between classical and folk tradi-tion is a South Asian reality that reflects the stratification between the literate and the less literate. Many of these popular religious narratives have been presented as television serials and also in the cinema. This has increased their popularity and has changed their status in both classical and folk traditions. It has brought the ethical and moral issues which these narratives portray to a wider, even domestic audience. The availability of these narratives has been enhanced through videos and cassettes. Far from lessening their popu-larity in the context of modernity, technology has greatly expanded their cultural significance as important facets of the Hindu tradition.

The two main Hindu epics *Ramayan* and *Mahabharat* concentrate on polarities of *dharma* and *adharma* that are contested and are in conflict on a wide variety of social, cultural and political issues. These stories constantly emphasise both the importance of *dharma* for the moral order and the intractable problems encountered when actors attempt to put their *dharma* ideal in practice, especially when it is in conflict at different levels. Never-theless, these epics provide pan-Hindu and pan-Indian themes that estab-lish what is correct moral behaviour and duty.[20] These epics portray obligations in an identifiable narrative form that establishes a framework for moral living. When an actor achieves a high degree of rectitude both in precept and practice, he may be called *dharmaraja*, or the king of *dharma*, as in the character of Yudhisthir in *Mahabharat*. Both the epics concentrate on action that is morally correct in almost a cosmological sense as the spirit of *dharma* pervades everywhere, enveloping humans, animals, spirits and the deities. Once these epic poems were translated in vernacular language, their recitals in various forms in local communities greatly increased their popu-larity. Tulsidas's *Ramacharitmanas* in Hindi demonstrates this in regular recitals of what has come to be known as *Tulsi Ramayan*.

The stories from *Mahabharat* are popular through readings and recitals in local communities. They appear and reappear in plays, dances and, more recently, in popular films and videos. It is not so much important that these episodes from *Ramayana* and *Mahabharat* teach people how to observe their moral obligations in relation to a particular set of actions than that they highlight the symbolic significance of *dharma*. They provide models to which people can refer for an assessment of their own norms and conduct. They also supply popular examples of behaviour that are compatible with recognised principles of morality as distinct from the behaviour that provides a clear demonstration of *adharma* rather than *dharma*. These classical stories, and the values they portray, reinforce the notion of what it is that constitutes the right conduct in the appropriation and use of *dharma* in everyday life.

So far, the argument has focused on the polarity of *dharma* and *adharma* as providing models of what is ethical in text and context. We wish now to move these general considerations of *dharma* to a particular realm, addressing questions of correct moral behaviour, of ways that relate to the ambitions of men and women to be virtuous.

In his analysis of religion as an institution in the pre-modern and the modern world, Weber saw the connection between religion, sexuality, and celibacy as one of the most important issues in major religious traditions.[21] Hindus believe in observing celibacy as a basis for self-knowledge and salvation, *moksha*. As a result, numerous texts prescribe and legitimise celibacy both as a precept and a practice. The relationship between desire, sexuality and self-control is treated at several different levels to conceptualise the idea of a 'pure self', one which is not simply reducible to the power of desire. To turn or to escape from the webs of desire, the self uses knowledge and discipline to seek the divine. This involves a difficult path in the pursuit of virtue. Thus, leading Hindu religious texts focus on the self and self-consciousness which might accomplish this virtuous task. The *Upanishads*[22] and *Bhagavada Gita*[23] teach the need to deny the impulses of desire through physical and mental self-control. These form the necessary conditions for spiritual self-enlightenment and the anchoring of the self in ways that are ultimately relatively untempered by fruits of desire. The importance of chastity, and the transcendence of desire, are related to the wish for self-knowledge through discipline, a point much emphasised in *Chandogya Upanishad*.[24] *Mundaka Upanishad* explicitly refers to desire, *kama*, as a cause of rebirth. Thus:

> [he] . . . who entertains desires, [in] thinking of them [he] is born (again) here and there on account of his desires. But of him who has his desire fully satisfied, who is a perfected soul, all his desires vanish even here (on earth).[25]

When Krishna instructs Arjuna on the nature of true yoga in *Bhagavada Gita*,[26] he reminds him that unless one has freed one's self from the power of desire, the true self will be obscured, the one which is transcendent and inseparable from the essence of the divine. Such a goal of self-knowledge is desirable as an ideal. The dynamics of desiring and not desiring are complex phenomena. Hindus recognise that the individuals who aspire to the goal of awareness of the self will vary in their ability to sustain the steadfastness necessary to achieve detachment and self-knowledge.

Celibacy as a virtue

Celibacy and self-control are important corollaries of Hindu aims of life. Following the logic of relationship between the four aims of life and the importance of self-control and self-regulation, this section will focus on socialisation into self-restraint as one of the most vital dimensions of becoming a person, both in social, religious and spiritual sense.

Brahamacharya, or celibacy as a virtue, is an essential aspect of the culture of Hindus, one that symbolises the self-control that is necessary for know-ledge of the self and, ultimately, for self-liberation. In the ancient Vedic texts, the concept of *brahamacharya* emerges as a category that goes well beyond the idea of celibacy.[27] It encompasses the notion of ascetic self-con-trol as one of the vital forces that regulate the rhythm of the cosmos. The ancient Hindu texts such as *Mahabharat* and *Ramayana* point to celibacy as a recurring theme and they explore the issue in the context of the question of fulfilment or non-fulfilment of human desire and its implications for relationships between men and women. *Mahabharat* provides a model of celibacy. In the story of Bhishma, he takes a vow of celibacy to ensure that he does not inherit the kingdom of his father. This vow would enable his father to fulfil his desire to make a beautiful fisherwoman his wife whose child would then inherit his kingdom. She will marry him only if her child could supersede Bhisma's right to inherit the royal throne. Bhisma's life-long vow of *brahmacharya* becomes one of the ideal models of celibacy as a virtue. The epic *Ramayana* provides a contrasting model of celibacy. After the abduction of his wife Sita, by Ravana, the king of Sri Lanka, Rama, the hero of this epic, observes *brahmacharya* for a period of fourteen years before he is reunited with his wife Sita. This is a recurrent theme in Hindu texts of diverse intellectual and devotional traditions.

As an ideal and a virtue, *brahmacharya* is an important principle of tradi-tional Hindu social organisation. It may be argued that the tradition that organised Hindu society into four categories of hierarchy of *varna* and the four stages of life of which *brahamacharya* is crucial, is no longer relevant in modern Hindu social life. This argument is often more apparent than real. In practice, it is not uncommon for even 'secular' Hindus to invoke the traditional categories which mark one's transition from the *bramacharya* stage of studentship to the householder stage followed by succession to forest dwelling and renunciation – the final two stages which mark and symbolise disengagement from bonds of social and material life and prepare one for the final stage leading to reincarnation or to the final release from the fetters of material existence according to the well-established tradition. *Brahmacharya* is not only about the control of one's desires and passions. It is an ideal of self-regulation in life. It even influences those among the urban Hindus in India whom Rupert Murdoch's satellite transmissions from Hong Kong bombard with graphic erotic images of material self-gratification and pleasure.

Celibacy and modernisation in Hindu life

Accounts of Indian society and its diasporic communities of Indians point to a complex and dynamic relationship between Westernisation and modernisation and its impact on traditional values of Hindu life. While the significance of modernity is an undeniable fact of life, the kind of impact it has on traditional behaviour is by no means a one-way street. The establishment of modern institutions and the increasing secular rationalisation of social life through science, education and modern forms of governance does not necessarily bring about an erosion of ethical values which have an impact on personal lives and 'conscience collective'. The concept of sanskritisation[28] that Srinivas has used in order to argue about transmission of Hindu values demonstrates consolidation rather than erosion of certain values including celibacy as a virtue. There is a number of different kinds of arguments about celibacy and its observance among the Hindus. As an attribute, celibacy is not constructed as a monolithic virtue applied equally to all.

Renouncers take on special obligations and forms of commitment. Those who take the vow of celibacy observe a strict avoidance of sex in deed and in thought, as both acts and images can bring about a decline of the religious and spiritual merit. For example, among the renouncers of the Gujarat-based Swaminaryan movement, there is a systematic body of rules and regulations which apply to renouncers should they lapse from their physical and mental celibate state. Concern with preservation of *virya* (semen) can become a source of deep anxiety that can be a further impediment to self-knowledge. Therefore the renouncers may work towards a state of 'natural' self-control preferably devoid of anxiety and excessive self-repression. The texts prescribe forms of penance and purification from sensual thoughts, practices that enable the renouncers to maintain their vow of celibacy. Sometimes texts prescribe severe sanctions if a renouncer incurs a lapse from a celibate state. What is most important for the renouncer is not only to follow the minutiae of rules and regulation but also to be a part of a religious culture that inculcates an ethic of self-control in relation to sexuality.

In contrast to renouncers, the rules of celibacy which apply to householders who make up families underline the ethics of restraint, even when erotic pleasure is recognised as part and parcel of relationships between men and women. The fact that householders recognise restraint as part and parcel of their circumstances in everyday living is a tacit and unstated ethic rather than an explicitly stated rule. Mahatma Gandhi illustrates this vividly in his autobiography when he juxtaposes his father's illness and death with his sexual desire which he regards as inappropriate.[29] While Gandhi massaged his father's legs to comfort him, he was aware that he had made his wife pregnant during the course of his father's illness. This upset him, for he wrote:

> every night whilst my hands were busy massaging my father's legs, my mind was hovering about the bedroom – and that too at a time when religion, medical science and commonsense alike forbade sexual intercourse. I was always glad to be relieved from my duty and went straight to the bedroom after doing obeisance to my father.[30]

Just before his father died, Gandhi's uncle had relieved him from his duty late in the evening. He returned to his bedroom and recorded that he 'was glad and went straight to the bedroom. My wife, poor thing, was fast asleep. But how could she sleep when I was there? I woke her up.'[31] The servant knocked his door in a matter of minutes to inform him that his father had died. This left him with a deep sense of guilt and shame, for he wrote:

> so all was over! I had to wring my hands. I felt deeply ashamed and miserable. I ran to my father's room. I saw that, if animal passion had not blinded me, I should have been spared the torture of separation from my father during his last moments.[32]

Without any hesitation, Gandhi admits that he was a lustful husband and that it took him a long time to free himself from attraction to sexual desire. Such a candid admission about sexual desire is rather uncommon, for Indian men and women are likely to talk about their own sex life only in very close and intimate company. Gandhi's own experience demonstrates the conflict between compulsion of desire and the virtue of self-restraint.

Gandhi's great concern with desire, sexuality and self-control provides one of the most important illustrations of *brahamacharya*, the notion of celibacy as a virtue. In his autobiography Gandhi has devoted two chapters to this topic.[33] It is useful to look at Gandhi's attitude to sexuality and celibacy in terms of distinction between primary and secondary celibacy.[34] Primary celibacy may refer to a lifelong vow of celibacy which the renouncers often take. Secondary celibacy may apply to married householders who are expected to observe self-restraint once they have fulfilled their duty of having a family. *Brahamacharya* which Gandhi wanted to put into practice in his own life is a case of secondary rather than primary celibacy. His own thoughts on the topic clearly show the way he struggled with desire, sex and lust. For him, the ideal of self-restraint meant the end of desire, and thus renunciation was a 'natural and inevitable fruit' of this effort.[35]

There is a sense in which it is possible to make some general comments on the virtue of celibacy on the basis of Gandhi's own experience. Hindus regard primary celibacy for those who renounce the world to become *sadhus* but expect householders to respect and accept the culture of self-control and self-restraint. Undoubtedly, in a complex interplay between eroticism and asceticism, the Hindu tradition highlights the volatile nature of desire and the need for self-control and self-regulation for human existence in ways that brings *dharma* and *karma* together in a normative harmony.

This chapter has attempted to outline the polarity of *dharma* and *adharma* and their relationship to human action, *karma*, as providing a basis for Hindu ethics and the observance of virtue. Celibacy or *brahamacharya* provides an example of a virtue that symbolises the supremacy of self-control over desire and immediate self-gratification. In a world that fragments and changes so rapidly, religious traditions can and do respond to a need for ethical foundations to social life and to guide individuals to virtues such as celibacy. Christianity – Catholicism in particular – has regarded celibacy as a virtue that parallels not only Hindu ideas about *dharma* and *karma* but also similar universal concerns with desire, self-control and moral order in Buddhism, Jainism and other world religions. The pursuit of such virtues is by no means peculiar to the West, but forms a crucial characteristic of religion and culture in the East.

Notes and references

1 Madan Sarup, *Identity, Culture and the Postmodern World* (Edinburgh: Edinburgh University Press, 1996).
2 Max Weber, *The Sociology of Religion*, trans. Ephraim Fischoff (Boston: Beacon Press, 1964).
3 Emile Durkheim, *The Elementary Forms of the Religious Life* (New York: Free Press, 1965).
4 Weber, *The Sociology of Religion*, p. 1.
5 Ian Hamnett, 'Sociology of Religion and Sociology of Error', *Religion*, vol. 3, 1973, pp. 1–12.
6 It is not surprising that the dictionary meaning of ethics should contain that which is prescribed along with that which is proscribed. See *The Compact Oxford English Dictionary* (Oxford: Oxford University Press, 1990), pp. 1672–3.
7 For instance, sects within the Swaminarayan movement use *Sikshapatri*, a text that clearly sets out rules of behaviour for different categories of people.
8 Sri Aurobindo, *The Foundations of Indian Culture* (Pondicherry: Sri Aurobindo Ashram, 1995), pp. 90–1.
9 Wilhelm Halbfass, *India and Europe: An Essay in Understanding* (Albany: State University of New York Press, 1988). See especially chapter 17, '*Dharma* in the

Self-Understanding of Traditional Hinduism', and chapter 18, 'Reinterpretation of *Dharma* in Modern Hinduism', pp. 310–48.

10   Wendy Doniger O'Flaherty and J. Duncan M. Derrett (eds), 'Introduction', in *The Concept of Duty in South Asia* (Delhi: Vikas Publishing House Pvt Limited; and London: School of Oriental and African Studies, 1978), pp. xiii–xix.

11   William K. Mahony, '*Dharma*', in Mircea Eliade (ed.), *The Encyclopaedia of Religion*, vol. 4, (New York: Macmillan, 1987), pp. 329–32.

12   That which is encompassing and that which is encompassed as an idea is derived from Dumont's discussion of 'pure' hierarchy. See Louis Dumont, *Homo Hierarchicus* (London: Weidenfeld & Nicolson, 1970), p. xii and p. 76.

13   Max Weber, *The Religion of India: The Sociology of Hinduism and Buddhism*, trans. and ed., Hans H. Gerth and Don Martindale (New York: Free Press, 1958), p. 25.

14   Halbfass, *India and Europe*, p. 312.

15   Julius Lipner, *Hindus: Their Religious Beliefs and Practices* (London: Routledge, 1994), p. 86.

16   As O'Flaherty and Derrett indicate, in their introduction to *The Concept of Duty in South Asia* (see note 10 above), the polarity between *dharma* and *adharma* is not dichotomous but rather they are to be conceived of as interdependent polar categories. See p. xiv.

17   Mahatma Gandhi, *Varnavyavastha* (Ahmedabad: Navjivan Press, 1950). In responding to both European and non-European Indian criticism of caste as a system of unequal social relations, Gandhi had to walk on a tightrope that carefully balanced the question of birth, based on belonging to *varna*, with the issue of action and merit that would determine one's position in its scheme of affairs. See especially the section on untouchability and *varnashram dharma* in Mohandas Karamchand Gandhi, *The Removal of Untouchability* (Ahmedabad: Navajivan, 1954), pp. 40–9.

18   There is an excellent introduction with a useful commentary on each verse of every chapter in Sarvepalli Radhakrishnan, *The Bhagavada Gita* (New Delhi: Harper Collins, 1993).

19   Edmund R. Leach, *Dialectic in Practical Religion* (Cambridge: Cambridge University Press, 1977), pp. 1–6.

20   The expression 'pan-Indian' is appropriate for these themes as the stories from these epics are also familiar to the non-Hindu Indian population.

21   Weber, *The Sociology of Religion*, pp. 223–45.

22   Sarvepalli Radhakrishnan, *The Principal Upanishads* (London: Unwin & Hyman, 1953).

23   Radhakrishnan, *Bhagavada Gita*.

24   Radhakrishnan, *The Principal Upanshads*, pp. 498–9.

25   Ibid., p. 689.

26   Radhakrishnan, *The Bhagavada Gita*, chapter 6, 'The True Yoga', pp. 187–211.

27   See Abinash Chandra Bose, *Hymns from the Vedas. Original Text and English Translation with Introduction and Notes* (Bombay: Asia Publishing House, 1966), pp. 73–8 for references on *brahamacharya*.

28   See Mysore Narsimhachar Srinivas, *Social Change in Modern India* (Berkeley: University of California Press, 1968), chapter 1 on sanskritisation, pp. 1–45; and also his study *The Cohesive Role of Sanskritisation and Other Essays* (Delhi: Oxford University Press, 1989).

29   Mohandas Karamchand Gandhi, *An Autobiography or the Story of My Experiments with Truth* (Ahmedabad: Navjivan, 1972).

30 Ibid., p. 20.
31 Ibid., p. 21.
32 Ibid., p. 22.
33 Ibid. See chapters 7–8, 'Brahmacharaya-1 and Brahmacharya-2', pp. 153–9.
34 Rohit Barot, 'Celibacy in the Swaminarayan Movement', in John Hinnells and Werner Menski (eds), *South Asian Religious Experience in the West* (forthcoming).
35 Gandhi, *An Autobiography*, p. 155.

9

New Age Utopianism, Cultural Extremities and Modernity

Paul Heelas

> We must say that the world in which what we see as incompatible values
> are not in conflict is a world altogether beyond our ken; that principles
> which are harmonised in this other world are not the principles with
> which, in our daily lives, we are acquainted; if they are to be transformed,
> it is into conceptions not known to us on earth. But it is on earth that we
> live, and it is here that we must believe and act.[1]

This essay is inspired by a song by The Eagles. Entitled 'Take it to the Limit',
the music captures a theme which was and continues to be widespread in
counter-cultural or alternative circles. The theme has to do with extremes:
excess; abandonment; with transgressing the rules and codes of mainstream
society; with the Dionysian fervour involved in 'break[ing]...through to
the other side', as The Doors sang; and indeed, not infrequently with that
utopia which can really work, the passage into oblivion.

Fuelled by drugs, music and alcohol, the Dionysian quest would appear to
owe little if anything to the values and assumptions of modernity. For as
well as involving rebellion, with participants often quite explicitly aiming
to reject the restrictive nature of life in conventional society, it also involves
states of consciousness that would not seem to be derived from what modernity has to offer. But even if it is accepted that the wilder excesses of the
Dionysian quest do indeed 'break' with modernity, it remains possible to
argue that many features of counter-cultural or alternative spiritualities are
nevertheless very much bound up with what modernity has to say and
promise.

The argument is that New Age spiritualities – the primary form of spirituality in alternative quarters, as well as being found elsewhere in the culture –
take various mainstream themes 'to their limit'. That is to say, the fact that
the spiritual realm is experienced as the ultimate state of affairs serves to
take a number of widely held cultural values and assumptions 'as far as they
can go'. Having explored this argument, and having drawn attention to an
important qualification (to do with the New Age ethic of humanity), this

chapter closes with attention being paid to the question of evaluating the New Age. Its spiritualities promise the utopian life. But as Isaiah Berlin and Karl Popper (amongst others) have argued, the utopian is dangerous.[2] The utopian prioritises particular values and assumptions, to the extent that they cannot be qualified or restrained by alternative values and assumptions. Thus, such cultural extremities involve the repression of alternative forms of life, hence the dangers they pose and also the question addressed later: can the same criticism be made with regard to New Age utopianism?

Cultural extremities

First, one wishes to comment on the concept of 'cultural extremities'. It must immediately be accepted that it is impossible to establish that an extremity has actually been reached. There is always the possibility that a further 'stretch' of the cultural 'imagination' will reveal that the (claimed) extremity is but a step on the path to yet more extreme states of affairs. Extremities, we might say, are always relative, but never definitive. This said, however, it remains possible to use the term when, *to the best of our knowledge*, things cannot be taken any further.

To illustrate, first with reference to cross-cultural studies, we certainly appear to be in the realm of extremities when anthropologists write of peaceful societies. What can be more peaceful than those societies, reported from central Malaysia, where participants claim that they do not even experience anger? Again, an extremity would appear to be reached when traditional Trobriand Islanders attribute pregnancy to *baloma* spirits rather than to intercourse. Can denial of the link between male impregnation and pregnancy, in favour of cultural assumptions to do with matrilineal transmission, be taken any further? Together with cross-cultural examples of this variety, extremities can also be illustrated by reference to historical developments within particular cultures. A good example, in this regard, is provided by beliefs found among the Puritan sects of early Western modernity. Many then took the human to be so 'fallen' as to be totally incapable of doing anything to obtain salvation. With salvation entirely in the hands of God, the doctrine of predestination was bound up with a view of human nature which – it is difficult if not impossible to imagine – could not be any more negative from a religious point of view.

Viewed historically, the cultural extremities of modernity are typically to be found in connection with attempts to develop the utopian life: for example the Enlightenment project and the valorisation of reason; or the Third Reich and the ultimate faith placed in the purity of the nation. Cultural extremities can also be thought of as providing radical, 'final' or 'completed' renderings of powerful cultural developments. Such cultural developments (trajectories or 'currents', to use Isaiah Berlin's term) point towards, or lead the way to, extremities: increasing faith in human reason in the case of the Enlightenment project; or the construction of nationhood and race in the case of the Third Reich. As for New Age spiritualities, to which we now turn, the key development surely concerns the cultural 'turn' to the self.

New Age self-spirituality

To introduce New Age spiritualities, and to highlight the absolute import-ance attached to the 'self', it is useful to think in terms of three central New Age assumptions. The first is that to live out of the 'ego' is to live a life which is not working. The 'ego', or 'lower self', is the product of socialisa-tion. It is what we are by virtue of family, education, the demands of work and the lures of consumer culture. It is therefore held to suffer from what are taken to be the defects of the culture at large: the stresses and strains of the family; the harmful over-reliance on rationality demanded by the examination system; and the trivialities of consumer culture.

The second key assumption is that what really matters lies beyond the ego. At heart, the person is a spiritual being; a God or Goddess (or both).[3] Rather than this spirituality being acquired from without, it is integral to the person. It is what we are by nature. It is our true, authentic selfhood and, being spiritual, it is perfect. It should also be pointed out – and this important consideration is returned to later – that although New Agers (by definition) have faith in themselves as spiritual beings, the 'self' of the New Age is rarely limited to the individual. The great majority of those involved take their 'own' spiritual selves to be intimately interconnected, if not fused, with the selves of 'others': people and the natural order as a whole.

As for the third key assumption, without exception New Agers know that it is possible to 'go within'. Practices are what matter. These range from meditation, to New Age astrology, to many forms of Paganism – which are held to liberate participants from the realm of the ego, with all its 'dis-ease', to enable them to experience the perfection of the spiritual realm. It has to be said that few if any New Agers suppose that it is possible to acquire permanent liberation (both the ego and the intent on its survival are consid-ered to be formidable opponents). Few, if any, New Agers, on the spiritual quest within, would deny the importance of 'working' on themselves in order to experience what 'life' itself has to offer.

New Age spiritualities teach that the utopian lies with the self: not merely the self of the experiencing subject, but the self which – in the same way as in many Eastern mystical traditions – is experienced as suffusing all life, all of nature, if not the cosmos as a whole. Finally, by way of introducing New Age spiritualities, a brief note on how those intent on the inner quest are catered for. Some provisions take the form of specific new religious move-ments, with headquarters, committed membership and, typically, a hier-archical organisational structure (a classic example, in this regard, being

Scientology). By far and away the majority of spiritual teachings and prac- tices, however, do not amount to organised new religious movements. They are much better thought of as 'new spiritual outlets'. Such outlets include alternative shops (as well as some mainstream ones), shamanic weekends, healing sessions, informal wiccan events, management trainings, medita- tion sessions, spiritually orientated Tai chi courses, growth seminars, 'out- ward bound for inward life' weekends, psychospiritual Jungian encounters, New Age astrology, and so on. More generally, in the culture, these 'new spiritual outlets' also include books, magazines (for example Feng Shui), articles and newspapers, music and films (for example of the back-to-nature or out-into-space varieties). It can be emphasised that New Age spiritualities are primarily provided by 'new spiritual outlets' from the book to the face- to-face session, rather than from new religious movements. 'New spiritual outlets' do not demand loyalty; they are very often run on a one-to-one basis (as with much alternative healing), or they simply require the engage- ment of the participant (as with reading a New Age book); and they are (relatively) egalitarian and non-authoritative.

Self-spirituality as a cultural extremity

Going back at least to the publication in 1878 of Jacob Burkhardt's classic study, *The Civilization of the Renaissance in Italy*,[4] scholars have drawn atten- tion to what can be described as the 'turn to the self'. This expression should not be taken to mean that the 'turn' is to some performed self; rather, it serves to emphasise the fact that modern times, specifically mod- ernity, have witnessed the 'elevation' and 'elaboration' of the self. In stark contrast to the 'fallen' self of the Puritans of early (Western) modernity, the self today is (culturally) highly valued. Cultural value is accorded to auto- nomy, the exercise of self-responsibility, freedom of expression, creativity, living life to the full, being one's self, exercising initiative, developing through personal relationships, and seeking one's own way.

Clearly, it cannot be denied that modernity has also witnessed powerful counter-currents (one need only think of the tyrannical utopian movements of the twentieth century). Equally clearly though, and in comparison with early modernity, it cannot be denied that what Charles Taylor describes as 'the massive subjective turn to modern culture' has taken place.[5] New Age spiritualities take the value, authority and 'subjectivity' of the self to the limit. The self, itself, is accorded ultimate value. For what could be more highly valued than being spiritual, actually being – at heart – a God or God- dess? What could possibly exercise higher authority when the 'Source' is taken to lie within? What 'subjectivity' could be more profound than the wealth and the wisdom which the inner spiritual life is taken to offer?

A related way of looking at the turn to the self is in terms of the process of detraditionalisation. The argument is that religious (and other) traditions –

authoritative realms existing over and above the individual or whatever the individual might aspire to be – have been eroded by the processes of modernisation. As traditional frames of reference and judgement have waned in influence, the argument continues, selves have had increasingly to serve as sources of significance and authority. This argument is primarily associated with a Germanic strand of thinkers, running from Simmel through Berger to Gehlen and Luckmann.[6]

Many forms of religion, today, are partially detraditionalised: liberal religions, for example, retain a number of traditional theistic beliefs, but, at the same time, are detraditionalised in that the critical use of *human* reason has resulted in the loss of faith in much transmitted from the past. New Age spiritualities, however, take this process further. The process of detraditionalisation is taken to its limit, its end-point, in that New Age spiritualities often claim (in effect) to be post-traditional. The experiencing self is taken to be the *only* authentic source of significance and judgement.

Without wishing to imply that this total reliance on the self applies to all New Age spiritualities, especially as they are practised,[7] the fact remains that New Age discourse is replete with evidence of the post-traditional; indeed, is characterised by the rejection of any external sources of authority, whether belonging to traditions or not. To illustrate by way of two examples, let us consider first Sheldon Kopp's injunction in his widely read *If You Meet the Buddha on the Road, Kill Him!*

> the Zen Master warns: 'if you meet the Buddha on the road, Kill him!' This admonition points up that no meaning that comes from outside of ourselves is real. The Buddhahood of each of us has already been obtained. We need only recognize it. Philosophy, religion, patriotism, are all empty idols. The only meaning in our lives is what we each bring to them. Killing the Buddha on the road means destroying the hope that anything outside of ourselves can be our master.[8]

Then consider secondly, Richard Adams and Janice Haaken who, writing of Lifespring, an enlightenment seminar organisation running in North America, note:

> anticultural culture refers to any meaning system or set of values that deny the legitimacy of meaning systems or values having their origin outside of the individual ... those participating in an anticultural culture do not believe that legitimate values exist outside of themselves. Thus the prescriptions of others, of tradition, of experts, of religious texts, and all such external sources are not considered to be legitimate.[9]

Countless similar examples of the post-traditional theme that meaning, significance and value come from the experiencing self, can be provided from New Age discourse. Examples can also be provided of how the (apparently) ultimate valorisation of the self is bound up with specific cultural extremities, to do with the source of ethicality, the exercise of freedom and responsibility, and the utilisation of power. Regarding ethicality, the widespread cultural theme that, on occasion, one should act 'according to one's conscience', is taken to the limit in that New Agers believe that one's own experience of inner spirituality provides the *only* grounds for making judgements. The widespread belief that freedom is a 'top priority' value is taken to its extreme in that New Agers believe that contact with the spirituality within provides total, spiritually-informed freedom: freedom from the constraints of the ego or lower self; freedom to express one's self; and, for those New Agers who emphasise magical power, freedom to do or to obtain what one truly wills. Regarding responsibility, the cultural emphasis in many quarters, not least among political parties, is on the exercise of self-responsibility. This is radicalised, for there are New Agers who hold that they are responsible for everything which happens in their world: their experiences, their health, even – for some – events like the birth of their parents.[10] Finally, to develop the theme of magical power, the widespread cultural belief in 'will-power' is radicalised in many New Age circles, it being believed that ritual practices, serving to make contact with what lies within, enable participants to achieve the (scientifically) impossible.

The expressive self and utilitarian individualism

In a somewhat more refined fashion, New Age cultural extremities can be explored by drawing on the language of Robert Bellah *et al*'s *Habits of the Heart* and the analytical distinction drawn between two forms of selfhood.[11] First, there is the self in the expressive mode. This self works with a relatively 'deep' understanding of what it is to be a person. Memories (perhaps repressed), emotions, stresses and strains, sense of well-being, one's 'life' itself, are given attention. The aims are to 'grow', to 'develop', to live 'life' to the full, to handle one's anxieties or angers, to express one's creativity, to be 'true to oneself', to enrich family life and personal relationships and to find harmony with nature. With between 10 and 20 per cent of Western populations born between 1946 and 1965 identifying with this mode of selfhood,[12] the language is predominantly psychological, therapeutic, or, more generally, humanistic (in the sense of being about human *life*). Providing a sacralised rendering of this kind of self-understanding, New Age spiritualities take it to its 'logical' conclusion or completion. From the point of view of New Agers, the 'self-development' or 'growth' of the humanistic expressivist is seen as being merely a matter of tinkering with 'ego-operations', growth therefore remaining stuck at the level of the lower self. From the point of view of New Agers, this is far inferior to 'self-actualisation' or what can be called 'self-sacralisation': the experience of ultimacy within.

Together with the radicalisation of humanistic expressivism, the New Age also involves the sacralisation of utilitarian individualism. This form differs from expressive selfhood in that the primary aim of this mode of self-understanding and action is to deploy various means, such as rational calculation or enterprise, to obtain various ends, in particular money, to satisfy those desires which one has by virtue of living in terms of capitalistic modernity. Rather than 'working' to explore the 'wealth' that one's inner 'life' and personal relationships have to offer, the emphasis now lies with what the 'externals' of consumer culture have to offer. What matters is obtaining (consuming and displaying) these externals, this incorporation satisfying the needs and desires aroused by the world of pleasure-promising commodities.

What can be thought of as the prosperity wing of the New Age radicalises utilitarian individualism in that the quest for gratification through prosperity is placed in the hands of the sacred. Putting it crudely, prosperity teachings and practices – at least of the most capitalistic-orientated variety – promise the perfect 'yuppie'. Participants no longer have to rely on the exercise of fallible human capacities. They are able to access their spirituality, one which (supposedly) then has the power automatically to effect desired states of affairs. Furthermore, prosperity teachings and practices accord ultimate significance to these desired states of affairs. Money, it is taught, is spiritual; to own a luxury car is to possess something which is spiritual; to dress in designer clothes is part and parcel of expressing one's spirituality. In sum, prosperity is perfected; the utilitarian individualist, the yuppie, is now absolute.[13]

The New Age and the sacralisation of the ethic of humanity

The ethic of humanity

Whereas the self, in utilitarian mode, is (typically) fundamentally individualistic, utilising its own powers to obtain its own ends, the self in expressive mode is (typically) holistic, experiencing 'itself' to be bound up with other selves, to life as a whole, if not all that belongs to the natural, authentic order of things. Expanding on the theme of holistic interconnectedness or interfusion, we now turn to consider the sacralisation of 'the ethic of humanity'.

Let us first look at this ethic in its more 'secular' guise. At least since Weber, it has frequently been noted that one of the great marks of modernity concerns functional and normative differentiation. Much less attention, however, has been paid to the converse process of de-differentiation, the quest for the universal which lies within or beyond differences. The ethic of humanity provides a powerful illustration of this point. This mode of relating to others, of evaluation and decision-making – with its assumptions, values, duties, obligations, sentiments, freedoms and rights – is driven by the claim that there is such a thing as a universal and unified 'humanity'. Beyond differences to do with biology, colour, age, ethnicity, class, nationhood and so on lies 'the same': that which we share or have in common by virtue of being human; that which belongs to the nature of man as such, as enshrined in UN declarations.

Writing towards the end of the nineteenth century, Durkheim claimed that what he variously called 'eighteenth-century liberalism', 'the religion of humanity' or 'the cult of man' has 'become a fact'. As he continues, 'it has penetrated our institutions and our mores, it has blended with our whole life, and if, truly, we had to give it up, we would have to recast our whole moral organisation at the same stroke'.[14] Little in evidence during earlier modernity, Durkheim clearly thought that this 'religion' had become the dominant tradition of his time. A century on, and despite (or because of) the tyrannical counter-movements of the twentieth century, what shall here be called the ethic of humanity is arguably stronger than ever. Postmodernists (Bauman, Baudrillard) and anti-feminists (Lonzi) might engage in forceful critiques, but there is ample evidence of the vitality of the ethic with its integral rights.[15] One can think of its diffusion into nature;[16] its institutionalisation within the workplace and the educational system; or in Bangladesh, from where I write, its pivotal role in underpinning that 'parallel state', the one run by Non-Governmental Organisations.[17] Or one can think of the ways in which the ethic has entered the field of religion: liberal religions (perhaps better called religions of humanity); the increasing use of the language and assumptions of human rights by the Catholic Church; and the sacralisation of humanity as in New Age quarters. In short, and comparing the situation with early modernity, there is absolutely no doubt that the development or construction of the ethic of humanity amounts to one of the great revolutions of modern times.

To pave the way for exploring how New Age sprituralities sacralise this ethic, let us devote a few words to its key values. Drawing on Durkheim's portrayal, since we are all humans and since the 'human personality' is of 'incomparable value', we are called to 'respect' all those who share humanity as much as we respect ourselves; to treat everyone with 'dignity'; to treat all humans 'as though we were equal'; to exercise 'sympathy', 'pity', our 'thirst for justice' and our responsibilities; to avoid killing ('except in cases allowed by law'); and to avoid 'unlawful attack' 'on the property of the human person'.[18] In addition, the ethic emphasises 'freedom'. By virtue of being human we are entitled to rights, most generally the right (or freedom) to live 'out' what it is to be human. We have the right to live; the right to be treated with dignity; the right to be treated as equal; indeed, all those rights which (supposedly) serve to protect us from those outside forces which threaten our freedom to live as human beings. Furthermore, people also have the right (or freedom) to be different: the importance attached to 'respect' is bound up with the importance attached to people having the freedom to live – at least within limits – different forms of life.

Despite the role played by freedom, however, this is a '*strong*' form of liberalism. The contrast is with 'weak' (relativistic, *laissez faire*) liberalism emphasising freedom (people being free to hold different values). 'Weak' liberalism attaches equal importance to equality, to respect and to toleration, and this means that one cannot judge the freedoms of others as wrong (for to do so would mean that they were no longer being treated as equals). The ethic of humanity, on the other hand, places 'freedom' under scrutiny. Some forms of life (and their associated exercise of freedom) are wrong, namely those forms of life which attack others whose values are bound up with 'being human'. Thus one cannot respect those who exercise their freedom to take away human dignity; which destroys human life in an unlawful fashion; and so on. In short, far from uncritically propounding that all forms of life, all freedoms, are equal, the ethic has a powerful cutting edge.

The sacralisation of the ethic of humanity

Famously, that great critic of Enlightenment thought, Joseph de Maistre, exclaimed, 'I have seen in my time Frenchman, Italians and Russians. I have known, thanks to Montesquieu, that one may be a Persian, but as for *Man*, I declare that I have never met him in my life; if he exists it is without my knowledge.'[19] The criticism has often be made that this ethic of humanity rests on the flimsiest of bases, if indeed it has a foundation at all – some indeterminate, unspecified if not entirely vacuous, 'intrinsic' and 'universal' 'human nature'.

To put it mildly, New Agers would not agree. As it says in the window of a bookshop near to where I live in the Yorkshire Dales, 'There are no strangers in the New Age'. At the spiritual level, we are all bound up with one another; are 'interdependent', 'interconnected' or 'interfused'; we are 'one' (formulations vary in new Age circles). At its essentialised, sacralised core, humanity can thus serve as a spiritual truth, one which lends absolute authority to the associated virtues of the ethic of humanity: equality, respect, dignity, compassion, responsibility, freedom. Accordingly, we should expect to find cultural extremities in evidence: total, unqualified equality, respect, freedom, compassion and responsibility. And indeed there are signs of the unqualified – those New Agers who do their very best not to destroy sentient life under any circumstances, for example.

Although the New Age radicalises the ethic of humanity by grounding it in the spiritual realm, one does not find the 'totalising', absolute or unconditional, extremities that one might expect. Thus New Agers do not respect *everything*; do not value freedom *whatever* form it might take; and do not hold that *all* cultural assumptions and activities are of equal value. The most obvious explanation of this is that New Agers (typically) think that much of life is in the hands of the ego or lower self. And when this is the case, the lower self generates states of affairs which do not deserve to be treated with dignity or respect. For the spiritually informed, these are not to be judged as 'equal'. Indeed, they are to be judged as erroneous, misguided forms of freedom. Just as the (more secular) ethic of humanity has an 'intolerant' cutting edge, criticising forms of life which do not accord with its human values, so does the New Age.

'True' New Agers, then, are far from being free to do whatever they like. The only freedoms which count are those in 'alignment' with inner truth. Again, 'true' New Agers should not respect (let alone love) or be responsible for whatever the world has to offer. They should only respect or be responsible for that which advances the spiritual life. In short, precisely because the New Age rendering of the ethic of humanity is spiritually informed, the values of the ethic are not taken to totalising, unconditional extremes.

Arguably, there is another reason why the sacralisation of the ethic does not result in unconditional, across-the-board adherence to its values. The reason is that the values of the ethic necessarily clash, and therefore – if they are to co-exist – must necessarily qualify or temper one another: and so cannot be taken to their extremes, their limits. Looking at this more closely, the general argument that values clash – especially when there are enough to inform a (relatively) distinctive way of life – has been forcefully argued by Isaiah Berlin. As he writes in a well-known passage, 'both liberty and equality are among the primary goals pursued by human beings through many centuries; but total liberty for wolves is death to the lambs, total liberty of the powerful, the gifted, is not compatible with the rights to a decent existence of the weak and the less gifted'. And he records, 'justice, rigorous justice, is for some people an absolute value, but it is not compatible with what may be no less ultimate values for them – mercy, compassion – as arises in concrete cases'.[20] Now applying Berlin's point to the ethic of humanity, it immediately becomes apparent that the ethic is riven with clashing values: liberty versus equality; respecting the freedom of others (which could include the freedom to be repressive) versus the freedom of human rights; and treating people with sympathy versus the rigorous application of justice.

As Berlin suggests in the passage which comes at the beginning of this chapter, 'the world in which what we see as incompatible values are not in conflict is a world altogether beyond our ken'. New Age sacralisation of the ethic of humanity *might* harmonise the values of the ethic of humanity, but – if Berlin is right – this cannot be picked up by way of this-worldly, human knowledge. And so we are left with the other possibility, namely that New Age 'sacralisation' *might* equally well do nothing to alleviate those value-clashes found in the more secular United Nations rendering of the ethic of humanity. And if this is indeed the case, we have an explanation as to why the values of the New Age ethic of humanity have their limits: they are continually held in check by other, competing, values.

Evaluation: New Age dangers?

One of the great refrains running through the work of Isaiah Berlin concerns the dangers of the search for the utopian. For Berlin, the search has been intimately bound up with widespread ideologies of progress and perfectibility. He also holds that it has been unwritten by widely held Platonic assumptions: that any given question has only one true answer; that there is a certain or dependable path to such truths; and that it is true, *a priori*, that all 'supreme' or 'great' truths will be compatible. The utopian is believed to come about when 'supreme' truths or goods are realised simultaneously. From Berlin's point of view, however, the inevitability of value clash (at least when there are enough values to sustain any particular form of utopianism) means that this simultaneous realisation is not possible. Hence his argument that to handle the problem of value conflict utopian projects have had to organise their values hierarchically. By according certain values priority over others, conflicts can be resolved. But for Berlin this only makes things worse. Value prioritisation (national or *volk* values over human rights or the rights of the individual, for example) can only too readily be associated with the repression of conflicting values and indeed result in inhumanity.[21]

Aiming to transform life from that run by defective institutions and lower selves to that informed by the realm of perfection, inner spirituality, New Age spiritualities certainly belong to the utopian tradition. Some New Age teachers and participants, it would appear, can be criticised for taking particular cultural values and assumptions to their (supposedly) utopian extremes. Criticisms of this variety hang on the claim that in going to particular extremes New Agers devalue – even ignore – alternative values and assumptions. To illustrate by reference to the absolute value attached to finding significance and authority by way of first-hand experience of inner spirituality, it can be argued that this is to ignore what supra-self or external voices might have to offer. If 'the Buddha' is killed, the danger (among others) is that nobody is left to enable people to see that there is more to life than the lower self or ego. To provide another illustration, it might well be argued that New Age yuppies, with their faith in what ownership and consumption of material goods has to offer and their belief in the infinite abundance of the earth's resources, have gone much too far along the path to some capitalistic utopia. Their path is dangerous, the argument continues, in that it amounts to a lopsided excess, paying little or no attention to what other values and assumptions have to offer.

There is no denying the fact that extremities are to be found in New Age circles, and from the point of view of those who hold other values and assumptions, such extremities can readily be criticised for distorting what life is 'really' about. This said, however, the New Age today is predominantly 'safe'. That is to say, the utopian thrust towards the extremity is held in check by the fact that the great majority of New Agers (it appears) are committed to a sacralised rendering of the ethic of humanity.[22] Accordingly, they are committed to competing or conflicting values. These have continually to be compromised, adjusted, jiggled and juggled rather than treated as operating as valorised extremities. Residents at Findhorn, the internationally renowned community in North East Scotland, know the truth of both freedom and equality. The history of Findhorn since the early 1960s is the playing out of these two truths. This posits people exercising their freedom to become authority figures as against people demanding an equal say. As a consequence, neither truth has been taken to a totalising extreme. So long as these two truths remain in ('creative') interplay, there is no danger of Findhorn either becoming an authoritarian cult or disintegrating into egalitarian chaos.[23]

The New Age and a danger of postmodernity

The New Age today is as 'safe' as that complex of interplaying and mutually restraining values, comprising the (relatively secular) ethic of humanity, which it sacralises. Much of what is known as 'postmodernity', it can now be claimed, also draws on this ethic. In contrast to New Age sacralisation, however, postmodern radicalisation would appear to let 'freedom' run riot. As Benhabib acutely observes, 'postmodernists...assume or even posit those *hyper-universalist and superliberal* values of diversity, heterogeneity, eccentricity and otherness'.[24] To value difference, one can then go on to argue, *ipso facto*, that this is to value 'respect' (for otherwise differences could not be positively evaluated), 'equality' (in that positive evaluations of differences mean that they must at least approximate to being equal), and 'freedom'. And the last – I think – is the key to the matter. From (at least) Nietzsche, the reason why *difference* matters, is evaluated as it is, is that it bound up with that great priority – the freedom to live as one wills (or as one's culture would have it).

   Postmodern ethicality thus involves the radicalisation – or valorisation – of the 'freedom' component of the ethic of humanity. However, whereas the traditional ethic of humanity of modernity serves to restrain the operation of freedom (one should not exercise one's freedom to engage in acts which run counter to what it is to be human by failing to treat people with dignity, for example), postmodern freedom tends to run riot. The reason is simple, for, as Squires suggests, postmodernity 'involves the rejection of all essentialist and transcendental conceptions of human nature'.[25] The exercise of postmodern freedom, in other words, can no longer be tested – that is, evaluated – by reference to the (essentialised) virtues taken to be bound up with what it is to be human – equality, dignity, responsibility for the welfare of others, and so on – hence the criticism so often levelled against postmodern ethicality, namely its inability to identify and deal with differences, such as the exercise of racism, by judging them to involve the wrong exercise of freedom.

Both New Age and postmodern ethicality might involve transformations of the ethic of humanity, the former by way of sacralisation, the latter by way of the prioritisation of freedom. However, whereas New Age ethicality is (largely) grounded in what are taken to be the truths of an essence, namely sacred human nature, the latter is radically de-essentialised. Accordingly, whereas the New Age prioritises the *truth* of what it is to be human, freedom only counting when it is informed by this truth, postmodern ethicality prioritises *freedom*, 'truth' (in particular the celebration of difference) being envisaged as that which is free. Again, New Age essentialism, with regard to what it is to be truly human, provides a (supposedly) infallible basis for distinguishing between the 'good' and the 'bad' life. In contrast, postmodern post-essentialism means that judgement is left with or as freedom and difference. In short, judgement – and thus politics – is possible for the New Ager; but for the postmodernist . . .?[26]

New Age spiritualities are very much '*of*' modernity in that the sacralisation of the self, in its expressive and utilitarian modes, as well as the sacralisation of the ethic of humanity, means that widespread cultural assumptions and values are (variously) empowered, radicalised, and – on occasion – taken to the limit.[27] In conclusion, the key point to emphasise is that the essentialised, sacralised ethic of humanity plays an important role in holding excesses in check. The values of this ethic, mutually holding themselves in check, do not operate – individually – in unconditional, absolute fashion. Thus one does not find that valorisation of freedom associated with postmodern thought. Taken as an essentialised complex of values, the sacralised ethic of humanity – like its more secular counterpart – can nevertheless function with a cutting edge, identifying and criticising misguided forms of life; those forms of life where the values of freedom, equality, respect, dignity, compassion, the values of life itself, are either missing or are not in the right balance.

Notes and references

1 Isaiah Berlin, *The Crooked Timber of Humanity. Chapters in the History of Ideas* (London: Fontana, 1991), p. 13.
2 Ibid. See also Karl Popper, *Conjecture and Refutation* (London: Routledge, 1963).
3 See Maxine Birch, 'The Goddess/God Within: The Construction of Self-Identity through Alternative Health Practices', in Kieran Flanagan and Peter C. Jupp (eds), *Postmodernity, Sociology and Religion* (Basingstoke: Macmillan, 1996), pp. 83–100.
4 Jacob Burkhardt, *The Civilization of the Renaissance in Italy* (London: George Allen & Unwin, 1928).
5 Charles Taylor, *The Ethics of Authenticity* (Cambridge, Mass.: Harvard University Press, 1991), p. 25.

6　See: Georg Simmel, *Essays on Religion*, trans. Horst Jürgen Helle (New Haven: Yale University Press, 1997); Peter L. Berger, Brigitte Berger and Hansfried Kellner, *The Homeless Mind. Modernization and Consciousness* (Harmondsworth: Penguin, 1974); Arnold Gehlen, *Man in the Age of Technology* (New York: Columbia University Press, 1980); and Thomas Luckmann, 'Shrinking Transcendence, Expanding Religion?', *Sociological Analysis*, vol. 50, no. 2, 1990, pp. 127–38.

7　It could well be the case that New Age spiritualities are much less detraditionalised with regard to practice and implementation than they are in terms of statements of intent. For further discussion see Paul Heelas, *The New Age Movement. The Celebration of the Self and the Sacralization of Modernity* (Oxford: Blackwell, 1996), especially chapter 8, pp. 201–26.

8　Sheldon Kopp, *If You meet the Buddha on the Road, Kill Him* (London: Sheldon Press, 1974), p. 140.

9　Richard Adams and Janice Haaken,' Anticultural Culture. Lifespring's Ideology and Its Roots in Humanistic Psychology', *Journal of Humanistic Psychology*, vol. 27, no. 2, 1987, pp. 501–17.

10　A good illustration of a New Ager taking self-responsibility to a radical extreme is provided by Shirley MacLaine, who claimed that she was responsible for the birth of her parents. See *It's All in the Playing* (London: Bantam, 1988), p. 143.

11　Robert N. Bellah, Richard Madsen, William M. Sullivan, Ann Swidler and Steven M. Tipton, *Habits of the Heart. Individualism and Commitment in American Life* (Berkeley and London: University of California Press, 1985).

12　Ronald Inglehart, *Culture Shift in Advanced Industrial Society* (Princeton: Princeton University Press, 1990), p. 91.

13　See Heelas, *The New Age Movement*, for more on prosperity New Age.

14　Emile Durkheim, 'Individualism and the Intellectuals', in Robert N. Bellah (ed.), *Emile Durkheim. On Morality and Society* (Chicago: University of Chicago Press, 1973), pp. 43–57, especially p. 47. See also W. Watts Miller, *Durkheim, Morals and Modernity* (London: UCL Press, 1996).

15　See: Zygmunt Bauman, *Postmodern Ethics* (Oxford: Blackwell, 1993); Jean Baudrillard, *The Transparency of Evil* (London: Verso, 1993), p. 85; and Carla Lonzi, *Sputiamo su Hegel* (*Spit on Hegel*) (Milan: Scritti di Rivolta Femminile, 1974), pp. 20–1.

16　Roderick Frazier Nash, *The Rights of Nature* (London: the University of Wisconsin Press, 1989).

17　On Bangladesh, see Ziauddin Sardar, *Postmodernism and the Other. The New Imperialism of Western Culture* (London: Pluto, 1998).

18　For details regarding Durkheim's portrayal of the ethic of humanity, see Paul Heelas, 'On Things not being Worse, and the Ethic of Humanity', in Paul Heelas, Scott Lasch and Paul Morris (eds), *Detraditionalization* (Oxford: Blackwell, 1996), pp. 200–19.

19　As quoted in Edmund R. Leach, *Social Anthropology* (London: Fontana, 1982), p. 56.

20　Berlin, *The Crooked Timber of Humanity*, p. 12.

21　See ibid. and also his *Against the Current* (Oxford: Oxford University Press, 1981).

22　Although it cannot be gone into detail here, a very considerable amount of evidence supports the view that New Agers typically adhere to a sacralised rendering of the ethic of humanity. An excellent concrete example is provided by the activities of one of Britain's leading spokesperson on matters to do with inner spirituality, William Bloom, who is becoming increasingly involved with UN concerns. A press release, dated 20 October 1998, is entitled 'United Nations Conference Recognises Holistic and New Age Approach'.

23 On such matters at Findhorn see, for example, Carol Riddell, *The Findhorn Community* (Forres: Findhorn Press, 1991).

24 Seyla Benhabib, *Situating the Self* (Cambridge: Polity, 1992), p. 16 (my emphases).

25 Judith Squires, introduction to the book she edited: *Principled Positions* (London: Lawrence & Wishart, 1993), p. 2.

26 In passing, it can be noted that the fact that the New Age and postmodern thought treat the ethic of humanity in such different ways serves to contribute to the ongoing debate as to whether or not the New Age is postmodern by strongly suggesting that the answer should be in the negative.

27 It should be emphasised that it has not been possible, in this essay, to explore other ways in which the New Age serves to encourage cultural extremities. Thus attention has not been paid to the important topic concerning how gendered identity has been radicalised by way of essentialised, gender-specific spiritualities. Nor has attention been devoted to ways in which discourses and practices sustaining the 'autonomous self' of modernity have been taken to extremes, perhaps those best highlighted by the reported practice of people marrying themselves.

10
From Religion to Ethics: Quaker Amillennialism

Pink Dandelion

This chapter attempts to explain the ambiguous relationship of Quakerism, largely in Britain, to two issues: first, the history of its changing relationships to its original belief that the Second Coming of Christ was taking place; and secondly, the emphasis the group currently places on 'seeking new Light' outside of a confessional or explicitly religious framework. The issue of Quaker attitudes to the unfolding of time and eschatology forms a distinctive experience in the sociology of religion.[1] It illustrates how the ordering of virtue is linked to the interpretation of time and the fates and choices it ordains for a religious group. Study of the evolving relationship of Quakerism to time and eschatology offers a useful counterpoint to received sociological thinking about the link between believing and belonging within present-day British culture.[2] It also offers a useful comparison with the other chapters in the present collection by Lindohf, Watts Miller and Jupp.

The management of time is about the issue of hope and the realisation of duty in this world and this forms an important facet of virtue ethics which the Quaker experience can illuminate. The duties, obligations and interpretations of time illustrate also a variability of response to the world and the relationship of Quakerism to it. These shift over time in a complex relationship to secularisation. They also point to efforts to characterise beliefs in relationship to the world as it evolves and modernises. In this process of interpretation, the Quaker relationship to the world shows some subtle shifts that mark changes in its approaches to ethics and the notion of how virtue ought to be established.

The chapter begins with a description of a Christian perspective on the temporary nature of history, and of the Church within that, as believers wait for the end of time and the end of history with the Second Coming. Whatever the relation to millennial thinking (the specific picture of a thousand-year rule of the saints in the book of Revelation) it is suggested that each Christian group has its own set of eschatological hopes, its own story of the endtimes. From a Christian perspective, the challenge for each group is how to remain faithful in the 'meantime'. The second and third sections of the chapter consider the claims of the first Quakers that the endtime was unfolding in the 1650s and how, typically for groups which are founded on prophecy about the present-day, those grand claims needed to be modified. The fourth section considers the dilemma of maintaining an ecclesiology in present time that fulfils those grand claims (those which eschew a set-apart priesthood, places, times and seasons, and outward sacraments) conceived in another era and time of experience of the founders. What has come to pass for Quakers in Britain today, 'Liberal Friends', is that they have left themselves without any explicitly religious forms. Unity around values and ethics has replaced the explicitly religious so that a concentration on the present has de-eschatologised Quaker religiosity. Their present dilemma is that Quakers have ended up working in their own time rather than God's.

Little sociological work has been done on present-day British Quakerism. Only two sociologists (Plüss and myself) have undertaken specialist research on this distinctive religious group. Earlier, Bryan Wilson had classified Quakers as a revisionist sect, seeking to achieve salvation through the reform of people's consciences. Neither Plüss nor Wilson has examined the historical underpinning of the present-day practices of Quakerism.[3] The Friends' self-conception, as a group seeking 'new Light' with the attendant concentration on process rather than content, belies the historical legacy of a lack of explicit outward religious signs and symbols, and the absence of such an apparatus of belief has left them prone to the possibility and actuality of secularisation in the group.

Quakers in Britain today hold a diversity of beliefs. Their emphasis on the primacy of experience, and thus the value of silence as a basis to worship, and prayer, coupled with the devaluation of speech, means that this diversity of belief is rarely voiced. It is rendered invisible and is marginalised. 'Correct' belief, other than in the *form* of Quakerism, is not required for membership and, indeed, it is hard to identify a normative set of theological beliefs amongst group members. Outward Quakerism is thus focused on the means to religious experience, silent worship, and what are claimed as its fruits, Quaker witness on issues of social justice. Such ethics can be nurtured in ways other than the spiritual and this lack of *necessary* connection has left the group particularly prone to a secularised version of what has previously been a religious witness. Significantly, both *look* the same. The issue of time and how it is handled draws out differences between these for it is argued that Quakers work now only in secularised time, within historical time, or even as if before the invention of the clock,[4] and have thus de-eschatologised their faith.

Time and time again: Christianity and history

Christianity differentiates between historical (constructed, human) time and God's time. From a union of God and humanity in Eden, of heaven and earth, the Fall situated humanity apart from heaven and God's realm. These two planes intersect again with the first coming of Christ. According to Paul, this life, death and resurrection of Christ allows humanity to become aware of its growth, as heirs, from a place of 'childhood' under the law, through its present adolescence, to a sense of what it will be to live by faith in a kind of spiritual adulthood. The 'New Testament' looks towards a future Second Coming of Christ, when this inheritance is fully realised, a point when the whole of humanity moves to full adulthood. At this point: humanity will be set free from sin; humanity will live by the faith of Christ; there will be a renewed intimacy with God for all, in a state akin to that of Eden but also beyond it in that the Fall will not be repeatable. It will be the end of historical time, or rather its final and complete intersection with God's time, a fulfilment of the Fall and of the promise of the first coming.[5] It will be the culmination of God's plan for the world.

What changes within the scriptural accounts is the timing of the end of time. Eschatological hopes become less immediate as the letters of Paul progress.[6] As Albert Schweitzer claimed, 'the whole of the history of Christianity...is based on the delay of the Parousia'.[7] Different Christian groups have placed different emphases on this part of Scriptural orthodoxy. Their theologies have contained this future transformation but the priority it is given in practice and daily faith differs. Yet, all such groups have needed to create and sustain a 'theology of the interim' where the focus is less on the endtime but on the meantime.

At the Second Vatican Council, the Roman Catholic Church made this explicit when it stated that

> the pilgrim church, in its sacraments and institutions, which belong to the present age, carries the mark of this world which will pass, and she herself takes her place among the creatures which groan and travail yet and await the revelation of the sons of God.[8]

Until the time of its new intimacy with God, humanity needs help. It needs to remind itself of what it is about. The Church is as it is, with its sacred buildings, priests, sacraments, and Christian calendar, in order to help humanity in its relationship with God until, and only until, the Second Coming makes such arrangements unnecessary and obsolete. This issue of time and the forms and responsibilities for waiting for the Second Coming were of particular importance in shaping Quaker assumptions about relating to the world. Their duties to the world were defined in terms of their beliefs about the Second Coming.

Quakers through time: Quakers and the Second Coming
When Quakerism began in the 1650s, George Fox and other early leaders of the movement claimed that the time for the end of the Church had come.

The Second Coming was unfolding and the outward forms were anachronistic. These early Quakers claimed: a direct relationship with God available to everyone; a doctrine of perfection; and a fulfilment of God's purposes for the world. Their experience of 'turning to the Light of Christ' placed them in a new relationship to God, to the world and to history.[9] Thus Fox wrote:

> now I was come up in spirit through the Flaming Sword, into the paradise of God. All things were new, and all creation gave another smell unto me than before, beyond what words can utter. I knew nothing but pureness and innocency and righteousness, being renewed up into the image of God by Christ Jesus, so that I say I was come up to the state of Adam, which he was in before he fell . . . But I was immediately taken up in spirit to see into another or more steadfast state than Adam's innocency, even into a state in Christ Jesus that should never fall.[10]

Quakers were back in Eden, experiencing heaven on earth, but were also beyond the possibility of falling. Early Friends were reunited with God in a new new-covenant which marked the fulfilment of God's plan for humanity and believed that theirs was the time of the Second Coming. They claimed they knew this through their dramatic transforming religious experiences.

Friends were not millennial in the strict sense of the word.[11] They never encouraged a theology of a thousand-year rule of the saints. Theirs was not an outward Second Coming but an inward one, as foretold in Jeremiah 31:31–34. This speaks of God writing a new covenant on the *hearts* of the people so that they would all know the Lord, and in a way that would set them free from sin. Thus, Friends claimed that 'Christ has come to teach his people himself'. For them, 'Christ is come and is coming'.[12] The Second Coming was realised *within* these Friends and would be realised amongst the whole world. Everyone could and should become a Quaker, one of 'his people' and those early years of enthusiasm saw missions sent as far afield as Constantinople and the Vatican in order to secure conversions.

In this *realising* eschatology, Friends were living in sharp contrast to those Christians who still looked back to the first coming for their sustaining inspiration, or to those other sects, who maintained vital millennial hopes, but placed them in the future. Friends formed a 'Second-Coming church' in contra-distinction to the Churches which focused on the first coming or those others still living in the meantime. Quakers based their ecclesiology on the belief that in this new intimacy with God there was no need for set-apart priests, buildings, special times, or the outward sacraments. Now that the Lord had come again, there was no need to break the bread in remembrance, as in 1 Corinthians 11:25–6. Thus Fox ordained that

> this work by Christ superseded all existing Church orders, governments, teachers, and ministers, which could only stand in the way of the full

exercise of his messianic offices. . . . The official temples and ministers of Christendom, which were not ordained in the New Testament, were thus an idolatrous offence which must give way to the true temples of God, the bodies of his faithful, and their true prophet, bishop, counsellor, and priest, Jesus Christ.[13]

For Quakers, the theology of the interim was no longer valid. Indeed, it held people back from the new new-covenant now available to them. Christ *had* come again according to Quakers and so outward sacraments were no longer necessary. As the Word of God was free to all, priests and churches were anachronistic. Mediation between humanity and God was no longer necessary in this renewed intimacy. This belief was sufficiently strong to lead to a degree of militancy.

Early Quakers disrupted services in 'steeplehouses' and interrupted 'hireling ministers'. Quakers protested against 'holy days (so-called)' and the celebration of times and seasons. They believed all time was equally sacramental and so Quaker shops opened on Sundays. Meeting for Worship (held in silence so as to facilitate the free ministry) was held on Wednesday. In terms of ethics, the fruits of the Spirit were an automatic consequence of the Quaker experience of the Spirit. Humanity was levelled. Quakers refused to differentiate by class. They would take their hats off to no one but God. They used 'thee' and 'thou' to everyone, rather than the polite form 'you' to peers and so-called betters. Whilst these 'fruits' continued, and indeed became institutionalised and regulated, the claims, however, around the nature of the powerful experience of the first Friends were modified as it became clear the Second Coming was not in fact taking place.

The problems of grand claims

Second-generation Quaker millennialism typically changes form.[14] Moore's meticulous analysis of the tracts of Friends through the 1650s reveals that as early as 1654, Quakers begin to modify some of their grand claims.[15] Not everyone had converted to Quakerism and the world had not been transformed. On a more mundane level, a doctrine of perfection had been difficult to maintain, given human fallibility.[16]

In 1659, following the death of Cromwell, there was a renewal of the hopes of earlier years. The restoration of the Monarchy, however, brought with it a new pragmatic Quakerism which survived the persecution of the State (which only ended with the Act of Toleration in 1689) but which, in turn, limited the consummation of eschatological hopes.[17]

Although Damiano argues that the eighteenth-century Quaker community lived a realised eschatology, that they lived as if 'God's created order was to be manifested on earth now' and that Friends experienced 'a daily nourishment of the inward person of Christ in those within whom he dwells',[18] other Friends claimed that this experience of the inward Christ operated within a different eschatological frame. In his systematic Quaker theology of 1676, which became a household text after his death in 1692, Robert Barclay tempered the doctrine of perfection in a significant manner. He located salvation on a God-chosen and 'singular day of visitation' as opposed to a continuous opportunity on the part of the believer to turn to the Light of Christ. In this shift, he helped to create an anxious community of those waiting and seeking.[19]

Instead of living in a state of heaven on earth, of a fully realised intimacy with God, eighteenth-century Friends explicitly spoke of the gulf between the natural and the supernatural. Now, their ability to be faithful was dependent on being wary of a corrupt and corrupting world. For them, the self was no longer the channel of potential global transformation but the site of human emotions and delusions. So an eighteenth-century Quaker could write:

> I'm often afraid lest by indulging my own ideals of what is good, and not labouring after a total resignation of mind,...I should frustrate the divine intention, which may be to humble and reduce self more than flesh and blood would point out.[20]

This period of Quakerism was also a time of increasing regulation over consumption. Dress and pastimes were constrained.[21] Outward appearance was deemed to symbolise inward authenticity. If early Friends had heard the alarm clock of the Second Coming ringing, 'restoration Quakerism' and the 'Quietism' which followed it pressed the snooze button. The construction of the Quaker household and its contingent disciplines in the eighteenth century marked an important shift in duty and obligation. It focused on the maintenance of purity in 'the meantime'. This movement raised some pertinent questions. Either earlier Friends had been wrong about the Second Coming, in which case a particular opportunity had passed, or its arrival was on a slower timescale than had been forecast. Instead of settling for an interim theology embodied in forms of worship, it is as if Quakers chose a set of 'meantime practices' to help them remember what they were about.

In the nineteenth century, a new social and religious context took the Quaker movement even further away from a sense of an imminent or unfolding Second Coming. Denied access to the professions, many Quakers had turned to industry and were increasingly moving in rich urban social circles where ethical boundaries were being continually modified. In this setting, these Friends found the evangelicalism of their Anglican contemporaries increasingly compelling, whilst also discovering that the range of Quaker 'peculiarities' seemed to have become awkward or anachronistic. Many of these Friends converted out of Quakerism,[22] whilst others strove to change Quakerism itself.

By the middle of the nineteenth century, a Quietist wariness of the world had been replaced by an increasing desire to pull down the 'hedge' that lay between Quakerism and the world. A Quaker evangelicalism had brought Friends firmly alongside mainstream Christianity, thus making them ecumenical in outlook for the first time. Quakers now sought to protect the Lord's Day from railway travel. This marked a significant shift in attitudes to time, where each and every moment had been regarded as part of the Day of the Lord. From the 1850s, the peculiarities of Quakerism were abolished. Friends could erect gravestones for their dead. They could marry non-Quakers without facing disownment. In 1861, the 'book of discipline' was amended to omit the advice on plain dress and plain speech (the use of 'thee' and 'thou' instead of the polite form 'you').[23]

From this point, it was possible to be invisible as a Quaker in the street and to live in a Quaker/non-Quaker household. Soon after, Meetings relinquished their authority to judge what was now a 'private life', and 'Quaker time' (the time an adherent spends explicitly as a Quaker) could be confined to Sunday worship. Scripture had superseded experience and revelation as the primary religious authority within the group. The concept of the 'inward light', central to earlier Friends, was questioned as unscriptural although 'unprogrammed' worship was maintained. For a time then, explicit theology replaced specific practices, in terms of dress and speech for example, as the way in which the Quaker movement remembered its aspirations. At the same time, the energy once spent on maintaining the purity of the group was channelled towards philanthropy.

In America, where the Quaker movement had divided twice in the 1820s–1840s, further splits took place over the introduction of pastors from 1875 and 'programmed' worship with music and a message.[24] Pastors were not priests – any Friend could still minister – but it was an ecclesiological reform which took that branch of the Quaker tradition closer to the interim practice of other Churches. In some traditions Barclay's systematic theology was not reprinted. Evangelical Quakers were now divided between pre- and post-millennial doctrines as they took on theology as well as form from other parts of Christianity.[25] Some argued for the right to baptise with water or to take communion. It was if the hands of the alarm clock had been wound back.

Such an apparently radical departure from earlier form is consistent, however, given the equally apparent departure of the Second Coming experience of the first Friends. For a Church established on Second Coming structures, which loses its sense of the Second Coming, reform makes sense, particularly if the concept of a theology or form of the interim is compelling. In this sense, parts of Quakerism became empathetic to other Churches and more focused on the First Coming than the Second. The move to a pastorate and programmed worship was not defended in terms of the loss of Second Coming experience. Rather the reasons for it (large numbers of newly affiliated and an absence of a teaching ministry)[26] and the theological emphases of these pastoral Friends indicate that these American Friends too no longer felt they were living in the endtimes.

In Britain, the evangelical domination of Victorian Quakerism would not last the century. There have never been Quaker pastors in Britain. Instead, the very freedoms evangelicals had pushed for, opening Quakerism to the world and increasing recruitment, would lead to a further reinvention of how Quakerism was to be defined as a religious group. By 1900, a Liberal Quaker revisioning of British Quakerism was under way. Influenced by Darwinian thinking and the critiques of Biblical scholarship, their theological enterprise reclaimed parts of original Quakerism in order to restore a distinctive non-conformity. Most importantly, they returned Quakerism in Britain to an emphasis on the authority of experience. They coupled this with the desire to be part of a faith always relevant to the age, and one which was always open to 'new Light'.[27] It was as if Friends had finally agreed to work only within historical time, to live fully 'in the world', rather than living in ways which, notionally at least, kept them apart from 'the world'. Quakers were now full citizens of the British State and they worked within it as MPs and magistrates. Progressivism, the chronological authority of revelation, which had become part of Quakerism since the 1870s,[28] became more explicitly adopted in a doctrine of continuing revelation. What was different, then, from the first Quakers is that these Liberal Friends did not seek to check revelation with Scriptural authority but relied on experience alone. They explicitly sought to be open to 'new Light' and new ideas and claimed that new revelation would necessarily replace old. They no longer saw themselves at odds with the culture around them. These changes laid the foundations for more radical change to take place within British Quakerism in the twentieth century.

No time like the present: twentieth-century British Quakerism

Based on experience alone, with an emphasis on continuing revelation but always open to 'new Light', belief-content in twentieth-century British Quakerism had no place to which it needed to be fixed to or to return. It did not need to tie in with Scripture or with tradition. Additionally, the continuing emphasis on silence and a renewed wariness of the universality of theological statements led it to regard theology as a private affair. Today, belief need never be voiced and rarely is.

In the last fifty years, British Quakerism has shifted from a position of Quaker-Christian hegemony to one of theological pluralism. 'New Light' now includes the non-Christian and today there are Buddhist and Muslim Quakers. The organisation is best described as post-Christian in the sense that there are many adherents who use an alternative language to describe their personal theologies.[29]

Liberal Quakerism is defined by its members in terms of its lack of form, the absence of a separated priesthood, of outward sacraments, music, programmed worship and means of management and recognition of sacred space. The answer to the question 'What do Quakers believe?' remains an elusive one to the enquirer. Present-day British Friends believe roughly what they like about the nature of God (or not). Belief is marginal in the life of a group committed to a non-creedal belief system but unified around a 'behavioural creed,' that is a creedal attitude to the way in which the group is religious.[30]

Such hesitation about an over-definition of belief is rooted in the rationalism which underlay Liberal Quaker concerns over having Scripture as a primary source of authority. It is a rationalism which also exposes religion itself as nonsensical, that 'God' is neither true nor false but meaningless. Friends are careful only to talk about their faith or even the frame of their faith to those who they know already share this extra-rational language game, or to those who have asked to hear about it. Instead of responding to modernity with faith as the Evangelicals had, Liberal Quakers responded with a 'reasonable' religion.

Emerging from the emphasis on experience and the wariness about theological statements, even private theology has become a story. In one of about ten ways in which Liberal and Evangelical Friends hold oppositional positions, Liberals maintain that theology is a constructed 'belief story' built on a real experience (realists) or a constructed one (non-realists). Even realists know that, either philosophically or within the constraints of the group life, they cannot claim theology is true except in a personal, partial or provisional way. Conversely, it means that they have never found the final complete truth. Seeking after continuing revelation becomes normative.[31] In a manual on Quakerism, it is stated:

> we do not in the least deprecate the attempt, which must be made, since man (*sic*) is a rational being, to formulate intellectually the ideas which are implicit in religious experience . . . But it should always be recognised that such attempts are provisional and can never be assumed to possess the finality of ultimate truth.[32]

Belief is marginal and is less important than the experience it can only describe partially. It is also personal. The inability to judge corporately the theology of another is inherent. As one respondent noted, 'the fact that the group allows the doubt of all beliefs surely means it should support the tolerance of all beliefs'.

It is by holding so carefully to the form, and to the sense of a continuous search which may have few definite or final answers, that these Friends maintain organisational cohesion. Those who disagree with the form are in tension with the group, whilst those who have a crisis of faith are encouraged to stay.[33] Individual adherents face a paradox, of holding to a personal belief story which helps them make sense of their religious experience, whilst belonging to a group in which statements of belief are considered marginal or even dangerous to group unity. In Plüss' study of modern Quakerism, interviewees claimed that they were wary of exposing their theological biases for fear of ostracisation or for fear of treading on the toes of their co-religionists. Those who wish to reform Quakerism have no authority with which to pronounce a 'true' Quakerism and may rather have to console themselves that they belonged to what had gone before. Not only is silence given a premium within the group as the medium through which God is approached and experienced and through which 'God's will' is known in vote-less business meetings, but it operates as organisational glue, one that masks difference and potential dissent.[34] This has led to a number of contradictions.

The organisation is in tension because its form is predicated on beliefs, and as these become open to individual interpretation and reinterpretation, the form itself may be challenged. Phrases like 'seeking the will of God', used officially to describe the purpose of Quaker business meetings, have become anachronistic to many. Their God may not be the kind of God who can have a will, or they do not believe in God, as such, or at all. The form around this partiality of religious truth is held with clear determination. The perhaps-ness of Liberal Quaker theology is absolute, as it were.[35] Those who have claimed they have been 'eldered' (disciplined) for explicitly Christian ministry in this post-Christian group sound too certain about the truth of what they had to say.

Gwyn[36] and Roof[37] have examined the phenomenon of seeking. Gwyn's research is amongst seventeenth-century sectarians and the group called Seekers, many of whom became ardent Quakers. Gwyn identifies two kinds of seekers, A and B. Seeker A types are those who look to restore what has been corrupted. Seeker B types look to a new dispensation, believing God would not take them backwards. In present-day British Quakerism, it is possible to identify a Seeker C type, who wishes only to seek, not to find. As one respondent stated: 'I know I will never have the answers, any of the answers... if I thought I had found any, I would know I was wrong ...Quakerism is better that way, more honest.'

Indeed, theoretically, Seeker C types can seek anywhere where they can be sure *not* to find. They reflect the saying 'to travel hopefully is better than to arrive'. It could be argued, first, that it would not be possible to be totally and truly sure of having arrived, for truth is not discernible in that kind of way. Secondly, the Quaker 'God' is not the type of God who brings a people of God to a final resting place. Thus, for some modern Quakerism, 'the spirit of seeking is still the prevailing one in our faith'.[38] Theologically speaking, all this group is corporately certain of is its uncertainty.

This has consequences for maintaining belief in the Second Coming. First, many Friends are not 'Christian' in the way that the Second Coming is traditionally important. Secondly, for non-Christian Friends, the First Coming itself is inappropriate or meaningless. Thirdly, for Friends at ease with 'the absolute perhaps', any consummation of God's plan for the world, or indeed any sense of finality, or even of future, may appear out of place within a theology of individual in-the-moment seeking. The alarm clock has been thrown out.

On a timeline running from the First to the Second Coming, Liberal Quakers do not move back towards the First Coming as their immediate predecessors did, but drop off the timeline altogether. They are in this sense amillennial or, more strictly speaking, operate a de-eschatalogicalised theology. If, as Lindhof suggests in this volume, interest in the apocalypse has been revitalised in popular culture, then, ironically, present-day Quakers find themselves out of tune with the times in the area where traditionally they were strong, a theology that focused on a future, one that marked the hope of time resolved which the notion of a Second Coming embodied. Without an apparatus of religion, they have also lost their distinctive witness to the apocalypse.

The loss of hegemonic Quaker-Christianity appears as a forerunner to the loss of explicit religion and the boundaries such explicitness creates. The behavioural creed masks this shift because the form *looks* exactly like the religious frame which has been in place for three centuries. It is also a form in which no outward aspect is explicitly religious. Silence may be a humble approach to God or may simply be silence.[39] There are no regularised vocal prayers, no outward religious practices, only the liturgy of silence.[40] Religious belief, or its lack, need never be voiced. Ministry is frequently in inclusive secular language, explicit religion being seen by some respondents as divisive and inappropriate in that words cannot get close to the reality of religious experience. Furthermore, there is a sense that any single pronouncement may be misunderstood by the listener to carry more 'weight' than its partial, provisional or personal truth-base warrants.[41]

Paradoxically, it is the maintenance of the form resulting from the early Quaker claims of the unfolding Second Coming which contributes to this outward secularisation. Liberal Friends did not at any stage take up the premise of mainstream Christianity that humanity needs the help of a separated priesthood, outward sacraments, with set-aside times and seasons for life *in the meantime*. From 1722, those with a 'gift of ministry' were 'recorded' by their Monthly Meetings (local business meetings), but this was abolished in 1924 as it was claimed that the practice inhibited the free ministry. From the turn of the century, Quakers have increasingly celebrated Christmas,[42] though this may be put down to increased 'worldliness' rather than a recognition that Quakers need times and seasons to help them in their spiritual life.[43] In 1903, Woodbrooke was set up as a training college for the Quaker 'priesthood of all believers' but attendance is voluntary. The organisation has never created a mechanism to enforce religious learning or remembrance amongst its members.

One consequence of dedication to form is that outward defining symbols of Quakerism are not challenged. For example, during the Gulf War in 1991, there were numerous interpretations of what maintaining a Peace Testimony might involve – one Friend suggested assassinating Saddam Hussein would alleviate further death and suffering. Whilst some favoured military intervention, evidence suggests no one questioned the validity of the Peace Testimony itself as part of what Quakerism embodied.[44]

It is in this way that explicit religion is replaced by a dedication to form and the fruits, if not the roots, of the 'testimonies' or witness, notably on peace and the integrity of humanity and of creation. The single universal Quaker belief is 'that of God in everyone', and whilst the 'that' and 'the God' and even 'everyone' is subject to individual interpretation, it is currently taken to signify an innate optimism about human nature and potential.[45] Quaker work in peace and justice projects continues world-wide and individual Friends are typically involved in numerous social action causes locally.

Attenders, those who attend regularly without formally joining, claim they are not 'good enough' to be Friends.[46] The cultural inheritance of philanthropists such as Elizabeth Fry, the post-World-Wars relief which led to the Nobel Peace Prize in 1947, or the founders of Oxfam being Quaker still frames and encourages a model of what it is to be a Quaker. In her influential 1980 address to Friends in Britain, Janet Scott answered the question as to whether Friends need to be Christian or not with the advice, 'it's not the label . . . but the life'.[47] Shared values have replaced a shared God.

Conclusion

British Quakerism offers an intriguing case-study of a significant sociological question: the extent to which pure experience and/or the 'pure search' can sustain a corporate and individual faith even after the explicit sharing of that experience has passed. It remains of critical interest to investigate longitudinally the way in which corporate expressions of religiosity are managed, both in their presentation to the world, and in negotiation with an increasingly theologically disparate membership. Can shared ethics sustain religiosity when the faith-basis of such ethics may be invisible to the group or non-existent?

The liberal Quaker case reveals that the believing-without-belonging hypothesis[48] may only apply to mainstream religion. In those groups with more of a sectarian culture, belonging may continue long after believing has dissipated or disappeared. The group may wish to retain those 'at home' in the group, for example, encouraging atheists to join or stay. Birthright participants, regardless of their belief, have remained in membership, because, as one respondent put it 'it's what I know.' Even where there are tensions around belief and parts of the practice, sectarian distinctiveness, such as the silent worship method or pacifism, may encourage those to stay simply for the reason they have nowhere else to go which offers similar forms of worship and experience. Additionally, the emphasis on seeking without finally finding not only accommodates some 22.9 per cent of a sample who are not sure whether they believe in God,[49] but it may act as the first step on the ladder of religious shopping. Eighty-five per cent of present-day Quakers have joined from outside the group,[50] 47 per cent of these having no immediately prior religious affiliation.[51]

If Perrin and Mauss are correct in their assessment that it is perceptions of 'seriousness' that precipitate conversion and switching,[52] then Quakerism can appear more 'serious' than solitary atheism and agnosticism, whilst not making any demands in terms of belief on the enquirer. The numbers of those attending Quaker worship remains level[53] at a time when other Christian groups are suffering huge losses of attendance.[54] In a religious group where one does not have to believe, it may be more attractive to belong. Rational-choice theory applied within Quakerism can only be based on rational rewards, as opposed to extra-rational ones.

This case-study also highlights the way in which attitudes to key pieces of doctrine, such as the Second Coming, can be used productively to delineate the theology and organisational culture of different religious groups within a single broad tradition. Further research might underline differing attitudes to 'time' between sect and church groups. In the Quaker case-study, denominationalisation has accompanied a more focused attitude to past-time and the authority of what has gone before, whether tradition or scripture. The sectarianism of present-day Friends is less interested in what has gone before, albeit in a different kind of a way from the detachment of the first Friends to tradition and history *per se*. The emphasis is on the present, the 'now', and on the personal journey. Time is only of interest in secular terms. Ethics are shared, unlike theologies, but, as such, their root may not be. Not only has the Quaker faith been de-eschatologised, but also de-divinised. A form which initially resulted from the power of the spiritual experience of the first Quakers has paradoxically left the group particularly vulnerable to the secular culture within which it finds itself embedded. All that remains is for somebody to either wind the alarm clock or sell it.

Notes and references

1   See also, for example, Richard K. Fenn, *The End of Time: Religion, Ritual, and the Forging of the Soul* (London: SPCK, 1997).

2   I am indebted to Richard Fenn, Timothy Peat and Douglas Gwyn for the intellectual stimulation which led to the production of this paper. It is based on ten years of qualitative and quantitative research and ongoing participant observation amongst Quakers in Britain.

3   Caroline B. Plüss, 'A Sociological Analysis of the Modern Quaker Movement', unpublished D.Phil. thesis, University of Oxford, 1996. See also Bryan R. Wilson, *Religious Sects* (London: Weidenfeld & Nicolson, 1970).

4   Richard K. Fenn, *The Persistence of Purgatory* (Cambridge: Cambridge University Press, 1995), p. 2.

5   Timothy Peat, 'Adulthood: Incarnation and the Kingdom of God', in Ben Pink Dandelion, Douglas Gwyn and Timothy Peat, *Heaven on Earth: Quakers and the Second Coming* (Kelso and Birmingham: Curlew & Woodbrooke, 1995), pp. 53–66.

6   E. P. Sanders, *Paul* (Oxford: Oxford University Press, 1991), p. 53.

7   Albert Schweitzer, *The Quest for the Historical Jesus* (New York: Macmillan, 1968), p. 360.

8   Austin Flannery (ed.), *Vatican Council II: The Conciliar and post-Conciliar Documents* (Dublin: Dominican Publications, 1975), p. 408. [cf. Romans 8:18–23]

9   Timothy Peat, 'Adolescence and the Church', in Dandelion, Gwyn and Peat, *Heaven on Earth*, p. 87.

10 John Nickalls (ed.), *The Journal of George Fox* (Cambridge: Cambridge University Press, 1952), p. 27.

11 Where 'amillennialism' is used, it may thus be more correctly interpreted as a complete de-eschatologisation of theology.

12 Nickalls, *The Journal of George Fox*, p. 48.

13 Douglas Gwyn, *The Apocalypse of the Word: The Life and Message of George Fox* (Richmond, IN: Friends United Press, 1987), p. 30.

14 See, for example, the analysis of the United Society of Believers in Christ's Second Appearing (Shakers), in Majorie Procter-Smith, '"In the Line of the Female"; Shakerism and Feminism', in Catherine Wessinger (ed.), *Women's Leadership in Marginal Religions* (Urbana: University of Illinois Press, 1993), pp. 23–40.

15 Rosemary Moore, 'The Faith of the First Quakers: The Development of Their Beliefs and Practices Before the Restoration', unpublished Ph.D. thesis, University of Birmingham, 1993.

16 Barry Reay, *Quakers and the English Revolution* (London: Temple Smith, 1985), p. 120.

17 Douglas Gwyn, *The Covenant Crucified: Quakers and the Rise of Capitalism* (Wallingford, PA: Pendle Hill, 1995), p. 218.

18 Kathryn Damiano, 'On Earth as it is in Heaven: Eighteenth Century Quakerism as Realised Eschatology', unpublished Ph.D. thesis, Union of Experimenting Colleges and Universities, 1988.

19 Ben Pink Dandelion, 'Fresh Light, Dimmer Hopes', in Dandelion, Gwyn and Peat, *Heaven on Earth*, pp. 161–5.

20 Sarah Grubb, *Some Account of the Life and Labours of Sarah Grubb* (London: James Phillips, 1794), p. 28.

21 According to Vann, even hair was brought under the control of the Meeting. He found a Dublin Half-Yearly Meeting minute of November 1714, where it was recorded that 'if any Friend wants hair, they should acquaint the men's meeting they belong to, and have their approbation, and consent before they get any'. Richard Vann, *The Social Development of English Quakerism* (Cambridge, Mass.: Harvard University Press, 1969), p. 192.

22 Notably Isaac Crewdson and his 'Beaconite' group in 1836. See ibid., p. 507. See also Elizabeth Isichei, *Victorian Quakers* (Oxford: Oxford University Press, 1970), pp. 45–53.

23 Ibid., p. 157.

24   Thomas D. Hamm, *The Transformation of American Quakerism: Orthodox Friends, 1800–1907* (Bloomington, IN: Indiana University Press, 1988), pp. 124–30.
25   Ibid., pp. 106–7 and 119–20.
26   Ibid., p. 127.
27   Martin Davie, *British Quaker Theology Since 1895* (Lampeter: Edwin Mellen, 1997), chapter 2, pp. 54–98.
28   Isichei, *Victorian Quakers*, p. 34.
29   Ben Pink Dandelion, *A Sociological Analysis of the Theology of Quakers: the Silent Revolution* (Lampeter: Edwin Mellen, 1996), chapter 4, 'Content', pp. 133–92.
30   Ibid., chapter 3, 'Frameworks', pp. 93–131. This 'behavioural creed' has been present from the early days of Quakerism and may be a feature of all sectarian movements. Quietism is an example of a period of Quaker history when a 'behavioural creed' was emphasised and this was less the case in the following Evengelical era.
31   Ben Pink Dandelion, 'Blood or Water? Liberal Quakers and Evangelical Friends', *The Seeker*, Autumn 1998, pp. 19–21.
32   *Quaker Faith and Practice: The Book of Christian Discipline of the Yearly Meeting of the Religious Society of Friends (Quakers) in Britain* (London: Britain Yearly Meeting, 1995) section 27.23. This book is the closest text to what may be considered 'orthodoxy'; although it is generally descriptive on matters of belief, it is prescriptive on matters of form.
33   Dandelion, *A Sociological Analysis of the Theology of Quakers*, p. 101.
34   See Plüss, 'A Sociological Analysis of the Modern Quaker Movement', for the high emphasis placed on unity within the group, through strategies of recruitment, socialisation, belief and theological epistemology, particularly when concerned with Quaker business methods.
35   Ben Pink Dandelion, 'The Absolute Perhaps: Towards an Understanding of Liberal Quaker Theology', in Janet Scott (ed.), *Papers from the International Quaker Consultation on Identity, Authority, Community* (forthcoming).
36   Douglas Gwyn, 'Early Quakers: When Seekers Become Finders', paper presented at Manchester College, Oxford, 12 May 1997.
37   Wade Clark Roof, *A Generation of Seekers: the Spiritual Journeys of the Baby Boom Generation* (San Francisco: Harper Collins, 1993).
38   *Quaker Faith and Practice*, section 26:16. Earlier in the book, section 1.02, one of the Advices asks 'are you open to new light from whatever source it may come?' Some of those who find great certainty choose to leave, although there is no requirement to, on matters of belief alone.
39   See Kieran Flanagan, *Sociology and Liturgy: Re-presentations of the Holy* (Basingstoke: Macmillan, 1991), p. 115, on the uncheckable nature of the rite and the potential for feigning piety.
40   Richard A. Baer, Jr., 'Silent Worship, Glossolalia and Liturgy: Some Functional Similarities', *Quaker Religious Thought*, vol. 16, no. 3, 1975, pp. 28–37.
41   See Dandelion, *A Sociological Analysis of the Theology of Quakers*, sections 3.2 and 6.2.1, on the value of silence and the inappropriateness of words. See pp. 93–100 and 239–42.
42   Ann Carrdus, 'The Quaker unChristmas', *The Friend*, vol. 151, no. 52, 1993, pp. 1659–60.
43   Winfred M. White, 'Keeping Christmas', *The Friend*, vol. 154, no. 51, 1996, p. 24, provides an exception.
44   Friends joined up in both World Wars. Brian D. Phillips suggests that one-third of all eligible male Quakers joined up in the First World War. See 'Friendly Patriotism:

British Quakerism and the Imperial Nation, 1890–1910', unpublished Ph.D., University of Cambridge, 1989. On the other hand, Thomas Kennedy has shown that those who resisted conscription most rigorously were given the most status in the inter-war years. See his essay, 'Why did Friends Resist?: The War, Peace Testimony, and the All-Friends Conference of 1920', *Peace and Change*, vol. 14, 1989, pp. 355–71. Following the Gulf War and the diversity of views expressed then, Ambler suggests looking afresh at the meaning of the Peace Testimony, but this sociologist has not found any evidence to suggest a desire for its removal from Quaker culture. Plüss and I have identified this maintenance of outward form as a dimension of unity-generation within the group. See Rex Ambler, *The End of Words: Issues in Contemporary Quaker Theology* (London: Quaker Home Service, 1994), p. 32

45 Dandelion, *A Sociological Analysis of the Theology of Quakers*, p. 268.
46 Alastair Heron, *Caring, Conviction, Commitment: Dilemmas of Quaker Membership Today* (London: Quaker Home Service, 1992), p. 27.
47 Janet Scott, *What Canst Thou Say? Towards a Quaker Theology* (London: Quaker Home Service, 1980), p. 70.
48 Grace Davie, *Religion in Britain Since 1945: Believing without Belonging* (Oxford: Blackwell, 1994).
49 Dandelion, *A Sociological Analysis of the Theology of Quakers*, p. 159.
50 Ibid., p. 331.
51 Heron, *Caring, Conviction, Commitment*, p. 13.
52 R. D. Perrin and Armand L. Mauss, 'Saints and Seekers: Sources of Recruitment to the Vineyard Christian Fellowship', *Review of Religious Research*, vol. 33, no. 2, 1991, pp. 97–111.
53 'Tabular Statement of the Yearly Meeting of Friends (Quakers) in Britain for the year ending 1997' (London: Britain Yearly Meeting, 1998).
54 Phillip Richter and Leslie J. Francis, *Gone but not Forgotten: Church Leaving and Returning* (London: Darton, Longman & Todd, 1998).

11
The Ethos of Modern Apocalyptic Stories: The Use of Judaeo-Christian Narrative in Popular Film

Jessica Lindohf

Contemporary notions of the apocalypse have arisen with growing fears of nuclear disaster and ecological catastrophe and with worries over the ending of the millennium. The meanings attached to the term are as diverse as are the themes related to the apocalypse which have emerged in popular culture and science fiction. In this chapter, the dual nature of apocalypse, as used in popular culture, is contrasted with its narrower and more classical use in its original theological context. Against this background, the potential of popular film to formulate apocalyptic narratives for our times will be investigated. Their relation to the apocalyptic themes of good versus evil, messianic heroes, the fallen society and the world to come will be outlined and examined.

In a theological context, the term 'apocalypse' signifies a particular genre of Biblical writings, such as those in the Books of Daniel and of Revelation. This literature sees itself as revealing God's purpose at the end of time.[1] In popular culture, the term 'apocalypse', or 'apocalyptic', has been appropriated to signify images of decay, disaster, social collapse and moral breakdown. This reflects properties of classical apocalyptic literature and millenarian movements in history. Millenarian movements support an eschatology (a belief in how God's purpose for history and humankind will be brought about) which affirms that a Second Coming of Christ will establish a 1000-year kingdom on earth, followed by judgement.[2] The concept of the apocalyptic and millenarianism, as Wilson rightly points out, is problematic in the context of non-Christian cultures which can also carry the traits of millenarian movements. His investigation of millenarianism outside the Western world raises many important questions about the essence of the apocalyptic.[3]

The popular versions of the apocalypse that are found in contemporary music and literature[4] seem to have lost touch with the more classical and theological forms. These popular versions are written for their own ends.

The result might seem that the notion of apocalypse has become banal, as Giddens would express it.[5] Yet people in late modern society have come to feel that they are living in a high-risk society. The proximity to ecological, nuclear and economical disasters is a real threat to cope with. The safe cocoon of a secluded society has been broken by the media which increasingly spread an awareness of living at risk. As a result, modern society's interest in the apocalypse has been revitalised. It has taken on a new significance as we stand on the brink of a new millennium. The postmodern marriage of reason, technology and nightmare in Ballard's vision has broken down our concepts of philosophy, history and time. This has created an even more ambiguous world with new opportunities but also one with new forms of paranoia.[6] Anticipation and fear mark a beginning, but also a sense of an end, as the year 2000 takes on a symbolic significance. The paranoia and fear connected to the new millennium corresponds to the anxiety raised by the human condition and the problems of living in a modern technological society. The fear of the End feeds on the fear of death and vice versa, giving rise to contemporary expressions of the apocalyptic and millenarianism in popular culture. These factors are creating a new language and a new imagery which expands the understanding of the classical apocalypse. They seem to fulfil Thompson's point that millenarian beliefs are a driving force in history.[7]

Kreuziger approaches the genre of apocalyptic in the context of science fiction as popular literature. In his dialectical comparison between science fiction and the apocalyptic he argues that both are user-oriented and that they reveal much of the reader's expectations and hopes as well as formulating a political critique.[8] He sees science fiction as a secular apocalyptic that can further a deeper understanding of classical biblical versions of the apocalyptic.[9] Working from a reader-orientated perspective, Kreuziger offers an understanding of the apocalyptic as literature that expresses a hope and a longing for emancipation and redemption.[10] His approach is valuable since it also allows science fiction film to be an expression of popular culture at the same time as it focuses on the importance of the apocalyptic in the genre. This makes it possible to interpret the apocalyptic stories of popular culture as part of a larger mythology and a long tradition of apocalyptic writings.[11] Kreuziger points out the similarities between the apocalyptic and science fiction. The most significant of these traits is the intense longing for a new world and a new age. Another important trait is how contemporary society is portrayed as occupying an epoch of crisis, where humanity waits for salvation to be brought to it from outside the concurrent reality. Science fiction and traditional notions of the apocalyptic similarly see themselves as foreshadowing future events, revealed to them in supernatural ways. Both traditions have evolved as subcultures out of similar social and political settings. Both are formed by marginal groups embracing their exclusiveness and re-appropriating old myths for dealing with origins and ends thus creating a future, whilst interpreting history in order to accommodate their own belief systems.[12]

Classical apocalyptic meets popular apocalyptic

Zamora sees the apocalypse as the least understood but also one of the most basic myths underlying American culture.[13] He notes that the application of the myth has been expanded to a context outside religion. This means that the notion of the apocalyptic has become secularised in order to explain our destiny. The apocalyptic outlook has become increasingly pessimistic as the concept becomes more historical than religious. Our history and experience of human self-destruction have fed into the concept of the apocalypse resulting in a negative outlook on the future to come.[14] The wider interpretations of the concept of the apocalyptic in Zamora and Kreuziger pick up on similar apocalyptic expressions in modern society, but differ in their understanding. Zamora's negative outlook is challenged by Kreuziger's reading of popular apocalyptic as potentially liberating.

In contrast to the wide and increasing usage of the term 'apocalypse' in secular society, theologians have tended to limit its use to a biblical or church-historical context.[15] In the Judaeo-Christian context, the apocalypse has to do with time or rather the interruption of time. It is the moment when time itself ceases to exist. The apocalyptic event stands outside history and looks at future, present and past from this a-temporal place.[16] In the biblical tradition, the apocalyptic is crisis literature which is formulated by a community in chaos to give hope for another existence. In its claims to reveal the purpose of God it offers not only hope but also assurance that the just will ultimately triumph.[17] The biblical tradition treats the apocalypse as the end of time when disaster, pain, and suffering occur but also when a new beginning is formed. The End is a time of grief and pain, traditionally depicted through a series of metaphoric images, and these serve as tools for revealing the future to humankind. These images are depicted in a very powerful way that seems to elude interpretation and can leave the reader disturbed.[18] This belief in a new beginning is the underlying theme of apocalyptic thought that has made the apocalypse something to long for and to fear.[19] In his unravelling of the apocalypse in American fiction Zamora notes that the classical apocalypse satisfies a need for wholeness, one that places our lives in a historical context and provides our existence with a greater meaning.[20] He stresses that even if the apocalypse in popular culture has become increasingly negative, in a religious context it has always been seen as God's fulfilment and not as a threat to the believer who is saved.[21] This means that in a secularised age, faced with the actual fears of human self-destruction, the apocalypse becomes more frightening than promising, something Zamora notes in his tracing of the apocalyptic in contemporary American fiction.

He argues that problematic historic reality is treated with irony or avoided rather than used as an expression of crisis, which would emphasise its critical potential.[22]

Apocalypse transformed

In the Christian tradition the apocalypse evokes both fear and hope. In its use in a secular society, the concept of the apocalypse has come into focus as a means of supplying a cultural understanding of the actual and continued threat of nuclear and ecological disasters. As Beck has suggested, modern life involves living in a risk society. In post-industrial society we are collectively faced with massive threats and global risks that gives rise to anxiety, repressed in the idea that everybody and no one is responsible.[23] As a result, the apocalyptic is brought out of context, the connection with new beginnings is lost and accordingly the end becomes something more to fear than to long for. What has happened is a suppression of the classical, religious concept of the apocalypse in contemporary secular society in favour of a concept that embraces historical incidents as well as the anxiety of life in a self-destructive society. Zamora makes the same point, seeing the modern apocalypse as more historical and less religious as a result of past events and humanity's inclination towards self-destruction.[24]

Paradoxically in his critique of the Church as institutionalised and provisional, Cox claims that the Church has become an anti-apocalyptic institution that is more interested in maintaining stability than in working for radical change.[25] He argues that the Church is holding on to an ideology of preservation and permanence when what is needed is one that works for social change. For him, a truly Christian Church is one less concerned about its traditions than with the way it deals with questions raised by modern society.[26] Kreuziger agrees with Cox but argues that the challenge to the Church is not only to deal with the third world but also with the secularised expressions of religion in popular culture.[27] This critique raises an important problem. Christianity has become more institutionalised and provisional as a result of focusing on tradition and its own survival rather than on developing forms of spirituality that would deal with particular and current unsettlements. The biblical stories seem to have little relevance in the modern world and the Church often does not provide a narrative that connects with the fears and questions of the secularised reader.

Altizer pursues the issue of the exclusion of the apocalyptic from modern theology and claims that now we have inherited a theological tradition that excludes the most central theme of Christianity.[28] It began with apocalypse and affirmation of belief in a new world. This apocalyptic grounding in Christianity, however, has been eroded by the emergence of the Christian Church.[29] Anyhow, as Altizer argues, even if modern theology has expelled the apocalyptic, it has still survived in literature and philosophy. As a result of this exclusion, a rebirth of theology has to take place in the contemporary atheistic and nihilistic world.[30] The modern realisation that God is dead makes it possible and even necessary to form a contemporary theology, one that aims at the absolutely new and which does not avoid facing the issue of the end.[31] Altizer's critique of modern theology as anti-apocalyptic has the radical implication that modern theology is not truly Christian. The belief in redemption and the new beginning, has in theology, as well as in society, become a belief in an end, not one of absolute emptiness but one in which it is possible to postpone by stability.[32] This raises the interesting paradox that Christianity, in the hands of the Church, has become anti-apocalyptic, whilst popular culture is struggling with the apocalyptic condition of the modern world. The answer to this paradox might lie deep in Altizer's and Cox's critique of the Church. For them, the institutionalised Church is more interested in is own survival and prosperity than in the human secularised conditions of the modern world. The extension of Altizer's argument means that for the Church to be truly apocalyptic, it needs to argue for a theology that would result in its own extinction.[33]

Liberating narratives

With Altizer's argument in mind let us turn to Kreuziger's call for new liberating narratives as guidelines. For Kreuziger, popular culture is offering the apocalyptic and liberating narratives that the Church no longer provides. According to Metz, the metaphor that is controlling the way the modern, western subject looks at human experience is emancipation, whilst the metaphor controlling theology has always been redemption. Eternity no longer carries a promise but follows an evolutionary eschatology that denies the possibility of the radically new.[34] Kreuziger argues that the immanent expectation in science fiction as well as in eschatology has gone through a process of domestication. This has reduced the apocalyptic in science fiction to a subjective fantasy or a structural principle of action. A similar reductionism has taken place in theology where the apocalyptic element is often confined to the subjective and esoteric literature of sectarian groups or simply to a literary genre within biblical studies.[35] The apocalypse has become domesticated through the emergence of a secular apocalyptic. The popular apocalyptic tends to simplify and reduce the content and meaning of the classical apocalypse. The result is that the chaos and complete otherness that is the strength of the classical apocalypse, has in popular apocalyptic been explained, made safe and comprehensible. In order to see beyond the reductionism and the individualisation of the apocalypse, Kreuziger uses Cox's narrative theology which enables him to interpret science fiction literature as apocalyptic narrative.[36] The core of Cox's narrative theology is the human need for a story, a narrative by which we can hear and live, that guides and provides answers to existential questions about existence, life and death. Cox turns to the third world's liberation theology to find appropriate contemporary narratives. He sees in 'the people's religion' the religion of the suppressed and marginalised, a model for how narrative can be used in a liberating way. He argues that liberating narratives can only be created out of people's experiences and that only through a communication with the world can theology be relevant.

Cox is critical of classical theology's a-historical and culture-bound position that tends to place itself outside suffering and outside the human as lived now. As a result of western theology's cultural position, redemption has become futuristic and the present suffering of anxiety and uncertainty is not a matter of its concern. In this way, the issue of redemption is postponed to an indefinite future and the present goal of the Churches is to preserve the status quo. Cox argues that in contrast to western theology, liberation theology finds a concern for suffering, a quest for redemption and an emancipatory use of contemporary narratives for immediate purposes. In order for a narrative to be truly liberating, a connection must be found between the suffering of people, and their history of expectation, redemption and emancipation. Only then, Cox believes, can narratives be used both to give hope and to effect actual change in the society in which we are living.[37]

Kreuziger turns to Metz to find a soteriology that bridges the gap between emancipation, which is needed, and redemption, which is longed for.[38] Metz argues that Christianity has become a bourgeois religion and has lost sight of a messianic future.[39] Bourgeois religion has increasingly focused on reconciliation, giving our present a certificate of political and moral innocence. By seeing reconciliation instead of revolution as the core of messianism, bourgeois religion preaches stagnation rather then freedom.[40] As a counterweight to stagnated bourgeois religion Metz provides a way of looking at soteriology that deals with suffering, emancipation and redemption. Like Cox he turns to the third world to find a memorative, narrative soteriology that is able to tell a story about redemption at the same time as it provides a narrative of the history of suffering. Remembering and telling become the centre for a theology which, for Metz, has to be political in order to preserve the memory of a messianic God.[41]

'The religion of the people' and its appropriate narrative can be found in our own contemporary society. Meaningful and emancipatory narratives are created and used in contemporary society, and the 'religion of the people' can be found in popular apocalyptic, for example in its expression in science fiction. Apocalyptic narratives were used during the inter-testamental period and are in their new forms still available to us outside high culture and respectability.[42] Kreuziger indicates that one of the central ideas used within science fiction is the supposition that humanity is not alone in the universe. This is an important characteristic of science fiction since it expresses community at the same time as it deals with otherness. 'We are not alone' can be interpreted as having a double meaning. The 'other' is also a believer and it is not just 'I' but 'we' who are not alone. According to Kreuziger, the sentence expresses the longing for community and interaction, and shows that at the centre of science fiction stories is a desire not only for community and for shared faith but also a longing for something new.

The central theme of the science fiction story, 'we are not alone', exposes this potential for radical change and bridges the gap between emancipation and redemption through its focus on changes and on community.[43] According to Kreuziger, this would open up a possibility of an emancipating faith and a narrative that can liberate and emancipate both spiritually and physically. The science fiction story as narrative has the ability to give hope and effect change if we read it not only as an expression of contemporary culture or as a criticism of contemporary society, but also as a horizon towards which people can act and live socially and politically.[44] These narratives of hope, expectation and 'otherness' as the horizons for action intertwine with the goals of redemption and emancipation, thus making physical liberation part and parcel of spiritual forms.

In this context, Metz sees humanity's memory as a dangerous and subversive force that ought to be encapsulated in the narrative to effect change. Memory becomes subversive in its role of helping the identification with the history of suffering and struggle and can thereby break the spell of a historical reconstruction based solely on abstract reason.[45] Kreuziger suggests that science fiction stories encapsulate this memory and have freed themselves from the history as seen by abstract reason. Now they have become subversive in their preoccupation with history, myth and suffering. On the one hand science fiction risks totalitarian plans, through its preoccupation with myth, history, beginnings and ends, but on the other it signifies the liberating expectation of something different. With a totalitarian approach it seems that science fiction has been declaring war on the poor in their attempts to create a utopia. Yet from a liberative perspective, science fiction has a basic faith in which the notion that 'we are not alone' provides a true hope for redemption and emancipation.[46] The science fiction story can thereby become a liberating narrative in a society where the traditional Christian narratives are seen as very far away from the lives and dreams of most people.

Exploring religion in science fiction

Science fiction is often regarded as a reflection of social attitudes and trends of the times. It may express ideologies that are not easily discernible at the level of the plot, thus requiring investigation at a deeper level.[47] In addition to the sub-textual elements, much of what is repressed in a story may appear in the form of metaphors and projections. Elucidation of these repressed forms requires a reading which focuses on the gaps and exclusions occurring in the text, as well as on their underlying messages. This requires an interpretation that recognises that film, in both its content and making, is essentially and inherently ideological.[48] To extract the apocalyptic mythology from science fiction texts, a perspective that takes into account the apocalyptic tradition and mythology is required. The application of a theological approach with a reader-orientated interpretation is capable of revealing these elusive messages and takes into account both theological and secular components.[49] This form of interpretation can be illustrated in the way facets of the apocalyptic emerge in some recent films. They carry forward in another format theological themes that relate to questions of hope and morality that mirror contemporary worries and fears about life in the future, where there seem to be good reasons for anxiety. It is useful to categorise these themes under particular headings that illustrate resonances of the classical and theological approaches to the apocalypse in modern use.

Apocalypse and after

Several films depict the world after a great disaster. The disaster is usually caused by humans and appears in the form of nuclear war, as in *Mad Max* (George Miller, 1979) and *Terminator 2* (James Cameron, 1991), or as an ecological disaster as in *Blade Runner* (Ridley Scott, 1982, 1990) and *Late Great Planet Earth* (Robert Amram, 1979). In *Late Great Planet Earth* the disaster is a result of nature taking revenge on its human offenders, whilst in *Blade Runner* the disaster appears to be the result of a gradual exploitation by humans of ecological resources.[50] The 1980s and 1990s featured many films with an apocalyptic theme. The computerised and technological society going wrong seems to be one of the earlier traits featuring in films like *Terminator*. Lately the technological nightmare seems to have faded and given rise to images of ecological disasters, such as in *Vulcano* and *Twister*, as well as in imageries of virtual reality in films like *Strange Days* and *Existenz*.[51] *Terminator*, *Blade Runner*, and more recent dystopian films, have a tendency to revel in the aftermath of a great disaster. *Terminator 2* is one such and the topic is technology turning against its creators.[52] The film begins with a scene in which a nuclear explosion destroys a playground in the foreground and an entire city in the background. This scene is replaced with a devastated landscape that is supposedly 2029. In this time nothing grows and people live underground in the aftermath of a nuclear holocaust which they call the 'day of doom'. They are fighting a war against the machines which are in control and which are attempting to annihilate humans because of the threat they pose to their power. Powerful imagery reminds us throughout the film of the nuclear explosion. Its depiction and the voice-over is reminiscent of passages in Mark 13:24–25 where it is written: 'but in those days, after the tribulation, the sun will be darkened and the moon will not give its light, and the stars will be falling from heaven, and the powers of the heavens will be shaken';

and in Revelation 8:9 that 'something like a great mountain, burning of fire, was thrown into the sea; and a third of the sea became blood'.

The account of the disaster in *Thunderdome* (George Miller, 1985), told in the narrative used by the lost tribe, is described in a similar way to Revelation 6, in which the fourth seal is broken, resulting in mass death by famine, pestilence and the sword. In *Road Warrior*, famine is used as a metaphor for the depth of depravity to which humanity has sunk. A striking image is the fight between a man and a dog over a can of dog food. A further example, in Revelation 6, is when the sixth seal is broken, the earth shakes, the sun becomes black and the moon becomes like blood. The lost tribe narrative tells a similar story. It describes how the earth started to shake, 'maybe by a gang called turbulence'. The narrative also explains their painful history in which they endured a nuclear holocaust. This was 'a fearsome time, a long winter, a crackling dust and many were taken by mister death'. The narrative of the lost tribe and the depiction of the landscape in *Road Warrior* and *Thunderdome* have many similarities with the apocalypse in the book of Revelation. In Revelation 8:7–12 we are told about the burning of the earth and how the water becomes bitter and kills people. Similarly the landscape in *Road Warrior* and *Thunderdome* is barren and burnt, without vegetation or animals, and where the water is polluted by radioactivity. The accounts of the apocalypse are similar in *Mad Max 2* and *3* and in *Terminator 2*. All three films have striking parallels with the accounts of the apocalypse in the Book of Revelation.

Symbols of a fallen society

Society on the brink of disaster is a common topic in this film tradition. In the pre-apocalyptic state, society is often depicted as having traditional values that are fragmenting, allowing individualism, violence and crime to dominate. *Mad Max* together with *Blade Runner* and *Terminator 1* focus on the time period before the apocalypse. We first meet Max in *Mad Max* while he is chasing a person who sees himself as the elect sent to strike down the unworthy. Max represents justice and kills the representation of evil in a race towards death. The race can be interpreted as an illustration of the Judaeo-Christian view of history, as a race down a linear path, finally culminating in a collision with the eschatological moment.[53] The strongest image of a society in breakdown is given in *Blade Runner*. In this film, society is depicted as racist and unequal and it is corporate capitalism that rules. Streets are filled with garbage as a sign of a consumer society in breakdown. Acid rain is constantly falling and causes buildings to deteriorate and people to suffer from 'accelerated decrepitude'. There is no sense of community in a society whose two most significant aspects are individualism and capitalism. This world is a one without blue skies or animals, where replicants are designed to do work, give pleasure and serve society. The replicants are enslaved and are created after the motto 'more human than human'. When the replicants become self-conscious they rebel, which causes the corporation to despatch Blade Runners to remove them. The replicant raises the question of what, and who, is human, an ethical dilemma around which the film is focused. As seen in *Mad Max* and *Blade Runner*, a dirty, barren and chaotic world is what is imagined to signify the pre-apocalyptic society. *Terminator 1* (James Cameron, 1984) differs to some extent from the usual barren and deserted chaos of pre-apocalyptic society and the society that is portrayed is a highly technological one. Such societies are fragile, as are the machines, which also makes them dangerous to people.[54] The pre-apocalyptic society is characterised by the fragmentation of society and traditional values in favour of the dominance of capitalism, individualism, privatisation and racism.

Messianic expectation

Messianic expectation is another powerful characteristic of the modern apocalyptic. The 'Alien Messiah' has been a pervasive figure in the science fiction genre since 1951 when the image first appeared in the film *The Day When the World Stood Still*. The film depicts an alien who warns humanity about an impending nuclear disaster. The film reflects the fear of a civilisation that has lost control and is about to destroy itself. The image of the messiah serves to give hope, and purpose, and to provide solutions in a world that is seemingly doomed.[55] The alien is depicted as having superior qualities to humans and serves as an inspiration for humanity that lives under a threatening technology and the banality of modern life.[56] In *The Day When the Earth Stood Still*, the saviour comes from the outside to save the world. In more recent films, it is more common that humans develop messianic traits and become the saviours of the world and humanity. In *Terminator 2*, John becomes the saviour elect to save humanity from extermination. The story of John is reminiscent of the story of Jesus' birth and Herod's search for the newly born saviour. John's father is sent from the future to make Sarah pregnant with the child who is going to save humanity from the machines. Later on, a terminator is sent out to protect John from the machines that are seeking to kill him, and prevent salvation history from happening just as Herod had sought to kill the king of the Jews.

The messianic expectations in *Mad Max* are more centralised around Max's struggle with his role as the saviour. When the lost tribe first meets Max he asks them who they are, and the answer is:

> We are the waiting ones.
> Waiting for who?
> Waiting for you.
> Who do you think I am?

The dialogue depicts the messianic expectations of the lost tribe, and Max asks the waiting ones a similar question to that Jesus in Mark 8:29 posed to his disciples 'who do you say that I am?'. Max struggles with being the saviour throughout the trilogy of films. He goes through a messianic struggle of denial, temptation and acceptance. In the first film he loses everything and takes refuge in the wasteland. In the second film, *Road Warrior*, his struggle stands between being the helper of the commune or minding his own business. He seeks solitude like an Old Testament prophet or hermit and lives alone in the desert. In the final film, *Thunderdome*, Max finally accepts the role of a saviour.

The messianic role in science fiction has several different faces. It is presented as the 'Alien messiah' who comes to save the world and as the human who struggles and grows to be a saviour. The characteristics of the Alien messiah, and the human messiah are similar to those of the messiah in the religious myths. He is human yet has divine traits. He is the champion of things to come and struggles with being the saviour.

Good versus evil in the fight over the world

The dualism of good and evil, righteousness and unrighteousness, is a dichotomy present in most science fiction films. For example, in the film *Aliens*, good and evil have very distinct boundaries where the human part of the crew are perceived as being good whilst the non-humans, represented by the android Ash, the company and the monster, are portrayed as evil.[57] Our heroine in the *Alien* trilogy, Ripley, is the most human on the ship and we see her sacrificing herself in order to kill the monster. In the first two films she exhibits the most human and emotional behaviour and she is the only one to survive the ordeal with the monster.

Ripley can be seen as surviving because she is the one who cares most about the group and other humans. She is not individualistic, and she does not take part in the colonising capitalism of the company who want the monster for their own strategic and monetary gain.[58] In *Terminator 2*, as in *Alien*, 'evil' is represented by the non-human, namely the computer Skynet. It represents the fear of a machine that develops outside human control and becomes self-conscious and power hungry. A war against humanity starts and terminators are sent out to kill John, who is the hope for the survival of humans. This bears a strong resemblance to Revelation 12:4 and 12:13 where the beast chases the woman who is pregnant with the saviour. She is saved twice, just like Sarah (the mother of John), and at the end of the film the terminator is thrown into molten steel, just as Satan is flung into a lake of fire in Revelation 20:10.

In contrast to the view of the human as righteous, and the machine as evil, stand the replicants in *Blade Runner*. Through their wish to be treated as humans they raise the important question of how to treat the 'other'. Of the films discussed here, the most complex view of the duality between good and evil, is featured in *Blade Runner*. The issue of human versus machine is the focus of the film. The machine in *Blade Runner* has feelings that are reportedly 'more human than human'. At the beginning of the film the replicant is evil. As the film progresses the replicant's character develops and the issue of human versus machine becomes more complicated. In the end, it is once again corporate capitalism, a symbol of evil, that triumphs at the same time as our hero starts to doubt that he is human. Ultimately the replicant Roy fulfils the motto 'more human than human' when saving the character Deckart from dying.[59] The film ends with an unusual twist, where the evil system is the winner and the machine the most human.

Salvation and expectation

Science fiction films whether they are utopias or dystopias express the possibility of a life and a world completely different and totally 'other'. Through the expression of something different, an alternative world, a utopian thinking and a hope have arisen which works as the starting point of actual change. *Blade Runner* has a very open ending. Deckart leaves his individualised existence out of love for a replicant. He is saved by Roy who until the end has been his enemy; and when this happens a white dove is released and flies into a blue sky. This dove stands for the hope and expectation of the life to come. It is part of another life where animals do exist and where the sky is blue. In *Alien 3*, Ripley sacrifices herself for the survival of humanity by diving into boiling steel, taking the monster with her. The film ends with the death of the monster, the sacrifice of Ripley and the failure of the company to bring ultimate devastation to the world. This messianic sacrifice brings hope for a new beginning. In essence, *Terminator* is an apocalyptic story. The termination of the terminator enables humanity to survive and postpones the apocalypse. The saviour is saved and can become the saviour of the future to come. The altruistic actions of a few people save humanity. There is goodness and salvation in the world and a better future is made possible.

Mad Max provides a classic example of expectation and salvation in science fiction film. The trilogy develops this theme, starting on a micro level and ending on the macro level. In *Mad Max*, Max is the hero set on revenge. In *Road Warrior* he becomes the saviour of a microcosm, symbolised by the community that hopes for a new life in paradise. Finally, by saving the lost tribe in *Thunderdome*, Max becomes the saviour of the world, which gives rise to the possibility of a new civilisation.[60] Joseph Campbell observed that 'the effect of the successful adventure of the hero is the unlocking and release again of the flow of life into the body of the world'.[61] This is exactly what happens in the concluding scene of *Thunderdome*. In the film, Savannah sits with a new-born child on her lap telling a narrative that signifies the new beginning: 'time counts and keeps counting and we know where to find the trick to what have been [*sic*], it's not an easy ride but it's our track and we gotta travel it and nobody knows where it's gonna lead'.

Science fiction: the apocalyptic of our time?

Society is at the end of the second millennium and its mythological associations with death and rebirth re-emerge as part of contemporary cultural consciousness. Humanity has recently realised its fragility and if it just sees the sense of an ending as a fear of death, it is overlooking the whole apocalyptic tradition, and the actual threat that gives these thoughts significance. Apocalyptic visions have taken on different forms at different times in history. What is important is that in the present time humanity has begun to see itself as the agent of its own destruction. Mankind is both victim and offender, responsible for exploiting the planet and for the construction of weapons that can destroy it several times over. In order to cope with the guilt and provide hope for something other, there is a great need for narratives that can provide alternative futures. This topic has been explored in films like *Terminator*. One example of such liberating narratives can be seen in science fiction as well as in other utopian literature and film.

It is hope upon which we need to be focused in films like *Terminator* and *Mad Max* because this dimension of hope and expectation opens up the genre to an interpretation that takes into account the redemptive and the liberating qualities of the narrative. Through the connection between narrative theology and the people's religion it is possible to transcend the debate concerning God's death and the secularisation of modern culture. The traditional Christian narratives regarding the end of times in contemporary society have lost their connection to people's beliefs and hopes. Christian institutions are following an eschatology that has become anti-apocalyptic, more in favour of maintaining stability and order than of effecting change. To make radical change possible it is necessary to have the apocalyptic serving as the horizon of a political and eschatological theology. Christianity needs to be revitalised to find a new relevance as well as new narratives appropriate for a secularised society. This means that historical and political action must be focused on both expectation and the hope that the apocalypse brings.

The world of science fiction is a world of immanent expectation, and it is to popular culture that one must turn in order to understand how contemporary expectations might be expressed. The problem is how to look at immanent expectations, and not to make them into instrumentalised and technologised programmes that betoken an oppressive apocalyptic. In order to avoid this reductionism, the apocalyptic should be treated as people's religion and as something worth taking into account as an expression of the hopes and fears of contemporary society. Science fiction has the ability to portray an alternative existence and in this lies its strength. In their creation of alternative futures the miracles of the past become as close as the miracles in the future. The narrative used in this way becomes subversive and opens up a possible 'other' world, and if the present is open for such a change, the future also becomes open rather than determined. As expressed by the narrator in *Terminator 2*: 'the future is not decided, Destiny doesn't exist. We are creating it. We are now on unknown territory and are changing history.'

Living in the modern era is living in a risk society with ecological, political and nuclear threats as well as the burden of everyday existence. The fear of the End is no longer addressed by institutionalised Christianity, which has become anti-apocalyptic, focusing on stability and reconciliation rather than on radical change. In an era when the Church is now turning its back to the apocalypse the challenge is being taken up by popular culture which expresses the fear and the hope of people in the end of times. The narratives of popular culture express the fear of extinction, but they also offer new alternatives and capacities to think of the 'Other' and to offer a hope for something different.

Notes and references

1 John J. Collins, 'Introduction: Towards a Morphology of a Genre', *Semeia: An Experimental Journal for Biblical Criticism*, no. 14, 1979, pp. 1–20. The definition used by Collins is one widely accepted by theologians and focuses on the apocalyptic as a biblical genre. His definition of the apocalypse is 'a genre of revelatory literature with a narrative framework, in which a revelation is mediated by an otherworldly being to a human recipient, disclosing a transcendent reality which is both temporal, insofar as it envisages eschatological salvation, spatial insofar it involves another, supernatural world' (p. 9). For more discussion on the classical definition of the apocalyptic, see: Christopher Rowland, *The Open Heaven: A Study of Apocalyptic in Judaism and Early Christianity* (London, SPCK, 1982); and Mitchell G. Reddish (ed.), *Apocalyptic Literature: A Reader* (Nashville: Abingdon Press, 1990).

2 See Norman Cohn, *The Pursuit of the Millennium: Revolutionary Millenarians and Mystical Anarchists of the Middle Ages* (London: Maurice Temple Smith, 1970), p. 13, and also the introduction to Reddish, *Apocalyptic Literature*, pp. 19–24.

3 Bryan R. Wilson, *Magic and the Millennium: A Sociological Study of Religious Movements of Protest Among Tribal and Third World Peoples* (London: Heinemann, 1973), pp. 484–6.

4 Malcolm Bull, 'On Making Ends Meet', in Malcolm Bull (ed.), *Apocalypse Theory and the Ends of the World* (Oxford: Blackwell, 1995), pp. 3–5. The popular notions of the apocalypse manifest themselves in film and music. Examples are disaster films such as *Volcano* and *Titanic* and arthouse films such as *Crash* and *Apocalypse Now*. In music, the apocalyptic is expressed in the anarchistic agenda of Johnny Rotten's 'I am antichrist' as well as in the more softly spoken and deeply ironic REM lyrics of 'It's the end of the world as we know it, and I feel fine'.

5 Anthony Giddens, *Modernity and Self-Identity: Self and Society in the Late Modern Age* (Cambridge: Polity Press, 1991), p. 183.

6 J. G. Ballard, introduction in *Crash* (London, Vintage, 1995).

7 For an investigation of contemporary apocalyptic and millenarian beliefs, see Damian Thompson, *The End of Time: Faith and Fear in the Shadow of the Millennium* (London: Sinclair-Stevenson, 1996), pp. 322–32.

8 Frederick A. Kreuziger, *Apocalypse and Science Fiction: A Dialectic of Religious and Secular Soteriologies* (Chica, CA.: Scholars Press, 1982), pp. 2–3.

9   Ibid., pp. 3 and 188.
10 Ibid., pp. 3 and 224–7.
11 Robert Lifton, 'The Image of the End of the World: A Psychological View', in Valerie Andrews, Robert Bosnak and Karen Walter Goodwin (eds), *Facing the Apocalypse* (Pallas: Spring Publication, 1987), p. 44.
12 Kreuziger, *Apocalypse and Science Fiction*, p. 187.
13 See the introduction to Louis Parkinson Zamora (ed.), *The Apocalyptic Vision in America: Interdisciplinary Essays on Myth and Culture* (Bowling Green: Bowling Green University Press, 1982), p. 6.
14 Ibid., pp. 1–2.
15 Among theologians who wish to limit the concept and term of apocalyptic to the context of a biblical genre, is Christopher Rowland, *The Open Heaven*, (see note 1 above). Another theologian who argues along these lines is Richard Bauckham, 'The Theology of the Book of Revelation', in James D. G. Dunn (ed.), *The Theology of the Book of Revelation* (Cambridge: Cambridge University Press, 1993.), pp. 1–22.
16 Zamora, *The Apocalyptic vision in America*, p. 3.
17 Reddish, *Apocalyptic Literature*, pp. 21–6.
18 Zamora, *The Apocalyptic Vision in America*, pp. 1–2.
19 Ibid., p. 3.
20 Ibid., p. 9.
21 Louis Parkinson Zamora, *Writing the Apocalypse: Historical Vision in Contemporary U.S. and Latin American Fiction* (Cambridge: Cambridge University Press, 1989), p. 2.
22 Ibid., pp. 179–80.
23 Ulrich Beck, *Risk Society: Towards a New Modernity*, trans. Mark Ritter (London: Sage, 1992), pp. 14–15 and 47–9.
24 Zamora, *The Apocalyptic Vision in America*, pp. 1–2.
25 Harvey Cox, *The Seduction of the Spirit: The Use and Misuse of People's Religion* (London: Wildwood House Ltd, 1973), p. 170. See also Kreuziger; *Apocalypse and Science Fiction*, pp. 194–6 and 206.
26 Harvey Cox, *The Secular City: Secularization and Urbanization in Theological Perspective* (London: SCM Press, 1965), pp. 105–8.
27 Kreuziger, *Apocalypse and Science Fiction*, p. 195.
28 Thomas J. J. Altizer, *Genesis and Apocalypse: A Theological Voyage Toward Authentic Christianity* (Louisville, Kentucky: Westminister/John Knox Press, 1990), pp. 9–11.
29 Thomas J. J. Altizer, *History as Apocalypse* (Albany: State University of New York Press, 1985), pp. 1 and 15.
30 Altizer, *Genesis and Apocalypse*, pp. 13 and 29.
31 Ibid, pp. 28–30.
32 Ibid, pp. 178–87.
33 Ibid, pp. 186–7. See also Cox, *The Seduction of the Spirit*, pp. 312 and 328–9.
34 Johann-Baptist Metz, 'Messianic or Bourgeois Religion', in Fiorenza Francis Schüssler (ed.), *Faith and the Future: Essays on Theology, Solidarity and Modernity* (Nijmegen, Netherlands: Counsilium Foundation, 1995), pp. 18–23. See also Kreuziger, *Apocalypse and Science Fiction*, p. 206.
35 Kreuziger, *Apocalypse and Science Fiction*, p. 215.
36 Although Kreuziger deals mainly with literary texts, his approach is, however, applicable to cinematic texts, especially in a postmodern situation where the text as written text is to a greater extent exchanged for images.

37 Cox, *The Seduction of the Spirit*, pp. 172–4 and 324–9.
38 Kreuziger, *Apocalypse and Science Fiction*, pp. 195–6.
39 Metz, 'Messianic or Bourgeois Religion', p. 17.
40 Ibid., pp. 20–1.
41 Johann-Baptist Metz, 'Theology in the Struggle for History and Society', in Schüssler, *Faith and the Future*, pp. 51–2.
42 Kreuziger, *Apocalypse and Science Fiction*, pp. 195–6.
43 Ibid., p. 219.
44 Ibid., pp. 210 and 212–13. Science fiction stories do not only inspire positive change but are often dystopic in their character. Whether the stories are dystopic or utopic, the important point is that the stories deal with a different world, which opens up for the utopian belief in something 'other'.
45 Johann-Baptist Metz, 'Future in the Memory of Suffering', in Schüssler, *Faith and the Future*, pp. 7–12.
46 Kreuziger, *Apocalypse and Science Fiction*, p. 224.
47 See the introduction to Anette Kuhn (ed.), *Alien Zone: Cultural Theory and Contemporary Science Fiction Cinema* (London and New York: Verso, 1990), p. 10.
48 Ibid., pp. 10 and 91–2.
49 A perspective which is both theological and literary allows the text to be a theological comment as well as being a secular narrative and an expression of popular culture.
50 See II. Bruce Franklin, 'Visions of the Future in Science Fiction Films from 1970 to 1982', in Anette Kuhn, *Alien Zone*, p. 22.
51 The blockbuster *Titanic* is an example of a disaster film that features human error and the unpredictable nature of the forces of nature. This film by James Cameron presents a familiar and historical disaster but manages to give voice to fear and anticipation.
52 Constance Penley, 'Time Travel, Primal Scene and the Critical Dystopia', in Kuhn, *Alien Zone*, pp. 116-17.
53 Mick Broderick, 'Heroic Apocalypse: Mad Max, Mythology, and the Millennium', in Christopher Sharrett (ed.), *Crisis Cinema: The Apocalyptic Idea in Post-Modern Narrative Film* (Washington DC: Maisonville Press, 1993), pp. 261–2.
54 Penley, 'Time Travel, Primal Scene and the Critical Dystopia', pp. 117–18.
55 Hugh Ruppersberg, 'The Alien Messiah', in Kuhn, *Alien Zone*, p. 32.
56 Ibid., p. 33.
57 Thomas B. Byers, 'Commodity Futures', in ibid., pp. 39–40.
58 Ibid., p. 42.
59 Ibid., p. 44.
60 Mick Broderick, 'Heroic Apocalypse: Mad Max, Mythology, and the Millennium', in Sharrett, *Crisis Cinema*, p. 260.
61 Cited in ibid., p. 260.

12
Hope Against Hope

W. Watts Miller

Hope's importance in our lives seems an ordinary moral intuition. It is a traditional Christian virtue. In theology, it remains a central concern. The situation is different in the secular 'mainstream' of contemporary social and ethical theory. This more or less neglects hope – and at the same time destroys its bases. So even if it saw a need for hope, can it offer any?

Gabriel Marcel and Ernst Bloch, who provide us with what are still the most important modern accounts of hope, wrote forty to fifty years ago, but this mainstream has passed them by. Perhaps this is not surprising. Marcel, a philosopher associated with existentialism, was a Catholic, and his at first secular-sounding account of hope ended up anchoring it in belief in God.[1] Bloch was inspired by a Marxist belief in progress, that he held on to despite everything, including his own persecution by the East German state and eventual exile.[2] In the 1970s came an important work by the French neo-Durkheimian sociologist, Henri Desroche.[3] It did not invoke God or progress and that mainstream has again passed by.

My own interest in hope arose through my work on Durkheim, but also on others important for understanding him, such as Guyau and Kant.[4] It has developed into an enquiry which links a number of concerns.[5] I shall say something about the first of these, since it leads to the worry I explore here, which is whether secularism, now an entrenched part of our world, has adequate bases of hope.

Can there be a morality without hope? Or at least how can modern morality, with its universalising ideals, keep going without hope? Sartre, at one point in *Existentialism and Humanism*, offered what is perhaps the only answer. It is action itself, in commitment to a belief. Indeed, it is this active *engagement* which makes something a belief, and gets away from 'dreams, expectations and hopes'. But he complains, at the end, that it misunderstands existentialists to 'describe us as without hope'.[6]

The underlying problem could be the inextricability of commitment, belief and hope. Or it could be the need, in facing up to freedom, for hope in our power to live by and enact it. But whatever it is, it is not easy to realise a morality without hope. Perhaps we should keep looking, in hope, for this. In the meantime, we hit the worries to do with the second question. Jacques Ellul wrote, 'then God is turned away, then, in the desert of information, nothing more is possible except hope...It is the virtue for a time which has no faith, no word and no escape.'[7] This is all very well, except that the 'desert' includes contemporary theory. What if it dries up the very sources of hope?

For Marcel these sources involve religion; for Bloch, some sort of historical 'grand narrative'; and perhaps, for Sartre, a confidence in our power to enact our freedom. In Kant, they involve all these things. His sources of hope are morality's three postulates – an immortal soul, God and freedom – together with philosophical history.[8]

Mainstream contemporary theory has little or no time for any of them. It dismisses the immortal soul – and God. It goes on about autonomy, but ignores freedom as a postulate. It generates almost knee-jerk reactions against stories of progress. It is also with little or no concern for them as sources of hope, and fails to come up with alternatives.

It is necessary to explore the contemporary 'desert', to see, nonetheless, if it contains bases of hope. Even in the case of the main candidate, the prospect of varieties of 'hope against hope' seems doubtful. There is another possibility, which does not show up much in the theoretical scene, yet seems of special importance nowadays. But it will need to combine with other bases of hope.

So it is also necessary to re-explore classic terrain. Do religious sources of hope have adequate secular counterparts? What is freedom's job as a postulate? Is there a way to revive philosophical history?

Hope against hope

Objects, modes and sources of hope lead to critical distinctions and one is what I wish to call 'positive' and 'negative' hope. This relates to its objects which, as fundamental rather than minor concerns, are answers to the Kantian question: what may we hope? A positive hope is for a society, or a commonwealth, in which everyone can develop and flourish as a person. A negative hope is that evil will not inherit the earth. Is this more 'realistic'? Kant is often criticised for setting his sights too high. Yet good and evil are mutually defining, and unless some of us hold on to ideals, can the rest of us hold on even to negative hopes? At any rate, idealism should not just be ruled out.

Another distinction is between what can be termed 'strong' and 'weak' hope. This relates to its modes, and should not be confused with expectations, or with the difference between fundamental and minor hopes. Viktor Frankl's work arose from his experience in Nazi concentration camps, and underlines how small, particular hopes can help to sustain a fundamental one.[9] But both fundamental and smaller hopes can represent strong hopes, insisting that something is possible, indeed, even that it will somehow obtain. This does not depend on probabilities and high expectations. It can cope with low ones. Marcel tended to emphasise a patient, constant hope, whereas for Bloch it signifies an explosiveness. Desroche took a more Durkheimian interest in rhythms of hope. It can well up in moments of collective ferment, but also outlast them – as in rhythms of a strong fundamental hope. This still has to involve feelings that something is possible, even though these ebb and flow, and in ways that do not just parallel expectations. It is still like the kind of hope – *espérance* – stressed by Marcel. A weak hope is like the kind of hope – *espoir* – he associated with expectations. It goes up and down with them, and is especially vulnerable to the 'surrender' and 'going to pieces' of despair.[10]

So, one way of understanding 'hope against hope' has to do with *espérance contre espoir*. This is a strong positive hope that does not go to pieces with low expectations. It might still clutch at straws, knowing that is what they are, and in encounters with despair – as in Nadezhda Mandelstam's moving account of her life with her husband during the Stalinist terror.[11] It survives as a hope that, despite everything, good can prevail, and as a commitment to going on in life on this basis. It is a way in which hope, commitment and belief are bound up with one another. But asking about sources of this 'hope against hope' returns us to a classic terrain. Marcel tried to capture key aspects of things in the formula: *'I hope in thee for us'*.[12] He was reluctant to lay down the exact identity of the 'thee' in whom hope is placed, and who is thus the source of hope. It involves, however, an absolute 'thou'. And for him it is God.[13]

'Hope against hope' can also have the sense of a rockbottom hope – a minimal negative hope, just this side of despair, that evil will not inherit the earth, that life is not totally pointless and absurd, etc. Thus, Max Charlesworth wrote:

in the grim world of Samuel Beckett, which at first sight appears to be denuded of any kind of human hope or expectation, his protagonists still exhibit a minimal kind of stoical persistence – a hoping against hope – which saves his view from utter nihilism. I believe that this kind of analysis of the work of symptomatic figures of the age such as Nietzsche, Freud, Sartre, Camus, Beckett, is a strictly philosophical task and one that could shed a great deal of light on the ontological basis of human hope.[14]

This brings out how a rockbottom hope can be strong enough to resist despair, however near to it. But its strength might turn into stoic resignation – which is different from 'stoical persistence'. Hope as a moral virtue is more than the integrity of not going to pieces. It is also the commitment of struggling on in a wider cause: 'I hope *for us*'. Can rockbottom hope sustain practical moral commitment? Worries about its 'ontological basis' include whether this just issues in a hope *for me*, or in a withdrawal from the world instead of engagement with it.

Disengagement from the world is a key to another kind of 'hope against hope'. It is perhaps the most modern of all, showing up, for example, in Richard Rorty's 'ironist' philosophy.[15] It stakes more or less everything on moral luck or, in a grander term, 'contingency'. So it is a finger-crossing, contingent hope. Its belief in chance is altogether different from belief in a coherent, intelligible story of things – and so it contrasts with *both* the fideistic hope of traditional religion *and* the reasoned human hope of enlightenment. For fideistic hope involves belief, not in a luck which is obscure or unfathomable to us, but in a story which is obscure or unfathomable to us – God does not play dice, even if He does not show us His hand. Reasoned human hope also invokes a logic of things. Only as in philosophical history can we have some sort of access to this. At the same time it emphasises our own power to act and take charge of our lives. Contingent hope is instead a disengagement from the world in its emphasis on passivity rather than on agential freedom, struggle and effort, on what is to be awaited rather than what is to be done. So what good, as a source of hope, is this kind of 'hope against hope'? It is not just that it gives up on stories of hope. If it drains away the sense of agency, it takes the life out of morality itself. Yet what is the good of rejecting what may be the last hope open to us? We need to refer to something else, to a metaphysical hope.

The 'metaphysics of morals' is a Kantian term we might take over for ethics, with all its questions about the understanding and evaluation of moral ideals, norms and beliefs. It contrasts with another older term, the 'physics of morals'. 'Metaphysical' is not meant here in a more esoteric sense, or, as often nowadays, just as a term of abuse. So how is metaphysical hope important as a basis of practical hope, commitment and belief?

Metaphysical hope

Guyau made an impression on such opposite characters as Durkheim, Kropotkin and Nietzsche. His work buzzes with ideas, and one of them helps to set up our problem. Kant had tried to base morality on the certainty of reason. Others then tried to base it on the certainty of faith. Instead we need to develop a morality either based on doubt or on its other side, hope – as Guyau shows.[16]

Faith seems paradoxical. It questions and sets limits to reason, yet suppresses doubt on going beyond these. But it also collides against the ideal of freedom and diversity of thought, so central to the modern worldview. Guyau baptised this as the ideal of *anomie*.[17] Nietzsche turned it into a world of 'infinite interpretations'.[18] In taking over the term, Durkheim converted it into a malaise of 'infinite desire'.[19] But he did not break with the ideal itself. The ethic of the person is a new religion, with autonomy as 'its first dogma', free-thought as 'its first rite',[20] and the only viable religions of the future will give individual initiative and free-thought 'a greater place than even the most liberal Protestant sects'.[21]

But what still drives a demand for faith? There are at least three key assumptions. One is that belief must come first, as the basis of commitment. For Guyau (and Sartre) it is the other way round. Guyau wrote, 'I do not ask you to believe blindly in an ideal; I ask you to work to realise it. Without belief? So as to believe. You will believe in it when you have worked to produce it.'[22] Another is that belief must come first, as the basis of hope. Again, for Guyau, it is the other way round: 'religions say: I hope because I believe...It is necessary to say: I believe because I hope.'[23] Miguel de Unamuno, the Catholic philosopher and man of letters, wrote some years later: 'we do not hope because we believe, but rather we believe because we hope. It is hope in God...that leads us to believe in him.'[24]

But it is the traditional view, reported by Guyau, which remains orthodox. Nor, perhaps, is it left behind in Moltmann's *Theology of Hope*: his emphasis on the promise held out to us by God seems an affair of belief in Him in the first place.[25] A third assumption combines with the other two and might be put this way: metaphysical certainty is necessary for practical belief, hope and commitment, which are at the heart of morality. So we need faith, given there is no certainty of reason. Indeed, there is a clear reluctance, nowadays, to come out and claim such certainty – despite the umpteenth reason in support, say, of a theory of justice.

Or perhaps certainty, and so faith, belongs to the museum, thanks to a modern approach concerned with judgement, and combining 'adequacy' with 'proportionality'. That is, there should at least be 'good', 'reasonable', 'adequate' grounds of practical beliefs and hopes. There should then be 'proportionality' between their grounds and the strength with which they are held.[26] The approach might seem not only modern but common sense. It seems to me poisonous. It misunderstands morality, the drive for certainty as a basis of commitment, and the need to explore metaphysical hope as an alternative.

Guyau helps with seeing what is wrong with reasonableness when he writes:

> it will be said, if it is irrational to affirm in thought as true that which is doubtful, it is still sometimes right and necessary to affirm it in *action*. Perhaps, yet it is always a provisional situation and a conditional affirmation: I do this only in *supposing* it my duty, even my absolute duty.[27]

Morality – even a liberal morality – is nothing without core convictions and commitments. It means hitting, somewhere along the line, things like a passion for justice and outrage at injustice, a sense of inviolable rights or absolute duties and a feeling of what is sacred. This is why for Durkheim morality is still a religion, however secular. It is also why the demand for certainty still has power. But given that we lack certainty, at least hope rises to the occasion. Even if not 'proportional' to the strength of core moral commitments, it fits their nature. With 'judgement', they must be watered down or surrendered altogether. Nor is it an answer to drop proportionality, and ask only for adequate, well-established grounds. This is a way to lose commitment, in the mires, twists, turns and controversies of reason. Part of the trouble arises if it is still assumed that commitment must follow belief. Instead of trying to fix which, if any, has priority, let us just see a continuing interaction of practical belief, hope and commitment.

Metaphysical hope, then, is the hope that we are correct about the worth of the practical moral beliefs and commitments we have formed, and about our practical hopes of insisting on their realisability. It does not start from scratch, 'reflective equilibrium', or the position of a spectator, and it does not lay down, in advance, any test they must pass. In contrast, it involves a hope in being able to develop our understanding of them – through efforts of interpretation, searches for different kinds of support (not necessarily 'grounds'), and through a culture empowering these attempts.

In asking what kind of culture, it is not a matter of starting from scratch, but from commitment to something like the ideal of free-thought, diversity and *anomie*, articulated by Guyau in his own fashion. This involves, as he has stressed, a culture ready to recognise the 'hypothetical character' of our ethical ideas.[28] That is, as 'hypotheses', they are not claims to certainty, but are also not just expressions of individual opinion. There are different ways of understanding how. One is that uncertainty links with respect for each other's views. But it does not just mean retreat into each other's opinions. For it also links with arguing with all the suasive force we can muster for our ideas, in the hope that we are right. All this entails risk (another of Guyau's themes[29]). In the labyrinth of reason, metaphysical hope lets us hold on to practical moral commitment – but not to the same fixed beliefs, immunised by faith against doubt and any process by which we might develop, revise or change them.

Yet although some of our beliefs might be liable, in such a process, to change, it might be wondered if it is possible to give up and change all of them, all at the same time. It might be wondered, in particular, if it is possible to give up the kind of belief discussed in Guyau's day as 'the presupposition'. He was especially critical of the faith that comes to rest in this – 'the greatest enemy of human progress is the presupposition'.[30] But is it for once, where faith, is right?

We might see presuppositions as key terms, ideas or intuitions at work in the very questions we ask and in arguments we construct, so that they themselves are not open to examination. How we can proceed with it must just be taken on trust. Distrust of this involved Guyau in attacks on the

Scottish 'philosophy of common sense', which tried to identify intuitions common to humanity. It resurfaces, pluralised, with a contemporary ironic twist and put through the modern linguistic turn, in Rorty's talk of an individual's or group's 'final vocabulary'. Its constitutive terms are as far as their users 'can go', without a discussion going round and round, in that 'if doubt is cast on the worth of these words, their user has no noncircular argumentative recourse'.[31]

Yet it is not an impasse. Rorty sees a way in which presuppositions (or 'platitudes', as he renames them) are open to criticism and change. This is the strategy of 'ironists'. It gives up on argument, in the sense of analytical reasoning. It also gives up on metaphysics, in the sense of a search for underlying essences, logics and realities. Instead, the ironist 'looks for a better final vocabulary', through metaphors of creation, diversity and novelty, thick-textured rather than thin, abstract language, redescription rather than inference, gradual, tacit substitutions of new terms for old, and a form of argument which is dialectical in taking 'the unit of persuasion to be a vocabulary rather than a proposition'.[32] It is still a concern, however linguistic, with an understanding and evaluation of 'webs of belief'.[33] So it is still, we can say, a metaphysical concern. But is it in a return to metaphysical certainty?

Rorty's ironists express doubt, yet seem very sure about a lot of things – life is a language-game; there are no foundations; all is contingent; analytical reason cannot escape circularity. Or maybe they just argue with all the force they can, in the hope they are right.

So let us consider another route out of circularity. Its challenge to the presupposition is more rationalist, but also more internalist, as against Rorty's view that 'nothing can serve as a criticism of a final vocabulary save another such vocabulary'.[34] Perhaps a web of belief cannot be tackled from the inside, whole and at once. It can change over time through the ways different individuals or groups approach one of its elements in terms not only of its available interpretations, but of other elements and their available interpretations. This can let in an upsurge of the new, which Rorty emphasises – but also lets in an unfolding logic of things, where all is not as contingent as he insists. There are various accounts, on these more rationalist, internalist lines, of a changing modern world-view. One of the most impressive is Alain Renaut's *The Era of the Individual*.[35] It also takes us to a basic general issue.

The presupposition is about limits to our knowledge and understanding, and so is about 'human finitude'. We might question views which lay down particular presuppositions or other conditions, frameworks, limits. This does not rule out the idea that there are limits. Put another way, we might question a faith which fixes such limits, without endorsing a rationalism set on certain, total, absolute knowledge. It is important to distinguish a tradition of enlightenment which has different strands, but which does not see absolute knowledge as possible for us – even if a necessary idealisation, and representable in God. Knowledge is limited, uncertain, provisional, in that it is the kind of knowledge on offer in our 'finitude', although a kind of knowledge we can still work with and try to develop. So metaphysical hope, as a hope that we are right in our ideas, applies as much as anything to the sciences and their search for and claims to knowledge. Indeed, a way of interpreting Kant is that this is a hope which applies above all to the sciences, and to our development of a knowledge within the limits of their 'theoretical reason'.

What about ethics, and the understanding on offer through 'practical reason'? Was Guyau correct, in thinking Kant claimed an absolute ethical certainty based on this? If so, a problem is that in ethics – as our understanding of the moral law – there is somehow an escape from the finitude which applies elsewhere, not least to our struggle to respect the law but also to the sciences. This problem is discussed by Renaut, via the controversy over Kantian interpretation between Ernst Cassirer and Martin Heidegger. He argues that Cassirer was undoubtedly correct to see, in the content of the texts, an escape in ethics to the absolute, and that Heidegger was undoubtedly mistaken to see, again in the content of the texts, a radical across-the-board finitude. But he rejects Cassirer's modern endorsement of a breakthrough to the absolute. Heidegger was right to look for radical finitude.[36] And it might be found not in the content of the texts but in their style, mode of expression and viewpoint – the viewpoint of a finite subject about the viewpoint, with regard to the world, of its infinite creator.[37]

We might redescribe this as our limited uncertain viewpoint about the viewpoint from an imagined ideal of absoluteness and certainty. Some such idealisation may be a necessary part of both science and ethics, and of arguing with whatever force we can for what seems to us to be true or right. Or it may express the practical commitment at the heart of morality, but again in feelings that we are limited and lack arguments guaranteeing this. In any case, why repeat an orthodox Kantian appeal to a 'practical rational *faith*'? It reeks too much of certainty. It is better, for ethics within the limits of reason, to appeal to hope.

Practical hope and the 'disenchantment of the world'

Marcel Gauchet's *The Disenchantment of the World* explores, like Renaut, a modern logic of things. It is in a long line of accounts of secularisation, but stands out in seeing Christianity as the religion which ends religion.[38] His concern is with religion's demise as something at the centre of social life, even if continuing at the margins.[39] However, he does not discuss it as a source of hope. Is the internal logic of Christianity really to blame if this has drained away in our society?

Gauchet's conventional idea of religion contrasts with Durkheim's idea of the sacred. So it need not be that Christianity leads to secular disenchantment. For Durkheim, it leads to a new secular sense of the sacred.[40] What is this, and is it a new secular source of hope?

The modern centre of the sacred is not at all just the individual, but also is not at all just society. Durkheim repeatedly referred to it as the person[41] – and saw this as a secular transformation of the soul.[42] So let us go on from these ideas to particular concerns here. Let us first ask about the person as a source of practical moral hopes, then see if these are in any way counterparts of the hopes involved in the soul.

Renaut brings out the importance, for understanding modernity, of the problematic of the individual and the person, and criticises accounts taken up with one of these in a blindness to the other.[43] The relationship between the individual and the person was crucial for Durkheim. A common mistake is just to approach his work through the relationship between the individual and society. The person involves, for him, a modern collective representation of a humanity we all share. It is essential for an ethic committed to a society in which everyone has the same basic status, respect and regard. This is impossible if there is only an emphasis on individuals and postmodern *différences*. Yet the idea of the person is not much good as a sacred centre of things unless it sacralises persons – particular, diverse, flesh-and-blood human individuals – and extends a similarily basic status not just to everyone but to *everybody*. This is partly why, in earlier work, I referred to a notion of the 'organic self', which Durkheim required to try to overcome the individual/person and individual/society dualisms. But it is not only an embodied self. It is also one with a deep attachment to others, in which they become an integral, organic part of our very sense of self. It is not, then, the individual as atom. It is the individual as an embodied, attached personality. Indeed, Durkheim often referred to the personality interchangeably with the person, in a fuller sense to do with the organic self. Let us now talk of 'the person' in this fuller sense, as distinct from the 'idea of the person' which is a key element of it.

As secular persons, we can have many hopes about the world after our own death, a whole range, let us say, of post-mortal concerns – for others close to us, for a wider group or society to which we belong, for humanity itself and for particular causes which are part of our lives. Post-mortal concerns are an ordinary, even taken-for-granted but altogether basic aspect of our moral experience. Few, if any, moral movements can get very far without effort over the generations and without the commitment of people – penal reformers, eco-warriors, anti-slavery campaigners, civil rights activists, suffragettes, women's liberationists – with hopes for what may be achieved, not just in their lifetime but after, even long after, their deaths. Together with the emotions at the death of others close to us, there are the concerns for them on our own death. Yet philosophical literature, asking if it is rational to fear death, tends to focus not only on one's own death but on concern for oneself about it. Some answers may express the outlook of the person. The focus does not, and is a preoccupation more to do with the individual as atom. There are many ways in which morality might be undermined if the individual as atom is the soul's secular successor. An important way is the erosion of post-mortal concerns. Perhaps, as in de Tocqueville's critique of individualism, we draw apart from society and retreat into a little circle of family and friends.[44] Or perhaps, as in Durkheim's anxiety over developing trends, we do not form any attachments.[45] But the horizon of concern is drawn tight round the individual's own situation and possibilities during this life. It does not extend much, if at all, to the world after the individual's own annihilation at death.

Yet the person might not do so well either, without the hopes connected with the soul – or rather, in the Christian case, with some kind of personal continuation and an eternal life. We need a broad picture of these, across different contexts and traditions – for example, as in the essays of Marcel, a lay Catholic, or as in *The Coming of God*, a long systematic work by Moltmann, professor of theology in the Protestant faculty at Tübingen,[46] or as in *The Hope of Immortality*, a series of radio talks by W. R. Matthews, at the time dean of St Paul's, which contains his responses to questions from listeners.[47] A widespread ordinary concern brought out by him is for a reunion with those close to us, a hope that death does not separate us from one another forever – and this was also a key case discussed by Marcel. Another kind of hope, at work in Kant's argument for immortality, is that death does not cut short our efforts at something like a moral life, that it does not just leave us where we are, a long way off from a vision of the good, that we can still struggle to attain. A gut hope, at work in appeals – including Kant's – to a God, is for a justice in which the evil do not forever escape their due, and there is at last a link between moral and happy and flourishing lives. It takes us to the 'hope of glory', the coming of the kingdom and a raising to eternal life in fellowship with God and with one another.

It does not seem to me that any of these hopes can be secularised, on Durkheimian lines, as metaphors of solidarity, moral commitment, justice, the human ideal of a commonwealth of persons – even though, through their interpretation in a developing modern Christian tradition, they are about such things. Another Durkheimian way into this is the importance of ritual, rather than only ideas and beliefs. But it is again difficult to envisage meaningful secularised forms of prayer, the ritual which, as an individual or collective petition to God, is central to Christianity and the individual or collective voicing of hope.[48]

The problematics of the individual, the person and society interweave with two other basic themes. One has to do with the continuity of social and moral life, death's rupture of this and how it separates us from a community that nonetheless joins past, living and future generations. The other is the sacred as transcendent, set apart from and above the profane mediocre world, but also as immanent, present within this world and able to govern it.

The hopes open to the secular person do not stand up as comparable counterparts of those offered by Christianity. In a secular world-view, the death of those close to us means that our relationship with one another is finally ended for them, even if it is not finally ended for us. They remain an integral part of us as organic selves. They continue to contribute to our personality. But they cannot continue to participate in it, through their own active influence in a developing relationship. Continuing to contribute and continuing to participate is a fundamental difference, involved in the rupture of the secular person's death. We cannot overcome it by seeing religion as a metaphorical expression of solidarity, moral commitment or the ideal of a commonwealth. Even with some of the commitment demanded by Kant, we can continue to contribute after our death to the development of a commonwealth, through the impact of individual or collective efforts during our lifetime and of individual or collective memories of these. But even with all the commitment demanded by him, we cannot continue to participate. Nor does this seem necessary, to have the concerns which are important for solidarity and moral commitment. For these, the hopes open to the secular person are adequate, though not comparable, counterparts of those held out by Christianity. Divine justice and the glory of the kingdom raise other problems, which underline the difference between hopes for this world and for the next. Yet they remain shared problems. It is Christianity which is inadequate if its hopes are pinned only on the next world.

Durkheim was right in seeing the person as a modern sacred centre of things and in seeing this notion as transcending the individual. But it is also immanent. It involves the human – all too human – person, rather than just the idea of the person. It is only in this context that, as he sometimes said, 'man is the new god for man'.[49] The person and a society of persons are limited. Whatever their sacredness, it is not one which can offer the kingdom's justice, glory and perfection. Nor, however, can God, unless the kingdom is already within us, an immanence in the world that is a seed of its transformation and transcendence – but again, as far as this world rather than the next is concerned, only in a limited form. That is, there is not such an opposition between secularism and Christianity if we focus on this world, drop hope for a complete realisation in it of an ideal of the good, but retain hope for the development of a commonwealth with a resemblance, even in its defects, to the ideal. In secularism, of course, it is a development which can take place without God's intervention and assistance. But it is odd to claim, like Gauchet, that the logic of Christianity leads to the same view. The picture of a remote God, without an active presence in the world, does not correspond with the hope in Him voiced through the Catholicism of Marcel, the Protestantism of Moltmann, or the Anglicanism of Matthews.

A fundamental practical difference between secularism and Christianity is over the need not just for an idea of a God and another world, but to turn to Him for help in this one.[50]

Yet although it is a divide between them, it is not a complete parting of the ways. They might disagree over the possibility, without God, of an adequate basis of hope for a commonwealth. Like secularism, Christianity still involves looking for other sources of this in our world itself – the person, human agency, an order or direction underlying human affairs. Indeed, a place to start in re-looking at philosophical history is with a secular rather than a religious fideistic hope that there is a story of things, which is yet obscure to us. Hope for a commonwealth does not have to have detailed accounts of how we might get to it. As a reasoned hope, it can involve trying to come up with these, revising them in light of events, or scrapping them altogether and beginning all over again. But there are times when it is difficult to see any way ahead, and we may wait, in fideistic hope, for the clouds to lift. It can still be a reasoned hope. It can draw on what is just a very basic story – as do attempts at a more detailed picture. What sort of story applies nowadays?

We need an alternative to the kind at work in Gauchet, say, or Francis Fukuyama's *The End of History*.[51] These seem modern updates of Hegelian and other tales of a logic that, despite twists, leads in a single inevitable direction. We should look for stories of a logic which might go in very different ways. This lets in a sense of contingency, but also belief in agential freedom. Indeed, instead of squeezing out any of these three things – an unfolding logic, contingency, freedom – it is important to try to manage with all of them and the tension each involves with the others.[52] Secularism introduces an ineliminable element of 'moral luck', and with it an ineliminable element of finger-crossing, contingent hope. But the more we rely on finger-crossing to get to a commonwealth, the more we undermine the idea of a commonwealth, the person at its centre, and belief in some kind of autonomous charge over our own lives. Hope in our power to develop and enact autonomy has to do with freedom as a Kantian moral postulate, but also with the difference between recognising our finitude and trying to fix what its limits are. This is a difference, put another way, between recognising an ineliminable element of contingent hope and closing things down so that it is almost all there is. The same can be said about closing them down with a logic of the inevitable.

Let me end, then, with the essentials of an ambivalent story of hope – or, rather, hope against hope. Renaut develops a story like this, concerned at how the idea of the person serves 'both as a source of ultimately dangerous illusions and as an unsurpassable value'.[53] So did de Tocqueville, in a tradition of thought concerned at how modern liberal society is itself the source of authoritarian and other currents that run against and can destroy it. The tradition includes Durkheim, and involves what my work on him discussed as his 'internalist program'. In trying to understand modern ideals, but also modern pathologies, it is about trying to understand them as tied up with one another in a same dynamic. Ideals to do with the individual and 'man' are not just created by individuals and are not just expressions of human nature or human reason. They are part of a dynamic of social processes in the modern world. But they are active at its core; they are not superstructural by-products. They help to drive change through criticism of injustice, exploitation, exclusion, degradation and other forms of 'man's inhumanity to man' in existing society. These, however, are not just rooted in the past, and do not just arise, haphazardly, from outside the dynamic. They are continuously generated from within its core. The basic pathologies Durkheim diagnosed as egoism and *anomie* link in one case with freedom of thought, in the other with freedom to manage our own interests. It is via the influence, in both cases, of the individual as atom – who is also central to his diagnosis of authoritarian and related tendencies in modern liberal 'democracy'. In looking for groups needed to overcome these, with attachments intermediate between the basic modern identities of individual and 'man', he was aware of the risks. We can become locked instead into narrow communitarianisms. This complicates announcements (perhaps premature) of the individual's eclipse in Michel Maffesoli's *The Time of the Tribes*.[54] Maffesoli recognises the risks and traps in a sociological exploration of the terrain that complements Renaut's philosophical one.

In sum, there can still be a story of hope in reaching a commonwealth – despite everything. The ideal is deeply embedded in modern society and its dynamic – though so are all kinds of forces that block the way. This is also how the ideal is limited rather than utopian. It is not the end of history, or a religious-like *eschaton*. A commonwealth, if we ever get one, is a society which continues to generate its own characteristic pathologies, which might destroy it. It is a society which continues to generate criticisms, calls for reform and new aspirations, which might wonder if it is a commonwealth at all.

Notes and references

1 See Gabriel Marcel, *Homo Viator*, trans. Emma Craufurd (London: Victor Gollanz, 1951); and 'The Structure of Hope', *Communio: International Catholic Review*, vol. 23, no. 3, 1996, pp. 604–11. For an excellent discussion, see Joan Nowotny, 'Despair and the Object of Hope', in Ross Fitzgerald (ed.), *The Sources of Hope*, (Oxford: Pergamon Press, 1979), pp. 44–66.

2 Ernst Bloch, *The Principle of Hope*, 3 volumes, trans. Neville Plaice, Stephen Plaice and Paul Knight (Oxford: Basil Blackwell, 1986). See also Wayne Hudson, *The Marxist Philosophy of Ernst Bloch* (London: Macmillan, 1982).

3 Henri Desroche, *The Sociology of Hope*, trans. Carol Martin-Sperry (London: Routledge & Kegan Paul, 1979).

4 W. Watts Miller, *Durkheim, Morals and Modernity* (London: UCL, 1996).

5   W. Watts Miller, *Hope* (forthcoming).

6   Jean-Paul Sartre, *Existentialism and Humanism*, trans. Phillip Mairet (London: Methuen, 1948), pp. 40–2 and 56.

7   Jacques Ellul, *Hope in Time of Abandonment*, trans. Edward Hopkin (New York: Seabury Press, 1973), p. 222.

8   On hope and the three postulates, see Alexis Philonenko, *L'Œuvre de Kant* (Paris: Vrin, 1993), vol. 2, ch. 3. See also Peter D. Fenves, *A Peculiar Fate: Metaphysics and World-History in Kant* (Ithaca: Cornell University Press, 1991).

9   Viktor E. Frankl, *From Death-Camp to Existentialism* (Boston: Beacon Press, 1959).

10   Marcel, *Homo Viator*, pp. 36–8.

11   Nadezhda Mandelstam, *Hope against Hope*, trans. Max Hayward (London: Collins & Harvill, 1971).

12   Marcel, *Homo Viator*, p. 60.

13   Ibid., pp. 46–7, and Marcel, 'The Structure of Hope', p. 609.

14   Max Charlesworth, 'Hope: An Ontological Foundation?', in Fitzgerald (ed.), *The Sources of Hope*, p. 175.

15   Richard Rorty, *Contingency, Irony and Solidarity* (Cambridge: Cambridge University Press, 1989).

16   Jean-Marie Guyau, *A Esquisse d'une morale sans obligation ni sanction* (Paris: Alcan, 1885), pp. 107–36.

17   Ibid., p. 3.

18   Friedrich Nietzsche, *The Gay Science*, trans. Walter Kaufman (New York: Vintage Books, 1974), p. 336.

19   Emile Durkheim, *Suicide*, trans. John Spaulding and George Simpson (London: Routledge & Kegan Paul, 1952), p. 287. Cf. Guyau's reference to 'infinite desire' in *Esquisse*, p. 149.

20   Emile Durkheim, 'Individualism and the Intellectuals', in W. S. F. Pickering (ed.), *Durkheim on Religion* (London: Routledge & Kegan Paul, 1975), p. 65.

21   Durkheim, *Suicide*, p. 375.

22   Guyau, *Esquisse*, p. 239.

23   Ibid., p. 240.

24   Miguel de Unamuno, *Tragic Sense of Life*, trans. J. E. Crawford Flitch (New York: Dover, 1954), p. 186.

25   Jürgen Moltmann, *Theology of Hope*, trans. James Leitch (London: SCM Press, 1967).

26   This general way of talking characterises some recent work in English on hope: John Patrick Day, *Hope: A Philosophical Inquiry* (Helsinki: Acta Philosophica Fennica, vol. 51, 1991); Joseph J. Godfrey, *A Philosophy of Human Hope* (Dordrecht: Martinus Nijhoff, 1987) and James L. Muyskens, *The Sufficiency of Hope* (Philadelphia: Temple University Press, 1979).

27   Guyau, *Esquisse*, p. 128.

28   Ibid., p. 229.

29   Ibid., pp. 205–52.

30   Ibid., p. 128.

31   Rorty, *Contingency, Irony and Solidarity*, p. 73.

32   Ibid., 77–8.

33   Ibid., p. 84.

34   Ibid., p. 80.

35   Alain Renaut, *The Era of the Individual: A Contribution to a History of Subjectivity*, trans. M. B. DeBevoise and Franklin Phillip (Princeton: Princeton University Press, 1997).

36   Ibid., pp. 174–93.
37   Ibid., p. 194.
38   Marcel Gauchet, *The Disenchantment of the World: A Political History of Religion*, trans. Oscar Burge (Princeton: Princeton University Press, 1997), p. 4.
39   Ibid., pp. 162–5.
40   Durkheim, 'Individualism and the Intellectuals', p. 68.
41   For a discussion, see Watts Miller, *Durkheim, Morals and Modernity*, chs 4 and 10, pp. 95–116 and 229–49. See also my essay, 'Teaching Autonomy', in Geoffrey Walford and W. S. F. Pickering (eds), *Durkheim and Modern Education* (London: Routledge, 1998), pp. 72–91.
42   See W. Watts Miller, 'Durkheim, Kant, the Immortal Soul and God', in N. J. Allen, W. S. F. Pickering and W. Watts Miller (eds), *On Durkheim's Elementary Forms of Religious Life* (London: Routledge, 1998), pp. 67–74.
43   Renaut, *The Era of the Individual*, criticises Martin Heidegger's preoccupation with the person/subject and Louis Dumont's preoccupation with the individual.
44   Alexis de Tocqueville, *Democracy in America*, trans. Richard Heffner (New York: Mentor Books, 1956), pp. 192–4.
45   See Watts Miller, *Durkheim, Morals and Modernity*, pp. 76–7 and 100–2.
46   Jürgen Moltmann, *The Coming of God: Christian Eschatology*, trans. Margaret Kohl (London: SCM Press, 1996), pp. 49–118. See also Richard Bauckham and Trevor Hart, *Hope Against Hope: Christian Eschatology in a Contemporary Context* (London: Darton, Longman & Todd, 1999).
47   W. R. Matthews, *The Hope of Immortality* (London: SCM Press, 1936).
48   It is noticeable that Durkheim's *The Elementary Forms of Religious Life* omits any discussion of prayer, although he had access to plentiful material on it, in Australia and elsewhere, since it was the subject of his nephew's doctoral dissertation. See Marcel Mauss, *La Prière* in *Œuvres* (Paris: Editions de Minuit, 1968).
49   Durkheim, *Suicide*, p. 334, and 'Individualism and the Intellectuals', p. 62.
50   This basic point – again linking with the centrality of prayer – also undermines Larmore's insistence, influenced by Gauchet, on secularisation via a remote, withdrawn God. See Charles Larmore, *The Morals of Modernity* (Cambridge: Cambridge University Press, 1996), pp. 41–4.
51   Francis Fukuyama, *The End of History and the Last Man* (London: Hamish Hamilton, 1992). For a discussion, see Howard Williams, David Sullivan and Gwynn Matthews, *Francis Fukuyama and the End of History* (Cardiff: University of Wales Press, 1997).
52   For a discussion, see Watts Miller, 'Teaching Autonomy', pp. 78–81; and 'Liberté de la volonté et science sociale', in Charles-Henry Cuin (ed.), *Durkheim d'un siècle à l'autre. Lectures actuelles des 'Règles de la méthode sociologique'* (Paris: Presses Universitaires de France, 1997), pp. 223–35.
53   Renaut, *The Era of the Individual*, p. xxix.
54   Michel Maffesoli, *The Time of the Tribes: The Decline of Individualism in Mass Society* (London: Sage, 1996). It is difficult, without a Durkheimian background, to savour Maffesoli's argument about the individual, the person and new forms of collectivity and of the sacred.

13
Virtue Ethics and Death: The Final Arrangements

Peter C. Jupp

The issue of virtue has a property of choice. To be virtuous is to have elected to be so. It is to develop the fortitude to cope with anxieties, fears and self-doubts. It is to have faith in a future and to trust that that future will validate acts of virtue. Virtue is needed to live the good and complete life. It is what characterises the struggle of and for life, hence the significance of hope and the striving for self-dignity. All persons want to be particular in the maximisation of their moral qualities. In the issue of virtue is a question of recognition, of judgement and entitlement, and that is so because people still alive have a future, even if it one is riddled with the risks and anxieties of life in late modernity. Yet its characterising quality in popular culture, in forms detached from traditional theologies, is also a concern with the apocalypse, which Lindohf has discussed in Chapter 11 above. In all these issues which virtue ethics raises, what is missing is a concern with death, for then there is no future, no struggle, no testing, for the life is ended. It is the one inescapable facet of life that any sociology dealing with virtue ethics has to consider.

In commemorating the dead, a list of virtues is often compiled of what they did that was good in their life. In this moral inquest, this ceremony of remembrance, the living are also called to reconsider their relationship to virtues. They are enjoined to remember what virtues they bring to these commemorations. Care, compassion and support, are some of these, but also the cardinal virtues of faith, hope and charity, for amidst the memorialisation of the dead, the living have to live on. Fittingly, to mourn the dead is to affirm the living. The safe departure of the dead and the giving of comfort and direction to the living requires rituals. These require safe management, lest the personal and social bewilderment that death often initiates turns into pathological grief or social chaos. When someone dies, personal and communal worlds are disturbed, indeed shaken, in proportion to the social role played by the one who died. If so vital, so necessary, a person has died, we say, what is there that can abide? Is there anything that can last? Individual deaths, therefore, challenge survivors to identify and to articulate the values and relationships that survive death, undefeated. Thus, death, in exposing transience, effects an affirmation of what is permanent. Thus, the threat of despair can also create the virtue of hope.

The issue of control of these rituals that embody so many virtues is of crucial importance. In dealing with virtue ethics, there is a risk of locking its issues into questions of character, goodness and recognition that do not take account of how these are regulated in particular grounds of culture. The setting for these arrangements for marking virtues points to an interchange between religion and culture, which the issue of death and its ritual marking greatly clarifies. The commemoration of the dead speaks much about the state of society, the place of religion and after-life beliefs within it and the forms of the social structure that mark their departure. This is well illustrated in the collective grief around the death of Princess Diana.[1] These events are now televised, for what Davies and Neal (see Chapter 4) would term 'perfect persons'. The public feel they have a right to display their virtues of mourning and, even through television, to belong to and to participate in such events that mark the identity of a nation. Tragedies such as those of Hillsborough[2] and Lockerbie required highly visible funerals to assuage public grief and to act as a channel for – perhaps to direct – the national sense of mourning.

The capacity to effect a transition for the departed involves a degree of ritual power, a capacity to control, comfort and regulate what could otherwise be dangerous.[3] The certification of the virtues of the dead for the living might seem the prerogative of traditional religion. It points to avenues of access to the after-life for the living, and confirms the hope that the dead have walked these successfully. The virtues of faith, hope and charity combine with considerable force in dealing with the dead. Yet, in contemporary society, this power of traditional religion has been weakened through the commodification of forms of mourning and social responses to death. Before the nineteenth century, the clergy had a controlling interest in many of the supplies of grief and comfort to the dead. They controlled the space, the rituals and the beliefs surrounding the internment of the dead in an orderly and religious manner. Rituals for the dead, however, have realised their own form of secularisation, that has weakened the power of the clergy in the areas of supplying hope of after-life, a service where one would have thought their powers were indisputable. This movement of power from the monopoly of the clergy to other competing agents, such as funeral directors and local government, marks a change in the understanding of death in contemporary culture.[4]

In this chapter, the functions of the funeral are treated as final arrangements that embody the critical virtue of giving comfort to the survivors. These need to be related to theological changes, such as those resulting from the Reformation. This prepared the way for the lessening of influence of the clergy. In the second and the third parts of the chapter, two other elements are discussed that have had a profound and perhaps unrecognised effect on the management of grief. These have increased the marginalisation of the clergy in their capacities to provide for a 'good funeral', one that embodies the virtues of giving comfort to those who mourn. These two elements are the shift of control of the site of burial, and its replacement by cremation. These two processes have had a profound influence on the management of virtues surrounding the need to mourn, and the way in which the Church could and should channel these for the benefit of the survivors. This poses a question of the regulation of the virtues of mourning and the manner in which these are subtly changed in social and technological processes that have profound but unscrutinised theological implications for the link between this life and the after-life. These implications are considered in the last section of the chapter.

The functions of the funeral: the virtues of commemoration

Rituals for the dead have evolved from emotional and practical necessity. In sociological terms, the funeral ritual has four functions. First, it is a rite of disposal for the orderly dispatch of a dead body. Secondly, marking the end of his social involvement in this world, the rite serves to transmit the dead person's identity safely to the next world. Thirdly, it enables the mourners to cope with their loss and to reincorporate them back into wider society. Fourthly, it provides a means of symbolising and interpreting people's beliefs about death, both as a specific event and as a universal fact. It supplies a collective purpose to the need to search for answers. It is proposed to treat each of these functions separately.

Disposal

Death is final: it takes away a physical presence from our everyday lives and assumptions; it removes an actor from the stage of our lives; and it has repercussions that are emotional, companionate, economic, authoritative and domestic. All of these elements will vary according to our relation to the person who has died. That relationship needs to be commemorated in some fitting social manner, for as Grainger has observed, the funeral marks the event of death, but is also its public consequence.[5] Our lives and social roles have henceforth to adjust to the new situation, of life without the significant other, and this involves a period of uncertainty. As van Gennep has suggested, the time between death and funeral is the liminal/threshold period when the dead person presents an ambiguity, of being both present yet absent, vulnerable yet threatening.[6] After the disposal of the body, the survivors start to move on to a new or revised form of normality and read-just to the new roles and circumstances their loss has precipitated. Thus, in discussing grief tasks, Worden has emphasised the importance of facing the fact of death.[7] The importance of the presence of the corpse at a funeral can be gauged by the effect of the First World War on attitudes to death when so many people died, whose funerals were never attended by their relatives. More recently, the concern of families after air-, sea- or oil-rig disasters to glimpse the body, or to have it restored to them, indicates the continuing importance of the confirmation of death so necessary for successful grieving. If the corpse is present at the funeral, the issue of its visibility emerges. The question arises as to whether it should be in a coffin, or open for view and inspection. In English society, the corpse is usually shrouded. Coffining became universal in the latter part of the seventeenth century.[8] Coffining functions to serve a public sense of decency but also indicates concerns of public health. Both municipal architects, liturgists and crematorium staff have sometimes contributed to a crematorium culture in which death has become more invisible.[9] As the National President of the Institute of Burial and Cremation Administration, in 1969, noted proudly, 'in these islands, I feel we have the finest funeral system in the world, with the impact of death on the community not too apparent. I want it to stay that way!'[10]

Transmission

Secondly, the funeral functions to transmit the dead person's identity safely to a next world. In all religions there is a well-articulated form of belief in an after-life, into which religious rituals help to conduct the soul or personality of the dead person. The purpose of these rituals varies according to the religious belief represented. Firth has shown how Hindus follow prescribed rituals which not only safeguard the transmission of the soul, but also ward off the evils that might attend both the dead and their survivors if these rituals are not correctly performed.[11] In Christianity, Orthodox, Catholic and Protestant groups have never entirely held that the correct funeral rituals guarantee the safe passage of the dead nor protect the living: their belief in the sovereignty of God insists that His is the last word over the destiny of the dead.

In Christianity, the functions of transmission relate to an uncertainty about the fate of the dead. Thus, in Catholicism, the concern of the living for the dead is shown by the practice of prayers for their relief from the temporary pains of Purgatory.[12] The dying may themselves show last-minute repentance which could lessen or absolve them from post-mortem punishments. Preparing for death and not presuming on the quality of these preparations marks a property of petition in issues of death. For example, in certain forms of classical Calvinism, the dying strove to cultivate correct and godly attitudes and thoughts when death was imminent.[13]

The arrangements for a funeral serve to mark theological or secular attitudes to the issue of transmission. They also serve to express attitudes to the after-life, whether of fear or presumption. As fear of punishment in Hell or Purgatory diminishes, so also does the power of the clergy. As the issue of

Final Judgement under the pressures of secularisation and modernity melts, this ultimate fear for the end of life, moves from a fiat ordained to an opinion often haphazardly cast. Accordingly the relationships between the virtues ascribed to the dead and those imposed on the living are also adjusted.

Increasingly, funerals serve secular needs, of recalling the life, achievements and character of the dead person, sometimes in the light of his death (if premature) and often his past role in the community.[14] The centrality of a secular rather than a religious criterion for commemoration marks a shift in attitudes to what should be a 'good' funeral. This concentrates on the biography of the individual, rather than on his fate in the after-life. It accounts for the increased annoyance felt when the funeral is skimpily performed, when it is enacted in an anonymous fashion or when the minister has failed to offer any personal narrative or characterisation of the diseased. These issues of attitudes to transmission have profound implications for the change in the balance of power between the clergy and funeral directors. As the latter, encouraged by contemporary funeral reform groups, move to offer greater choice in more personalised and individualised rites of transmission, minimising inconvenient religious issues of commitment and obligation, they fit better than the clergy to the prevailing marketplace, where it is believed anything can be commodified. Funeral directors and local governments seek increasingly to give their 'clients' a greater choice in commemoration in ways the clergy are often not in a position to emulate.

Reincorporation and survival

A crucial function of the funeral is to enable bereaved people to cope with their situation.[15] Throughout history, the loss felt by bereaved people is closely related to the emotional and economic dependence upon the (now) dead person. Marking the end of this is a necessity far less common now when the old are dependent on the young.[16] Whether dependent or independent on the dead person, the mourners require the funeral to function as a distinct stage in their journey on to a readjusted mode of life. There is no return to the old normality, but a new normality must now be established for death may well have altered economic, domestic, companionate and sexual patterns of living. The price of the secularisation of the funeral and its adjustment to a culture of commodification has led to a degree of impoverishment, or privatisation, of grieving. The individual mourners often receive few benefits of social succour once the 'funeral tea' is over. This evokes a degree of nostalgia for past forms of funerals when religion *and* community embodied strong social bonds. Some like Gorer would have felt that Edwardian commemorative rituals represented 'a golden age of mourning' especially in restriction of costume and social activity, and that present forms are nugatory in the comforts they supply to enable reincorporation and survival to occur in a healthy manner of adjustment.[17]

Meaning/interpretation: religious or secular

The past 200 years have witnessed to the fragmentation of the grip of Christianity in English society and this has profound implications for the way in which the issue of death is handled and for the virtues it is deemed to embody. In a large number of areas, the Church no longer has a monopoly over ritual, burial grounds, sites for disposal, and, indeed, the beliefs that responses to death embody. The Church now faces many competitors in its sacerdotal role and it is increasingly weakened in resisting their interventions. The decline of the fear of death and Hell;[18] the effects of the First World War;[19] the secularisation of society compensated for by a growth of implicit religion, a believing without belonging;[20] and the context of a healthier and longer living society; have all weakened the ground of culture and faith upon which funeral rites of the Churches used to stand so solidly.

Changes in religious history, especially at the Reformation, had a profound impact on attitudes to the funeral, its meaning and basis of interpretation. The critical consequence was a fracture of relations between the communities of the living and of the dead. As long as Purgatory was accepted, both dying people and their successors could influence (through Christ) post-mortem destiny. When Protestants placed Purgatory out-of-bounds, the funeral service lost half of its effect: it could help only the bereaved and no longer those who were mourned. As Gittings observed, 'the ritual ties connecting the living and the dead were severed'.[21] This reflects a comment of Keith Thomas, that the effect of the Reformation was that 'each generation could be indifferent to the fate of its successor'.[22] This issue is returned to below. For the moment it is sufficient to note that the Reformation marked the beginning of the dismantling of the post-mortem superstructure of salvation and made the clergy the increasingly dispensable servants of its vision.

A sense of impersonality has arisen as a feel of liturgical history becomes lost in a world less familiar with the forms and words of religious faith. For Trasler, 'apart from the words of committal, there is probably not much of the funeral service that can be quoted among the general population. Changing liturgies and less church attendance have distanced people from the ritual they will experience at the crematorium.'[23] There is now an uncoupling between Church and people, an insecurity about what liturgical form 'works' and how it should be personalised to meet all needs.[24] In this the clergy, in so far as they exemplify theological virtues that ameliorate grief for the dead, find themselves less able to deliver what is required.

Clerical loss of control: the burial site

The passing of the accountability and control of the burial site from the realm of the clergy to civil and secular authorities had a profound effect on the relationship of the clergy to the funeral. During the eighth century, churchyards were developed in town and country.[25] From one angle, people wished to strengthen their guarantees of a heavenly future by burial near a church, and preferably – according to status and ability to pay – within one. From another angle, the clergy strengthened their earthly authority by promoting the symbolism of the churchyard as post-mortem security, assisted – if not guaranteed – by burial liturgies and burial fees. Thus the churchyard came to function as a representation of the local community and its constituent family and feudal structures. It symbolised the continuity of the parish and its inhabitants, dead and alive, past and present. It also symbolised a boundary between the law-abiding and the out-lawed: unbaptised babies were usually be buried on the north side, and suicides were excluded.

At the Reformation, churchyards became Anglican. This later affected relationships with other denominations and religions if they sought space on the same site. It marked a period of unmatched power for the Established Church. From the Uniformity Act 1662, the symbolism of the English parish, as a multi-hinged union of the parish as church and as a bounded geographical community, was unchallenged. This power applied to the control of burial sites. This had particular significance for it marked a site for all, living and dead, to identify with the parish. Those who went their separate ways, such as Catholics, Baptists, and Quakers, were in effect in exile and beyond the ecclesial pale. This power did not outlast two centuries. The Church of England found itself undermined by an unexpected point: a shortage of land.

With the urbanisation consequent upon industrialisation, the Church of England failed to plan for burial space that would be adequate for an expanding population. This failure had important implications, as the new industrial towns had sharply higher mortality rates than the countryside and pressure on available burial spaces grew steadily. Between 1820 and 1850, private cemetery companies sprang up to meet the needs which the Church of England could not supply. These were often established by the increasingly wealthy Dissenters.[26] Pressure on space finally lost the Church of England its now partly fractured monopoly on the provision of burial sites especially as that monopoly was confronted by funeral reformers and cholera epidemics in the context of the growing public health movement.

The Burial Acts of the 1850s closed churchyards in towns of over 5,000 inhabitants by Orders in Council and initiated the establishment of local cemeteries run by local government authorities. These were financed by rates and burial fees. Associated factors helped an erosion of the Church's monopoly over burial sites. The campaigning activities of reformers like Walker and Chadwick, who saw churchyards as a public health issue made their mark, as did the financial success of the private cemetery movement, where the cemetery also took on an unexpected importance as a site for leisure.

Three consequences from these changes in the nineteenth century are especially significant for our purpose. First, the new public cemeteries were established beyond the environs of the towns. This removed the dead from the neighbourhood where they had lived. This necessitated the development of appropriate forms of funeral transport to convey the dead to their new home of rest. It also ushered in cultural expectations that the dead could be distanced from the living. Secondly, the symbolisation of death in the closed churchyards was softened by their adoption for recreational use. Some of the mystery and fear that generated deference to the Christian religion was taken away. This change needs to be understood in relation to the public parks movement with such legislation as the Churchyards and Gardens Act 1884 and the Playing Fields Act 1906. Today, cemeteries are increasingly being valued for reasons other than as a burial place for the dead, e.g. for wildlife preservation, for recreation and as a resource for local history. This means that burial land is coming to be seen as a wider community resource. Thirdly, once public cemeteries became the norm, clergy interest in the care and function of their own burial grounds was reduced, especially now that their proprietorial responsibilities had been removed by law. The marginalisation of the Church from responsibility for the dead was extended with the development of cremation. In response to the economic pressures on burial space and cemetery management, local authorities, for whom budgetary not Biblical constraints were the guiding principles, resorted to cremation to discharge their twentieth-century duties to bereaved families. English people responded, increasingly adopting cremation instead of burial.[27] This shift in attitude removed the commemoration of the dead further away from clerical influence. The clergy had to operate on secular grounds in handling the dead. Unlike in Sweden, for example, English crematoria are entirely in secular hands. While evidence is currently fragmentary, this chapter contends that the clergy's role as gatekeepers for their dead was marginalised by their loss of control over burial grounds. Whilst the relationships are complex, it is clear that in the later nineteenth century, clergy turned their attention increasingly to the (more visible) needs of the living, parallel with people's rising political aspirations, increasing health and longevity, and the moderation of the harsh doctrines about Judgement and Hell after death.

Other forces are making their mark of cultural expectations surrounding the funeral and its site. The funeral service itself is becoming consumer-led and subject to democratic decisions as to what the ritual ought to contain.[28] In certain settings, families are pressing their own values upon death and its symbols. The hospice movement has prompted many people to express greater degrees of autonomy in terminal illness. Pre-paid funeral plans have the potential to enable people to budget for funeral costs. In utilising consumer culture, funeral reform groups paved the way for forms of choice over the style of rite also to be made in advance. Whilst about 28 per cent of people are buried, it has become apparent that significant numbers of people are using graves not only for remembrance of the dead but as a continuing focus for family identity.[29] This is paralleled in the realisation that grave-stones in churchyards are of far more importance to families than had been realised. The Freckleton case, in 1994, indicated that families place great value on the phrases they choose to express relationships between the living and the dead.[30] One historical context for this is the Churches' increased acceptance of the legitimacy of prayers for the dead, and the rise (largely outside the Churches) of heterodox beliefs in spiritualism and reincarnation. Most recently, the debate in bereavement counselling about 'bereavement and biography'[31] is a further indication that the Protestant culture of England, which had insisted on a strict separation of the living from the dead, has been seriously eroded.

Given the combination of reduced Church adherence, the majority choice of cremation and the rise of the consumer movement, families have begun to exercise their rights to conduct their own funerals without the assistance of religious professionals. The growth of the crematorium as the exemplary site for disposal of the dead further marked the marginalisation of the clergy from committal proceedings.[32] It also marked the rise of consumer dissatisfaction with the contemporary basis of the funeral in such settings.[33] The crematoria might well have resolved land problems, issues of public health and consumer-led needs, but they did so at a theological and sociological price, one which is still not fully considered or realised. A host of contradictions emerge, of freedom to choose the form of service involving dependence on the funeral director; a personalised choice being deemed impersonal in operation; and the location and custody of dead people about whom religious authorities have constructed post-mortem expectations which are administered by secular government.

Cremation: a burning issue of disposal for the secular and religious alike

Burial had been the traditional mode of disposal for Christians. The establishment of Christianity brought the spread of burial grounds, and nearness to a church was understood to be beneficial. Resurrection would be followed by some form of final judgement. Belief in the resurrection of the body to judgement survived the Reformation. As Protestant funerals forbade any ritual acts on behalf of the dead, so the secular use of funerals, churchyards and memorials to celebrate the earthly status of the dead increased. The first Protestant instinct, that funerals were religious occasions for reminding the survivors of their own mortality, rather than offering opportunities for prayer to speed the departed heavenwards, was matched by a nineteenth-century concern that the disposal of the dead might actually be medically harmful to the living. The miasmic theory of disease lay behind the ambition of the rising public health movement to remove burial grounds from the centres of urban areas to their fringe. This not only took from the Church a very profitable source of income, it also removed its responsibility for providing and maintaining ground for the dead to lie in peace. It also undermined the ring of authority which the Church had traditionally wielded over and on behalf of the dead. This authority held control over the theology of death and of being dead. It represented the custody of symbolic values and the power to ascribe these to dead bodies. The sites where they lay until the Day of Judgement were the only witnesses of their former lives visible to the eye and community of faith. Once the Church had lost control of burial grounds, it began to lose its interpretative power over death and its memorialisation.[34]

The surrender of burial ground responsibilities to local authorities had another consequence: secular government had inherited the very financial problems which the Church had been unable to solve. These included: the cost of extending burial grounds in urban areas; their cost of maintenance given the vagaries of the English climate; and the geographical mobility of an industrial population which meant that descendants would no longer travel to maintain the graves they owned. This all meant that by the end of the century, local government was looking for ways of discharging its burial obligations more cheaply. In England, the Cremation Society, a reforming charity, was founded in 1874. It initiated a movement which first achieved legal recognition in 1884 and Parliamentary approval by the Cremation Act 1902.[35] Backed by local medical authorities, and largely the work of local authorities, cremation later resolved many of the problems over the issue of burial space. Unfortunately, the Church was not the beneficiary of this new technology of disposal.

The advance of cremation in Britain in the twentieth century may be characterised as the steady concurrence of the various interest groups promoting its use. In the inter-war years, local authorities were increasingly concerned with problems of burial space in a society where the expanding middle class sought housing in new suburbs on the cities' edge, and where the poorer victims of the Depression found it increasingly difficult to pay for traditional funerals. The war years saw both the Churches and the funeral industry realise the benefits of cremation: for the latter the advances of motor transport would enable them to exploit crematoria funerals to increase their trade.[36] After the war, changes in the organisation of the medical profession and the health service encouraged doctors to realise the benefits of cremation. Local authority investment in cremation enabled them both to meet their budgets and to enable families to benefit from the considerably lower charges of a crematorium funeral.

At first the Church of England was divided about cremation. Bishops with a social conscience saw its social benefits. Consecrating the Anglican section of a new cemetery at Stockport 1877, the Bishop of Manchester had two thoughts: 'in the first place, this is a long distance for the poor to bring their dead;...second...here is another hundred acres of land withdrawn from the food-producing areas of the country for ever'.[37] For the more traditional Bishop of London, the needs of the bereaved were outweighed by the social and spiritual benefits these beliefs carried. He understood cremation as a mode of disposal which, claiming to have economic and sanitary concerns rather than doctrinal ones, was actually a proposal to secularise death. Thus, he argued that 'the adoption [of cremation] would be to undermine the faith of mankind in the doctrine of the resurrection of the body, and so bring about a most disastrous social revolution'.[38] Cremation as a neat technological solution to a problem of public health and land space had a spiritual and a social cost that few seemed to grasp. Once cremation had been legalised in 1902, the Churches neglected to develop theologies and liturgies for cremations so they were unable to take advantage of the increasing trend for these new modes of disposal.

The First World War affected attitudes to death in many ways.[39] Three are pertinent to the growing resort to cremation. First, war-time funerals encouraged the preference for simplicity in funerals, exemplified in the decline of mourning dress and customs, simpler memorialisation and the privatisation of grief. Secondly, traditional religious meanings of death changed under the impact of mass death and mass bereavements. At the level of Church pastoral practice, old beliefs in the resurrection of the body, the reality of Hell and the illegitimacy of prayers for the dead were found to be increasingly less relevant and beneficial. Thirdly, the political changes effected by the war bringing Labour to power, enhanced the role of local authorities, with their responsibilities for burial grounds. The economies of land and financial investment which crematoria could provide were realised by local governments. By 1939, 4 per cent of people were cremated, and, by 1945, 9 per cent.

Once cremation had been established by law in 1902, the Church of England had to form its own policy. This was laid down by the Convocation of Canterbury in 1911. Contemporary Anglican divisions can be gauged from the Convocation's decision. First, clergy were not obliged to conduct cremation services for their own parishioners, but could not forbid other clergy from being asked in their place. Secondly, the liturgy for the Burial Service would still be used. Thirdly, ashes were to be interred in consecrated ground. By such concessionary policies did the Church of England encourage competition in its traditional role in funeral services, but this was to weaken the position of the parish priest and to legitimise and encourage those who chose cremation and to seek it from secular and non-local authorities. Thus, the Church started to lose control of the one area where it should have been strong and unassailable: the regulation of ritual forms of disposal of the dead.

The growing desire of Christian parishioners for cremation placed pressure on clergy for this form of disposal. The debates in the Convocation of

Canterbury between 1937 and 1944 formed a new (if not yet common) mind in raising questions.[40] Was cremation legitimate for Christians, and would Church support for it undermine those who believed in bodily resurrection? Since 1911, there had been no liturgy or even prayers authorised for cremation. Evidence was given that ashes were being scattered at crematoria and on unconsecrated ground. The debates reveal a clear separation between the Lower House (clergy) and the Upper House (Bishops). The latter argued that cremation was an acceptable alternative to burial. The former (with the greater pastoral experience) argued that cremation was acceptable only as a preliminary to burial; that ashes should be buried and not scattered; and that the burial of the ashes should take place in consecrated ground. Bishops supported scattering, but only in cemeteries. Parish clergy were defending the Church's traditional positions in seeking to ensure that the mode of disposal should not alter traditional practices of rite, site, interpretation/doctrine and presidency.

Few clergy noted that crematorium procedures had introduced secondary funeral procedures, hitherto unknown in Christian England which would further upset clerical authority to preside over rituals. The action of cremation broke the unity both of the liturgy and of the body. The words of committal were not simultaneous with the commitment to destruction (unlike burial); the cremation process left a residue of ashes. If ashes were to be buried, should that be the proper place for the committal prayer? If ashes were to be buried, could the mourners be expected to reassemble for the occasion? At what point was the body to be regarded as separated or dismissed from the community of the living? At what point was the prayer of committal appropriate?[41]

Three reasons can be discerned for the Bishops' support for cremation. First, they saw, correctly, no incompatibility between belief in the resurrection and the cremation process; secondly, cremation was to be recommended on social and hygienic grounds; and thirdly, ordinary Church members were already choosing it, and the Church should respect their wishes. They did not seem to notice that the trend was being set not by traditional theologies of death but by the preferences of the bereaved. Although paradoxically, in a Protestant country, neither clergy rituals nor survivors' actions were believed to have a beneficial effect upon the destiny of the dead; the wishes and preferences of survivors about the most fitting disposal of their dead were more than legitimate. Convocation's acceptance of cremation began with the words, 'the practice of cremation has no theological significance'.[42] The seal was set on Anglican approval by the death on 26 October 1944 of Dr Temple, the Archbishop of Canterbury. After a funeral service in Canterbury Cathedral, he was cremated.

The conversion of the Established religion to the idea of cremation was followed swiftly by a combination of interests. The Labour Government elected in 1945 found 200 local councils already planning applications for crematoria, a cost-effective means to help both bereaved people and local authority budgets. The Cremation Commission of 1947–1951 assuaged the concerns of medical authorities, the penultimate interest group to be persuaded. The cremation rate steadily rose, at 2 per cent per annum, for the next twenty years. By 1964, the cremation rate had reached 48 per cent. In that year, the Catholic Church accepted cremation.

The curious thing, as yet unexplained, is that after 1944, the Anglican Church paid little formal attention to cremation. Clergy both accompanied their parishioners to the crematorium and were generally prepared to take their turn as rota clergy at the crematoria, as they had at cemeteries. Liturgies for cremation were approved in prayer-book revisions of the 1960s. Cremation became widely accepted as an alternative to burial. Most ashes were scattered at crematoria, overwhelmingly without the attendance of clergy or mourners. Churchyards once full were rarely extended. The voices were rare which questioned the liturgical consequences of the funerary processes that cremation involved.[43] The Church has rarely sought to persuaded crematoria owners to introduce such reforms as, for example, extending times allowed for the funeral service (sometimes as little as twelve minutes). The lack of time not only enforces the truncation of funeral liturgies authorised by the Church; it also encourages clergy to impose limits upon family behaviour and participation.[44] In short, the Church concurred with the role of secular authorities in arrangements for the disposal of the dead.

Whilst there were occasional reassessments of their doctrines of life after death, for forty years no serious thought was given to the articulation of any theology for cremation. This only commenced with Davies.[45] It is noticeable that the General Synod debate (18 November 1998) neither questioned the practice of cremation, nor argued that the Church's practice at funerals rested upon belief in Christ's resurrection.[46] It appears that in most respects the Church has been content to let responsibility for the disposal of the dead to remain largely in secular, public or commercial, hands. It has concentrated on reserving for itself the role of presiding at the funeral service, a role increasingly challenged by contemporary bereaved families.

Sociology and the theology of the final arrangements: virtues gained and lost

Any theology has to give comfort to the living about their prospects in the next world. Burial has remained the dominant form of Christian disposal for Catholic, Orthodox Christians and (until the mid twentieth century) for Protestants. Burial symbolised the post-mortem future of Christians by employing an agricultural metaphor: Christ's resurrection was the first fruits of a whole harvest of the dead (1 Corinthians 15.20). Burial places provided both a focus and a symbol for the living and the dead. It effected the union of local and family identities. For individuals, it provided the place where dead bodies lay to await the post-mortem destiny that – in uneasy tension – it hoped that both they deserved and God purposed.[47]

Christian theology developed a two-edged concept of the dead involving both resurrection and immortality. The body lay dead and the soul slept: both awaiting the day of resurrection when the body would arise, to be reunited with the soul, to face the process of judgement. Various folk-loric fears about the state of the corpse and the danger to which it was exposed were countered by the Church with rituals of sacrament and prayer for the dying and the dead, and of course the protection afforded to the burial ground by its proximity to the Church. On the Day of Resurrection, God would assemble all bodies to reunite with souls – even the sea would give up its dead – and the Last Judgment would consign the wicked to Hell and the good and godly to Heaven. The preaching of this theology was undergirded and symbolised by the Church's control of funeral rites, its ownership/custodianship of burial grounds, and its growing control over local, domestic and family life – especially as that control was marshalled and organised in a feudal, rural society. This was organised, for example, in the weekly Bede roll, in prayers, bequests and guilds – all with the effect of maintaining a concept and an awareness of a living community – centred on the local – of people both alive and dead.[48]

As indicated earlier, the imaginative notion of Purgatory, that imposed a duty of prayer on the living, was swept away in the Reformation. The accountability of the living for the fate of the dead was denied and the virtues of commemoration which these embodied, were swept away. The funeral services were truncated, reflecting the Reformers' beliefs that, after death, no earthly good could be performed for those who had died. No word could be uttered which would influence – let alone counter – the post-mortem judgement of God. The funeral liturgy instructed the priest to commit the body, but not to commend the soul. Any preaching should be to the mourners, touching the nature of death and their need of repentance.[49] These changes had profound implications, for they effected a contraction of the virtues which duties to care for the dead imposed. Thus, for Duffy, the truncation of ceremonies for the dead impoverished opportunities for the virtue of neighbourliness: hitherto, intercessory customs had been an act of religious charity that neighbours could contribute, and expect to have done for them in their turn.[50]

The twentieth century has seen a continuous decline in institutional religion, which has affected younger people even more intensely than older people. What has been effected in the twentieth century is a general assumption that death is no longer a religious threat, or a fact for which religion can offer any more than the fleeting help on the occasion of funerals. All Christian rites of passage attract fewer participants.[51] It appears that Protestantism has proved its own grave-digger. As I have written elsewhere,[52] whilst Catholics had Purgatory to offer, Protestants offered only

Heaven or Hell. When they dropped Hell, Heaven was the only option left. Once the Great War had locked Heaven's gate open, there was no risk after death. Once men could reject the very idea of an after-life without reproof, there remained no risk in death. Fear drained from death, to congeal around the event of dying. People may fear dying, they may fear old age or abandonment, but they no longer fear what follows – death.

In short, the Church has severed the link between death and ethics, between post-mortem options of a life to come and ethical behaviour and sanctions this side of the grave. This process may be said to have begun with the Protestant Reformation, and continued with debates over the existence and functions of Hell,[53] and promoted by pastoral practice in a century which experienced both total war, better health and longevity and increasing secularisation. There are signs that Catholicism may be following a similar course.[54] This need not, however, be interpreted as entirely threatening to the Churches. Their vocation has always been to develop the relationship (however tense) between theological development and pastoral practice to serve people in their need.[55]

If metaphysical nature abhors a vacuum, then the place of Hell has been replaced by a notion of extinction. First secularists and then Freethinkers, followed by the Secular Society and the British Humanist Association, have vigorously promoted 'funerals without God'.[56] Funerals may legitimately be organised for atheist corpses, preaching an atheist gospel and confirming the convictions of atheist mourners that their faith that life ends at death can be articulated even in the face of death. The availability of alternative religions, with their concomitant death practices and beliefs, has extended the religious 'supermarket' where, in a consumer society, people may 'pick and mix' from the range of available beliefs on offer. After-life beliefs are thus chosen on the basis of personal need, and marketed according to their suitability for the customer rather than their traditional authority.

The context of this widening plurality of after-life beliefs involves a consciousness engendered by discoveries in medicine, science and public health. This leads to a belief that death is a natural and predictable event, not a Divine nor a random one. Just as God has withdrawn from the burial-ground (or vice versa), He has discarded death as one of His goads. When premature death was a daily occurrence and a nightly fear, ordinary people might be excused if they did not stand back and view death objectively.[57] Yet the Birth and Death Registration Acts of 1837, the rise of the life assurance industry, developments in medical and public health all worked together in complex ways, to convince people that life-chances were not random. As medical analysis and registration procedures developed, there grew predominant a medical frame of reference for life and death in which God was not required as an explanatory hypothesis[58] and in which the moral worth of sufferers was not a factor in treatment.

As death today usually strikes the dependent elderly it presents few spiritual or economic disadvantages for survivors. Nevertheless, reduced family sizes, career opportunities for women, and social and geographical mobility have combined to promote a need for bereavement support services. In the present secular climate, the needs of the bereaved (none the less real) are seen to be paramount. It is not surprising that funerals have become increasingly, in the Australian phrase, 'life-centred'. Death is no longer considered to be a threat to the future life of dead people. Not surprisingly, funerals are now rituals serving increasingly to mark their previous life. Thus, in Davies's phrase, funeral rituals increasingly represent 'the retrospective fulfilment of identity'.[59] They celebrate the character, the relationships and the achievements of those who have died, whereas in more religious societies, the rituals represented the 'prospective fulfilment of identity' and looked forward to the deceased's life in heaven: looking not forward to a future perfect with God but, if mourners are frank enough, a past imperfect, warts and all. In all these final arrangements are the questions that unite sociology and theology, but also divide them over the issue: where does virtue lie and ultimately to which world is virtue accountable, even, if not especially, in matters of life and death?

Notes and references

1   Tony Walter (ed.), *The Mourning for Diana* (Oxford: Berg, 1999).
2   Tony Walter, 'The Mourning after Hillsborough', *Sociological Review*, vol. 39, no. 3, 1991, pp. 599–625.
3   See Douglas J. Davies, *Death, Ritual and Belief* (London: Cassell, 1997).
4   The wider context of this process is discussed in Tony Walter, *The Eclipse of Eternity: A Sociology of the Afterlife* (Basingstoke: Macmillan, 1996).
5   Roger Grainger, *The Social Symbolism of Grief and Mourning* (London: Jessica Kingsley, 1998) p. 130.
6   Arnold van Gennep, *The Rites of Passage*, trans. Monika B. Vizedom and Gabrielle L. Caffee (Chicago: University of Chicago Press, 1960).
7   William J. Worden, *Grief Counselling and Grief Therapy*, 2nd edn (London: Routledge, 1991), pp. 10–18.
8   Julian Litten, *The English Way of Death: The Common Funeral Since 1450* (London: Hale, 1991). See especially pp. 85–118.
9   Paul J. Sheppy, 'The Dance of Death – a Liturgist Considers Cremation', *Pharos International*, vol. 64, no. 2, Summer 1998, pp. 4–8.
10 Quoted in *The Observer*, 13 July 1969.
11 Shirley Firth, *Dying, Death and Bereavement in a British Hindu Community* (Leuven: Peeters, 1997). For a general discussion, see Julia Neuberger, *Dying Well: A Guide to Enabling a Good Death* (Hale, Cheshire: Hochland & Hochland, 1999).
12 Jacques Le Goff, *The Birth of Purgatory*, trans. Arthur Goldhammer (London: Scholar, 1984). See also Richard K. Fenn, *The Persistence of Purgatory* (Cambridge: Cambridge University Press, 1995).
13 David E. Stannard, *The Puritan Way of Death: A Study in Religion, Culture and Social Change* (New York: Oxford University Press, 1977).

14 A trend characterised as the 'retrospective fulfilment of identity' by Davies, *Death, Ritual and Belief*, p. 31.

15 This is represented by the third of the three stages van Gennep hypothesised for understanding rites of passage, including funerary rituals of separation, transition and incorporation. See van Gennep, *The Rites of Passage*.

16 See Robert Blauner, 'Death and Social Structure', *Psychiatry*, vol. 29, no. 4, 1966, pp. 378–94.

17 Geoffrey Gorer, *Death, Grief and Mourning in Contemporary Britain* (London: Cresset, 1965). For a recent discussion of Gorer's study, see Tony Walter, 'A Sociology of Grief', *Mortality*, vol. 3, no. 1, 1998, pp. 83–7.

18 See Geoffrey Rowell, *Hell and the Victorians. A Study of the Nineteenth Century Theological Controversies concerning Eternal Punishment and the Future Life* (Oxford: Clarendon, 1974).

19 Alan Wilkinson, *The Church of England and the First World War* (London: SPCK, 1997).

20 For implicit religion, see Edward Bailey, *Implicit Religion: An Introduction* (London: Middlesex University Press, 1998). For 'believing without belonging', see Grace Davie, *Religion in Britain Since 1945: Believing without Belonging* (Oxford: Blackwell, 1994).

21 Clare Gittings, *Death, Burial and the Individual in Early Modern England* (London: Croom Helm, 1984), p. 40.

22 Keith Thomas, *Religion and the Decline of Magic* (Harmondsworth: Penguin, 1973), p. 721.

23 Graham Trasler, '"Mind the Gap": Funerals at the Crematorium', unpublished, 1998. Available from Revd Graham Trasler, 37 Jacklyns Lane, New Arlesford, Hants. S024 9LF.

24 For a recent discussion, see Keith Denison, 'The Theology and Liturgy of Funerals: A View from the Church in Wales', *Mortality*, vol. 4, no. 1, 1999, pp. 63–74.

25 Christopher Daniell and Victoria Thompson, 'Pagans and Christians: 400–1150', in Peter C. Jupp and Clare Gittings (eds), *Death in England: An Illustrated History* (Manchester: Manchester University Press, 1999), pp. 65–89. See also Christopher Daniell, *Death and Burial in Medieval England, 1066–1550* (London: Routledge, 1997).

26 Julie Rugg, 'The Rise of Cemetery Companies in Britain, 1820–53', unpublished Ph.D. thesis, University of Stirling, 1992.

27 Peter C. Jupp, 'The Development of Cremation in England: A Sociological Analysis', unpublished Ph.D. thesis, University of London, 1993.

28 See, for example, Nicholas Albery, Gil Elliot and Joseph Elliot, *The Natural Death Handbook*, second edition. (London: The Natural Death Centre, 1997); The Institute of Burial and Cremation Administration (IBCA), *Charter for the Bereaved*, revised edition (London: IBCA, 1997); and The National Funerals College, *The Dead Citizens Charter*, revised edition (Bristol: The National Funerals College, 1998).

29 Doris Francis, Leonie Kellaher and Georgina Neophytou, 'Sustaining Cemeteries: The User Perspective', *Mortality*, vol. 5, no. 1, March 2000, pp. 34–53.

30 Diocese of Blackburn: Judgement in the Consistory Court, 16th July 1994.

31 The debate followed the paper by Tony Walter, 'A New Model of Grief: Bereavement and Biography', *Mortality*, vol. 1, no. 1, 1996, pp. 7–25.

32 For a contrasting view, that crematoria may also be fostering a sense of the sacred, see Douglas J. Davies, 'The Sacred Crematorium', *Mortality*, vol. 1, no. 1, 1996, pp. 83–94.

33   One common example concerns the choice over ministers presiding at crematoria. For a recent discussion, see Malcolm Lesiter, 'Clergy Rota', *Pharos International*, vol. 64, no. 4, Winter 1998, pp. 26–7.
34   Peter C. Jupp, 'The context of Funeral Ministry Today', in Peter C. Jupp and Tony
Rogers (eds), *Interpreting Death: Christian Theology and Pastoral Practice* (London:
Cassell, 1997), pp. 3–16.
35   Peter C. Jupp, 'History of the Cremation Movement in Great Britain: The First
125 years', *Pharos International*, vol. 65, no. 1, Spring 1999, pp. 18–25.
36   See Glennys Howarth, 'Professionalising the Funeral Industry in England
1700–1960', in Peter C. Jupp and Glennys Howarth (eds), *The Changing Face of
Death. Historical Accounts of Death and Disposal* (Basingstoke: Macmillan, 1997),
especially pp. 125–33. For a full-length treatment of changing funeral directing
practices, see Brian Parsons, 'Change and Development of the British Funeral
Industry in the 20th Century with special reference to the period 1960–1994',
unpublished Ph.D. thesis, University of Westminster, 1997.
37   Quoted in *The Undertakers' Journal*, 15 October 1911.
38   Quoted in *The Times*, 6 July 1874.
39   See Aidan Gregory, *The Silence of Memory. Armistice Day 1991–1946* (Oxford: Berg,
1994); Jay Winter, *Sites of Memory, Sites of Mourning: The Great War in European
Cultural History* (Cambridge: Cambridge University Press, 1995); and Wilkinson,
The Church of England and the First World War.
40   For a discussion of the relevant Church of England debates 1942–4, see Jupp, 'The
Development of Cremation in England', pp. 312–28.
41   For a contemporary discussion of this problem, see John Lampard, 'Theology in
Ashes – The Failure of the Churches to think Theologically about Cremation', in
Bereavement and Belief (London: the Churches' Group on Funeral Services at
Cemeteries and Crematoria, 1993), pp. 28–36.
42   *Debates of the Lower House of the Convocation of Canterbury*, 11 October 1944.
43   See Douglas J. Davies, *Cremation Today and Tomorrow* (Nottingham: Alcuin/Grow
Liturgical Study 16), 1990, especially p. 33.
44   Jenny Hockey, 'The Acceptable Face of Human Grieving? The Clergy's Role in
Managing Expression during Funeral Rites', in David Clark (ed.), *The Sociology of
Death. Theory, Culture, Practice* (Oxford: Blackwell, 1993), pp. 129–48.
45   See Douglas J. Davies, 'Theologies of Disposal', in Jupp and Rogers, *Interpreting
Death*, pp. 67–84.
46   See *Good Funerals. A background paper prepared on behalf of the ecumenical Churches'
Group on Funeral Services at Cemeteries and Crematoria in support of the Southwark
Diocesan Synod Motion*, 'Funerals: Business and Vocation' (London: General Synod
of the Church of England, 1998), GS Misc. 539. For the debate, see *General Synod
November Group of Sessions 1998. Report of Proceedings*, vol. 29, no. 3, pp. 940–67.
47   For a full discussion, see Caroline Walker Bynum, *The Resurrection of the Body in
Western Christianity, 200–1336* (New York: Columbia University Press, 1995).
48   Geoffrey Rowell, 'Changing Patterns: Christian Beliefs about Death and the
Future Life', in Jupp and Rogers, *Interpreting Death*, pp. 21–3.
49   Geoffrey Rowell, *The Liturgy of Christian Burial* (London: Alcuin Club/SPCK,
1977), pp. 84–7.
50   Eamon Duffy, *The Stripping of the Altars: Traditional Religion in England, 1400–1580*
(New Haven and London: Yale University Press, 1992), pp. 474–5.
51   William S. F. Pickering, 'The Persistence of Rites of Passage: Towards an Explanation', *The British Journal of Sociology*, vol. 25, no. 1, March 1974, pp. 63–78.

52 Peter C. Jupp, *From Dust to Ashes: The Replacement of Burial by Cremation in England 1840–1967* (London: Congregational Memorial Hall Trust (1978) Ltd, 1990), pp. 28–9.

53 See Phillip C. Almond, *Heaven and Hell in Enlightenment England* (Cambridge: Cambridge University Press, 1994).

54 Michael Hornsby-Smith, *Roman Catholic Beliefs in England: Customary Catholicism and Transformations of Religious Authority* (Cambridge: Cambridge University Press, 1991), pp. 98–102.

55 For a full discussion of the issues involved in the development of future Christian theologies about death and after-life, see David L. Edwards, *After Death? Traditional Beliefs and Real Possibilities* (London: Cassell, 1999).

56 Jane Wynne Wilson, *Funerals without God: A Practical Guide to Non-Religious Funerals* (London: British Humanist Association, 1988).

57 C. E. Lawrence, ' The Abolition of Death', *Fortnightly Review*, vol. CI, N.S., 1917, pp. 326–31.

58 Lindsay Prior, 'Actuarial Visions of Death: Life, Death and Chance in the Modern World', in Jupp and Howarth, *The Changing Face of Death*, pp. 177–93.

59 Davies, *Death, Ritual and Belief*, p. 31.

Conclusion

Kieran Flanagan

Few more fundamental questions face society and, indeed, sociology itself, than the circumstances in which social bonds endue. If they do not, the public weal withers. Recent political and social thought has been much directed to reversing a fall in public confidence in how the social bond is to be made. Individualism marks a retreat from the language of giving and this erosion of commitment lies at the root of the perceived failure to re-make communities. There is a feeling that society has lost its capacities to repro-duce itself. The indifference that destroyed religion in the context of modernity, has now spread to any form of belief system in postmodernity. It is not only a public mood of cynicism with politics, religion and any belief system that accentuates the present crisis. The trouble is that techno-logy is forming a means of living without community, via the internet and via an easeful life of gazing at virtual realities, where the social and com-munal are seen as old-fashioned distractions that make untidy demands on the self.

It is against this background that the issues generated by virtue ethics take on an unexpected significance for sociology. They supply it with a means of re-casting itself away from the nihilism of postmodernity. The legacy of this intellectual form of dry rot still percolates into present culture in some fated and fixed manner. It penetrates so many areas of public life, culture and reli-gion, so that fragmentation and pastiche are deemed the marks of present society. Is sociology doomed to accept this state of affairs? Reversing this trend, by attending to the issues generated by virtue ethics, is to bring what is valuable in the human condition into focus in ways that offer sociology numerous opportunities to reclaim its prophetic mantle. It enables soci-ology to re-cast its disciplinary legacy to return to a question of central and enduring importance: the social circumstances of trust.

These issues point to something more than ethics can answer or contain by its appeal to individual reason and calculation of consequence. They direct attention to properties of identity, of character and moral worth, intrinsic traits for which the actor is accountable. These elements of virtue ethics overspill into matters of sociological concern that make them more than mere movements in philosophical fashions. They relate to issues very much the concerns of Weber and Durkheim, two figures who hover over the collection. They also point to considerations that lie within the writings of two enormously significant figures who have shaped sociological thought in its characterisations of late modernity and postmodernity. Giddens and Bauman have brought to the fore issues of trust, of obligation and commitment to what lies beyond the mere self. In their writings they express issues of anxiety and concern with the moral commitment at the level of the individual where questions of trust lie. Issues of virtue ethics lie tantalisingly adjacent to their concerns.

Any number of virtues could have been considered, but this collection centred on those such as celibacy, hope, mourning and the worth of the person, to name a few. Themes of recognition, secularisation, and sociology's own ethical duties marked the concerns of the collection. In the collection some issues came forward as specific questions sociology finds hard to handle, hence the diversity of positions amongst the contributors. Tester and McMylor showed how difficult these issues were in their treatment of Weber, MacIntyre and Bauman. One particular question that becomes apparent is how self-sufficient sociology can be in dealing with virtue. This relates to an endemic question that goes back to the foundations of the discipline and its roots in the Enlightenment. It is the question of whether sociology can treat issues of virtue from within its own frame of reference without recourse to religion or if it has to defer to properties of revelation that lie outside reason.

In the collection, McMylor, Tester, Flanagan, Archer, Barot, Watts Miller and Jupp treated issues of virtue and religion in terms of an insufficiency in sociology. Set against MacIntyre, whose writings have been oddly neglected in sociology, Tester and McMylor reflected on a disquiet, that asks questions for which there were no easy answers, about ultimate fate and moral worth, and which lie heavily and unacknowledged on the agenda of the discipline. In claiming that MacIntyre had misunderstood Weber, both were marking out a ground for sociology to make its own dispositions in relation to the issue of virtue. It is interesting to note the comparisons made between MacIntyre and Bauman. For Watts Miller, this insufficiency in sociology is endemic in handling questions of hope, which for him, seems a hopeless task without reference to theology, a point whose punch he pulled at the end of his essay.

Flanagan and Archer seemed concerned to push sociology into a theological test doomed to fail in two areas. For the former, the endemic ambiguity of virtue and vice posed a test that sociology could not pass, whereas for the latter the strengths of sociology in relation to individualism and community could not penetrate into the theological issues surrounding the virtues of sainthood. Barot's treatment of celibacy reminds one of the insularity of Western culture which seems to have a limited notion of virtue. In Jupp's contribution, the regulation of the virtues of mourning over which the Church had presided unchallenged up to the recent past, has become unravelled. This unstitching had arisen over a failure to read the sociological omens surrounding cemeteries and crematoria. His concerns are less with the insufficiency of sociology regarding the handling of virtue, and more with the failure of theologians sufficiently to grasp changes in the reproduction of mourning in a culture where anything could be commodified. It is theology rather than sociology that is picked out as being in some way insufficient.

Some contributions seemed to accept the sufficiency of sociology in dealing with issues of virtue without reference to religion in its traditional sense as that which is defined in some form of theological formulation that imposes obligations. Thus, Heelas, Collins and Davies and Neal place their contributions about virtue in ways that do not presuppose a theology. For Collins the disjunction between youthful attitudes to ontological insecurities in late modernity points to a crisis of recognition of the transcendent and a disbelief in the authority of traditional religions, such as Anglicanism or Catholicism. She argues for recognition of an immanent religion, one where young people find their own circumstances of the making of virtue. This question of recognition without reference to their theological properties governs Herbert's approach. His concerns are with the politics of recognition surrounding virtue when treated as a property of an ethnic or a religious group, but this time as part of an agenda of assimilation in post-Christian civil societies. Like Barot, he seeks to find a site for another tale of virtue in another religious tradition. Likewise, Heelas treats the management of cultural extremities in the context of ethics and New Age religion. His concerns are with the humanity embodied in sociology, evident not least in Durkheim, that would ameliorate cultural excesses, and that would appeal to some general notion of human dignity.

The issue of sufficiency relates also to mechanisms of the reproduction of religion in relation to virtue, and here one finds an interesting if not unexpected division between Lindohf and Dandelion. Both are concerned with the issue of time and the unfolding of obligations which it imposes on religion. For Lindohf, popular culture has caught better the moods and fears surrounding the apocalypse than traditional theologies which are supposed to give witness to its unfolding basis. These properties of the apocalypse, the fears and hopes it embodies, have been discarded as incredible by traditional theologies who have underestimated the needs of the times. For Lindhof, they also face crises over the credibility of their mechanism of reproduction of belief. These structures and traditions of authority and ritual order seem to her impediments for the Churches as they try to link traditional interpretations to contemporary fears which popular culture articulates much more effectively. By contrast, Dandelion sees the absence of such structures as the source of the problem of Quakerism's emptying of a distinctive belief and witness. It has secularised its teaching that stood close to the unfolding of time just at the point when society needs such a definite religious witness. Thus, whereas Lindohf sees the structures of ecclesial culture as disabling, Dandelion regards these as enabling, as entities that might have saved Quakerism from the forces of secularisation to which it has so unwittingly capitulated. Like Jupp, he sees a failure to conserve a distinctive form of belief as leading to a weakening of a claim to represent virtue in some authentic theological sense. Both see capitulation to forces of secularisation as being a form of own-grave-digging that weakens their power to proclaim virtues of fidelity and a concern with the last things.

Clearly the issue of virtue needs to be made more specific. It is a property of the human condition, covering manifold literatures, philosophies, religions and cultures, and none can claim a monopoly on its definition or basis of realisation, although some would claim privileged access. Laxity or tightness of definition depends on sociological and theological expectations, those that enjoin and specify what is virtue and how to realise it.

The most obvious sociological path to proceed on lies in the contextualisation of the issue of virtue. This opens out the issue of habit, formation and communal conditions of realisation. A way forward would be for sociology to explore Cottingham's notion of an ethical culture. This would be to study the communal setting in which exemplars are formed. In some sense, this would be to hope for a coming of an exemplar who would establish a completely new communal setting for the realisation of virtue. This would echo MacIntyre's hope for a new, albeit much different, St Benedict, fit for the times of present hopelessness.

Wider contextual demands could be made on sociology in the study of virtue, not least a cataloguing of its own. Sociology's values of affiliation to science, which Weber so ably portrayed in 'Science as a Vocation', affirm the exemplification of duty, but in an educational setting. The issue of virtue points to sociology's own witness within the institution within which many sociologists pursue their calling: the university. The current tyranny in the United Kingdom, of rendering research and teaching accountable to inspection, is itself a problem of virtue ethics which sociologists are well qualified to explore. One group profoundly distrusted, and so required to undergo bureaucratic scrutiny and accountability, are academics themselves.

The moral landscape of the university is increasingly constructed on paper requirements, and in these fictions more fundamental questions of character have become obscured. The only character that counts is that which can be rendered fit for bureaucratic accountability in terms of research and teaching. Bizarrely, academics themselves have colluded in their own bureaucratic entrapment. They have become willing victims of Bourdieu's notion of symbolic violence. Without a vision of virtue, they have no means of ameliorating their own fate.

Within reflexivity, the notion of self-awareness peculiar to the discipline, lurks a higher question, one of calling to a higher duty, and that is what the study of virtue yields for sociological scrutiny. It could be that the study of virtue might offer instruments of redemption from the present plight into which university education is being so remorselessly cast. This would be a context that would matter, not least to sociologists themselves.

To some extent the questions posed by virtue ethics relate to concerns sociology already has in hand. Habitus points to the cultivation of disposition. It resolves a methodological problem of the disjunction between agent and structure, but it also points to traits and characteristics, and that is what virtue ethics seeks to amplify. The issue of character is of central importance in Weber and, indeed, in all aspects of sociology. Virtue is not pointing to something new to sociology in so emphasising the significance of the issue of character. It simply asks for clarification of the moral traits that character does and ought to embody. Likewise, the formation of virtue relates to issues of education, socialisation, and expectation. Virtue takes over an existing agenda. As suggested earlier, the whole debate on identity and sexual politics is about moral traits, imputed to, or supposedly characterising an actor and his or her community of affiliation. It is not far-fetched to argue that the present wars over culture and gender are about the imputation of virtue or its denial to particular groups. They are about credit and discredit in the issue of virtue and the moral judgements so made. Within the question of virtue lies an issue of power that is presently masked.

The questions that sociology poses to virtue ethics, within disciplinary terms, are conventional. The first and most important question is that of the power to define virtue and to mark its boundaries. This relates to the way definitions of virtue have contested properties. Social means of realisation are required and these are linked to questions of empowerment, to confer and to receive. The issues raised relate to legitimacy and authority, to deem what is virtuous and what is not and who is or is not. This is to return the question of virtue to a very broad terrain. The question of power does have one particularly important implication: it rehabilitates the notion of judgement, of marking differences to what often might pass as matters of indifference. Simply saying that attitudes have changed is not an argument in accounting for changes in virtue. One wants to know *how and why* they have changed.

The second area ripe for speculation, is that of context of belief. This relates not only to the setting of virtue and its recognition (an issue on which some contributors have focused) but also to the belief systems that govern what is to be read as virtuous. This has formed a crucial strand of the collection and accounts for the diversity of readings of virtue so made. Precept and practice, civic or religious, are all elements of value brought to the context of virtue. Within this setting are very orthodox issues of the sociology of knowledge. How are ideas of virtue grounded, recognised and realised? What are the agendas of social construction that surround the realisation of the traits which virtue ethics generates as questions?

The third area open to elaboration is the issue of the practice of virtue. This relates to manners of disclosure, but also a return to the issues of socialisation that might effect an agenda of virtue ethics. This returns, again, to the question of virtue in the setting of an ethical culture which Cottingham has explored. Virtue ethics points to curricular demands more specific than broad questions of civic values and those embodied in sex education. It is about a change in moral expectation. The issue of virtue ethics, education and religion is wide open for sociological exploration, for it is a debate that can only unfold.

Fourthly and finally, the question emerges of how virtue needs to be related to the cultural circumstances of its reception. This means exploring how virtue is perceived and what are the conditions surrounding its misperception. This would involve going against the whole grain of media culture in the United Kingdom, which is cast solidly against such issues being raised. Virtue has no media image. As said in the introduction, this is because it is not an issue for a media that thrives on accounts of its demolition.

The only essay in the collection that embodied research in the field on the topics of virtue ethics is that of Collins. Here is a wide-open territory for exploration of how virtue ethics is grounded in practices of self-understanding. The notion of testimony which is so central to qualitative research methods in sociology could be well harnessed to exploring this terrain. If nothing else, such research would turn back the tide that regards giving voice to exemplars of virtue as some sort of betrayal of the naturalised beliefs of sociology that only the study of vice matters.

The issue of what are the existing and active virtues that best reflect the domestic needs and expectations of sociology requires considerable further exploration. In the collection, the contributors have placed a lot of conceptual meat on the table. MacIntyre, Bauman, Giddens Weber and Durkheim have been targets of especial interest; the person, fortitude, hope, fear, anxiety, death and moral justice, all worked from a variety of positions on religion, have been others; and in all, there has been a struggle to connect sociology to questions that matter. If the contributors have sought anything, it is to open out opportunities for sociology to take further the questions that virtue ethics pose to the discipline.

Bibliography

Abbinnett, Ross, 'Postmodernity and the Ethics of Care: Situating Bauman's Social Theory', *Cultural Values*, vol. 2, no. 1, 1998, pp. 87–116.

Abbinnett, Ross, *Truth and Social Science. From Hegel to Deconstruction* (London: Sage, 1998).

ABPI, *ABPI Facts and Figures* (London: Association of the British Pharmaceutical Industry, 1992).

Adams, Richard and Janice Haaken, 'Anticultural Culture. Lifespring's Ideology and Its Roots in Humanistic Psychology', *Journal of Humanistic Psychology*, vol. 27, no. 2, 1987, pp. 501–17.

Albery, Nicholas, Gil Elliot and Joseph Elliot, *The Natural Death Handbook*, second edition (London: The Natural Death Centre, 1997).

Almond, Phillip C., *Heaven and Hell in Enlightenment England* (Cambridge: Cambridge University Press, 1994).

Alston, William, *Perceiving God* (Ithaca, New York: Cornell University Press, 1991).

Altizer, Thomas J. J., *History as Apocalypse* (Albany: State University of New York Press, 1985).

Altizer, Thomas J. J., *Genesis and Apocalypse: A Theological Voyage Toward Authentic Christianity* (Louisville, Kentucky: Westminster/John Knox Press, 1990).

Ambler, Rex, *The End of Words: Issues in Contemporary Quaker Theology* (London: Quaker Home Service, 1994).

Anscombe, G. E. M., 'Modern Moral Philosophy', in Roger Crisp and Michael Slote (eds), *Virtue Ethics* (Oxford: Oxford University Press, 1997), pp. 26–44.

Aquinas, St Thomas, *Summa Theologiae*, trans. Reginald Masterson and T. G. O'Brien (London: Eyre & Spottiswoode, 1965), vol. 60.

Archer, Margaret S., *Realist Social Theory: The Morphogenetic Approach* (Cambridge: Cambridge University Press, 1995).

Aristotle, *The Ethics of Aristotle*, trans. J. A. K. Thomson (Harmondsworth: Penguin, 1976).

Ashford, Sheena and Noel Timms, *What Europe Thinks: A Study of Western European Values* (Aldershot: Dartmouth, 1992).

Augustine, St, *City of God*, trans. Henry Bettenson (Harmondsworth: Penguin, 1972).

Aurobindo, Sri, *The Foundations of Indian Culture* (Pondicherry: Sri Aurobindo Ashram, 1995).

Baechler, Jean, *Suicides* (Oxford: Blackwell, 1979).

Baer, Jr., Richard A., 'Silent Worship, Glossolalia and Liturgy: Some Functional Similarities', *Quaker Religious Thought*, vol. 16, no. 3, 1975, pp. 28–37.

Bailey, Edward, 'The Religion of the People', in Tony Moss (ed.), *In Search of Christianity* (London: Firethorn Press, 1986), pp. 178–88.

Bailey, Edward, *Implicit Religion: An Introduction* (London: Middlesex University Press, 1998).

Ballard, J. G., *Crash* (London: Vintage, 1995).

Baron, Marcia, Philip Pettit and Michael Slote, *Three Methods of Ethics* (Oxford: Blackwell, 1997).

Barot, Rohit, 'Celibacy in the Swaminarayan Movement', in John Hinnells and Werner Menski (eds), *South Asian Religious Experience in the West* (Basingstoke: Macmillan) (forthcoming).

Barrientos, Alberto (ed.), *Introducción a la lectura de Santa Teresa* (Madrid: Editorial de Espiritualidad, 1978).

Bauckham, Richard, 'The Theology of the Book of Revelation', in James D. G. Dunn (ed.), *The Theology of the Book of Revelation* (Cambridge: Cambridge University Press, 1993), pp. 1–22.

Bauckham, Richard and Trevor Hart, *Hope Against Hope: Christian Eschatology in a Contemporary Context* (London: Darton, Longman & Todd, 1999).

Baudrillard, Jean, *The Transparency of Evil* (London: Verso, 1993).

Bauman, Zygmunt, *Legislators and Interpreters* (Cambridge: Polity, 1987).

Bauman, Zygmunt, *Modernity and the Holocaust* (Cambridge: Polity Press, 1989).

Bauman, Zygmunt, 'The Social Manipulation of Morality: Moralizing Actors, Adiaphorizing Action', *Theory, Culture and Society*, vol. 8, no. 1, 1991, pp. 137–51.

Bauman, Zygmunt, *Modernity and Ambivalence* (Cambridge: Polity, 1991).

Bauman, Zygmunt, *Postmodern Ethics* (Cambridge, Polity, 1993).

Bauman, Zygmunt, *Intimations of Postmodernity* (London: Routledge, 1993).

Bauman, Zygmunt, *Life in Fragments: Essays in Postmodern Morality* (Oxford: Blackwell, 1995).

Bauman, Zygmunt, 'What Prospects of Morality in Times of Uncertainty', *Theory, Culture & Society*, vol. 15, no. 1, February 1998, pp. 11–22.

Beaudoin, Tom, *Virtual Faith. The Irreverent Spiritual Quest of Generation X* (San Franciso: Jossey-Bass Publishers, 1998).

Beck, Ulrich, *Risk Society: Towards a New Modernity*, trans. Mark Ritter (London: Sage, 1992).

Beck, Ulrich and Elisabeth Beck-Gernsheim, *The Normal Chaos of Love*, trans. Mark Ritter and Jane Wiebel (Cambridge: Polity Press, 1995).

Bellah, Robert N., Richard Madsen, William M. Sullivan, Ann Swidler and Steven M. Tipton, *Habits of the Heart. Individualism and Commitment in American Life* (Berkeley and London: University of California Press, 1985).

Benhabib, Seyla, *Situating the Self* (Cambridge: Polity, 1992).

Berger, Peter L., *A Far Glory. The Quest for Faith in an Age of Credulity* (New York: Doubleday, 1992).

Berger, Peter L., Brigitte Berger and Hansfried Kellner, *The Homeless Mind. Modernization and Consciousness* (Harmondsworth: Penguin, 1974).

Berlin, Isaiah, *The Crooked Timber of Humanity. Chapters in the History of Ideas* (London: Fontana, 1991).

Bewes, Timothy, *Cynicism and Postmodernity* (London: Verso, 1997).

Bhaskar, Roy, *Reclaiming Reality* (London: Verso, 1989).

Birch, Maxine, 'The Goddess/God Within: The Construction of Self-Identity through Alternative Health Practices', in Kieran Flanagan and Peter C. Jupp (eds), *Postmodernity, Sociology and Religion* (Basingstoke: Macmillan, 1996), pp. 83–100.

Blauner, Robert, 'Death and Social Structure', *Psychiatry*, vol. 29, no. 4, 1966, pp. 378–94.

Bloch, Ernest, *The Principle of Hope*, 3 volumes, trans. Neville Plaice, Stephen Plaice and Paul Knight (Oxford: Basil Blackwell, 1986).

Bokun, Bruno, *Spy in the Vatican, 1941–45* (London: Vita, 1973).

Bose, Abinash Chandra, *Hymns from the Vedas. Original Text and English Translation with Introduction and Notes* (Bombay: Asia Publishing House, 1966).

Brierley, Peter, *Christian England: What the English Church Census Reveals* (London: Marc Europe, 1991).

Brierley, Peter (ed.), *UK Christian Handbook. Religious Trends 1998/1999* (London: Christian Research, 1997).

British Medical Association, *Living with Risk* (Chichester: John Wiley, 1987).

British Muslims and Islamophobia (London: The Runnymede Trust, 1997).

Broderick, Mick, 'Heroic Apocalypse: Mad Max, Mythology, and the Millennium', in Christopher Sharrett (ed.), *Crisis Cinema: The Apocalyptic Idea in Post-Modern Narrative Film* (Washington, DC: Maisonville Press, 1993), pp. 258–83.

Bruce, Steve, *Religion in the Modern World: From Cathedrals to Cults* (Oxford: Oxford University Press, 1996).

Buckley, Michael, *At the Origins of Modern Atheism* (New Haven: Yale University Press, 1987).

Bull, Malcolm (ed.), *Apocalypse Theory and the Ends of the World* (Oxford: Blackwell, 1995).

Burkhardt, Jacob, *The Civilization of the Renaissance in Italy* (London: George Allen & Unwin, 1928).

Burnstall, Michael and Bryan Reuben, *Critics of the Pharmaceutical Industry* (London: Remit Consultants, 1990).

Butler, Samuel, *Erehwon or Over the Range* (London: Jonathan Cape, 1927).

Byers, Thomas B., 'Commodity Futures', in Anette Kuhn (ed.), *Alien Zone: Cultural Theory and Contemporary Science Fiction Cinema* (London and New York: Verso, 1990), pp. 39–50.

Bynum, Caroline Walker, *The Resurrection of the Body in Western Christianity, 200–1336* (New York: Columbia University Press, 1995).

Carey, John (ed.), *John Donne* (Oxford: Oxford University Press, 1990).

Carrdus, Ann, 'The Quaker unChristmas', *The Friend*, vol. 151, no. 52, 1993, pp. 1659–60.

Catechism of the Catholic Church (London: Geoffrey Chapman, 1994).

Chapman, John W. and William A. Galston, *Virtue, NOMOS, XXXIV* (New York: New York University Press, 1992).

Charlesworth, Max, 'Hope: An Ontological Foundation?', in Ross Fitzgerald (ed.), *The Sources of Hope* (Oxford: Pergamon Press, 1979), pp. 165–75.

Charter for the Bereaved (revised edition) (London: IBCA, 1997).

Clissold, Stephen, *St. Teresa of Avila* (London: Sheldon Press, 1979).

Cohn, Norman, *The Pursuit of the Millennium: Revolutionary Millenarians and Mystical Anarchists of the Middle Ages* (London: Maurice Temple Smith, 1970).

Collier, Andrew, *Being and Worth* (London: Routledge, 1999).

Collins, John J., 'Introduction: Towards a Morphology of a Genre', *Semeia: An Experimental Journal for Biblical Criticism*, no. 14, 1979, pp. 1–20.

Collins, Sylvia, 'Immanent Faith: Young People in Late Modernity', in Leslie J. Francis (ed.), *Sociology, Theology and the Curriculum* (London: Cassell, 1999), pp. 165–74.

Conquest, Robert, *The Great Terror* (Harmondsworth: Penguin, 1974).

Cottingham, John, 'Religion, Virtue and Ethical Culture', *Philosophy*, vol. 69, 1994, pp. 163–80.

Cox, Harvey, *The Secular City: Secularization and Urbanization in Theological Perspective* (London: SCM Press, 1965).

Cox, Harvey, *The Seduction of the Spirit: The Use and Misuse of People's Religion* (London: Wildwood House Ltd, 1973).

Damiano, Kathryn, 'On Earth as it is in Heaven: Eighteenth Century Quakerism as Realised Eschatology', unpublished Ph.D. thesis, Union of Experimenting Colleges and Universities, 1988.

Dandelion, Ben Pink, 'Fresh Light, Dimmer Hopes', in Ben Pink Dandelion, Douglas Gwyn and Timothy Peat, *Heaven on Earth: Quakers and the Second Coming* (Kelso and Birmingham: Curlew & Woodbrooke, 1995), pp. 159–65.

Dandelion, Ben Pink, *A Sociological Analysis of the Theology of Quakers: The Silent Revolution* (Lampeter: Edwin Mellen, 1996).

Dandelion, Ben Pink, 'Blood or Water? Liberal Quakers and Evangelical Friends', *The Seeker*, Autumn 1998, pp. 19–21.

Dandelion, Ben Pink, 'The Absolute Perhaps: Towards an Understanding of Liberal Quaker Theology', in Janet Scott (ed.), *Papers from the International Quaker Consultation on Identity, Authority, Community* (forthcoming).

Daniell, Christopher, *Death and Burial in Medieval England, 1066–1550* (London: Routledge, 1997).

Daniell, Christopher and Victoria Thompson, 'Pagans and Christians: 400–1150', in Peter C. Jupp and Clare Gittings (eds), *Death in England: An Illustrated History* (Manchester: University Press, 1999), pp. 65–89.

David, Edward (ed.), *Inside Asquith's Cabinet, from the Diaries of Charles Hobhouse* (London: John Murray, 1977).

Davie, Grace, *Religion in Britain Since 1945: Believing without Belonging* (Oxford: Blackwell, 1994).

Davie, Grace, 'God and Caesar: Religion in a Rapidly Changing Europe', in Joe Bailey (ed.), *Social Europe* (London: Longman, 1998), pp. 231–53.

Davie, Martin, *British Quaker Theology Since 1895* (Lampeter: Edwin Mellen, 1997).

Davies, Christie, *Permissive Britain* (London: Pitman, 1975).

Davies, Christie, 'Religion, Politics and the "Permissive" Legislation', in Paul Badham (ed.), *Religion, State and Society in Modern Britain* (Lewiston: Edward Mellen, 1989), pp. 319–40.

Davies, Christie, 'The British State and the Power of Life and Death', in Richard Whiting and Simon Green (eds), *The Boundaries of the State in Modern Britain* (Cambridge: Cambridge University Press, 1996), pp. 341–74.

Davies, Christie, 'Moralism, Causalism and Rights: The Contrasting Arguments about Abortion, Capital Punishment and the Law that are Used in Britain and America', in Paul Badham (ed.), *Ethics at the Frontiers of Human Existence* (New York: Paragon) (in press).

Davies, Douglas J., *Cremation Today and Tomorrow* (Nottingham: Alcuin/Grow Liturgical Study 16, 1990).

Davies, Douglas J., 'The Sacred Crematorium', *Morality*, vol. 1, no. 1, 1996, pp. 83–94.

Davies, Douglas J., *Death, Ritual and Belief* (London: Cassell, 1997).

Day, David and Phillip May, *Teenage Beliefs* (Oxford: Lion Publishing, 1991).

Day, John Patrick, *Hope: A Philosophical Inquiry* (Helsinki: Acta Philosophica Fennica, vol. 51, 1991).

de Dios, Efrén de la Madre and Otgar Steggink, *Tiempo y vida de Santa Tesesa* (Madrid: Biblioteca De Autores Cristianos La Editorial), 1968.

de Tocqueville, Alexis, *Democracy in America*, trans. Richard Heffner (New York: Mentor Books, 1956).

de Unamuno, Miguel, *Tragic Sense of Life*, trans. J. E. Crawford Flitch (New York: Dover, 1954).

de Wendel, Catherine Wihtol, 'Muslims in France', in Wasif Shahid and Sjord van Konigsveld (eds), *Muslims in the Margin: Political Responses to the Presence of Islam in Western Europe* (Kampen: Kok Pharos, 1996), pp. 52–65.

Debates of the Lower House of the Convocation of Canterbury, 11 October 1944.

Denison, Keith, 'The Theology and Liturgy of Funerals: A View from the Church in Wales', *Mortality*, vol. 4, no. 1, 1999, pp. 63–74.

Desroche, Henri, *The Sociology of Hope*, trans. Carol Martin-Sperry (London: Routledge & Kegan Paul, 1979).

Dews, Peter (ed.), *Autonomy and Solidarity: Interviews with Jürgen Habermas*, revised edition (London: Verso, 1992).

Di Masi, Joe, 'Rising Research and Development Costs for New Drugs in a Cost Containment Environment', *Pharmaco-Economic*, 1 (Supp), 1992, pp. 13–20.

Diocese of Blackburn: Judgement in the Consistory Court, 16 July 1994.

Dostoevsky, Fyodor, *The Idiot*, trans. David Magarshack (Harmondsworth: Penguin 1955).

Dostoevsky, Fyodor, *Notes from Underground*, trans. Mirra Ginsburg (New York: Bantam, 1974).

Dowd, James J., 'Revising the Canon: Graduate Training in the Two Sociologies', *Teaching Sociology*, vol. 19, no. 3, July 1991, pp. 308–21.

Dryzeck, John, *Discursive Democracy* (Cambridge: Cambridge University Press, 1990).

Dryzeck, John, 'Critical Theory as a Research Programme', in Stephen White (ed.), *The Cambridge Companion to Habermas* (Cambridge: Cambridge University Press, 1995), pp. 97–119.

du Gay, Paul, 'Alasdair MacIntyre and the Christian Genealogy of Management of Critique', *Cultural Values*, vol. 2, no. 4, 1998, pp. 421–44.

Duffy, Eamon, *The Stripping of the Altars: Traditional Religion in England, 1400–1580* (New Haven and London: Yale University Press, 1992).

Dumont, Louis, *Homo Hierarchicus* (London: Weidenfeld & Nicolson, 1970).

Duncan, David, *The Life and Letters of Herbert Spencer* (London: Methuen, 1908).

Dunn, Robert G., *Identity Crises: A Social Critique of Postmodernity* (Minneapolis: University of Minnesota, 1998).

Durkheim, Emile, *Suicide*, trans. John Spaulding and George Simpson (London: Routledge & Kegan Paul, 1952).

Durkheim, Emile, *The Elementary Forms of the Religious Life* (London: Allen & Unwin, 1964).

Durkheim, Emile, 'Individualism and the Intellectuals', in Robert N. Bellah (ed.), *Emile Durkheim. On Morality and Society* (Chicago: University of Chicago Press, 1973), pp. 43–57.

Durkheim, Emile, 'Individualism and the Intellectuals', in W. S. F. Pickering (ed.), *Durkheim on Religion* (London: Routledge & Kegan Paul, 1975), pp. 59–73.

Edwards, David L., *After Death? Traditional Beliefs and Real Possibilities* (London: Cassell, 1999).

Ehrlich, Isaac, 'The Deterrent Effect of Capital Punishment, A Question of Life and Death', *American Economic Review*, vol. 68, June 1975, pp. 397–417.

Ellul, Jacques, *Hope in Time of Abandonment*, trans. Edward Hopkin (New York: Seabury Press, 1973).

Ester, Peter, Loek Halman and Brigitte Seuren, 'Environmental Concern and Offering Willingness in Europe and North America', in Peter Ester, Loek Halman and Ruud de Moor (eds), *The Individualizing Society: Value Change in Europe and North America* (Tilburg: Tilburg University Press, 1993), pp. 163–83.

Etzioni, Amitai, *The New Golden Rule. Community and Morality in a Democratic Society* (London: Profile Books, 1997).

Featherstone, Mike, Mike Hepworth and Bryan S. Turner, *The Body. Social Process and Cultural Theory* (London: Sage, 1991).

Feirabend, Jeroen and Jan Rath, 'Making a Place for Islam in Politics', in Wasif A. R. Shahid and Sjord van Konigsveld (eds), *Muslims on the Margin: Political Responses to the Presence of Islam in Western Europe* (Kampen: Kok Pharos, 1996), pp. 243–58.

Fenn, Richard K., *The Persistence of Purgatory* (Cambridge: Cambridge University Press, 1995).

Fenn, Richard K., *The End of Time: Religion, Ritual, and the Forging of the Soul* (London: SPCK, 1997).

Fenves, Peter D., *A Peculiar Fate: Metaphysics and World-History in Kant* (Ithaca: Cornell University Press, 1991).

Feuerbach, Ludwig, *The Essence of Christianity*, trans. George Eliot (Buffalo: Prometheus Books, 1989).

Firth, Shirley, *Dying, Death and Bereavement in a British Hindu Community* (Leuven: Peeters, 1997).

Fisher, Geoffrey, Archbishop of Canterbury, *Hansard, House of Lords*, vol. 201, col. 1194, 21 February 1957.

Flanagan, Kieran, 'J.-K. Huysmans: The First Post-Modernist Saint?', *New Blackfriars*, vol. 71, no. 838, May 1990, pp. 217–29.

Flanagan, Kieran, *Sociology and Liturgy: Re-presentations of the Holy* (Basingstoke: Macmillan, 1991).

Flanagan, Kieran, 'Postmodernity and Culture: Sociological Wagers of the Self in Theology', in Kieran Flanagan and Peter C. Jupp (eds), *Postmodernity, Sociology and Religion* (Basingstoke: Macmillan, 1996), pp. 152–73.

Flanagan, Kieran, *The Enchantment of Sociology. A Study of Theology and Culture* (Basingstoke: Macmillan, 1996).

Flanagan, Kieran, *Virtue Ethics and Vocation: A Sociology of Edification* (forthcoming).

Flannery, Austin (ed.), *Vatican Council II.: The Conciliar and post-Conciliar Documents* (Dublin: Dominican Publications, 1975).

Fontaine, J. S. La, *Speak of the Devil. Tales of Satanic Abuse in Contemporary England* (Cambridge: Cambridge University Press, 1998).

Foot, Phillipa, *Virtues and Vices, and Other Essays in Moral Philosophy* (Oxford: Blackwell, 1978).

Francis, Doris, Leonie Kellaher and Georgina Neophytou, 'Sustaining Cemeteries: The User Perspective', *Mortality*, vol. 5, no. 1, March 2000, pp. 34–52.

Francis, Leslie, 'Christianity Today: The Teenage Experience', in Jeff Astley and David Day (eds), *The Contours of Christian Education* (Great Wakering: McCrimmons, 1992), pp. 340–68.

Francis, Leslie J. and William K. Kay, *Teenage Religion and Values* (Leominster: Gracewing, 1995).

Frankfurt, Harry G., *The Importance of What We Care About* (Cambridge: Cambridge University Press, 1988).

Frankl, Viktor E., *From Death-Camp to Existentialism* (Boston: Beacon Press, 1959).

Franklin, H. Bruce, 'Visions of the Future in Science Fiction Films from 1970 to 1982', in Anette Kuhn (ed.), *Alien Zone: Cultural Theory and Contemporary Science Fiction Cinema* (London and New York: Verso, 1990), pp. 19–31.

Fukuyama, Francis, *The End of History and the Last Man* (London: Hamish Hamilton, 1992).

Fuller, Steve, *Science* (Buckingham: Open University Press, 1997).

Gandhi, Mahatma, *Varnavyavastha* (Ahmedabad: Navjivan Press, 1950).

Gandhi, Mohandas Karamchand, *The Removal of Untouchability* (Ahmedabad: Navajivan, 1954).

Gandhi, Mohandas Karamchand, *An Autobiography or the Story of My Experiments with Truth* (Ahmedabad: Navjivan, 1972).

Gauchet, Marcel, *The Disenchantment of the World: A Political History of Religion*, trans. Oscar Burge (Princeton: Princeton University Press, 1997).

Gehlen, Arnold, *Man in the Age of Technology* (New York: Columbia University Press, 1980).

General Synod November Group of Sessions 1998. Report of Proceedings, vol. 29, no. 3, pp. 940–67.

Gennep, Arnold van, *The Rites of Passage*, trans. Monika B Vizedom and Gabrielle L. Caffee (Chicago: University of Chicago Press, 1960).

Giddens, Anthony, *Modernity and Self-Identity: Self and Society in the Late Modern Age* (Cambridge: Polity Press, 1991).

Giddens, Anthony, *The Transformation of Intimacy. Sexuality, Love & Eroticism in Modern Societies* (Cambridge: Polity, 1992).

Giddens, Anthony and Christopher Pierson, *Conversations with Anthony Giddens. Making Sense of Modernity* (Cambridge: Polity Press, 1998).

Gilbert, William Schwenck, *The Bab Ballads* (London and New York: George Routledge, 1898).

Gill, Robin, *Churchgoing & Christian Ethics* (Cambridge: Cambridge University Press, 1999).

Gilligan, Carol, *In a Different Voice: Psychological Theory and Women's Development* (Cambridge, Mass.: Harvard University Press, 1982).

Gittings, Clare, *Death, Burial and the Individual in Early Modern England* (London: Croom Helm, 1984).

Godfrey, Joseph J., *A Philosophy of Human Hope* (Dordrecht: Martinus Nijhoff, 1987).

Good Funerals. a background paper prepared on behalf of the ecumenical Churches' Group on Funeral Services at Cemeteries and Crematoria in support of the Southwark Diocesan Synod Motion, 'Funerals: Business and Vocation' (London: General Synod of the Church of England, 1998), GS Misc. 539.

Gorer, Geoffrey, *Death, Grief and Mourning in Contemporary Britain* (London: Cresset, 1965).

Gouldner, Alvin, *The Coming Crisis of Western Sociology* (London: Heinemann, 1970).

Gowricharn, Rubin and Bim Mungra, 'The Politics of Integration in the Netherlands', in Wasif A. R. Shahid and Sjord Konigsveld (eds), *Muslims in the Margin: Political Responses to the Presence of Islam in Western Europe* (Kampen: Kok Pharos, 1996), pp. 114-29.

Grainger, Roger, *The Social Symbolism of Grief and Mourning* (London: Jessica Kingsley, 1998).

Gray, John, *Enlightenment's Wake: Politics and Culture at the Close of the Modern Age* (London: Routledge, 1995).

Gregory, Aidan, *The Silence of Memory. Armistice Day 1991–1946* (Oxford: Berg, 1994).

Grubb, Sarah, *Some Account of the Life and Labours of Sarah Grubb* (London: James Phillips, 1794).

Guyau, Jean-Marie, *A Esquisse d'une morale sans obligation ni sanction* (Paris: Alcan, 1885).

Gwyn, Douglas, *The Apocalypse of the Word: The Life and Message of George Fox* (Richmond, IN: Friends United Press, 1987).

Gwyn, Douglas, *The Covenant Crucified: Quakers and the Rise of Capitalism* (Wallingford, PA: Pendle Hill, 1995).

Gwyn, Douglas, 'Early Quakers: When Seekers Become Finders', paper presented at Manchester College, Oxford, 12th May 1997.

Habermas, Jürgen, *The Structural Transformation of the Bourgeois Public Sphere* (Cambridge: Polity, 1989).

Habermas, Jürgen, 'Struggles for Recognition in the Democratic Constitutional State', in Charles Taylor with Amy Gutmann, (ed.), *Multiculturalism: Examining the Politics of Recognition* (Princeton: Princeton University Press, 1994), pp. 107–48.

Halbfass, Wilhelm, *India and Europe: An Essay in Understanding* (Albany: State University of New York Press, 1988).

Hall, Robert T., 'Communitarian Ethics and the Sociology of Morals: Alasdair MacIntyre and Emile Durkheim', *Sociological Focus*, vol. 24, 1991, pp. 93–105.

Halman, Loek and Ruud de Moor, 'Religion, Churches and Moral Values', in Peter Ester, Loek Halman and Ruud de Moor (eds), *The Individualizing Society: Value Change in Europe and North America* (Tilburg: Tilburg University Press, 1993), pp. 37–66.

Hamm, Thomas D., *The Transformation of American Quakerism: Orthodox Friends, 1800–1907* (Bloomington, IN: Indiana University Press, 1988).

Hamnett, Ian, 'Sociology of Religion and Sociology of Error', *Religion*, vol. 3, 1973, pp. 1–12.

Harding, Stephen and David Phillips with David Fogarty, *Contrasting Values in Western Europe: Unity, Diversity and Change* (Basingstoke: Macmillan, 1986).

Hartley, Keith and Alan Maynard, *The Costs and Benefits of Regulating New Product Development in the UK Pharmaceutical Industry* (London: Office of Health Economics, 1982).

Heelas, Paul, 'On Things Not Being Worse, and the Ethic of Humanity', in Paul Heelas, Scott Lasch and Paul Morris (eds), *Detraditionalization* (Oxford: Blackwell, 1996), pp. 200–19.

Heelas, Paul, *The New Age Movement. The Celebration of the Self and the Sacralization of Modernity* (Oxford: Blackwell, 1996).

Hennis, Wilhelm, *Max Weber. Essay in Reconstruction*, trans. Keith Tribe (London: Allen & Unwin, 1988).

Heron, Alastair, *Caring, Conviction, Commitment: Dilemmas of Quaker Membership Today* (London: Quaker Home Service, 1992).

Hockey, Jenny, 'The Acceptable Face of Human Grieving? The Clergy's Role in Managing Expression during Funeral Rites', in David Clark, (ed.), *The Sociology of Death. Theory, Culture, Practice* (Oxford: Blackwell, 1993), pp. 129–48.

Hollis, Christopher, *The Homicide Act* (London: Gollancz 1964).

Hollis, Martin, *The Cunning of Reason* (Cambridge: Cambridge University Press, 1987).

Holton, Robert J. and Bryan Turner, *Talcott Parsons on Economy and Society* (London: Routledge, 1986).

Hornsby-Smith, Michael P., *Roman Catholic Beliefs in England: Customary Catholicism and the Transformation of Religious Authority* (Cambridge: Cambridge University Press, 1991).

Howarth, Glennys, 'Professionalising the Funeral Industry in England 1700–1960', in Peter C. Jupp and Glennys Howarth (eds), *The Changing Face of Death. Historical Accounts of Death and Disposal* (Basingstoke: Macmillan, 1997), pp. 118–33.

Hoyt, Edwin P., *The Kamikazes* (London: Panther, 1985).

Hudson, Wayne, *The Marxist Philosophy of Ernst Bloch* (London: Macmillan, 1982).

Hunt, Lester H., *Character and Culture* (Oxford: Rowman & Littlefield, 1997).

Huysmans, J. K., *Against Nature*, trans. Robert Baldick (Harmondsworth: Penguin, 1959).

Huysmans, J. K., *La Bas* (London: Dedalus, 1986).

Huysmans, J. K., *En Route*, trans. W. Fleming (London: Dedalus, 1989).

Inglehart, Ronald, *Culture Shift in Advanced Industrial Society* (Princeton: Princeton University Press, 1990).

Inman, Bill, '30 Years in Post-Marketing Surveillance: A Personal Perspective by Professor Bill Inman', *PEM News*, no. 8, November 1993, pp. 26–8.

Isambert, François-André, 'La sécularisation interne du christianisme', *Revue Français de Sociologie*, vol. 17, no. 4, 1976, pp. 573–89.

Isichei, Elizabeth, *Victorian Quakers* (Oxford: Oxford University Press, 1970).

Jamieson, Lynn, 'Intimacy transformed? A Critical Look at the "Pure Relationship"', *Sociology*, vol. 33, no. 3, August 1999, pp. 477–94.

Jaspers, Karl, *Leonardo, Descartes, Max Weber. Three Essays*, trans. Ralph Mannheim (London: Routledge & Kegan Paul, 1965).

Jervis, John, *Exploring the Modern. Patterns of Western Culture and Civilization* (Oxford: Blackwell, 1998).

Johnson, Daniel, 'Why We Should Have Killed Hitler', *The Times*, 24 July 1998, p. 20.

Jupp, Peter C., *From Dust to Ashes: The Replacement of Burial by Cremation in England 1840–1967* (London: Congregational Memorial Hall Trust (1978) Ltd, 1990).

Jupp, Peter C., 'The Development of Cremation in England: A Sociological Analysis', unpublished Ph.D. thesis, University of London, 1993.

Jupp, Peter C., 'The Context of Funeral Ministry Today', in Peter C. Jupp and Tony Rogers (eds), *Interpreting Death: Christian Theology and Pastoral Practice* (London: Cassell, 1997), pp. 3–16.

Jupp, Peter C., 'History of the Cremation Movement in Great Britain: The First 125 years', *Pharos International*, vol. 65, no. 1, Spring 1999, pp. 18–25.

Kant, Immanuel, *Critique of Practical Reason*, trans. Thomas Kingsmill Abbott (London: Longmans, 1909).

Kant, Immanuel, *Political Writings*, second edition, ed. Hans Reiss (Cambridge: Cambridge University Press, 1991).

Kant, Immanuel, *Groundwork of the Metaphysics of Morals*, ed. Mary Gregor (Cambridge: Cambridge University Press, 1998).

Kennedy, Thomas, 'Why Did Friends Resist?: The War, Peace Testimony, and the All-Friends Conference of 1920', *Peace and Change*, vol. 14, 1989, pp. 355–71.

Kierkegaard, Soren, 'The Present Age', in Robert Bretall (ed.), *A Kierkegaard Anthology*, trans. Alexander Dru (Princeton: Princeton University Press, 1946), pp. 258–69.

Kilmuir, Viscount, *Hansard, House of Lords*, vol. 201, col. 1168–9, 21 February 1957.

Kopp, Sheldon, *If You Meet the Buddha on the Road, Kill Him* (London: Sheldon Press, 1974).

Kreeft, Peter, *Back to Virtue. Traditional Moral Wisdom for the Modern Moral Confusion* (San Francisco: Ignatius Press, 1992).

Kreuziger, Frederick A., *Apocalypse and Science Fiction: A Dialectic of Religious and Secular Soteriologies* (Chica, CA.: Scholars Press, 1982).

Kruschwitz, Robert B. and Robert C. Roberts (eds), *The Virtues. Contemporary Essays on Moral Character* (Belmont, California: Wadsworth, 1987).

Kuhn, Anette (ed.), *Alien Zone: Cultural Theory and Contemporary Science Fiction Cinema* (London and New York: Verso, 1990).

Kymlicka, Will, *Liberalism, Community and Culture* (Oxford: Oxford University Press, 1989).

Kymlicka, Will, *Multicultural Citizenship* (Oxford: Oxford University Press, 1995).

La Rochefoucauld, François, *Maxims*, trans. Leonard Tancock (Harmondsworth: Penguin, 1959).

Lampard, John, 'Theology in Ashes – The Failure of the Churches to Think Theologically about Cremation', in *Bereavement and Belief* (London: The Churches' Group on Funeral Services at Cemeteries and Crematoria, 1993), pp. 28–36.

Larmore, Charles, *The Morals of Modernity* (Cambridge: Cambridge University Press, 1996).

Lasch, Christopher, *The True and Only Heaven: Progress and its Critics* (New York: Norton, 1991).

Lawrence, C. E., 'The Abolition of Death', *Fortnightly Review*, vol. CI, N.S., 1917, pp. 326–31.

Le Goff, Jacques, *The Birth of Purgatory*, trans. Arthur Goldhammer (London: Scholar, 1984).

Leach, Edmund R., *Dialectic in Practical Religion* (Cambridge: Cambridge University Press, 1977).

Leach, Edmund R., *Social Anthropology* (London: Fontana, 1982).

Lesiter, Malcolm, 'Clergy Rota', *Pharos International*, vol. 64, no. 4, Winter 1998, pp. 26–7.

Leveau, Rémy, 'Islam in France: New Perspectives', in Wasif A. R. Shahid and Sjord van Konigsveld (eds), *The Integration of Islam and Hinduism in Western Europe* (Kampen: Kok Pharos, 1991), pp. 122–33.

Levine, Donald N., 'Sociology after MacIntyre', *American Journal of Sociology*, vol. 89, no. 3, 1983, pp. 700–7.

Lewis, C.S., *The Screwtape Letters*, revised paperback edition (New York: Collier, 1982).

Lifton, Robert, 'The Image of the End of the World: A Psychological View', in Valerie Andrews, Robert Bosnak and Karen Walter Goodwin (eds), *Facing the Apocalypse* (Pallas: Spring Publication, 1987), pp. 41–57.

Lipner, Julius, *Hindus: Their Religious Beliefs and Practices* (London: Routledge, 1994).

Litten, Julian, *The English Way of Death: The Common Funeral Since 1450* (London: Hale, 1991).

Lonzi, Carla, *Sputiamo su Hegel (Spit on Hegel)* (Milan: Scritti di Rivolta Femminile, 1974).

Luckmann, Thomas, *The Invisible Religion* (London: Collier-Macmillan, 1967).

Luckmann, Thomas, 'Shrinking Transcendence, Expanding Religion?', *Sociological Analysis*, vol. 50, no. 2, 1990, pp. 127–38.

Luhmann, Niklas, 'The Sociology of the Moral and Ethics', *International Sociology*, vol. 11, no. 1, March 1996, pp. 27–36.

Luker, Kristin, *Abortion and the Politics of Motherhood* (Berkeley: University of California Press, 1984).

Lukes, Steven, 'Alasdair MacIntyre: The Sociologist versus the Philosopher', in Steven Lukes, *Moral Conflicts and Politics* (Oxford: Clarendon Press, 1991), pp. 248–56.

Luntley, Michael, *Reason, Truth and Self* (London: Routledge, 1995).

Lyman, Stanford, M., *The Seven Deadly Sins*, revised and expanded edition (New York: General Hall, 1989).

MacIntyre, Alasdair, 'Notes from the Moral Wilderness', *New Reasoner*, no. 7, Winter 1958–59, pp. 90–100.

MacIntyre, Alasdair, *Secularisation and Moral Change* (Oxford: Oxford University Press, 1967).

MacIntyre, Alasdair, *After Virtue* (London: Duckworth, 1981).

MacIntyre, Alasdair, *After Virtue*, second edition (London: Duckworth, 1985).

MacIntyre, Alasdair, 'Rationalities as Forms of Social Structure', *Irish Philosophical Journal*, vol. 4, 1987, pp. 3–19.

MacIntyre, Alasdair, *Whose Justice? Which Rationality?* (London: Duckworth, 1988).

MacIntyre, Alasdair, *Three Rival Versions of Moral Enquiry* (London: Duckworth, 1990).

MacIntyre, Alasdair, *How to Seem Virtuous Without Actually Being So* (Lancaster: Centre for the Study of Cultural Values, 1991).

MacIntyre, Alasdair, 'A Partial Response to My Critics', in John Horton and Susan Mendus (eds), *After MacIntyre* (Cambridge: Polity, 1994), pp. 283–304.

MacLaine, Shirley, *It's All in the Playing* (London: Bantam, 1988).

Maclean, Fitzroy, *Eastern Approaches* (Harmondsworth: Penguin, 1991).

McMylor, Peter, *Alasdair MacIntyre. Critic of Modernity* (London: Routledge, 1994).

Maffesoli, Michel, *The Time of the Tribes: The Decline of Individualism in Mass Society* (London: Sage, 1996).

Mahony, William K., 'Dharma', in Mircea Eliade (ed.), *The Encyclopedia of Religion*, vol. 4 (New York: Macmillan, 1987), pp. 329–32.

Mandelstam, Nadezhda, *Hope against Hope*, trans. Max Hayward (London: Collins & Harvill, 1971).

Marcel, Gabriel, *Homo Viator*, trans. Emma Craufurd (London: Victor Gollanz, 1951).

Marcel, Gabriel, 'The Structure of Hope', *Communio: International Catholic Review*, vol. 23, no. 3, 1996, pp. 604–11.

Marshalls, Jane, 'French Row Over Race Poll', *Times Higher Education Supplement*, 27 Nov. 1998, p. 56.

Martin, Bernice and Ronald Pluck, *Young People's Beliefs* (London: General Synod Board of Education, 1977).

Martin, David, *A General Theory of Secularization* (Oxford: Blackwell, 1978).

Matthews, W.R., *The Hope of Immortality* (London: SCM Press, 1936).

Mauss, Marcel, *La Prière* in *Œuvres* (Paris: Editions de Minuit, 1968).

Maynard, Alan and Keith Hartley, 'The Regulation of the Pharmaceutical Industry', *Symposium on Pharmaceutical Economics* (Berlin: Liber Forlag, 1984), pp. 123–37.

Metz, Johann-Baptist, 'Future in the Memory of Suffering', in Fiorenza Francis Schüssler (ed.), *Faith and the Future: Essays on Theology, Solidarity and Modernity* (Nijmegen, Netherlands: Consilium Foundation, 1995), pp. 3–16.

Metz, Johann-Baptist, 'Messianic or Bourgeois Religion', in Fiorenza Francis Schüssler (ed.), *Faith and the Future: Essays on Theology, Solidarity and Modernity* (Nijmegen, Netherlands: Consilium Foundation, 1995), pp. 18–29.

Metz, Johann-Baptist, 'Theology in the Struggle for History and Society', in Fiorenza Francis Schüssler (ed), *Faith and the Future: Essays on Theology, Solidarity and Modernity* (Nijmegen, Netherlands: Consilium Foundation, 1995), pp. 49–56.

Milbank, John, *Theology and Social Theory. Beyond Secular Reason* (Oxford: Blackwell, 1990).

Modood, Tariq, *et al.*, *Ethnic Minorities in Britain: Diversity and Disadvantage* (London: Policy Studies Institute, 1997).

Moltmann, Jürgen, *Theology of Hope*, trans. James Leitch (London: SCM Press, 1967).

Moltmann, Jürgen, *The Coming of God: Christian Eschatology*, trans. Margaret Kohl (London: SCM Press, 1996).

Moore, Rosemary, 'The Faith of the First Quakers: The Development of Their Beliefs and Practices Before the Restoration', unpublished Ph.D. thesis, University of Birmingham, 1993.

Morris, Lord, of Borth-y-Gest, *Hansard, House of Lords*, vol. 268, cols. 535–8, 19 July 1965.

Morrison, Blake, *As If* (London: Granta, 1997).

Musil, Robert, *The Man Without Qualities*, vol. 1, trans. Eithne Wilkins and Ernst Kaiser (London: Martin Secker & Warburg, 1954).

Muyskens, James L., *The Sufficiency of Hope* (Philadelphia: Temple University Press, 1979).

Nagel, Thomas, *The Possibility of Altruism* (Oxford: Oxford University Press, 1970).

Nash, Roderick Frazier, *The Rights of Nature* (London: University of Wisconsin Press, 1989).

Neal, Mark, *Keeping Cures from Patients: The Perverse Effects of Pharmaceutical Regulations* (London: SAU, 1995).

Neuberger, Julia, *Dying Well: A Guide to Enabling a Good Death* (Hale, Cheshire: Hochland & Hochland, 1999).

Newman, John Henry, *The Dream of Gerontius and Other Poems* (London: Oxford University Press, 1914).

Nickalls, John (ed.), *The Journal of George Fox* (Cambridge: Cambridge University Press, 1952).

Nielsen, Jørgen, *Muslims in Western Europe* (Edinburgh: Edinburgh University Press, 1992).

Nietzsche, Freidrich, *The Gay Science*, trans. Walter Kaufman (New York: Vintage Books, 1974).

Norris, Kathleen, *The Cloister Walk* (Oxford: Lion, 1999).

Nowotny, Joan, 'Despair and the Object of Hope', in Ross Fitzgerald (ed.), *The Sources of Hope* (Oxford: Pergamon Press, 1979), pp. 44–66.

O'Donoghue, Noel D., *Mystics for our Time* (Edinburgh: T. & T. Clark 1989).

O'Flaherty, Wendy Doniger and J. Duncan M. Derrett (eds), *The Concept of Duty in South Asia* (Delhi: Vikas Publishing House Pvt Limited; and London: School of Oriental and African Studies, 1978).

O'Hear, Anthony, 'Diana, Queen of Hearts, Sentimentality Personified', in Digby Anderson and Peter Mullen (eds), *Faking It: The Sentimentalisation of Modern Society* (London: SAU, 1998), pp 181–90.

O'Neill, John, *Modes of Individualism and Collectivism* (London: Heinemann, 1973).

Pareto, Vilfredo, *Sociological Writings* (London: Pall Mall, 1966).

Parker, Lord, of Waddington, *Hansard, House of Lords*, vol. 269, col. 541, 26 October 1965.

Parsons, Brian, 'Change and Development of the British Funeral Industry in the 20th Century with Special Reference to the Period 1960–1994', unpublished Ph.D. thesis, University of Westminster, 1997.

Paul, Ellen Frankel, Fred D. Miller, Jr. and Jeffrey Paul (eds), *Virtue and Vice* (Cambridge: Cambridge University Press, 1998).

Peat, Timothy, 'Adulthood: Incarnation and the Kingdom of God', in Ben Pink Dandelion, Douglas Gwyn and Timothy Peat, *Heaven on Earth: Quakers and the Second Coming* (Kelso and Birmingham: Curlew and Woodbrooke, 1995), pp. 53–66.

Peat Timothy, 'Adolescence and the Church', in Ben Pink Dandelion, Douglas Gwyn and Timothy Peat, *Heaven on Earth: Quakers and the Second Coming* (Kelso and Birmingham: Curlew and Woodbrooke, 1995), pp. 67–87.

Peers, E. Allison, *Handbook to the Life and Times of St Teresa and St John of the Cross* (London: Sheed & Ward, 1954).

Peers, E. Allison (ed.), *The Complete Works of Saint Teresa of Jesus*, vol. 1 (London: Sheed & Ward, 1982?)

Pence, Gregory E., 'Recent Work on Virtues', *American Philosophical Quarterly*, vol. 21, no. 4, October 1984, pp. 281–97.

Penley, Constance, 'Time Travel, Primal Scene and the Critical Dystopia', in Anette Kuhn (ed.), *Alien Zone: Cultural Theory and Contemporary Science Fiction Cinema* (London and New York: Verso, 1990), pp. 116–27.

Perrin, R. D. and Armand L. Mauss, 'Saints and Seekers: Sources of Recruitment to the Vineyard Christian Fellowship', *Review of Religious Research*, vol. 33, no. 2, 1991, pp. 97–111.

Phillips, Brian D., 'Friendly Patriotism: British Quakerism and the Imperial Nation, 1890–1910', unpublished Ph.D, University of Cambridge, 1989.

Philonenko, Alexis, *L'Œuvre de Kant*, vol. 2 (Paris: Vrin, 1993).

Pickering, William S. F., 'The Persistence of Rites of Passage: Towards an Explanation', *The British Journal of Sociology*, vol. 25, no. 1, March 1974, pp. 63–78.

Plüss, Caroline B., 'A Sociological Analysis of the Modern Quaker Movement', unpublished D.Phil. thesis, University of Oxford, 1996.

Poole, Ross, *Morality and Modernity* (London: Routledge, 1991).

Popper, Karl, *Conjecture and Refutation* (London: Routledge, 1963).

Porpora, Douglas V., *Landscapes of the Soul* (forthcoming).

Portis, Edward Bryan, *Max Weber and Political Commitment. Science, Politics and Personality* (Philadelphia: Temple University Press, 1986).

Potter, Ralph B. Jr., 'The Abortion Debate', in Ralph B. Potter, Jr. (ed.), *The Religious Situation* (Boston: Beacon, 1969), pp. 120–136.

Prior, Lindsay, 'Actuarial Visions of Death: Life, Death and Chance in the Modern World', in Peter C. Jupp and Glennys Howarth (eds), *The Changing Face of Death, Historical Accounts of Death and Disposal* (Basingstoke: Macmillan, 1997), pp. 177–93.

Procter-Smith, Majorie, '"In the Line of the Female"; Shakerism and Feminism', in Catherine Wessinger (ed.), *Women's Leadership in Marginal Religions* (Urbana: University of Illinois Press, 1993), pp. 23–40.

Putkowski, Julian and Julian Sykes, *Shot at Dawn* (London: Leo Cooper, 1992).

Quaker Faith and Practice: The Book of Christian Discipline of the Yearly Meeting of the Religious Society of Friends (Quakers) in Britain (London: Britain Yearly Meeting, 1995).

Radhakrishnan, Sarvepalli, *The Principal Upanishads* (London: Unwin & Hyman, 1953).

Radhakrishnan, Sarvepalli, *The Bhagavada Gita* (New Delhi: HarperCollins, 1993).

Ravitch, Norman, *The Catholic Church and the French Nation* (London: Routledge, 1990).

Reay, Barry, *Quakers and the English Revolution* (London: Temple Smith, 1985).

Reddish, Mitchell G. (ed.), *Apocalyptic Literature: A Reader* (Nashville: Abingdon Press, 1990).

Renaut, Alain, *The Era of the Individual: A Contribution to a History of Subjectivity*, trans. M. B. DeBevoise and Franklin Phillip (Princeton: Princeton University Press, 1997).

Report of the Interdepartmental Committee on Proposed Disciplinary Amendments of the Army and Air Force Acts, Cmnd 2376 (London: HMSO, 1925).

Report of the Royal Commission on Capital Punishment 1949–53, Cmnd 8932 (London: HMSO, 1953).

Report of the Committee of Inquiry into Human Fertilisation and Embryology, Cmnd 9314 (London: HMSO, 1984).

Richter, Phillip and Leslie J. Francis, *Gone But Not Forgotten: Church Leaving and Returning* (London: Darton, Longman & Todd, 1998).

Riddell, Carol, *The Findhorn Community* (Forres: Findhorn Press, 1991).

Robertson, Roland, 'After Nostalgia? Willful Nostalgia and the Phases of Globalisation', in Bryan Turner (ed.), *Theories of Modernity and Postmodernity* (London: Sage, 1990), pp. 45–61.

Roof, Wade Clark, *A Generation of Seekers: The Spiritual Journeys of the Baby Boom Generation* (San Francisco: HarperCollins, 1993).

Roof, Wade Clark, Jackson W. Carroll and David A. Roozen, *The Post-War Generation Establishment Religions: Cross-Cultural Perspectives* (Boulder: Westview Press, 1995).

Rorty, Richard, *Contingency, Irony and Solidarity* (Cambridge: Cambridge University Press, 1989).

Rose, Gillian, *The Broken Middle: Out of Our Ancient Society* (Oxford: Blackwell, 1992).

Rose, Gillian, *Judaism and Modernity: Philosophical Essays* (Oxford: Blackwell, 1993).

Rose, Gillian, *Mourning Becomes the Law: Philosophy and Representation* (Cambridge: Cambridge University, 1996).

Rose, Gillian, 'The Final Notebooks of Gillian Rose', *Women: A Cultural Review*, vol. 9, no. 1, Spring 1998, pp. 6–18.

Rosen, Stanley, *Hermeneutics as Politics* (Oxford: Oxford University Press, 1987).

Rowell, Geoffrey, *Hell and the Victorians. A Study of the Nineteenth Century Theological Controversies concerning Eternal Punishment and the Future Life* (Oxford: Clarendon, 1974).

Rowell, Geoffrey, *The Liturgy of Christian Burial* (London: Alcuin Club/SPCK, 1977).

Rowland, Christopher, *The Open Heaven: A Study of Apocalyptic in Judaism and Early Christianity* (London: SPCK, 1982)

Rugg, Julie, 'The Rise of Cemetery Companies in Britain, 1820–53', unpublished Ph.D. thesis, University of Stirling, 1992.

Rummel, Rudolf J., *Death By Government* (New Brunswick, Transaction 1990).

Rummel, Rudolf J., *Lethal Politics, Soviet Genocide and Mass Murder since 1917* (New Brunswick: Transaction 1990).

Rumney, Jay, *Herbert Spencer's Sociology* (New York: Atherton, 1966).

Ruppersberg, Hugh, 'The Alien Messiah', in Anette Kuhn (ed.), *Alien Zone: Cultural Theory and Contemporary Science Fiction Cinema* (London and New York: Verso, 1990), pp. 32–8.

Sanders, E.P., *Paul* (Oxford: Oxford University Press, 1991).

Sardar, Ziauddin, *Postmodernism and the Other. The New Imperialism of Western Culture* (London: Pluto, 1998).

Sartre, Jean-Paul, *Existentialism and Humanism*, trans. Phillip Mairet (London: Methuen, 1948).

Sarup, Madan, *Identity, Culture and the Postmodern World* (Edinburgh: Edinburgh University Press, 1996).

Saunders, Nicholas, *Ecstasy Reconsidered* (Exeter: BPC Wheatons, 1997).

Schweitzer, Albert, *The Quest for the Historical Jesus* (New York: Macmillan, 1968).

Scott, Janet, *What Canst Thou Say? Towards a Quaker Theology* (London: Quaker Home Service, 1980).

Shalit, Wendy, *A Return to Modesty. Discovering the Lost Virtue* (New York: The Free Press, 1999).

Sheppy, Paul J., 'The Dance of Death – a Liturgist Considers Cremation', *Pharos International*, vol. 64, no. 2, Summer 1998, pp. 4–8.

Simmel, Georg, *Essays on Religion*, trans. Horst Jürgen Helle (New Haven: Yale University Press, 1997).

Sjostrom, Henning and Robert Nilsson, *Thalidomide and the Power of the Drug Companies* (Harmondsworth: Penguin, 1972).

Skolnick, Jerome H., 'The Social Transformation of Vice', *Law and Contemporary Social Problems*, vol. 51, no. 1, 1988.

Smart, Barry, *Facing Modernity: Ambivalence, Reflexivity and Morality* (London: Sage, 1999).

Smith, A. C. and Brian Hogan, *Criminal Law*, 4th edition (London: Butterworths, 1978).

Smith, A. T. H., 'Warnock and After: The Legal and Moral Issues Surrounding Embryo Research', in Mark Ocketton (ed.), *Medicine, Ethics and the Law*, ARSP Beiheft 32, 1986, pp. 744–75.

Soskice, Janet M., *Metaphor and Religious Language* (Oxford: Oxford University Press, 1985).

Soysai, Yasmin, *Post-National Citizenship* (New Haven: Yale University Press, 1994).

Spears, Edward, *Assignment to Catastrophe*, vol II, *The Fall of France, June 1940* (London: Heinemann, 1954).

Spohn, William C., 'The Return of Virtue Ethics', *Theological Studies*, vol. 53, 1992, pp. 60–75.

Squires, Judith (ed.), *Principled Positions* (London: Lawrence & Wishart, 1993).

Srinivas, Mysore Narsimhachar, *Social Change in Modern India* (Berkeley: University of California Press, 1968).

Srinivas, Mysore Narsimhachar, *The Cohesive Role of Sanskritisation and Other Essays* (Delhi: Oxford University Press, 1989).

Stafford, J. Francis, 'The Religious Sense', *Communio*, vol. 25, no. 4, Winter 1998, pp. 663–78.

Stannard, David E., *The Puritan Way of Death: A Study in Religion, Culture and Social Change* (New York: Oxford University Press, 1977).

Statman, Daniel (ed.), *Virtue Ethics. A Critical Reader* (Edinburgh: Edinburgh University Press, 1997).

Stauth, George and Bryan Turner, *Nietzsche's Dance: Resentment, Reciprocity and Resistance in Social Life* (Oxford: Blackwell, 1988).

Stone, Brad Lowell, 'The Newest Weber', *Sociological Forum*, vol. 5, no. 4, 1990, pp. 669–676.

'Tabular Statement of the Yearly Meeting of Friends (Quakers) in Britain for the year ending 1997' (London: Britain Yearly Meeting, 1998).

Taylor, Charles, *Human Agency and Language, Philosophical Papers 1* (Cambridge: Cambridge University Press, 1985).

Taylor, Charles, *Sources of the Self: The Making of Modern Identity* (Cambridge, Mass.: Harvard University Press, 1989).

Taylor, Charles, *The Ethics of Authenticity* (Cambridge, Mass.: Harvard University Press, 1991).

Taylor, Charles with Amy Gutmann (ed.), *Multiculturalism: Examining the Politics of Recognition* (Princeton: Princeton University Press, 1994, expanded edition).

Tester, Keith, *Civil Society* (London: Routledge, 1992).

Tester, Keith, *The Life and Times of Post-Modernity* (London: Routledge, 1993).

Tester, Keith, *Moral Culture* (London: Sage, 1997).

Tester, Keith, 'Weber's Alleged Emotivism', *The British Journal of Sociology*, vol. 50, no. 4, December 1999, pp. 563–73.

The National Funerals College, *The Dead Citizens Charter*, revised edition (Bristol: The National Funerals College, 1998).

The Observer, 13th July 1969.

The Oxford Dictionary of Quotations, second edition (London: Oxford University Press, 1955).

The Times, 6 July 1874.

The Undertakers' Journal, 15 October 1911.

Thomas, Keith, *Religion and the Decline of Magic* (Harmondsworth: Penguin, 1973).

Thompson, Damian, *The End of Time: Faith and Fear in the Shadow of the Millennium* (London: Sinclair-Stevenson, 1996).

Tillich, Paul, *The Courage To Be* (London: The Fontana Library, 1962).

Tinker, C. B. and H. F. Lowry (eds), *Arnold. Poetical Works* (London: Oxford University Press, 1950).

Titmuss, Richard M., *The Gift Relationship. From Human Blood to Social Policy* (London: George Allen & Unwin, 1970).

Tracey, David, *The Analogical Imagination: Christian Theology and the Culture of Pluralism* (New York: Crossroad, 1981).

Trasler, Graham, '"Mind the Gap": Funerals at the Crematorium', unpublished, 1998.

Trianosky, Gregory, 'What is Virtue Ethics All About ?', *American Philosophical Quarterly*, vol. 27, no. 4, October 1990, pp. 335–44.

Trigg, Roger, *Rationality and Religion* (Oxford: Blackwell, 1998).

Turner, Bryan, 'A Note on Nostalgia', *Theory, Culture and Society*, vol. 4, no. 1, 1987, pp. 147–56.

Turner, Stephen, 'Whose Tradition About Tradition?', *Theory, Culture and Society*, vol. 7, no. 4, 1990, pp. 175–85.

Tuttle, Elizabeth Orman, *The Crusade Against Capital Punishment in Britain* (London: Stevens, 1961).

United Kingdom Action Committee on Islamic Affairs (UKACIA), *Need for Reform: Muslims and the Law in Multi-Faith Britain* (London: UKACIA, 1993).

Vann, Richard, *The Social Development of English Quakerism* (Cambridge, Mass.: Harvard University Press, 1969).

Walter, Tony, 'The Mourning after Hillsborough', *Sociological Review*, vol. 39, no. 3, 1991, pp. 599–625.

Walter, Tony, 'A New Model of Grief: Bereavement and Biography', *Mortality*, vol. 1, no. 1, 1996, pp. 7–25.

Walter, Tony, *The Eclipse of Eternity: A Sociology of the Afterlife* (Basingstoke: Macmillan, 1996).

Walter, Tony, 'A Sociology of Grief', *Mortality*, vol. 3, no. 1, 1998, pp. 83–7.

Walter, Tony (ed.), *The Mourning for Diana* (Oxford: Berg, 1999).

Watts, Miller, W., *Durkheim, Morals and Modernity* (London: UCL, 1996).

Watts, Miller, W., 'Liberté de la volonté et science sociale', in Charles-Henry Cuin (ed.), *Durkheim d'un siècle à l'autre. Lectures actuelles des 'Règles de la méthode sociologique'* (Paris: Presses Universitaires de France, 1997), pp. 223–35.

Watts, Miller, W., 'Durkheim, Kant, the Immortal Soul and God', in N. J. Allen, W. S. F. Pickering and W. Watts Miller (eds), *On Durkheim's Elementary Forms of Religious Life* (London: Routledge, 1998), pp. 66–77.

Watts, Miller, W., 'Teaching Autonomy', in Geoffrey Walford and W. S. F. Pickering (eds), *Durkheim and Modern Education* (London: Routledge, 1998), pp. 72–91.

Watts, Miller, W., *Hope* (forthcoming).

Weber, Marianne, *Max Weber: A Biography*, trans. Harry Zohn (New York: John Wiley, 1975).

Weber, Max, *The Protestant Ethic and the Spirit of Capitalism*, trans. Talcott Parsons (London: George Allen & Unwin, 1930).

Weber, Max, *From Max Weber. Essays in Sociology*, trans. and ed. Hans H. Gerth and C. Wright Mills (London: Routledge & Kegan Paul, 1948).

Weber, Max, *The Methodology of the Social Sciences*, trans and ed. Edward A. Shils and Henry A. Finch (New York: The Free Press, 1949).

Weber, Max, *The Religion of India: The Sociology of Hinduism and Buddhism*, trans. and ed. Hans H. Gerth and Don Martindale (New York: Free Press, 1958).

Weber, Max, *The Sociology of Religion*, trans. Ephraim Fischoff (Boston: Beacon Press, 1964).

White, Stephen, *The Recent Work of Jürgen Habermas* (Cambridge: Cambridge University Press, 1989).

White, Winfred M. ,'Keeping Christmas', *The Friend*, vol. 154, no. 51, 1996, p. 24.

Wiggins, David, 'The Person as Object of Science, as Subject of Experience and as Locus of Value', in Arthur Peacocke and Grant Gillett (eds), *Person and Personality* (Oxford: Blackwell, 1987), pp. 54–74.

Wilkinson, Alan, *The Church of England and the First World War* (London: SPCK, 1997).

Williams, Bernard, *Moral Luck* (Cambridge University Press, 1981).

Williams, Clifford, 'Teaching Virtues and Vices', *Philosophy Today*, vol. 33, Fall 1989, pp. 195–203.

Williams, Howard, David Sullivan and Gwynn Matthews, *Francis Fukuyama and the End of History* (Cardiff: University of Wales Press, 1997).

Williams, Raymond, *Politics and Letters* (London: New Left Books, 1979).

Williams, Rowan, *Teresa of Avila* (London: Geoffrey Chapman, 1991).

Wilson, Bryan R., *Religious Sects* (London: Weidenfeld & Nicolson, 1970).

Wilson, Bryan R., *Magic and the Millennium: A Sociological Study of Religious Movements of Protest Among Tribal and Third World Peoples* (London: Heinemann, 1973).

Wilson, Jane Wynne, *Funerals without God: A Practical Guide to Non-Religious Funerals* (London: British Humanist Association, 1988).

Winter, Jay, *Sites of Memory, Sites of Mourning: The Great War in European Cultural History* (Cambridge: Cambridge University Press, 1995).

Worden, William J., *Grief Counselling and Grief Therapy*, 2nd edn (London: Routledge, 1991).

Young, Francis, *The Art of Performance* (London: Darton, Longman & Todd, 1990).

Zamora, Louis Parkinson (ed.), *The Apocalyptic Vision in America: Interdisciplinary Essays on Myth and Culture* (Bowling Green: Bowling Green University Press, 1982).

Zamora, Louis Parkinson, *Writing the Apocalypse: Historical Vision in Contemporary U.S. and Latin American Fiction* (Cambridge: Cambridge University Press, 1989).

Index

Abortion
  and potential persons, 76–80
  and thalidomide, 87
  youth attitudes, 97–8
Adams, Richard and Janice Haaken,
    anticultural culture, 159
Adharma, as opposite of *dharma*, 144–9
    passim
Alarm clock, 18, 175, 176, 180, 182
Altizer, Thomas J. J.
  theological exclusion of
    apocalypse, 189–90
Ambiguity
  as bread of love, 113
  and postmodernity, 121
  as redemptive, 9
Amillenialism, defined, 183 n.11
Anglican Church
  attitudes to cremation, 226–9
  and municipalities, 223–4
Apocalypse
  and American Society, 188–9
  Church as anti-apocalyptic, 189
  definition, 199 n.1
  in films, 193–4
  and hope, 197–8
  images, 18, 186–201 *passim*
  loss in Quaker witness, 19, 180
  popular culture, 186–7, 190
  science fiction, 187–8, 191–3, 198–9
  secularisation, 187–190
  and *Terminator 2*, 193–8 *passim*
  and theology, 189–190
Aquinas, St Thomas, on vice and
    virtue, 118
Archer, Margaret
  collectivist accounts of virtue, 128–31
  individualist accounts of virtue,
    127–8, 130
  the Enlightenment and God, 131–4
  on living in love, 134–8
  on theology and sociology, 125–6, 138
  virtue and sainthood, 15–16
  Max Weber and St Teresa, 138

Arnold Matthew, 'twixt vice and virtue',
    106
Aristotle
  virtue ethics, 31
  on virtuous activities, 12
Augustine, St
  incompatibility of apathy and
    morality, 132
  on inversions of moral standards, 105–6

Barot, Rohit
  celibacy and the Hindu tradition,
    13, 149–52
  Dharma, adharma and Hindu ethics,
    142–6
  ethics and epics, 146–9
Bauman, Zygmunt
  ambiguity, 9, 113
  bureaucracy, 9–10
  choice between good and evil, 121
  and ethics, 28–30
  on evil, 8, 110
  and the Holocaust, 8, 10, 110
  identity and postmodernity, 121
  and Emmanual Levinas, 29–30, 47,
    49–50 n.52
  and Alasdair MacIntyre, 9–10, 28–9
  morality and choice, 8
  and postmodernity, 28–9
  and Gillian Rose, 30
  on Max Weber, 9–10, 47
Bellah, Robert, *et al.*, forms of selfhood,
    160
Beaudoin, Tom, crisis of spirituality,
    110
Benedict, St, 14, 239
Benhabib, Seyla, 166
Berlin, Isaiah
  incompleteness of the world, 155
  value clashes, 164–5
Bewes, Timothy
  on cynicism, 116
  des Esseintes, 116, 124 n.35 and 38
Bhagavada Gita, 146–9

Fox, George
  and paradise, 173
  and the theology of the interim, 173–4
Frankl, Victor E., and hope, 203–4
Fukuyama, Francis, 213
Funerals
  comfort of the survivors, 218–19
  and Hinduism, 220
  François la Rochefoucauld, 13
  and secularisation, 221, 231–2
Funeral directors, and the clergy, 221, 225

Gal.5:22 and 25, 13
Gandhi, Mahatma, 151–2 and 153 n.17
Gauchet, Marcel, and disenchantment,
    209–10
Gennep, Arnold van, liminality, death
    and funerals, 219, 233 n.15
Giddens, Anthony
  on homosexuality, 112
  intimacy management, 111–12
  ontological security, 93
  plastic sexuality, 97, 111
  'pure relationships', 1–2, 30, 110–13,
    115
  trust defined, 1, 113
Gilbert, William Schwenck, vice as
    virtue, 104
Gittings, Clare, ritual ties with the
    dead, 222
Gluttony, Screwtape's diagnoses, 108
Goffman, Erving,
  and Alasdair MacIntyre, 25–6
  vacuous characters, 9, 107, 118
Good, youth attitudes, 94–5
Good and evil
  Zygmunt Bauman on choice, 121
  in *Blade Runner* and *Terminator 2*, 196–7
  interdependence, 114, 203
  youth attitudes, 94–6
Gorer, Geoffrey, golden age of
    mourning, 221
Grainger, Roger, public consequences of
    death, 219
Guyau, Jean-Maire, and metaphysical
    hope, 205–9

Habermas, Jürgen
  participative democracy, 63–4
  and the public sphere, 65 n.3

Heelas, Paul
  cultural extremities, 156–60 *passim*
  sacralisation of the ethic of humanity,
    161–4
  self-spirituality, 157–60
  virtue and the New Age, 17
Hennis, Wilhelm, 20 n.14
Herbert, David
  Jürgen Habermas, 63–4
  Alasdair MacIntyre and social
    criticism, 58–61
  politics of virtue, 16
  virtue ethics and ethical
    theories, 56–8
  virtue ethics and the politics of
    recognition, 64–5
  virtue ethics and social policy,
    56–8
  women's movements and religious
    minorities, 63–4
Hinduism
  Bhagavada Gita, 146–9
  and celibacy, 13, 149–52
  dharma and *adharma*, 142–6
  and funerals, 220
Holocaust
  and Zygmunt Bauman, 8, 10, 110
  and modernity, 64
Homosexuality
  Anthony Giddens, 112
  youth attitudes, 96, 100
Hope
  and the apocalypse, 197–8
  Blade Runner, 197
  and Christianity, 212–13
  as contingent, 205
  and death, 210–11
  and Jacques Ellul, 203
  and Victor E. Frankl, 203–4
  Jean-Marie Guyau, 205–9
  against hope, 203–5
  metaphysical, 205–9
  Jürgen Moltmann, 206
  power and autonomy, 213
  and Jean-Paul Sartre, 202
  secularisation, 202, 210–13
  as virtue, 17, 203–5
Huysmans, J. K.
  a study of evil, 123 n.14
  evil and monasticism, 124 n.46

Millenialism
and Quakers, 173–4
second generation Quakers, 174–7
see also Second Coming
Moltmann, Jürgen, hope and God, 206
Monasticism
and John Donne, 119
and existence of evil, 124 n.46
Mourning
forms of mourning, 217–18
golden age, 221
impersonality, 222
and virtue, 217–18
Murder and capital punishment, 73–5
Musil, Robert, 37, 42, 45, 48 n.12
Muslims
foulard ('headscarf'), 51–3
integration in France, 53–4
representation in Holland, 54–5
recognition in the United
Kingdom, 55
recognition and virtue, 16

New Age
and ethic of humanity, 162–4, 167,
168 n.22
and ethics, 166–7
and postmodernism, 159 n.26
self-spiritualities, 157–8
spiritual freedoms, 160
Newman, John Henry, on virtue and
vice, 106
Nostalgia
golden age of mourning, 221
Christopher Lasch, 26–7
and Alasdair MacIntyre, 23–7, 32 n.8

Pacifism and Quakers, 184–5 n.44
Pareto, Vilfredo, 75
Permissiveness, 102 n.18
Person and Durkheim, 211–17
Persons, *see under* particular, potential
and statistical
Persons (particular)
anti-drugs and perfect forms, 85–6
defined, 69, 75
perfect forms, 84–7
and potential persons, 75–80
and statistical persons, 70–5, 83–4, 87
in wartime, 70–2

Persons (potential)
abortion 76–80
defined, 69–70
and infanticide, 76–8
and particular persons, 75–80
Persons (statistical)
defined, 69
and particular persons, 70–5,
83–4, 87
and pharmaceutics, 80–4
and thalidomide, 80–3
Plato, 37–8, 40–1, 45
Postmodernity
and ambiguity, 121
and Zygmunt Bauman, 28–9
and cynicism, 116
dangers and the New Age, 166–7
ethics and the New Age, 166–7
and identity, 121
as moral vacuum, 6–7
Judith Squires, 166
and virtue, 106–7
Prayer
and Durkheim, 211, 216 n.48 and 50
for the dead, 220, 230
Protestantism
and the character of modernity, 64
as its own grave-digger, 230
prohibition of ritual acts, 222, 225–6,
230–1
and Max Weber, 36, 43
Proverbs 2:1–9, 14
'Pure relationships', 1–2, 30, 110–13, 115
Purgatory and intercession, 220,
222, 230–1

Quakers
ecclesiology, 173–4
eschatology, 170, 173–5
First and Second Comings, 172
Millenialism, 173–4
and the 'new Light', 171, 173, 177
and pacifism, 184–5 n.44
provisional nature of belief, 178
as revisionist sect, 171
Janet Scott, 181
Second Coming, 172–6 *passim*
Second Coming uncertainties, 176–81
secularisation of time, 18, 170–85
passim